LETTERS TO THE CONTRARY

Stanford Studies in Human Rights

LETTERS TO THE CONTRARY

A Curated History of the
UNESCO Human Rights Survey

Edited and Introduced by Mark Goodale

Stanford University Press • Stanford, California

Stanford University Press
Stanford, California

Printed in the United States of America on acid-free, archival-quality paper

Library of Congress Cataloging-in-Publication Data

Names: Goodale, Mark, editor.
Title: Letters to the contrary : a curated history of the UNESCO human rights
  survey / edited and introduced by Mark Goodale.
Description: Stanford, California : Stanford University Press, 2018. |
  Series: Stanford studies in human rights | Includes bibliographical
  references and index.
Identifiers: LCCN 2017040633 (print) | LCCN 2017041867 (ebook) |
  ISBN 9781503605350 (e-book) | ISBN 9780804799003 (cloth : alk. paper) |
  ISBN 9781503605343 (pbk. : alk. paper)
Subjects: LCSH: Human rights—History—Sources. | United Nations. General
  Assembly. Universal Declaration of Human Rights—History—Sources. |
  Unesco—History—Sources.
Classification: LCC K3240 (ebook) | LCC K3240 .L477 2018 (print) |
  DDC 341.4/8—dc23
LC record available at https://lccn.loc.gov/2017040633

Cover design and photo: George Kirkpatrick
Text design: Bruce Lundquist
Typeset at Stanford University Press in 11/15 Adobe Garamond

What song then should [we] teach the youth of the world to sing? It must be a song that looks war in the face and yet continues to sing of better things. The heart must be strong enough to conquer hate, and the mind clear enough to see the Question from the point of view of the whole world. It will be the hardest song to learn that the race has ever been called upon to sing.

Ernest Henry Burgmann, aka the "Red Bishop" (1947)

Contents

Foreword

Samuel Moyn

In 1947 and 1948, UNESCO, the new United Nations agency for international cooperation in education and culture, surveyed some intellectuals. Its goal: to clarify the philosophical bases of human rights, which were then going through a separate process of canonization in the Universal Declaration of Human Rights, approved by the United Nations General Assembly on December 10, 1948. E. H. Carr, the English political scientist and founder of the field of international relations, was approached to participate in the inquiry and went to work, writing his own contribution to the symposium on the topic that was eventually published. As Mark Goodale narrates in this book, Carr chaired a committee of experts that attempted, albeit with more acrimony than had been known until now, to elaborate a unified report on the basis of the survey results. (Like Carr's personal response, the committee report is reproduced in this book.) But Carr was not done. He went on to write up a review of the entire symposium for the *Times Literary Supplement*, which was published in November 1949.[1] It is a revealing document, for Carr stressed two facts about the UNESCO process, and its relation to the Universal Declaration, that have since been ignored.

One fact was the sheer undeniability of the insuperable differences among the thinkers. What is perhaps the most cited legacy of the UNESCO survey today is the conclusion by French Catholic thinker Jacques Maritain—originally delivered at a UNESCO summit in Mexico City as Maritain's own assessment of the state of philosophical opinion, and which was then used as the preface to the symposium's 1949 publication—that all those surveyed agreed on the importance and substance of human rights, "so long as no one asks why." For his part, Carr emphasized that, actually, any agreement among philosophers of the day about human rights was patently fragile and profoundly incomplete. And for Carr, it was very important to ask why.

Then there was the other fact: the UNESCO symposium's essential point of distinction was that it featured these disagreements openly when diplomats in the separate processes leading to the Universal Declaration could or would not. The UNESCO survey and the Universal Declaration have regularly been conflated

---

1. E. H. Carr, "Rights and Obligations," *Times Literary Supplement*, November 11, 1949, also in Carr, *From Napoleon to Stalin, and Other Essays* (London, 1980).

with each other, as if both proved Maritain's point about universal prior agreement concerning human rights. In fact, they were critically distinct enterprises. Unlike the concurrent Universal Declaration project, Carr remarked, the symposium was "immune from political preoccupations and inhibitions." And the truth about human rights in the 1940s that came through more clearly thanks to the publication of the symposium was, Carr reported, that "the unqualified upholders of the eighteenth-century bill of rights are surprisingly few—perhaps rarer among intellectuals than among the politicians who directed the proceedings of the United Nations." In the original symposium publication, the text of the Universal Declaration appeared at the end, following Maritain's preface and a compilation of selected responses. Carr took this placement to be a revealing commentary all by itself. "Had the promoters of the Unesco inquiry into human rights desired to provide a justification for their work, they could hardly have done so more eloquently than by printing without comment in an appendix the declaration," Carr explained. "After all, "since [the] authors [of the Universal Declaration] were certainly not ignorant of the real issues, it can only be supposed that political expediency made it necessary to keep them decently out of sight."

Goodale has now placed them back into view. His extraordinary work in augmenting and republishing the documentary record of the UNESCO symposium is a gift to human rights scholarship. Grounded in impressive research, it finally allows a return to the 1940s as they were lived by the organizers of and participants in the survey, beyond the fictions, sustained by recent commentary, of ideological and multicultural communion around the principles. For Carr's disarming perspectives on the unavailability of agreement in the era of the Universal Declaration and the distance between the critical inquiry of thinkers and the diplomatic evasions of the Declaration's drafters simply did not fit with the role that the 1940s were later called upon to play, in public and in scholarship, as the moment of the birth of human rights universalism. Both in gathering these materials and in interpreting them so incisively, Goodale helps show that the realities of intellectual life at the time were far more uncertain and open-ended than that.

The UNESCO symposium, which had long been forgotten, was rediscovered in the course of the shockingly recent turn to investigate the historical origins of the Universal Declaration itself, especially in a short chapter of Mary Ann Glendon's now classic *A World Made New: Eleanor Roosevelt and the Universal Declaration of Human Rights* (2001). Like Maritain's dictum, the mere existence of the symposium has been routinely cited to settle contemporary debates about the cross-cultural and trans-ideological validity of human rights. Goodale reports that the origins of the present compilation stretch back to a rebuke he received at a conference for not knowing of Glendon's ostensible proof, using the UNESCO symposium, of the transcultural and -historical validity of human rights. In a classic act of unsettlement, Goodale's compilation singlehandedly deprives the symposium of this role.

To get a sense of the beliefs that Glendon's treatment and the ideological ambience of its time created around the topic, there is no better source than Cass Sunstein's review of her book. Published in *The New Republic* in February 2002, Sunstein's article predictably begins with Maritain's assurance that everyone agreed at the time. Sunstein treated this assertion, which has been infinitely repeated since Glendon retrieved it, as a factual truth to reflect upon rather than a contentious hypothesis to investigate, participating in the ideological work of the anecdote rather than subjecting it to critical analysis. Sunstein saw not only the Universal Declaration but also the UNESCO inquiry as specifically proving that "diverse people can often agree on particular practices even when they disagree on more general questions. . . . Sometimes we do best to bracket our theoretical disagreements and to see whether we might agree not on what to think but on what to do."[2] This is unexceptionable wisdom, of course, but emphasizing it as the main lesson of the 1940s now seems like a device to avoid controversy, to win more consensus for human rights than they may deserve without more evidence of consensus, by indulging in the pretense that they had obtained unanimity when they were famously first propounded and before more adventitious skepticism later set in. As this book shows, it is the wrong lesson to learn from the symposium, not least because what the symposium allowed was in fact the kind of unvarnished thinking in the philosophical surveys that diplomatic processes forbade.

It is far more interesting, Goodale shows, to bracket the fictions that have accreted around the 1940s in order to experience the remnants of those years firsthand. Not only does *Letters to the Contrary* allow for unprecedented factual clarity about the survey, it forces us to abandon many of our presumptions, notably about the precise relationship of the UNESCO enterprise to the parallel but separate drafting of the Universal Declaration and about Maritain's own frequently exaggerated role in the conception and organization of the survey. Read this book, then, to allow yourself to come to grips with the true diversity of opinions about human rights in the 1940s before those pivotal years had been retroactively scripted as a moment of overlapping consensus or incompletely theorized agreement of cultures and ideologies. If your interest is in the plurality of cultures past or present, the text shows that it is impossible to take up the

---

2. Cass R. Sunsten, "Rights of Passage," *The New Republic*, February 24, 2002.

Universal Declaration without reflecting that it was born into a still imperial world, while the popular notion of multicultural communion around human rights became edifying in a later era of emancipated but subordinated new states, which had attempted a revolt against prevailing world order in the 1960s and 1970s only to suffer the neoliberal depredations of national disempowerment in our own era. The fact that the original set of survey responses was "absurdly unrepresentative," in Goodale's choice but fitting phrase, with nearly half coming from just two countries, is a prophylaxis against any retroactive universalization of human rights in the 1940s, but then so is the basic fact that only fifty-odd countries were yet extant in December 1948 to vote on the Universal Declaration. If your interest is in the contention of ideologies, the materials make very clear how many open questions there were about the viability of rights principles and, to the extent that they were regarded as viable, the relative importance of duties compared to rights, economic rights as opposed to political ones, and the significance of socialist and social democratic commitments before human rights became popular in our own age, when such commitments nearly vanished.

The fuller compilation of materials and Goodale's historical and interpretive chapters allow us to return to the 1940s with a "period eye," to avoid freighting it with more recent expectations of what must have been going on at the time. This is not to say that there was no agreement across cultures (those few represented) and ideologies (more than exist now), particularly when it came to economics. It was a moment of unprecedented consensus about the welfarist tasks of the twentieth-century state, even if nobody concurred about what kind of state would best shoulder them. Otherwise, intellectual conceptions at the time differed profoundly among themselves—and from the pretenses and shortcuts of diplomacy.

As Goodale cites Carr insisting in an archival letter, "You can compromise in politics, but not—unless you are either stupid or intellectually dishonest—in philosophy." Revisiting the survey means measuring its differences from the political camouflage of unity in the Universal Declaration and the more honest registration of difference that the survey required. In turn, this book can lead human rights scholarship today to become more philosophical, using Goodale's second retrieval of the UNESCO symposium to escape from the oversimplifications of the first retrieval.

A Technical Note on the Text

Letters to the Contrary reproduces some of the responses, reports, memoranda, and letters that were part of the 1947–1948 UNESCO human rights survey and the meetings that were held to publish a selection of these responses. The materials are organized into thematic clusters identified by the volume's editor in the course of curating these diverse texts. Some of the documents have been translated from French into English, and those are marked as such. A few documents were submitted in English by non-native English writers, and the resulting texts therefore reflect differing levels of mastery of the language. Nevertheless, because the responses are interventions on the question of human rights at a key moment in history and documents that themselves have historical value, we are reproducing them, for the most part, as they were written. Minor typographical errors, misspellings, and punctuation errors have been silently corrected, but the wording of the responses has otherwise been left as it was.

Roughly half of these materials were published by UNESCO in 1949, in a volume that long since went out of print. The volume was reprinted in 1973, in an edition that also went out of print long ago. The publication here of all of the known remaining responses to the UNESCO human rights survey, along with the inclusion of additional letters from artists and thinkers such as W. H. Auden and T. S. Eliot, allows us to see this important period in the history of human rights in a new and critical light.

LETTERS TO THE CONTRARY

PART I

READING HUMAN RIGHTS HISTORY WITH A PERIOD EYE

Introduction

This project began its life as a mystery. In October 2005, I found myself amongst a group of junior scholars meeting in Berlin under the auspices of the Irmgard Coninx Stiftung, a small private foundation that had been created in 2001 in order to organize a set of yearly roundtables on the theme of transnationality. The 2005 meeting was dedicated to the problem of reframing human rights. Although the meeting was formally interdisciplinary, most of the participants came from the fields of political theory, philosophy, international relations, and law. Around an actual oversized roundtable, the thirty-five attendees engaged in several days of spirited and sometimes heated debate over highly abstract problems such as the relationship between human rights and collective goals, implementation versus universality, human rights and cosmopolitan justice, the idea of imaginary global communities, and arguments for a nonreligious grounding for human rights in a pluralistic world.

I was the only anthropologist at the meeting. It was clear that both the organizers and the other participants expected me to dutifully fill the anthropological slot by providing timely reminders of real-world human rights conflicts so that the proper thinkers around the table would have something more than arid philosophical categories to work with. Nevertheless, it was during these encounters that I learned that a concept like "normativity" could be deployed to certain effect when the ethnographer's magic begins to wear off.

After one particularly long and grueling exchange on the question of the universality of human rights had continued into the hallways, I confronted a razor-sharp political theorist. I had been working for several years on the anthropology of human rights, a nascent specialty within the wider discipline that focuses on empirical research into what one volume describes as "culture and rights" (Cowan, Dembour, and Wilson 2001). The idea was to conduct ethnographic studies on human rights practices in different parts of the world in order to understand more about the possibilities and tensions within what Kofi Annan (2000) described as the "age of human rights," that is, the first decade and a half after the end of the Cold War, during which the "last utopia" (Moyn 2010) became a powerful force in global politics, international law, and socioeconomic development.

I explained that the growing database of anthropological research challenged claims for the universality of human rights. Moreover, I said, the problem of cultural diversity had been anticipated even before the Universal Declaration of Human Rights (UDHR) was adopted in 1948. As part of my wider interest in anthropology and human rights at the time, I was editing a major special issue of *American Anthropologist* entitled "Anthropology and Human Rights in a New Key." During the research for this special issue, I had learned about something called the "Statement on Human Rights," a document that claimed to have been "submitted to the Commission on Human Rights, United Nations by the Executive Board, American Anthropological Association" in 1947 when it was published in the late-1947 number of *American Anthropologist*. As I put it to the political theorist, the collective body of anthropological data did not support the assertion of human rights universality even in 1947 (as the Statement on Human Rights had emphasized) and the more recent ethnography of human rights had done nothing to change this conclusion.

The political theorist regarded me with a look that seemed to indicate that he had a definitive, if surprising, answer to these objections: "But what about the UNESCO Philosophers' Committee?" I paused for a moment as I desperately searched my internal mental files, a search that came up painfully empty. With a heavy if nervous skepticism that I hoped would check his advance, I asked, "*what* UNESCO Philosophers' Committee?" He smiled and triumphantly explained that UNESCO had conducted a global survey on human rights in order to support the work of the Commission on Human Rights, chaired by Eleanor Roosevelt. Although it was not well-known (as my own ignorance demonstrated), UNESCO's survey had proven that the underlying principles of human rights, principles that would later be codified in the UDHR, were in fact (not just in theory) universal, meaning that they were present within all the world's cultures and belief systems despite the apparent surface diversity at which anthropologists had been scratching.

This was quite a stunning claim, and I asked the political theorist for his sources. He referred me to one volume: Mary Ann Glendon's recently published *A World Made New*, which I later learned included a chapter on this mysterious UNESCO "Philosophers' Committee." Once I turned to this chapter in Glendon's book, the question then became what her sources were for the discussion of this committee, whose world-historical findings on human rights universality would figure so prominently at different moments in what was otherwise a landmark study of Eleanor Roosevelt. Glendon's primary source, as it turned out, was a book entitled *Human Rights: Comments and Interpretations*, published by UNESCO in 1949 with an introduction by the French Catholic natural rights philosopher Jacques Maritain. And that 1949 UNESCO publication did, indeed, reveal more information about a certain UNESCO process that had taken place during the drafting of the UDHR: a survey that had been undertaken, responses that had been received, and a consensus on general human rights principles that had supposedly been uncovered through the survey.

Yet these discoveries only deepened the mystery, since even a cursory reading of the 1949 UNESCO publication raised more questions than it answered: How was this survey conducted? Who authorized it? What kinds of questions were asked? To whom was the survey sent? How many surveys were sent and how many responses were received? What criteria were used in the analysis of the responses? Did the UN Commission on Human Rights (CHR) authorize UNESCO to conduct the survey? Did the CHR consider the report written by UNESCO based on this survey? And, perhaps most important, did the findings of the UNESCO survey "prove" the universality of human rights despite the various critiques, including those included in the 1947 "Statement on Human Rights"? Very little had been written about the UNESCO human rights survey and by 2005, almost all references led back to Glendon's 2001 book, which was based on the elusive 1949 UNESCO publication. Without knowing more about both the circumstances that had given rise to the UNESCO survey and the specific details of UNESCO's work on human rights, it was impossible to answer these underlying questions.

Since I am an anthropologist and not a historian, I would have normally left this admittedly important historical puzzle aside to focus on more pressing contemporary ethnographic problems, particularly since the "age of human rights" was unfolding with such methodologically challenging intensity. Yet in a case of intellectual historical serendipity, it turned out that I was destined to pursue the case of the UNESCO survey further. For an early historical chapter in a book I was working on throughout 2007, a book on anthropology and human rights, I needed to know more about the Statement on Human Rights. During research in the United States National Anthropological Archives in Suitland, Maryland, I came across correspondence from 1947 between the Executive Committee of the American Anthropological Association (AAA) and one anthropologist, Melville Herskovits, in which Herskovits writes to the AAA president (Clyde Kluckhohn), "here is the draft of the statement I sent to the UNESCO Committee, revised in accordance with the idea that it would be forwarded to the Commission on Human Rights of the United Nations, from the Association" (US National Anthropological Archives, Presidential Correspondence, Box 2, 1947).

This meant that the Statement on Human Rights, with which I was very familiar, and the UNESCO human rights survey, with which (as we have seen) I was not, were in fact connected. This came as yet an additional surprise, since by this time I had written extensively about anthropology and human rights, and Herskovits's statement was not mentioned at all in UNESCO 1949. Yet I still could not bring myself to commit to the historical detective work that was clearly necessary in order to solve the enigma of the UNESCO human rights survey and thus Herskovits's (and by extension the AAA's, and by even further extension, anthropology's) connection with it. Even Mary Ann Glendon, in a personal communication, had acknowledged that even though "there is so little material to go on . . . the important thing is to figure out what really happened in that committee."

In the end, professional circumstances allowed me to figure out what really happened in that committee. This is not to say that every detail is now known, or that every important question can be answered. Indeed, given what has come before, a heavy dose of historical humility is called for, especially since, as I have learned, historical research is as much about establishing what cannot be known (for practical, if not epistemological reasons) as it is about establishing what is known. Nevertheless, over the course of several years, research was conducted in three important archives for the project: the UNESCO archives in Paris; the special collections of the University of Chicago Library (which hold the papers of Richard McKeon, an important protagonist); and the Woodson Research Center in the Fondren Library at Rice University in Houston, Texas (which houses the Julian Huxley papers). This volume is the result of this research.

STRUCTURE OF THIS VOLUME
Given the centrality of UNESCO 1949 to debates taking place decades later over the UNESCO human rights survey of 1947–1948, the contents of the 1949 publication form the foundation for what appears here. Indeed, since UNESCO 1949 is so difficult to locate, either in its original British (Allan Wingate) or American (Columbia University Press) edition or in the 1973 Greenwood Press reprint, the publication of a new edition limited to the original contents would be easy to justify. UNESCO 1949 contains 35 separate entries: an introduction by Jacques Maritain; an uncredited foreword that was written by (and credited here to) Jacques Havet, the head of UNESCO's philosophy section at the time of the survey; 30 responses to the UNESCO survey on human rights; 1 commissioned essay on the "conception of the rights of man in the U.S.S.R." by the Soviet legal scholar Boris Tchechko (for which he was paid); a copy of the survey and accompanying memorandum on human rights distributed by UNESCO; and a report based on the findings of the survey sent by UNESCO to the UNCHR in August 1947. All of these entries are included in the current volume.

In the course of finding out "what really happened" during the UNESCO survey, however, a much wider collection of relevant sources was located in the archives. These include 22 additional responses to the survey; 1 submission (by Emmanuel Mounier) that was a reprint of an essay written in 1945; and, perhaps most surprisingly, a set of substantive refusals to formally respond to the UNESCO survey, which constitute important contributions to the question of human rights in their own right. I have only included the most interesting and consequential of these refusals, since the archives contain many other letters, telegrams, and other forms of correspondence that likewise refuse the invitation but for logistical reasons such as time, preexisting professional commitments, or confusion over the goals and methods of the project.

The various sources reproduced in this volume, both those that appeared in UNESCO 1949 and those that were discovered in the archives, have been relatively lightly annotated. I have retained most of the original footnotes as well as the varying composition styles that appear in the original. Abridgments have been kept to a minimum, since part of the rationale for this volume is to present the full body of materials related to the UNESCO human rights survey. Nevertheless, for reasons of economy, a few selections, including those of Merriam, Dutt, Blaha, Hessen, and Tchechko, have been somewhat abridged. Moreover, some of the chapters in UNESCO 1949 use ellipses, which suggests that some minor editing had already been done by the UNESCO Committee in 1947 and 1948, prior to publication. In order to distinguish between original footnotes and editorial additions new to this volume, the abbreviation "ed." is used to indicate the latter. Finally, considerable effort has been made to include biographical notes on all the contributors to the volume, even though many of them (including Gandhi, Eliot, Auden, Aldous Huxley, Schoenberg, and Nehru) will be well-known to readers.

In addition to the original sources, the volume includes two expository chapters. The first is a detailed history of the UNESCO human rights survey within the broader context of the history of human rights in the years and decades after the Second World War and the creation of the United Nations. The second explains the organizational and interpretive logic behind the clustering of sources in Part III. Although a basic purpose of this volume is to provide, for the first time, the full range of materials associated with the UNESCO human rights survey so that others may come to their own conclusions about its meaning, interpretation, and historical significance, the volume's second expository chapter does explain why it is implausible to argue that the UNESCO survey demonstrated the universality of human rights.

The volume concludes with a note on sources, describing the current state of research on the UNESCO survey and the role of various archives in this history, as a guide to future research.

UNDERSTANDING THE UNESCO SURVEY
THROUGH A "PERIOD EYE"

The process of revealing the richness, complexity, and ultimate ambiguity in the UNESCO human rights survey has reinforced the importance of understanding it—and the history of human rights more generally—through what the British art historian Michael Baxandall (1972) calls a "period eye." Baxandall argues that one must develop the capacity for comprehending paintings and other forms of art by learning how they would have been perceived and appreciated in their own terms and times. The reason for adopting a "period eye" is to avoid imposing later—often much later—standards and expectations on works of art that were created against the backdrop of very different aesthetic, cultural, and historical conditions.

Working through the primary sources around the UNESCO survey, it is striking to what extent the proposal for a new "declaration of the rights of man" was regarded with skepticism, confusion, even incredulity. While important actors and institutions were certainly committed to liberal human rights as the primary legal, political, and moral response to the horrors of the Holocaust and world war, many others, particularly those on the left, viewed human rights as a framework firmly rooted in the late eighteenth century and therefore long since obsolete. As Morris L. Ernst, cofounder of the American Civil Liberties Union, put it in his refusal to formally respond to the UNESCO survey, "It seems to me that we are finished with the era of passing general resolutions in regard to liberty and freedom" (see his entry in Part III, in "From Repudiation to the Play of Fancy").

The period during which the UNESCO survey was undertaken, early 1947 to late 1948, was a time in which many proposals for the postwar order were being developed. These proposals were influenced by a range of currents and ideologies, not all of which were complementary. The discussions around human rights at the time took place within a swirl of debate and contention that involved widespread support for Soviet and socialist projects; a belief in the progressive aspects and dominance of technology; and the often conservative retreat into the certainties of religious faith and institutions. It is important to understand this liminal postwar but pre-UDHR period as one in which the idea of human rights was associated by its critics with a small cluster of Western national traditions (notably the American and French); viewed as the unmistakable normative underpinning of capitalism; and held in a certain disdain by many intellectuals, who regarded the "rights of man"—much as Jeremy Bentham had a hundred and fifty years earlier—as pernicious, since their metaphysical abstractness seduced people into ignoring other, more concrete, approaches to solving social and economic problems. In describing this relatively short period of about two years as a prehistory, it is not my intention to assign undue importance to the ratification of the UDHR in the broader historiography of human rights. Rather, it is to underscore the fact that at the time, at least for certain key actors and institutions in Europe and the United States, these months in which a declaration of human rights was being developed were seen as an important moment in the wider economic, political, and legal reconstruction of a fractured world.

Yet developing a period eye is not only necessary for gaining a fresh perspective on this critical moment when the UNESCO human rights survey took place, in the year and a half before the adoption of the UDHR in December 1948. It is also necessary in order to better appreciate how and why the UNESCO survey was interpreted in particular ways by scholars decades later. By the time the UNESCO survey was rediscovered by a small group of historians of human rights in the late 1990s, the geopolitical, ideological, and cultural background conditions had changed dramatically. With human rights (humanity's "last utopia" [Moyn 2010]) under increasing pressure from Asian intellectuals and politicians and postcolonial critics, among others, the findings of the UNESCO survey seemed to provide a conclusive rebuttal to charges that the expanding post–Cold War human rights movement was based on Western norms. As the two expository chapters explain in more detail, this was the charged broader context in which the UNESCO human rights survey was often used as a trump card in debates over universality, cultural relativism, and the status of Western human rights activism.

CONCLUSION:
REWINDING THE HISTORY OF HUMAN RIGHTS

If the rediscovery of the UNESCO survey in the 1990s took place during a time of both a rapid expansion of human rights activism and a growing critique of this transformative mode of contemporary world-making, the publication of this volume takes place during yet a different moment in the wider history of human rights. The promotion of the UNESCO human rights survey as a refutation of charges of Western-centrism was simply one aspect of a broader current of optimism bordering on triumphalism, for many scholars as much as for politicians, international aid workers, and social movement activists. This was a time in which history had apparently ended, with the triple pillars of late liberalism—capitalism, democracy, and human rights—the sole remaining foundations on which societies could be reinforced or rebuilt. It is striking how strong the belief was in the inevitability of human rights, at least until the early 2000s, when a series of international turning points—the attacks of

September 11, 2001; the launch of the so-called War on Terror; the rise of the global security state; the revelation that torture was an accepted practice among well-established Western powers—marked, in retrospect, the beginning of the end of the "age of human rights."

During the debates that took place in the mid-1990s over the question of "Asian values," for example, Aryeh Neier, one of the founders of Human Rights Watch, engaged in a lively series of exchanges with the Singaporean ambassador, Bilahari Kausikan (Neier 1993). At one level, this was a high-stakes international debate over universalism, relativism, historical contingency, and whether or not, as Kausikan put it, the "extent and exercise of rights and freedoms is a product of the historical experiences of particular peoples" (1995, 265). But at another level, this was a debate about whether or not global politics was converging around a well-defined set of norms. Neier, for his part, was willing to concede that different cultural and national traditions interpreted human rights in different ways. Yet what was never in doubt was the fact that a global culture of human rights would continue to take root as part of the broader process of globalization. If Neier could readily dismiss Kausikan's arguments for Asian values as a sophisticated attempt to rationalize authoritarian political practices, he did so believing that time was ultimately on the side of human rights, that a culture of human rights would eventually become so persuasive that the very idea of cultural difference itself would be rendered meaningless.

From the perspective of 2017, however, the "age of human rights" seems increasingly distant. Instead, we confront a period characterized by a widespread "backlash" (Venice Academy of Human Rights 2016) against human rights; a time in which the "rise and fall" (Allen 2013) of human rights has led to disenchantment and even hopelessness; and the realization that "we are living through the endtimes of the civilizing mission," a period of closure caused not by "transient misfortunes but [by] fatal structural defects in international humanism" (Hopgood 2013, 1). If the status of human rights was already "unsettled" as of June 2001 (Sarat and Kearns 2001), by 2017, with a Donald Trump presidency, the withdrawal of Britain from the European Union, and the strengthening of nationalism and identitarian politics in many parts of the world, it is clear that "the prospect of one world under secular human rights law is receding" (Hopgood 2013, 1) faster than ever.

Thus it is with a sense of some urgency that this volume, despite its idiosyncrasy, appears at this moment of crisis in the broader history of human rights. What, we might ask, is the precise nature of the "structural defects" at the core of the human rights project? If they are indeed structural, this would imply that the problem—now and in the future—is not merely political: not merely an issue of the failure of implementation, bad faith on the part of cynical state actors, institutional complexity, tensions between state sovereignty and international law, the obstructing hand of global capitalism, and so on.

Rather, if Hopgood and countless other contemporary critics—many from *within* the centers of "international humanism"—are right, the problems must be more basic; they must relate to how human rights are understood both conceptually and historically. In this sense, then, the sources in this volume offer us the ability to rewind the history of human rights back to an important moment when the basic concepts were still very much in flux and the first lines of the postwar story of human rights had not been written. Perhaps the rudiments of an alternative model of human rights are to be found among the diverse responses to the UNESCO survey and the surrounding debates, discussions, and various expressions of dissent.

REFERENCES CITED

Allen, Lori A. 2013. *The Rise and Fall of Human Rights: Cynicism and Politics in Occupied Palestine.* Stanford: Stanford University Press.

American Anthropological Association. 1947. "Statement on Human Rights." American Anthropologist 49(4): 539–43.

Annan, Kofi. 2000. "The Age of Human Rights." In Project Syndicate. http://www.project-syndicate.org/commentary/the-age-of-human-rights?barrier=true.

Baxandall, Michael. 1972. *Painting and Experience in Fifteenth-Century Italy: A Primer in the Social History of Pictorial Style.* Oxford: Clarendon.

Cowan, Jane, Marie-Bénédicte Dembour, and Richard A. Wilson, eds. 2001. *Culture and Rights: Anthropological Perspectives.* Cambridge: Cambridge University Press.

Glendon, Mary Ann. 2001. *A World Made New: Eleanor Roosevelt and the Universal Declaration of Human Rights.* New York: Random House.

Hopgood, Stephen. 2013. *The Endtimes of Human Rights.* Ithaca: Cornell University Press.

Kausikan, Bilahari. 1995. "An East Asian Approach to Human Rights." The Buffalo Journal of International Law 2(2): 263–83.

Moyn, Samuel. 2010. *The Last Utopia: Human Rights in History.* Cambridge, MA: Belknap Press of Harvard University Press.

Neier, Aryeh. 1993. "Asia's Unacceptable Standard." Foreign Policy 92(Autumn): 42–51.

Sarat, Austin and Thomas R. Kearns. 2001. "The Unsettled Status of Human Rights." In *Human Rights: Concepts, Contests, Contingencies*, edited by Austin Sarat and Thomas R. Kearns, 1–24. Ann Arbor: University of Michigan Press.

UNESCO. 1949. *Human Rights: Comments and Interpretations.* New York: Columbia University Press.

Venice Academy of Human Rights. 2016. "Backlash Against Human Rights?" July 4–13. https://www.eiuc.org/research/venice-academy-of-human-rights.html

History
UNESCO in the Paradigmatic Transition

As the years between us and the catastrophe of the Second World War grow in number, as memories of the first half of the twentieth century fade and the numbers of those who lived through that time become fewer, and as the world-historical tragedy of the Holocaust continues to be followed—though never overshadowed—by other, more recent, genocides, other moments of mass atrocity loosed upon the world, the archives of history serve to remind us just how much those who were charged with putting the world back together again were fully conscious of the extraordinary nature of their task.

INTRODUCTION:
UTOPIAN VISIONS FROM THE ASHES OF WAR
For the protagonists of the great powers, the models for a postwar global architecture were many, but they can be usefully grouped into those that were grounded in some form of technocratic or institutional vision and those grounded in bolder, even utopian, visions, those that imagined a new world order constructed along radically different lines. As the early post-1945 years soon revealed, however, it was the institutional visions that ultimately shaped the postwar world. From the committees and regulations of the United Nations to the International Monetary Fund, and from the International Court of Justice to the World Bank, the global postwar structure crystallized around the creation of new institutions that depended upon national sovereignty, the protection of great-power prerogative, the expansion of global capitalism, and the development of an international bureaucracy.

Within this institutional, essentially Westphalian, postwar charter, other visions were allowed to take root, even if they emerged largely symbolically, exceptional projects whose eventual marginality on the postwar landscape merely served to reinforce the general patterns of the coming international order. Among these marginal and utopian initiatives, that of human rights was the most important. Although the preamble to the UN Charter had proclaimed its "faith in fundamental human rights, in the dignity and worth of the human person, in the equal rights of men and women and of nations large and small," as against the record of "untold sorrow to mankind" that marked recent history, there was no question in the minds of those who promoted this faith that it would confront a world that would either reject it, not be ready for it, or simply not understand it. Indeed, as Eleanor Roosevelt—the chair of the commission that oversaw the drafting of the 1948 Universal Declaration of Human Rights (UDHR)—herself acknowledged, the work of "setting before men's eyes the ideals which they must strive to reach" was "frankly educational" rather than of practical consequence (Roosevelt 1948, 477).

Yet another—even more marginal and more utopian—vision of the time was the one that drove Julian Huxley to imagine a new global culture in which the world's differences would be overcome in a final synthesis of both ideas and practices organized around universal themes of reason, evolutionary humanism, moral progress, and the application of science to human society. Huxley believed that a new and singular international organization was required to direct such a large-scale project, and he therefore played a fundamental role on the preparatory commission that worked to create the United Nations Educational, Scientific and Cultural Organization (UNESCO). Indeed, his magisterial sixty-page blueprint for the incipient organization, "UNESCO: Its Purposes and Its Philosophy" (1946), constitutes an extended argument for how the world's ideological and economic conflicts could be definitively resolved through what he describes as "the emergence of a single world culture, with its own philosophy and background of ideas, and with its own broad purpose," the most important of which was the prevention of a third world war between "East and West" (1946, 61). In this, UNESCO would take the leading global role and serve as the vanguard in "the quest, so urgent in this time of over-rapid transition, for a world philosophy, a unified and unifying background of thought for the modern world" (41).

Thus, with "UNESCO: Its Purposes and Its Philosophy" as the guiding intellectual and moral framework, the organization was born during a first "general conference" held at what became known as "UNESCO House," the hastily retrofitted Hotel Majestic on the Avenue Kléber in Paris.[1] Huxley himself was elected UNESCO's first director-general during its inaugural 1946 meeting, though in a sign of how the business of politics would come to constrain the scope of UNESCO as the leading international organization charged with global unification around a single philosophy, his term was set for only two years, despite the fact that UNESCO's 1946 constitution specified a term of six years (Sewell 1975).[2]

----

1. At the Hotel Majestic, "working conditions were not exactly ideal. The largest bedrooms were allocated to secretaries, several of whom had to share them and store their files in the wardrobes, while middle-grade professionals were put in disused bathrooms, where the only place to keep their papers was the bathtub" (UNESCO 2017).

2. In addition to shortening Huxley's term, UNESCO also later took steps to distance itself,

During this first general conference, the organization was subdivided into a number of units that would be responsible for carrying forward Huxley's grand project. One of these units was at the very heart of UNESCO's global quest: the philosophy section, headed by the "brilliant young" French philosopher Jacques Havet (Weindling 2010, 127–28), an acolyte of Jean-Paul Sartre's who was at the head of the 1939 graduating class of the prestigious *École normale supérieure*, France's historic breeding ground for influential philosophers and other intellectuals (Israël 2005). Of the several tasks given to Havet's philosophy division for the following year, one of them would come to take on world-historical importance. Working in close coordination with Huxley and UNESCO's Secretariat, the philosophy division was charged with the following:

> D. Rights of Man
> The Secretariat should organize, in collaboration with the United Nations Commission on the Rights of Man, an International Conference in order to clarify the principles on which might be founded a modern declaration of the Rights of Man. (UNESCO 1947, 236)

However, beyond these rather general instructions—the idea for which had been introduced first by the Mexican delegation to the UNESCO Preparatory Commission and then supported by the French and British delegations (UNESCO 1947, 177)—nothing else was specified regarding the scope of UNESCO's work on human rights.

This ambiguity was a result of the unsettled nature of the emerging international system of the early postwar years, and it had significant consequences for how the visionary Huxley would come to view the relationship between human rights and UNESCO's mission to unify the world through the development of a meta-philosophy that would transcend all existing differences. A mandate of the UN Economic and Social Council had created an international commission on human rights in 1946, with 18 members and Eleanor Roosevelt as chair. However, beyond its own charge to produce an "international bill of rights," as US president Truman described it (Morsink 1999, 4), the actual working guidelines for the commission, its intended collaboration with other agencies, and, most importantly, the broader principles upon which such a bill of rights would be based, were all unspecified at the time UNESCO boldly inserted itself into the process.

---

as an institution, from "UNESCO: Its Purposes and Its Philosophy," going so far as to append a statement in subsequent publications that indicated that the manifesto reflected the personal views of Huxley. Nevertheless, while he served as director-general, the document served as an accurate framework for how Huxley envisioned UNESCO and its global role.

PHILOSOPHERS BY THE SEASIDE

Huxley immediately recognized the possibilities presented by human rights: UNESCO's work to uncover the universal principles upon which to base the first international bill of rights would be the mechanism through which a "single world culture" would emerge. But how to uncover these principles, particularly in such a relatively short time? Although the UN Commission on Human Rights (CHR) was not going to have its first meeting until early 1947, it was clear to Huxley and Havet that the process they developed would have to take place rather quickly so that what it produced would both precede and form the basic foundation for any later work undertaken by Roosevelt and her commission. Even at this early stage, Huxley viewed the role of the CHR—and the wider UN system itself, of which UNESCO was nominally a part—with deep skepticism, since it was seen as an essentially political arrangement shaped by partisan national interests. And the sense that UNESCO should take the leading role in developing the intellectual and ethical content for what would become the UDHR was only reinforced by the outsized role being played by the United States on the other side of the Atlantic. If the United States had viewed Huxley's candidacy for the director-generalship of UNESCO with alarm, given his cosmopolitan orientation and promotion of evolutionary humanism, this hostility was met in kind by Huxley, who saw in the postwar United States a major and brash world power that was nevertheless more suited to military and economic affairs than those that demanded a universal vision and a willingness to transcend the destructive conflict between "East and West" (in which the United States was a key protagonist).

In mid-January 1947, with a clear sense of destiny, Huxley and Havet began planning in earnest for an international conference of intellectuals that would play the central role in developing the philosophical basis for an international bill of human rights. Drawing on his national networks, Havet reached out to the mayor of the seaside town of Nice, who promptly offered to host such a major gathering in his city. Nice was considered to be an ideal location, not only for its congenial and relaxing surroundings but because it made it more likely that the philosopher Gaston Berger would be able to participate, as he had recently taken up a post at the University of Aix-en-Provence and lived in the region (memo from Havet to Huxley, 24 February 1947).[3] At the same time, the planning for this international conference in Nice was taking on a growing

---

3. UNESCO Archives, AG 8 Secretariat Records, Central Registry Collection, file Human Rights—Enquiry, Public Opinion 342.7 (100): 301.153 A 151. Unless otherwise indicated, all memoranda and letters cited hereafter refer to the same archive. In this case, only the name and date of the document will be used.

urgency. Havet emphasized to Huxley that the Easter and Pentecost holiday periods were on the near horizon and that it would be difficult to organize the event before mid-April at the earliest.

FROM A GROUP OF TWELVE TO "NEARLY ALL THE WORLD'S NATIONAL GROUPS AND NEARLY ALL IDEOLOGICAL APPROACHES"

In early March 1947, Huxley canceled the plans for an international conference in Nice. His concern was twofold. First, he was worried that a gathering of philosophers in a distant part of the country would be too independent and its relation with UNESCO's mission to unify the world under Huxley's close watch therefore too tenuous. As he put it, "it would be very difficult to exercise any supervision, or even keep an eye on what they were doing, if they met at the other end of the country" (memo from Huxley to Havet, 3 March 1947). And second, Huxley had begun receiving reports from the United States regarding the activities of the CHR, which had met for the first time in January. Surprisingly, during the commission's first session, the substance of a potential bill of rights had been taken up directly, even before the drafting committee created by the commission at that meeting had done any work (Roosevelt 1948; Morsink 1999). Huxley clearly saw this as an unexpected intrusion into the course of UNESCO's fundamental work on human rights as global culture, work which would now have to proceed in the face of competition from Lake Success, New York, where the CHR was based.

Huxley thus made the decision to hold the international conference at UNESCO House in Paris instead and to limit participation to a small number of participants, whose attendance could be secured at very short notice. As he put it in a memo to Havet, "I hope to hear from you in the very near future as regards the names of those people you think we should get for the Conference on the Rights of Man. Personally I feel we should limit it to about twelve people, if possible all of them from Western Europe, *as the matter is urgent* (Huxley to Havet, 3 March 1947; emphasis mine). With the place and general time (between May 26 and May 30) now set, Havet got to work on invitations. For reasons of both time and money, Havet recommended that the ranks of UNESCO's offices in Paris be surveyed to see if any specialists could be found there, along with scholars "living nearby," which meant that Havet assumed that the majority of participants would be comprised of French intellectuals drawn from his own extensive networks from the *École normale supérieure*.

The list Havet sent Huxley for review the next day, March 4, is indeed filled with leading French thinkers: Georges Gurvitch, Étienne Gilson, Gaston Berger,

René Le Senne, Jean Hyppolite, and "either Sartre or Merleau-Ponty." In addition, Havet lists two possible participants from Belgium, one from Norway, and one from the Netherlands. So as not to exclude possible participation from Huxley's home country, Havet suggests "Bertrand Russell and perhaps someone else you know." Regarding the sensitive topic of possible American participation, Havet writes that "although it might be impossible to invite them," certain American thinkers are capable of making a "constructive contribution." To this he adds the names of the idealist philosopher William Ernest Hocking, of Harvard University, and the recently retired Harvard professor Ralph Barton Perry, who had won the 1936 Pulitzer Prize for his two-volume biography of his former teacher William James.

Between March 4 and March 27, UNESCO's plans for uncovering the basic principles of human rights and therefore determining the form and content of what later became the UDHR underwent a profound transformation. Through discussions among Huxley, Havet, and Richard McKeon, an influential member of the United States delegation to UNESCO who was visiting Paris at the time, it was decided to abandon the original idea to hold a small private conference of philosophers in Paris. On the one hand, Huxley simply could not afford to delay the process for three more months while the CHR in the United States continued to organize and advance its efforts, which now included requests to governments and institutions to forward draft bills of rights and other conceptual and political materials to the CHR for its consideration.[4] At the same time, the various exigencies meant that the original UNESCO human rights process could not aspire to the global reach that Huxley so desired. Even for someone with his level of self-assurance, it was difficult to imagine how a hastily convened meeting of office mates, friends, and close colleagues could succeed in using a consideration of human rights to establish a "unified and unifying background of thought for the modern world."

McKeon was a legendary University of Chicago philosophy professor who inspired "cold sweat and raw fear" in a long list of students, including Susan

---

4. In hindsight, Huxley's worry about whether the work of the CHR would compete with UNESCO's contributions to the form and content of what became the UDHR would prove to be quite irrelevant, not because of what happened later but because by March 1947, the first and most important draft of the UDHR had already been written. By late February, even before the CHR drafting committee had met for the first time, John P. Humphrey, the director of the United Nations' Division of Human Rights, produced what became known as the "Humphrey Draft" under instructions given by Roosevelt herself at her apartment in Washington, DC, on February 14. Thus, despite the fact that Huxley and Havet were just ramping up UNESCO's fundamental intervention, "the baby was [already] born" (Morsink 1999, 5, 29; see also Hobbins 1989, Humphrey 1984).

Sontag, Richard Rorty, Paul Rabinow, and Robert Pirsig (who used McKeon as the model for the character of the dreaded "Chairman" in his 1974 novel *Zen and the Art of Motorcycle Maintenance*) (Obermiller 1994). With this luminary agreeing to oversee robust participation from the American side, Havet was instructed by Huxley to draft a questionnaire and background paper that would be sent out with all dispatch to people and institutions well beyond the boundaries of France and Western Europe. These documents (UNESCO/Phil/1/1947, see Part II) were prefaced with a cover letter that explained, somewhat ambiguously, that UNESCO had been tasked with considering the underlying principles of human rights "so as to permit the formulation of a Declaration of Human Rights for the modern world in its present circumstances." The letter then invited people to respond to the accompanying "aide-mémoire"—which provided a short history of human rights declarations and ended with a list of potential rights to include in a declaration—in the form of a two-to-four-thousand-word essay written "preferably, though not necessarily, . . . in English or French."

Given the limitations of time, space, and the correspondence technology of the time (this was the age of dictation and the ubiquitous carbon copy), these materials were sent to an impressive range of individuals, states, and educational, cultural, religious, and political organizations. Nevertheless, the list of recipients was based largely on Havet's and Huxley's very different professional and personal networks. Havet took charge of sending the materials to French speakers or those he assumed would be more comfortable working in French than in English, a group that included many recipients from the Soviet Bloc. Although Huxley also circulated the documents largely within his own networks, these just happened to include many of the most influential intellectuals, writers, theologians, political leaders, and social activists of the late-colonial British (mostly English) world, a largely upper-class and Oxbridge world of wealth, power, and privilege of which Huxley—the grandson of T. H. Huxley, "Darwin's Bulldog"; brother of Aldous Huxley; and half-brother of the Nobel-Prize-winning scientist Andrew Huxley—was very much at the center.

To give just one example of what the inside of this world looked like: Huxley sent the UNESCO documents to his close friend the English poet Stephen Spender. In his reply, from his regular retreat at the Chalet Waldegg in Gstaad, Switzerland, Spender says that he won't burden Huxley with his own views on human rights, since he doesn't have anything "worth saying" on the topic, but then goes on to suggest that Huxley send the documents to some of his acquaintances. This curious list of the great and the good includes the psychiatrist and philosopher Karl Jaspers, the first and second presidents of Czechoslovakia (Tomáš Masaryk and Edvard Beneš), the Italian philosopher Benedetto Croce,

Isaiah Berlin, A. J. Ayer, and W. H. Auden. Spender even gives Huxley some advice about whom to avoid: "I honestly don't think there are any outstanding Belgians."

On the American side, with the collaboration of UNESCO's US National Commission and the American Council of Learned Societies, which was represented by a delegation to the US National Commission, McKeon systematically and tirelessly devoted himself to developing an extensive list of recipients. Indeed, McKeon's work on the UNESCO human rights process was in many ways much more organized and collaborative than the ad hoc process undertaken by Huxley and Havet themselves from UNESCO headquarters in Paris. McKeon eventually sent UNESCO/Phil/1/1947 to a diverse list of nearly fifty people, including John Dewey, Norman Cousins, Reinhold Niebuhr, Henry Wallace (vice president under Franklin D. Roosevelt), W. H. Auden (who had recently become a naturalized US citizen), J. B. Conant (president of Harvard University), Paul Robeson, Arnold Schoenberg, and Richard Wright. Among this wide group, only twelve eventually responded, including Auden and the composer Schoenberg but with the bulk of the responses coming from academia.

In the end, it is not possible to know for certain precisely how many people considered the UNESCO request to participate in the "formulation of a Declaration of Human Rights for the modern world in its present circumstances." This uncertainty is mostly due to the fact that Huxley's letters to states and national organizations were accompanied by the suggestion that the materials be forwarded to "whomever might be suitable."[5] Unlike McKeon, Huxley and Havet did not maintain a complete list of recipients of UNESCO/Phil/1/1947, only several changing lists of the responses received back at UNESCO headquarters. But given that Huxley and Havet assumed that the process would produce roughly a one-third response rate, and the fact that 57 to 59 responses were eventually received,[6] we can conclude conservatively that between a hundred

---

5. For example, the Belgian socialist newspaper Le Peuple printed UNESCO/Phil/1/1947 in its July 27 and 28 editions, with a note to readers to respond. One of these responses, from a "Mr. Nicolay, Honorary Director of the Ministry of Labour and Social Welfare," is reproduced in the section entitled "The Universal Declaration of Human Duties" in Part III.

6. The slight uncertainty over the number comes from the fact that at least three of the responses on the final list are in a special category. The essay by René Maheu on freedom of expression was commissioned by Havet at the beginning of the process, since Maheu, as the head of UNESCO's Division of Free Flow of Information (he later became a two-term director-general of UNESCO, 1962–1974), was an office mate of Havet's. The essay by the Soviet legal scholar Boris Tchechko was not a response to UNESCO/Phil/1/1947 but rather a commissioned study of human rights from the Soviet perspective. And the essay submitted by the French personalist philos-

and fifty and a hundred and eighty sets of materials were considered (including those that were passed along by direct recipients).

The distribution of responses to the UNESCO human rights documents paints a confusing picture. On the one hand, by contemporary standards, the range is almost absurdly unrepresentative. Nearly 45% of all the replies came from just two countries: the United States and the United Kingdom.[7] Another 40% of the replies came from several countries in Western Europe, South Africa (2 responses), Australia (2), and Canada (1). The remaining 15% of the responses was divided among several Soviet Bloc countries (5), India (3), all of Latin America (2), and China (1), although the response attributed to China was submitted by Chung-Shu Lo while he was a UNESCO consultant (in a letter to Sartre, Havet describes Lo as a "Chinese philosopher passing through Paris"). And although several more women were asked, there was only one woman who replied to UNESCO/Phil/1/1947, the English Quaker prison reformer Margery Fry.

Yet on the other hand, this range was depicted almost from the beginning as a triumph of global scope, the first empirical study to comprehensively measure global diversity of opinion on the principles of human rights. In an article in the *UNESCO Courier* in August 1948, UNESCO's "world-wide symposium of the philosophic bases of Human Rights" was described by Havet in revealing terms: a survey on human rights was "despatched to philosophers, scientists and political figures throughout the world" and the responses received by UNESCO "represented nearly all the world's national groups and nearly all ideological approaches" (Havet 1948, 8). It is difficult to know whether these first public representations of the UNESCO process were meant in earnest: that is, perhaps the final tally of responses did appear to the main actors to reflect the world's diversity of opinion as they understood it at the time.

Certainly the problem of diversity—and thus, the legitimacy of the results—was a basic concern that structured the way in which Huxley and Havet envisioned the process after it had been transformed from a private conference in Paris to a "world-wide symposium." But since both Huxley and Havet had every interest in the success of the project, and since this success depended on both the global representativeness of the responses and the extent to which these responses revealed "the principles on which might be founded a modern declaration of the Rights of Man," I believe that the public presentation of the

---

opher Emmanuel Mounier was also not a response to the UNESCO documents but was a reprint of one of Mounier's essays on human rights published in the May 1945 issue of the journal *Esprit*.

7. Huxley and Havet themselves used country of origin as a way to track the representativeness of the process, something they were acutely concerned with from the beginning.

UNESCO survey was an intentional construction meant to conceal the fact that it had actually fallen far short of its ambitions.

THE UN REJECTS A "VERY DANGEROUS PRECEDENT"
While the responses to the UNESCO survey were beginning to trickle in, Huxley and Havet made plans to convene a grandly—and, as we will see below, ill-advisedly—titled "UNESCO Drafting Committee" to analyze the results and prepare a report to be sent to the CHR. Time pressures continued to mount, since the CHR's own drafting committee was scheduled to meet for the first time in June 1947. The composition of the "Committee of Experts Convened by UNESCO on the Philosophical Principles of the Rights of Man," as it was also called, shifted right up to the day of the meeting, but the group did finally gather in Paris from June 26 to July 2, 1947. It consisted of the following: the British political scientist and historian E. H. Carr (chair); McKeon (rapporteur); the French nuclear physicist and education official Pierre Auger; the pro-Soviet French sociologist Georges Friedmann; the French philosopher Étienne Gilson (recently elected to the French Academy); the British political theorist and socialist Harold Laski; the Belgian communist and civil servant Luc Somerhausen (who had survived political imprisonment at the Nazi concentration camp Esterwegen); and the Chinese philosopher and UNESCO consultant Chung-Shu Lo, who had been added just the day before as a replacement for the Mexican scholar and diplomat Manuel Cabrera Maciá, who was then studying for a doctorate at the Sorbonne.

Over the course of the week, the UNESCO committee considered the forty-four responses that had been received so far, more than half of which came from American and British respondents. Subsequent correspondence indicates that the proceedings were dominated by the native English speakers and that the problem of language was significant (the French speakers frequently asked for translations of documents, and francophone frustration with the Anglocentrism of the process is palpable in the archival record). Within two weeks of the end of the meeting, the imperious McKeon had produced a report to be sent to the CHR, entitled "The Grounds of an International Declaration of Human Rights" (see Part II). With the exception of minor corrections, and a request by Somerhausen to have the document translated into French, no major revisions were made to McKeon's document by any of the other committee members.

On August 1, 1947, Huxley sent "The Grounds of an International Declaration of Human Rights" to Henri Laugier, UN Assistant Secretary-General for social affairs, and at the same time had fifty copies of the document sent directly to John P. Humphrey, the director of the United Nation's Division of Human

Rights, in Geneva, where the CHR was scheduled to meet in full session for the second time in December. Yet despite the fact that Laugier's reply to Huxley was courteous, even asking Huxley to "send some more copies for use here at Lake Success," the broader UN system, and the US government in particular, had by this time awoken to UNESCO's ambitions in the field of human rights and was intent on restraining or, if need be, suppressing them.

These behind-the-scenes machinations against the UNESCO human rights process reached an important turning point on December 3, 1947. In a closed second session of the CHR in Geneva, the question of UNESCO's survey and resulting report were discussed. Eleanor Roosevelt and John P. Humphrey were both closely questioned by other members of the commission about the curious "The Grounds of an International Declaration of Human Rights," which seems to have appeared without warning and without the knowledge of most of the members of the CHR. Roosevelt and Humphrey both knew much more about the UNESCO process than they acknowledged during these heated exchanges, in which the Belgian, Soviet, and Australian delegates in particular railed against the unwanted intrusion of a mere "specialist agency" into the important work of the CHR in producing a human rights declaration.

The Belgian delegate, Fernand Dehousse, in particular, was adamant that the efforts of UNESCO should be rejected, since its unsolicited participation constituted a "very dangerous precedent." Because UNESCO "had not consulted the United Nations, . . . there had been no co-operation or liaison . . . [and because] the UNESCO document claimed to define the philosophical principles of an International Bill of Human Rights and even the implementation of such a Bill" (CHR, E/CN.4/SR/26, 3 December 1947), as the Australian delegate (Colonel William Hodgson) put it, a proposal was made to officially censure "The Grounds of an International Declaration of Human Rights" and refuse to consider it during the drafting of the UDHR. The proposal was accepted by a vote of eight to four (with one abstention). And with this, Huxley's dream of using human rights as a means through which UNESCO would articulate a "world philosophy, a unified and unifying background of thought for the modern world," came to an end.

THE UNESCO HUMAN RIGHTS SURVEY LIVES ON
AND IS REDISCOVERED

"The Grounds of an International Declaration of Human Rights" was not the only document to be produced by the UNESCO human rights committee. As Huxley began to realize that timing, institutional resistance, and intellectual content were working against the realization of the original grand vision to definitively "clarify the principles on which might be founded a modern declaration of the Rights of Man," he added a second rationale for the project: the publication of a collection of the responses. In the correspondence, this shift in emphasis is unmistakable. As criticism of the UNESCO survey mounted, from both international officials and those whose responses had been solicited, Huxley's replies increasingly moved the attention away from the grand vision toward a more limited, academic justification for UNESCO's participation. For example, in a late-April 1947 letter to Henry Wallace, in which Huxley seeks a response to UNESCO/Phil/1/1947, Huxley adds, "the book which we hope will result from [the survey] should be extremely important (more important to my personal view than any attempt to make a precise formulation of Human Rights as is being attempted by the Human Rights' [sic] Commission)."

To this end, Huxley and Havet convened a smaller subgroup from the original committee of experts to meet two more times: once in the fall of 1947 and the second, and final, time in July of 1948. The goal was to select a set of responses that reflected a certain ideological and intellectual diversity, although, in the end, many of the most important and provocative responses were not included. At the end of the September 1947 meeting of what was now called the "Editorial Committee," the manuscript had been largely assembled, minus an introduction. Indeed, it had proven to be a contested and difficult task among the committee simply to agree on the selection of 31 responses to be published. This was because of a major disagreement over the fundamental question of human rights itself, with Havet (acting as the committee's secretary) and McKeon on one side, and E. H. Carr, Luc Somerhausen, and Pierre Auger on the other. By this time, Carr had even begun to distance himself from the broader UNESCO project. In a letter to Huxley sent a few days after the contentious "Editorial Committee" meeting, Carr argued that the actual diversity of global perspectives, some of which were represented in the UNESCO responses, simply could not be simplified into a set of principles that were universally valid across cultures. As he put it, the problem is "not a difference of opinion, but a difference of starting point, method and conception, which does not permit of compromise or synthesis. You can compromise in politics, but not—unless you are either stupid or intellectually dishonest—in philosophy."

What this meant was that although Havet managed to convince the committee to agree on the basic structure of the volume, the project itself was leaderless—there was no editor to organize a collective analysis of the responses, summarize that analysis, and then oversee the publication of a book that would amount to more than the sum of its parts. Havet and Huxley were thus forced to look outside the committee for someone to write an introduction, a less-than-ideal solution given that this meant that someone who had not participated in the project would be undertaking the important task of giving broader form to the volume.

The question of the introduction was raised during UNESCO's Second General Conference, which took place in December 1947 in Mexico City and at which the French Catholic natural law philosopher (and future monk) Jacques Maritain had given the opening address. Yet at least until April 1948, no one had yet been identified to write the introduction. In correspondence, Huxley acknowledged that his two top candidates were the Dutch phenomenologist Hendrik Josephus Pos and Charlie Dunbar Broad, who was at the time the Knightbridge Professor of Moral Philosophy at Cambridge University. With time running short, Huxley made the surprise decision to ask Maritain to write the introduction. Huxley had been much impressed by Maritain's speech in Mexico City and, perhaps even more important, took the practical attitude that Maritain's address could be readily and quickly adapted for the UNESCO book.

Indeed, Maritain's introduction is largely modeled on his Mexico City speech and makes no attempt to analyze the 31 responses reproduced in the book. As a Catholic natural law philosopher, he had already established his own position on human rights long before, one in which the divine spark of God manifests itself through human institutions (including human rights) as an immutable truth. As he had put it in his 1932 *The Degrees of Knowledge*, "What we need is not truths that serve us but a truth we may serve" (1959 [1932], 4).[8] In the end, UNESCO's *Human Rights: Comments and Interpretations* was published in 1949 simultaneously in both London (Allan Wingate) and New York City (Columbia University Press).

On a practical level, the influence of the volume in the years after its publication was negligible. It obviously played no role in the deliberations that led to the adoption of the UDHR in December 1948, and the original hope for the book as an "extremely important" contribution seems to have faded with Huxley's departure from UNESCO, also in December 1948, at the end of his abbreviated term as director-general. As a contribution to scholarship, meanwhile, *Human Rights: Comments and Interpretations* was met with puzzlement.

---

8. Maritain's role in the UNESCO survey and book has been frequently mischaracterized, both as to the extent of his participation and as to the content of the introduction; he has been represented as the avatar of a kind of practical human rights pluralism, a characterization clearly at odds with his published philosophy of human rights. For an analysis of the ways in which Maritain's influence on human rights has been conventionally mistaken, sometimes farcically so (for example, he has been described as "the signatory of the Declaration of Human Rights"), see Stibora 2013.

In a particularly devastating review of the volume in *The Philosophical Review*, the philosopher George Holland Sabine writes that the haphazard and unexplained logic and organization of the book make it "quite impossible to make any general statements about the essays that make up the body of the volume" (1951, 105). In addition, the "scope of the topics included in the questionnaire [UNESCO/Phil/1/1947] was so broad that a contributor might write relevantly on almost anything from the abstract principles of a general social philosophy to relatively detailed questions about special subjects, such for example as the rights of primitive and dependent peoples" (105). In fact, as Sabine puts it, the only thing the contributions "have in common is a sense of the desperate seriousness—not to say the hopelessness—of the world situation, and in this respect they probably differ little from the opinions that might have been gathered from persons who were not professional scholars" (105).

Despite the fact that both the record of the UNESCO human rights survey and the volume *Human Rights: Comments and Interpretations* soon disappeared into a postwar history in which human rights more generally was plagued by the geopolitical logics of the Cold War, the UNESCO project was kept alive—at least for a time—by at least one person: its rapporteur (immortalized by Pirsig as the "Chairman"), Richard McKeon. In 1950 or 1951, McKeon participated in the University of Chicago's famous Round Table radio program, a weekly national radio broadcast by university faculty and guests that introduced the general public to important themes and civic discussions. His presentation was entitled "Human Rights" and accompanied a home study course based on *Human Rights: Comments and Interpretations*. A syllabus, of sorts, for this course directs students to read the volume in full and then write answers to questions such as "What are the contributions of various cultures and religions to the meaning of human rights and what are the means by which these contributions may be made effective?"

The impact of McKeon's efforts to promote *Human Rights: Comments and Interpretations* in this way is difficult to measure, although one intriguing piece of evidence points to at least some broader reach. For a January 1953 edition of *The Indianapolis Recorder*, one of the oldest African-American publications in the United States, T. C. Johnson, a *Recorder* columnist and "retired Hoosier schoolmaster,"[9] contributed an opinion piece entitled "Some Conclusions about Human Rights" based on his participation in McKeon's Round Table course, for which Johnson had "received a citation from the University of Chicago, Home Study Department." In his piece, written as civil rights battles were raging in the

---

9. "Hoosier" is the common nickname for someone from the US state of Indiana.

United States—indeed, a political cartoon just above Johnson's article depicts several Ku Klux Klan members putting debris on a railroad track as a train called "Freedom" bears down; one of the Klansmen says "Some here are taking this freedom business literally!"—Johnson argues that "attempts to realize human rights rarely have been in the interest of the masses. Legal equality in most Western countries has meant little to working people in general, and particularly so as regards American Negroes."

Yet except for the fact that *Human Rights: Comments and Interpretations* was reprinted by Greenwood Press in 1973, the volume, its origins, and its contents were largely forgotten for almost fifty years. But then something curious happened: the book, and through it the UNESCO human rights survey, was rediscovered at the end of the first decade of the post–Cold War era, during a critical moment in history in which the new "age of human rights" (Annan 2000) was being challenged by various forms of criticism based on the postcolonial argument that human rights was a form of Western moral imperialism masquerading as a set of universal truths.

Since scholars' ideological and political beliefs on the question of human rights often overlapped with their research agendas, the difficult problem during this period was how to respond to such challenges. Despite the nuances, the matter revolved around one basic and even urgent dilemma: were human rights, in fact, universal, even if they were closely associated with key moments in Western history, such as the promulgation of the French Declaration of the Rights of Man and of the Citizen and the American Declaration of Independence? And even more basic: how should this dilemma be resolved, once and for all? Was it possible to prove, empirically, the universality of human rights?

The rediscovery of *Human Rights: Comments and Interpretations* by a small group of prominent historians and researchers during the late 1990s seemed to provide just such empirical evidence; indeed, it seemed to be the ultimate trump card to be used against those who wanted to historicize, culturalize, and relativize the grand project of human rights. In a series of studies (e.g., Lauren 1998; Morsink 1999), scholars reacted with delighted surprise to learn that at the same time in which the CHR was going about the bureaucratic business of drafting the UDHR, another, hitherto hidden, process had been taking place, one with much farther-reaching implications. Adopting the characterization from *Human Rights: Comments and Interpretations* itself, these scholars discovered that UNESCO had conducted an empirical survey of "nearly all the world's national groups and nearly all ideological approaches" (to recall Havet's description in the 1948 *UNESCO Courier*) and found that the principles of human rights *were*, in fact, universal. That this survey took place before the adoption of the UDHR was even more significant, since that meant that this startling finding was not the result of any rhetoric or policies following the adoption of the UDHR in December 1948.

Among the influential wielders of *Human Rights: Comments and Interpretations* as a trump card, none were as important or consequential as Mary Ann Glendon. In a series of articles published in 1998 and 1999 (e.g., Glendon 1998, 1999), she establishes the building blocks for the argument that the findings of the UNESCO survey marked a key turning point in the history of human rights. As she explains:

> In 1946, UNESCO appointed a committee of philosophers to try to figure out whether it was feasible to frame a "bill of rights" for all peoples and nations. The committee, which included many of the leading thinkers of the day, sent a detailed questionnaire to statesmen and scholars in every part of the world. To their surprise, they found that the lists of basic rights and values they received from their far-flung sources were essentially similar. (Glendon 1998, 613)

As her research on what became *A World Made New: Eleanor Roosevelt and the Universal Declaration of Human Rights* (2001) advanced, Glendon's appreciation for the implications of the UNESCO survey deepened into a full-blown campaign to meet any challenges to the universality of human rights. As a fellow Harvard Law School faculty member, Martha Minow, put it at the time, "my colleague, Mary Ann Glendon, writes powerfully about the negotiations over the U.N. Declaration of Human Rights. She directly rebuts the charges that the document, and by implication, the human rights movement, is an imposition by the West on the rest of the world" (Minow 2002, 166).

Finally, at the end of *A World Made New*, Glendon puts her cards on the table most directly and forcefully. In a chapter entitled "Universality Under Siege," the rediscovery and promotion of the UNESCO survey and the resulting *Human Rights: Comments and Interpretations* receives its most influential and lasting expression. To those who might question the universal truth of human rights, Glendon gives this rejoinder:

> No one has yet improved on the answer of the UNESCO philosophers: Where basic human values are concerned, cultural diversity has been exaggerated. The group found, after consulting with Confucian, Hindu, Muslim, and European thinkers, that a core of fundamental principles was widely shared in countries that had not yet adopted rights instruments and in cultures that had not embraced the language of rights. Their survey persuaded them that basic human rights rest on "common convictions," even though those convictions "are stated in terms of different philosophic principles and on the background of divergent

political and economic systems." (Glendon 2001, 222; quoting from UNESCO 1949, 258–59)

A World Made New eventually went on to become the principal source for the UNESCO human rights survey, one of the most widely cited books on human rights in history, and an inspiration for any future scholar or human rights practitioner who likewise wanted a nonideological, nonpolitical, empirical answer to the challenge to the universality of human rights. Indeed, in this sense, *A World Made New* supplanted the problematic and difficult-to-obtain *Human Rights: Comments and Interpretations* itself, whose contents now lived on through *A World Made New* and the hundreds of other writings that drew appreciatively from that book.

CONCLUSION: MYTH, HISTORY, IDEOLOGY

As we have seen, UNESCO's ill-fated intervention into the process through which the "Magna Carta for all mankind" was eventually adopted by the United Nations General Assembly marks an extraordinary and even tragic moment in the prehistory of human rights, that liminal period, at the end of the catastrophic first half of the twentieth century, in which basic principles of value, dignity, and belonging were debated.[10] Despite the fact that the report produced by the UNESCO committee, "The Grounds of an International Declaration of Human Rights," did reach the UNCHR in August 1947, its contents and analysis played no role in the deliberations that led to the UDHR, the all-important first draft of which had already been written some five months before. Even so, a majority of the members of the CHR were outraged to learn of UNESCO's survey and report and voted to formally suppress it and refuse to distribute it "to all Members of the United Nations" (E/CN.4/SR/26, 3 December 1947).

Yet if the UNESCO human rights survey, report, and eventual published volume did not serve their original and intended purposes, there was another way in which they might be said to "clarify the principles . . . of the Rights of Man." Because the UNESCO survey took place at the same time in which the CHR was doing its more political and bureaucratic work, the findings of UNESCO's project were able to provide an independent confirmation of the universal claims of human rights, particularly since UNESCO's survey purported to be an empirical process undertaken at a global level.

---

10. As Isaiah Berlin put it, looking back at this period, "I have lived through most of the twentieth century without, I must add, suffering personal hardship. I remember it only as the most terrible century in Western history" (quoted in Hobsbawm 1995, 1).

The UNESCO survey was not, however, in fact undertaken at a global level. Despite the admirable and even heroic way in which Havet and Huxley went about the task of radically transforming the original closed conference of philosophers into a much more open process, the fact remained that the constraints of time, politics, and communication technology meant that what resulted, while fascinating and important in its own right, reflected those structural limitations. However, from the very beginning, there was a mythic narrative being developed about how the UNESCO survey was sent to "philosophers, scientists, and political figures throughout the world" and responses were received that represented "all the world's national groups and nearly all ideological approaches" (Havet 1948, 8). Fifty years later, as a response to critiques of human rights at the end of the first decade of the post–Cold War era, in which the "curious grapevine" (Korey 1998) of global activism had made human rights a powerful mode of contemporary world-making, scholars rediscovered this mythic narrative and invested it with foundational importance. In 1947 and 1948, "statesmen and scholars in every part of the world" had long ago provided the empirical proof for what contemporary human rights scholars and activists were vigorously arguing: that "cultural diversity has been exaggerated." The principles of human rights were universal after all, as UNESCO's "far-flung sources" revealed.

But even if the actual UNESCO human rights process was much more limited than this mythic narrative suggests, what about the content of the responses that *were* received? That is, even if we agree that the UNESCO survey was undertaken amongst a relatively small, if distinguished, sample, what did the replies to it reveal about the question of human rights during this important historical moment? Were they "essentially similar"? Did these 57 to 59 responses to UNESCO/Phil/1/1947 rest on "common convictions"? As we will see in Part III, despite the great variety in the responses, they do reveal certain patterns and similarities. Yet if any "common convictions" can be said to emerge from them, they would be those that either doubt the value of the entire project of human rights itself, or prefer to understand it as a temporary, historically contingent, reaction to the horrors of world war, a reaction whose relevance would diminish in the course of time and technological advancement.

REFERENCES CITED

Annan, Kofi. 2000. "The Age of Human Rights." In *Project Syndicate*. http://www.project-syndicate.org/commentary/the-age-of-human-rights?barrier=true.

Glendon, Mary Ann. 1998. "Rights Babel: The Universal Rights Idea at the Dawn of the Third Millennium." *Gregorianum* 79 (4): 611–24.

Glendon, Mary Ann. 1999. Foundations of Human Rights: The Unfinished Business. American Journal of Jurisprudence 44 (1):1–14.

Glendon, Mary Ann. 2001. *A World Made New: Eleanor Roosevelt and the Universal Declaration of Human Rights*. New York: Random House.

Havet, Jacques. 1948. "Distinguished World Thinkers Study Bases of Human Rights." *UNESCO Courier* 1 (7): 8.

Hobbins, A. J. 1989. "René Cassin and the Daughter of Time: The First Draft of the Universal Declaration of Human Rights." *Fontanus* II: 7–26.

Hobsbawm, Eric. 1995. *Age of Extremes: The Short Twentieth Century, 1914–1991*. London: Abacus.

Humphrey, John P. 1984. *Human Rights and the United Nations: A Great Adventure*. New York: Transnational Publishers.

Huxley, Julian. 1946. *UNESCO: Its Purposes and Its Philosophy*. London: Preparatory Commission of The United Nations Educational, Scientific, and Cultural Organization.

Israël, Stéphane. 2005. *Les Études et la Guerre: Les normaliens dans la tourmente (1939–1945)*. Paris: Éditions rue d'Ulm.

Johnson, T. C. 1953. "Some Conclusions About Human Rights." *The Indianapolis Recorder*, January 3.

Korey, William. 1998. *NGOS and the Universal Declaration of Human Rights: "A Curious Grapevine."* New York: St. Martin's Press.

Lauren, Paul Gordon. 1998. *The Evolution of International Human Rights: Visions Seen*. Philadelphia: University of Pennsylvania Press.

Maritain, Jacques. 1959 [1932]. *The Degrees of Knowledge*. London: Geoffrey Bles.

Minow, Martha. 2002. "Lawyering for Human Dignity." *Journal of Gender, Social Policy & the Law* 11 (1): 143–70.

Morsink, Johannes. 1999. *The Universal Declaration of Human Rights: Origins, Drafting, Intent*. Philadelphia: University of Pennsylvania Press.

Obermiller, Tim Andrew. 1994. "Will the real Richard McKeon please stand up?" University of Chicago Magazine. December. http://magazine.uchicago.edu/9412/Feat4.html.

Roosevelt, Eleanor. 1948. "The Promise of Human Rights." *Foreign Affairs* 26(3): 470–77.

Sabine, George Holland. 1951. "Review of *Human Rights: Comments and Interpretations* by UNESCO." *The Philosophical Review* 60 (1): 104–6.

Sewell, James Patrick. 1975. *UNESCO and World Politics: Engaging in International Relations*. Princeton: Princeton University Press.

Stibora, Carrie Rose. 2013. "Jacques Maritain and Alasdair MacIntyre on Human Rights." PhD diss., School of Philosophy, The Catholic University of America.

UNESCO. 1947. Proceedings of the First General Conference, held at UNESCO House, Paris, From 20 November to 10 December 1946. http://unesdoc.unesco.org/images/0011/001145/114580e.pdf.

UNESCO. 1949 *Human Rights: Comments and Interpretations*. New York: Columbia University Press; London: Allan Wingate.

UNESCO. 2017. "UNESCO House." http://www.unesco.org/new/en/unesco/about-us/who-we-are/history/paris-headquarters/ (accessed May 17, 2017).

United Nations Economic and Social Council. 1947. Commission on Human Rights, Second Session, Summary Record of the Twenty-Sixth Meeting, Palais des Nations, Geneva. E/CN,4/SR/26, 3 December.

Weindling, Paul J. 2010 *John W. Thompson: Psychiatrist in the Shadow of the Holocaust*. Rochester: University of Rochester Press.

Interpretations

From a "Hollow Sham" to a "Plurality of Cultural Values"

As we saw in the introduction, the conventional wisdom about the UNESCO human rights survey of 1947 and 1948 has involved two lines of interpretation. The first is that the UNESCO intervention into the process that led to the adoption of the Universal Declaration of Human Rights (UDHR) in 1948 constituted a parallel, and largely hidden, history, one in which a specialized agency of the United Nations independently confirmed the empirical foundations of the UDHR's universal principles. These foundations were established through a global inquiry among "all the world's national groups and nearly all ideological approaches" (Havet 1948, 8). And second, the results of this global survey demonstrated that the underlying values of human rights were held in common despite being expressed through "different philosophic principles and on the background of divergent political and economic systems" (UNESCO 1949, 258–59).

It is this second dimension to the conventional wisdom that is the subject of this chapter. As I emphasize in the introduction, the purpose of the present volume is, at the broadest level, to provide readers with the full range of responses to the UNESCO survey, including those published in UNESCO 1949, those received but not published, and the various items of correspondence, including refusals to respond, that constitute substantive contributions to the question of human rights. If the argument is that the UNESCO survey and what resulted have formed the basis for an ideologically shaped mythic narrative that both "rebuts the charges that . . . the human rights movement . . . is an imposition by the West on the rest of the world" (Minow 2002, 166) and sees human values and cultural diversity as opposed to each other, then one must be careful not to claim too much for an alternative interpretation.

Yet my argument is also that for the reasons described in the previous chapter, the creation of the UNESCO survey, the distribution of requests, the analysis of responses, the editing of UNESCO 1949, and the inclusion of an introduction to that volume did not take place in a recognizably systematic or critical way; rather, the entire process was, in a sense, predetermined by the objective toward which it was directed, namely, the discovery of a set of "principles on which might be founded a modern declaration of the Rights of Man" (UNESCO 1947, 236). The possibility that the UNESCO process might not discover such principles was never considered. Indeed, such an outcome was both politically and ideologically impossible. As the *UNESCO Courier* put it at the time as the lead-in to an article by Jacques Havet, the UNESCO survey was "undertaken following history's most terrible conflict—a conflict by the peoples of the world against the denial of Human Rights" (Havet 1948, 8). To not reaffirm the truth behind human rights would be to deny them once again.

In this volume, however, in the absence of that kind of historical immediacy, what I have attempted to do is to subject the various responses, correspondence, and reports to editing, critical synthesis, annotation, and analysis properly speaking. In so doing, the following questions have guided the logic of organization and interpretation:

1. How does the author respond to both the general and specific questions posed in UNESCO/Phil/1/1947?
2. Does the author reveal any predispositions toward the idea of human rights, either as a concrete response to the exigencies of the historical period or as a normative question?
3. How does the author use the invitation to reflect more generally on the contemporary world as it was understood at the time?
4. What analytical, philosophical, or cultural patterns emerge across the 57 to 59 responses, such that one can say that the UNESCO survey, such as it was, revealed any "common convictions"?
5. And finally, based on the responses, is it reasonable to conclude that a "core of fundamental principles was widely shared" in the world and that therefore arguments for the universality of human rights—whether in the UDHR or otherwise—are justified?

Working under these editorial criteria, I was able to identify nine thematic clusters within which the responses could be organized. These clusters are by no means equal in terms of numbers or their importance to the broader project. The description and organization of these clusters are also obviously open to further interpretation and revision. Indeed, it is my hope that this volume will stimulate other readings, other ways of understanding what these responses to the question of human rights can teach us more generally about the role of human rights in the contemporary world. Nevertheless, before describing the rationale for each cluster, several more general points should be made.

First, it soon became clear that the presentation of the UNESCO survey, particularly through McKeon's report on findings that was sent to the UN Commission on Human Rights (CHR) ("The Grounds of an International Declaration of Human Rights"; see Part II), suppressed the importance of the many responses that challenged the idea of human rights as an outdated framework that was no longer adequate to meet contemporary economic, political, and ideological challenges. This fundamental skepticism toward human rights was most commonly grounded in Marxist or socialist theories of historical development, which located the age of human rights in the late eighteenth century, when liberal philosophies of the person were closely tied to the overthrow of the feudal order and the rise of a commercial bourgeoisie. Indeed, many respondents expressed outright incredulity that UNESCO—and, by extension, the postwar international system—would so easily embrace human rights as the basis for the new settlement, since they associated liberal human rights with a capitalist mode of production that they believed was at the root of global conflict.

Second, despite the fact that Jacques Havet's *aide-mémoire* and questionnaire (UNESCO/Phil/1/1947; see Part II) were intended to shape responses around the specific consideration of particular proposed rights and freedoms, it is notable how rarely these directions were followed. Instead, respondents used the opportunity to discuss a wide range of issues, many of which were only tangentially related to the immediate task of preparing a "Declaration on the Rights of Man for the entire world," as Havet's cover letter put it. The diversity of responses, both in form and content, provides evidence for how the "rights of man" was either a vague referent, even for leading intellectuals and political thinkers at the time, or a nostalgic concept that paled in comparison with the challenges of technological conflict, population growth, and colonialism.

Third, for those who did structure their responses as an answer to the UNESCO questionnaire, it is important to underscore the way in which the normative expectations of human rights, as described historically by Havet in UNESCO/Phil/1/1947, created a kind of conceptual straitjacket that led respondents to produce what appear, in retrospect, to have been contrived efforts to play along. This is perhaps nowhere as clearly present as in the small group of much-misinterpreted "non-Western" responses, particularly those of S. V. Puntambekar and Humayun Kabir. Their essays, which—along with those of Chung-Shu Lo (who, as was mentioned in the previous chapter, was actually a UNESCO consultant at the time in Paris) and Mahatma Gandhi—have been taken as evidence that responses "poured in" (Lauren 1998, 210) from around the world, are not really arguments for how human rights are consistent with Hindu and Islamic traditions. Rather, in responding to the dictates of UNESCO/Phil/1/1947, they read as attempts to demonstrate how even a Hindu or a Muslim can support a Western, liberal conception of the "rights of man."

Finally, despite the impression given by McKeon's report to the CHR, and, more generally, the way in which the UNESCO survey has been characterized in histories of human rights (see the previous chapter), the full body of responses, private correspondence, and substantive refusals to respond to UNESCO/ Phil/1/1947 expresses a pervasive and ideologically diffuse apprehension about making human rights the centerpiece of the postwar system. Even the American respondents, who comprise most of the clearly supportive advocates for a declaration of human rights, were not wholly enthusiastic about the idea. Indeed, two of the strongest critiques of human rights were made (for very different reasons) by Americans, the philosopher and ethicist John Somerville and the anthropologist Melville Herskovits. Taken as a whole, then, one must conclude that these materials do not reflect a "core of fundamental principles" and that if any "common convictions" are to be associated with them, it is, with notable exceptions, a sense of indifference toward human rights in relation to other, more justifiable, blueprints for the postwar world order.

* * *

For reasons of space and economy, it is not possible to provide lengthy introductions to each response, piece of correspondence, and substantive refusal. Nevertheless, it is important to explain the logic behind each cluster of materials and to highlight certain key features.

LIBERALISM FROM THE ASHES

The first cluster of responses to the UNESCO survey consists of those that most unequivocally embrace the project of writing a "Declaration on the Rights of Man for the entire world." In responding to UNESCO/Phil/1/1947, they most directly endorse the liberal framework of rights as established in the earlier American and French declarations. The responses range from Arnold Lien's full-throated argument for a libertarian conception of rights grounded in the emancipatory potential of self-interest to McKeon's insistence that a new human rights declaration should be structured by the same universal ideals expressed in the eighteenth-century declarations, "which had a profound influence in improving the relations of men and in advancing the practice of justice." Quincy Wright's response addresses the debates that were then raging over the relationship between individual and social and economic rights. On the one hand, as he puts it, "social claims are in danger of snuffing out any real personal liberty." But on the other hand, social and economic rights are "less susceptible of universalization than are the more individualistic rights." For these reasons, he concludes that a new declaration should focus only on universal individual human rights. Lewis Mumford's response is more philosophical. What is a human right? he asks. It is that which "establish[es] those characteristics without which a person is not a person, but a mere biological organism or a slave." And finally, since

McKeon, as rapporteur for the UNESCO Committee of Experts, was responsible for writing the draft of the report to the CHR, it is not surprising that "The Grounds of an International Declaration of Human Rights" largely mirrors his own contribution and imparts a strained sense of consensus to the actual diversity of responses to the UNESCO survey.

BEYOND EGOTISTIC MAN—COMMUNIST, SOCIALIST, AND SOCIAL-DEMOCRATIC CHALLENGES

The essays in this thematic cluster directly challenge the idea of human rights, particularly in the largely liberal form that eventually was codified in the UDHR. The authors in this section come from a range of national backgrounds—the United Kingdom, the United States, Belgium, the Soviet Union, Sweden—and they offer, as an alternative to human rights, various programs for global social change and peace based in Marxist, socialist, social-democratic, and trade-union ideologies. It is notable that three members of the UNESCO Committee of Experts itself (Laski, Somerhausen, and Carr, the committee chair) wrote essays that were deeply critical, even dismissive, of the project of human rights. Numerically, this cluster contains the second largest number of responses to the UNESCO survey.

A unifying argument that links all of the contributions in this cluster is the idea that socialist societies represented a historical advance over the bourgeois approaches to politics and economy that arose in the eighteenth century. This was obviously not an argument that would appeal, in particular, to the American advocates for a universalist declaration of human rights centered on liberal individualism, and it is likely the reason that the lengthy, substantive, and numerous socialist and Marxist critiques of human rights among the responses were given short shrift by McKeon in "The Grounds of an International Declaration of Human Rights." It is one thing to make vague references to a certain amount of diversity of opinion among the responses to the UNESCO survey while at the same time concluding that this diversity does not detract from a core basis of support for human rights. It is quite another thing to acknowledge that this diversity includes, as it does in this important cluster, a fundamental challenge to human rights declarations based on the argument that they are central to a mode of production (capitalism) that has been the primary cause of global inequality and conflict.

Moreover, as Carr argues in his response, the liberal model of human rights declarations rests on a basic contradiction, one that feeds the division of wealth within societies and creates social relations that are characterized by narrow self-interest. In recognizing the individual rights of citizens without also demanding duties of them, particular those that can be harnessed to "direct the productive capacities of the entire society," human rights declarations become a "hollow sham." And in his response, Harold Laski takes this critique of human rights even further. It is not simply the empirical problem that liberal human rights declarations underwrite the exploitative conflicts of capitalism. This is, according to Laski, true enough. Yet in addition, the principle of "equality before the law" is itself false, since it is based on the idea that the pursuit of enlightened self-interest will lead to the good of the whole community "by some mysterious alchemy." In fact, as he puts it, "'equality before the law' has not meant very much in the lives of the working-class in most political communities, and still less to Negroes in the Southern states of the United States."

RIGHTS IN A SACRED UNIVERSE

Another cluster of responses to the UNESCO survey does not directly challenge the idea of human rights per se but instead takes issue with an overly humanist or liberal grounding. These essays, including Jacques Maritain's introduction to UNESCO 1949, emphasize the spiritual origins of all rights and duties and invoke the shaping hand of the divine to greater or lesser degrees. The extent to which these responses can be reconciled with the largely liberal, secular UDHR varies. It is notable that all of the essays in this section were written by Catholic scholars or theologians.

For example, Pedro Troncoso Sánchez, president of the Supreme Court of the Dominican Republic (and future Dominican ambassador to the Holy See), takes a strong stand against any conception of human rights that is grounded in secular values. Instead, humans pursue worldly objectives like liberty, freedom, and moral knowledge within the boundaries of a greater, spiritual order, one that gives us our ultimate meaning and purpose. To base a declaration of rights on purely economic or political considerations, Troncoso Sánchez argues, is to "lower . . . man to an animal condition."

The conservative Belgian philosopher and monarchist Marcel de Corte, in his response, makes a veiled but unmistakable attack on conceptions of human rights that remain abstract and theoretical, since all rights and duties ultimately come from "God, who gave [us] this concrete individual and social life."

Finally, in his own contribution, Jacques Maritain—whose December 1947 Mexico City speech formed the basis of the introduction to UNESCO 1949—makes it clear that the "true metaphysical connotations" of human rights lie well beyond any rational justifications. Although later commentators have described Maritain's position on human rights as one that focuses on practical agreement, they misconstrue the reason for his argument against "arbitrary dogmatism." It is not that human rights are the result of cross-cultural compromise and tolerance, but rather that any human institutions can only ever approximate what he calls the "Absolute greater than this world." In other words, for Maritain, natural law is the hand of God working through his imperfect creations.

THE UNIVERSAL DECLARATION OF HUMAN DUTIES

A smaller but important group of responses to the UNESCO survey challenges the project of human rights on the basis that it should be duties, not rights, that form the foundation of an international declaration. The authors in this cluster make this argument from a variety of positions. The most famous of these responses was sent by Mahatma Gandhi in the form of a letter to Julian Huxley written "in a moving train," eight months before Gandhi was assassinated. In Gandhi's pithy reply to UNESCO/Phil/1/1947, he explains that duties, including the "duty of citizenship of the world," are the genuine basis for everything "worth fighting for." Rights, in and of themselves, are a mere "usurpation" of this true moral order.

In his analysis of human rights and the "Chinese tradition," Chung-Shu Lo argues that the "basic ethical concept of Chinese social political relations is the fulfillment of the duty to one's neighbor, rather than the claiming of rights." Given the long influence of Confucian philosophy within Chinese history, duties can be understood in relation to a series of fundamental social dyads that define obligations that must be discharged—from subjects to ruler, from children to parents, from wife to husband, from younger to elder brother, and from friend to friend. Even though he acknowledges that "human rights" had no relevance in Chinese history until the "conception was introduced from the West" (via a Chinese translation of an 1868 Japanese text on "Western Public Law"), Lo's response to the UNESCO survey has been among the most misinterpreted by later writers and historians. Instead of reading it to say that a universal declaration of human rights would be antithetical to China's Confucian tradition, later authors, perhaps all too willing to accept Lo's own strained attempt to square the circle, have taken it as evidence that Confucianism and Western liberalism rested on the same "core of fundamental principles."

THE TECHNOLOGICAL SOCIETY OF THE FUTURE

Another surprising finding of this project is that during the late 1940s, many people looked to science and technology as the source of transformative insights about basic questions of war, peace, politics, and morality, this despite the fact that rapid developments in science had made possible the development of the two atomic bombs that were used by the United States against Japan at the end of the war (actions that would be classified as "crimes against humanity" according to current definitions). Several respondents to the UNESCO survey offer scientific approaches as an alternative to human rights as the basis for the new world order.

The American chemist W. Albert Noyes, Jr., for example, argues that any development of human rights will have to wait until the techniques of science have managed to reduce the burdens of the "struggle of mankind for prosperity and happiness." Until problems like poverty, disease, and population growth have been addressed by science, the question of human rights will have to be postponed. And if and when this time comes, the "Rights of Man" will have to be "redefined" in order to "fit the human race into a scientific world."

Julian Huxley's brother, the author Aldous Huxley, used his response to the UNESCO survey to make a lengthy argument for the relationship between unchecked global population growth and international conflict. As he puts it, the "increasing pressure of population upon resources and the waging, threat of, and unremitting preparation for total war—these are, at the present time, the most formidable enemies to liberty." Huxley's principal concern was the rate of population growth. He worries that by "the end of the present century world population will have increased . . . to about 3.3 billions." (As it turned out, global population had already reached 3.5 billion by 1965, and almost 6.1 billion by the end of the twentieth century, nearly double Huxley's anxious prediction.) In light of these broader, truly global challenges, Huxley is dismissive of the project to write a universal declaration of human rights. He argues that the UDHR will be just a set of "paper restrictions, designed to curb the abuse of a power already concentrated in a few hands, . . . the mitigations of an existing evil. Personal liberty can be made secure only by abolishing the evil altogether."

UNIVERSALITY IN A COLONIAL WORLD

As we saw in the previous chapter, the distribution of human rights surveys sent out and received back by UNESCO in 1947 and 1948 reflected several factors, including the rushed nature of the process, the scope of Julian Huxley's and Jacques Havet's professional and personal networks, and the challenges of communicating with potential respondents in different parts of the world through typed and handwritten documents sent through traditional postal services (telegraph messages do appear in the archives but these were appropriate only for brief communications).

Yet there was another, broader factor that indelibly shaped the UNESCO survey: the fact that the world of 1947 was still influenced by colonialism. Although the seeds of international decolonization had been planted in different ways, most notably in the 1941 Atlantic Charter and then in the 1945 UN Charter, much of Africa and large parts of South and Southeast Asia, among others, were still under direct colonial control at the time of the UNESCO survey. When Huxley and Havet considered the problem of measuring perspectives on human rights from "all the world's national groups and nearly all ideological approaches," as Havet had put it, the distortions of colonialism were an important reason for the deeply unrepresentative sample that eventually participated. For example, in 1947, there were only four independent states in Africa (Liberia, South Africa, Egypt, and Ethiopia). The entire continent is represented in the UNESCO survey by only two responses, both from South Africa: the first from the British–South African educational reformer Maurice Webb and the second from the Afrikaner classicist and University of the Witwatersrand professor Theodore Johannes Haarhoff.

Nevertheless, despite these geopolitical and ideological boundaries, Huxley and Havet did make an effort to broaden the human rights survey beyond the Anglo-European world, in terms of both the identities of respondents and the expected topics of their responses. Three of the respondents (Kabir, Puntambekar, and Lo) had been chosen as the result of a specific concern to receive ideas on human rights from what is referred to in correspondence and among the Committee of Experts as "the East." The American philosopher F. S. C. Northrop's volume *The Meeting of East and West: An Inquiry Concerning World Understanding* had just been published (in 1946), and its dualistic framework of cultural diversity shaped the way that "all the world's national groups and nearly all ideological approaches" were understood by the survey's main protagonists.

In addition, two responses were received that examine the broader question of colonialism and human rights. In his essay on the "rights of dependent peoples," Leonard Barnes makes a full-throated and deeply felt critique of colonial rule as fundamentally incompatible with human rights. And the Australian anthropologist A. P. Elkin uses his research among Australian aborigines to enumerate a lengthy list of "rights of primitive peoples" that should be taken into consideration during the drafting of the UDHR.

HUMAN RIGHTS AS HISTORY AND PRACTICE

This cluster of responses (along with the grouping of communist, socialist, and social democratic challenges) is both the most numerous and the most significant of the clusters. These responses are more varied in tone and background, but what they share is the fact that they reject the natural law and natural rights legacies of human rights. Each, in its own way, argues for the role of history, contingency, and politics in the understanding of rights and duties within society. Some of the essays propose an essentially cultural approach to the question of human rights; others are more skeptical and argue that the historical record does not lend support to the effort to draft yet another bill of rights as the foundation for the postwar settlement.

For example, in a withering critique of natural rights declarations, the Belgian legal scholar Jean Haesaert dismisses the drafters of such documents as "turbulent improvisers" who use the language of rights to cloak their own ambitions for power and advancement during times of political transition. As he puts it, "on the occasion of each fresh social change, the new masters have advanced their own ideals by clothing them with the name of rights." At the same time, values that are central to rights declarations either quickly become a "dead letter" or are altered beyond recognition. With reference to the value of equality, it has "been reduced to the narrow civic equality that we know so well. Political equality has barely begun and economic equality is not considered."

In his response to the UNESCO survey, the aging Italian humanist Benedetto Croce argues that all declarations of "natural and inalienable" rights are based on a theory that centuries of critiques "on many sides" have managed to destroy—the theory of universal human rights. Instead, Croce urges UNESCO to develop an alternative approach, one in which rights are understood "not [as] eternal claims but simply [as] historical facts." At the same time, before any such statement of "the rights of man in history" can be articulated, UNESCO should occupy itself with a prior, and more important task, according to Croce: to encourage a "formal, public and international debate on the necessary principles underlying human dignity and civilization."

Finally, in a response that examines most directly what would be understood today as the cultural dimensions of human rights, F. S. C. Northrop develops a robust pluralist approach that is "rooted in at least some of the accepted institutions and social doctrines of each and every people." Otherwise, the default position, that is, the one associated with history's great liberal rights declarations, assumes "that the traditional modern French and Anglo-American concept of freedom and its attendant Bill of Rights exhausts the meaning of the concept." The negative consequences of such a default position have been both political and moral. As Northrop puts it, the "price of a society rooted in the traditional modern Bill of Rights has tended to be a culture of laissez faire businessmen's values, with all the other values and aspirations of mankind left anemic and spiritually and ideologically unsustained."

SPECIFIC FREEDOMS

Several of the respondents to the UNESCO survey analyze (or argue for) specific freedoms rather than a declaration of human rights as such. This small cluster includes the only submission by a woman, a powerful mini-treatise on prisoners as a "limiting case" for human rights by the 73-year-old English prison reformer Margery Fry. Also included is an idiosyncratic essay on children's rights by the Hungarian scientist Albert Szent-Györgyi, winner of the 1937 Nobel Prize in Medicine for his discovery of vitamin C. In a response that echoes particularly loudly at the current moment in history (late 2017 at the time of this writing), René Maheu argues that the right to information should be seen as the most fundamental right, that which enables all others. When information is not free, when it is tainted by the forces that benefit from disinformation, the entire democratic order is in peril, either "torn by passion or possessed of the devils of credulity." The freedom of information is not a perfect tool, however. Even in societies in which the right to expression is protected, there is the possibility that bad information will influence political decisions. But Maheu believes this risk to be both inevitable and worth the struggle. As he argues, "is there any liberty without risk? Risk abides in the heart of man, for man exists only by inventing himself."

FROM REPUDIATION TO THE PLAY OF FANCY

The final cluster of responses to the UNESCO survey, which includes a number of letters and substantive refusals, is both the most literary and the most difficult to sort analytically. This is perhaps not surprising given that the grouping contains several previously unknown contributions from respondents who were at the time world-famous writers and artists. I describe their responses as the play of fancy, since what they produced has little connection to either the documents in UNESCO/Phil/1/1947 or the question of human rights more generally. At the same time, this cluster features the most sustained and systematic repudiation of what would become the UDHR, namely the essay by the American anthropologist Melville Herskovits, which was the contribution that first stimulated my own intellectual and historical interest in the UNESCO process (see my introduction).

This cluster begins with a substantive letter of refusal from Morris L. Ernst to Richard McKeon. Ernst, one of the founders of the American Civil Liberties Union, who had just left the hospital after a serious illness, was not able to write at great length. But in refusing UNESCO's invitation, he expresses great skepticism about a human rights declaration. As he puts it, "it seems to me that we are finished with the era of passing general resolutions in regard to liberty and freedom. I am not opposed to the creation of new, neatly worded symbols for man to use as goals. But the continued yapping . . . for the free flow of thought seems to me at this time to be doing little more than creating cynicism." Ernst would prefer to put energy behind specific areas of practical concern rather than into the fruitless quest for a set of core global human rights principles. Yet he realizes that his opposition will likely fall on deaf ears: "Huxley, wonderful dream boy that he is, is obviously not excited about small concepts like postage barriers or customs rates."

The response by the Australian theologian Ernest Henry Burgmann, a legendary figure known as both the "bushman bishop" and the "red bishop" (for his left-wing political positions), is a highly creative reflection on how historical ideas like human rights become problematic myths that demand to be served with "idolatrous passion." Instead of yet another modern myth, Burgmann argues, what the world needs is a compelling "song of hope." As he puts it, "what song then should [we] teach the youth of the world to sing? It must be a song that looks war in the face and yet continues to sing of better things. The heart must be strong enough to conquer hate, and the mind clear enough to see the Question from the point of view of the whole world. It will be the hardest song to learn that the race has ever been called upon to sing."

Further selections in this final cluster include responses by the composer Arnold Schoenberg (who invented 12-tone music) and the English writer W. H. Auden, whose essay rises—perhaps not surprisingly—to the level of literature (at one point, he quotes Shakespeare's line from *The Tempest*, "Hell is empty, And all the devils are here"). The cluster ends with two substantive refusal letters from the English anarchist and literary critic Herbert Read and the Nobel-Prize-winning poet T. S. Eliot, both of whom reject the idea of human rights—Eliot from a conservative perspective that echoes Edmund Burke's critique of the French Revolution and Read from a position of despair over the violence and inhumanity that plagued the first half of the twentieth century.

REFERENCES CITED

Havet, Jacques. 1948. "Distinguished World Thinkers Study Bases of Human Rights." *UNESCO Courier* 1 (7): 8.

Lauren, Paul Gordon. 1998. *The Evolution of International Human Rights: Visions Seen.* Philadelphia: University of Pennsylvania Press.

Minow, Martha. 2002. "Lawyering for Human Dignity." *Journal of Gender, Social Policy & the Law* 11 (1): 143–70.

Northrop, F. S. C. 1946. *The Meeting of East and West: An Inquiry Concerning World Understanding.* New York: The Macmillan Company.

UNESCO. 1947. Proceedings of the First General Conference, held at UNESCO House, Paris, From 20 November to 10 December 1946. http://unesdoc.unesco.org/images/0011/001145/114580e.pdf.

UNESCO. 1949. *Human Rights: Comments and Interpretations.* New York: Columbia University Press.

PART II

KEY DOCUMENTS

Memorandum and Questionnaire Circulated by UNESCO on the Theoretical Bases of the Rights of Man

COVER LETTER

The Commission on Human Rights of the U.N. is to prepare this summer a Declaration on the Rights of Man for the entire world. There is no need to underline the importance of this event, an importance both philosophical and practical, with both immediate and lasting effects. UNESCO has been informed by the Chairman of the Commission [Eleanor Roosevelt] that its views on the principles underlying any such Declaration would be welcomed.

The General Conference of UNESCO had already envisaged a Conference of Philosophers to undertake a general discussion of the subject. However, in view of the immediacy of the task, it has proved necessary to alter this procedure and to ask for contributions in written form, from Governments and from individuals, requesting them to lay before their National Commissions, Co-operating Bodies, or other appropriate groups, the problem of formulating an analysis of the problem of human rights and its underlying principles, so as to permit the formulation of a Declaration of Human Rights for the modern world in its present circumstances.

The Director-General is also inviting a number of individual thinkers to submit a statement on the subject or on a particular aspect of it, to serve as suggestions for a background to the work of the Commission, and is informing Governments of the individuals thus invited.

It is then proposed to submit all contributions received to a small Drafting Committee convened by UNESCO, which will utilize them as the basis for a single document, to be sent to the Chairman of the Commission on Human Rights, to aid in the framing of a Declaration of the Rights of Man.

In addition, the UNESCO Drafting Committee will act as an Editorial Committee, with a view of publishing a comprehensive selection of the contributions received in book form under the auspices of UNESCO.

It is requested that contributions should be dispatched, by air-mail, addressed to:

Monsieur J. Havet
Section de Philosophie

UNESCO,
19 Avenue Kléber,
Paris 16e

(who will act as Secretary to the Drafting and Editorial Committee), so that they may be considered by the Drafting Committee. They should preferably, though not necessarily, be written in English or French, and should be between 2,000 and 4,000 words in length.

An aide-mémoire is appended, setting forth the general framework of ideas in which we hope contributors will treat the problem.

AIDE-MÉMOIRE AND QUESTIONNAIRE

The classical formulations of Human Rights which have been influential in Western culture were first stated in the eighteenth century. They were drawn up on the basis of a conception of individual human rights as absolute and inherent. They thus followed out for the individual the conception which had inspired the idea of the Divine Right of Kings and the imprescriptible rights divinely conferred on the Church, although they attempted to set up against the notion of Divine Right an equally absolute but non-theological formulation of inherent Natural Rights.

Two historical events had been mainly responsible for preparing the way for this formulation of human rights—first, the Reformation with its appeal to the absolute authority of the individual conscience, and secondly the rise of early capitalism with its emphasis on freedom of individual enterprise from the shackles of Church or State authority.

The eighteenth century formulation of Human Rights was truly revolutionary, as shown by its importance in the American and French revolutions and its subsequent effects on political thought in the early nineteenth century; and the subsequent 150 years have been devoted to attempts towards the realization of the ideals therein embodied. Great progress has been made in this effort, despite temporary setbacks and obscurations. Thus, after the first half of the nineteenth century, the principle of religious freedom has been scarcely questioned in the Western democracies, and the right of the individual to the franchise has been progressively rendered more general. Similarly, the principle of the right of national groups to self-determination was much extended.

On the other hand, the passage of time also revealed various unexpected shortcomings and difficulties. Thus it soon became apparent that political freedom by no means guaranteed economic or social freedom. The industrial workers of the mid-nineteenth century were certainly no better off than those of earlier ages, and the freedom to choose one's employment appeared a dubious privilege when the alternative was not to be employed at all. Again, the freedom of individual enterprise became profoundly modified through the rise of even larger business and financial combinations, culminating in the enormous trusts and cartels, often international in their operation, of the twentieth century. Freedom of the press was similarly, though to a less extent, curtailed by the twentieth century developments which so largely converted the press into an affair of big business, of State policy or of party politics, and led to the formation of newspaper chains and syndicated news.

Meanwhile, there were developments in thought which profoundly affected men's general outlook. Among these, two of the most important were the promulgation and general acceptance of the theory of evolution, and the rise of Marxism. The chief effect of both of these on the question of Human Rights was to provide a dynamic and relativistic frame of reference for their consideration. It was realized that all the manifestations of life, including human societies, evolve and change, and accordingly that human rights, whether of individuals or of groups, can be properly considered only in relation to the conditions of time and place.

In addition, Marxist theory laid especial stress on material and economic conditions, thus re-emphasizing the need to analyze the effects of technological advance and of changes in socio-economic structure on human rights, as ideals, as working conceptions and as effective instruments. One of the most important effects of technological advance on our problem was the increased power of military weapons, which made rebellion against authority far more difficult and dangerous.

In the international field, the end of the first World War saw an early attempt at a general formulation of the rights of groups, in the shape of the principle of national self-determination; but its incompleteness and vagueness were speedily realized when the results of efforts to put it into practical operation were appraised. To the last few decades also belong the attempts to formulate the rights of nations and similar groups in relation to the rights of international or supranational groupings—attempts which are still continuing.

Finally, the widespread unemployment of the inter-war period, with its acute financial depression, spelled a crisis for the development of the eighteenth century formulation of the rights of man: among other things, it led to a rapid development of schemes of social security, which ran counter to many of their traditional individualist conceptions.

Meanwhile, these conceptions had been challenged in another way—by the development of the U.S.S.R. after the revolution of 1917. Historically, Russia had never passed through a period comparable to that which had marked the Reformation and the early rise of capitalism in the west, when the emphasis had been on the freedom of the individual, in regard both to conscience and opinion and to economic enterprise, as against organized authority whether of Church or State. Furthermore, events soon drove it to adopt the principle of over-all planning and of one-party Government.

However, one new individual right of freedom was incorporated into Soviet constitutional theory and practice—namely freedom from exploitation for private profit. Further, the principles of racial non-discrimination and of cultural self-determination for the so-called nationalities of the U.S.S.R. have been thoroughly implemented in practice.

Under these circumstances, a quite different working conception of human rights grew up in the Soviet sphere, as is witnessed by the present frequent opposition of the western and the communist usage of the word "democracy."

In addition, the revolutionary situation, which was accompanied by both external and internal threats to the stability of the regime, made it inexpedient to allow full freedom of opinion and conscience, of expression, of press, or information.

In this connexion, it is to be recalled that all nations restrict some or all of these freedoms in situations of emergency such as war or revolution; and further that, as a matter of historical fact, political and other conditions have often affected the degree of freedom allowed in particular spheres (for instance, in the case of the Roman Catholic minority in Britain).

We must also note that the twentieth century has witnessed a trend towards organized economic and social planning in a number of countries other than the U.S.S.R., including some of the western democracies. Since organized planning automatically restricts certain traditional individual freedoms, this has led to renewed interest in a consideration of their theoretical basis.

Thus from one angle the present state of the subject may be regarded as a confrontation of two different working conceptions of human rights, which have arisen from different historical formulations and have developed in relation to different sets of social circumstances. The one started from the premise of inherent individual rights, and with a bias against a strong central authority and against government interference, while the other was based upon Marxist principles and the premise of a powerful central government, and early wedded to total planning (which automatically magnifies the central power) and to one-party Government (which inevitably restricts certain political freedoms). Each has become modified in the course of its history, and in both cases many of the modifications have been in the direction of the other system.

These two working conceptions are in some ways complementary, in others opposed. One of the major tasks immediately ahead of us is thus clearly to find some common measure for the future development of the two tendencies, or in the terms of the Marxist dialectic to effect a reconciliation of the two opposites in a higher synthesis.

In this connection it is worth remarking that the ideal held up by both tendencies is far from dissimilar. The western formulation presupposed that liberty would be followed by equality and fraternity, in economic and social as well as political opportunity, while Marx expressly laid down that the dictatorship of the proletariat, once it has been successfully implemented, will be followed by a "withering away of the State." Again, many western social philosophers incline to the view that truly free enterprise in an age of abundance made possible by the application of science will be able to dispense with all kinds of restrictions on individual freedom and opportunity, while conversely Marxist theory maintains that collectivism properly applied will eventually permit the fullest degree of individual development and variety.

We must not, however, neglect the fact that in other parts of the world other theories of human rights have emerged, are emerging, or are destined to emerge. Fascism is one such. Most thinkers agree that it can be shown to be untenable on theoretical grounds, and in any case it has been discredited and defeated in practice.

Then a quite new formulation of human rights would be required to embody the views of a man like Mahatma Gandhi, or of those numerous Indian thinkers who believe in the social importance and individual value of meditation and mystical experience. And we can be reasonably sure that the ferment of thought now apparent in the peoples of black and brown and yellow skin-colour, from Africa to the Far East, is destined to result in still other formulations.

Meanwhile the immediate issue is clear. The world of man is at a critical stage in its political, social and economic evolution. If it is to proceed further on the path towards unity, it must develop a common set of ideas and principles. One of those is a common formulation of the rights of man. This common formulation must by some means reconcile the various divergent or opposing formulations now in existence. It must further be sufficiently definite to have real significance both as an inspiration and as a guide to practice, but also sufficiently general and flexible to apply to all men, and to be capable of modification to suit peoples at different stages of social and political development while yet retaining significance for them and their aspirations.

These considerations point to several lines of enquiry, both general and special.

(A) <u>GENERAL</u>

1. What are the relations between the political, the social and the economic rights of individuals (of different sexes and ages) and of groups, in societies of different types and in different historical circumstances?

2. How far are the differences between the divergent formulations of ideal human rights and freedoms in different societies accurate indications of the material differences in economic and social conditions in the regions concerned?

3. How far have the personal relations and group relations (e.g. class, national and international) of man been altered in the main advanced regions of the world during the last hundred years,

(a) by intellectual and cultural developments in the fields of the sciences, the arts and philosophy.

(b) by material and social developments in the field of applied science and technology, social and economic structure and national and international organization?

4. In particular;

(a) how far have the traditional human rights of the 18th Century Declarations been affected by the industrial revolution and its consequences before the first World War?

(b) to what extent have the rights of individuals and groups been modified, in theory and in practice, by developments since that time?

5. What are the relations between rights and duties? (a) for individuals (b) for groups? And what are the relations of individual freedoms to corporate or social responsibilities?

6. What emergencies justify the restriction or abrogation of normal rights and freedom?

(B) <u>SPECIAL</u>

What, in the world to-day, are the theoretical grounds, the practical extent, and the efficient guarantees of specific rights or freedoms, such as:

1. Freedom of conscience or worship (a) for individuals (b) for organized religious groups:

2. Freedom of speech (the right to free speech) and freedom of opinion:

3. Freedom of assembly:

4. Freedom of association and freedom for consequent action (the right to strike):

5. Freedom of movement (a) within (b) across national boundaries (c) freedom to leave one nation for another:

6. Freedom of communications and the right to accurate information (a) within (b) across national boundaries (freedom of the press etc.):

7. Political freedom and equality (a) for organized political parties (b) for individuals in the exercise of the franchise (the right to vote):

8. Freedom of expression (including freedom of the writer and the artist);

9. Freedom and equality of economic, social and educational opportunity:

10. Freedom of opportunity for pursuit of the good life:

11. Freedom of teaching:

12. Freedom of scientific and philosophic enquiry and publication:

13. The right to work or not to work; the right of leisure:

14. Freedom and equality of access to the means of subsistence (a) for individuals (b) for nations:

15. Freedom from fear (the right to protection):

16. Freedom from want (economic rights: the right to economic security and to a basic level of material well-being):

17. Freedom from exploitation and oppression (social rights):

18. The right to justice:

19. Freedom from preventable disease (the right to health):

20. The right to property:

21. The rights and freedoms of minorities (a) racial (b) political (c) religious (d) cultural or linguistic, including the right to self-determination:

22. The rights and freedoms of politically dependent (non-self-governing) peoples:

23. The rights of nations in relation (a) to each other (b) to existing or possible international or supra-national organizations:

24. The rights of women, of children, of the disabled and of the aged:

25. Any other rights and freedoms?

Paris, March 1947

The Grounds of an International Declaration of Human Rights[1]

An international declaration of human rights must be the expression of a faith to be maintained no less than a program of actions to be carried out. It is a foundation for convictions universally shared by men however great the differences of their circumstances and their manner of formulating human rights, it is an essential element in the constitutional structure of the United Nations. In order that all peoples and all governments shall be made aware that the authority and goodwill of the United Nations will be exercised with ever increasing power to apply these means for the advancement of human happiness in the great society, it is fitting that its members solemnly proclaim a declaration of rights to the civilized world. Such a declaration depends, however, not only on the authority by which rights are safeguarded and advanced, but also on the common understanding which makes the proclamation feasible and the faith practicable.

The preparation of a Declaration of Human Rights faces fundamental problems concerning principles and interpretations as well as political and diplomatic problems concerning agreement and drafting. For this reason the Unesco Committee on the Philosophic Principles of the Rights of Man has undertaken, on the basis of a survey of the opinion of scholars in the various parts of the world, an examination of the intellectual bases of a modern bill of rights, in the hope that such a study may prove useful to the Commission on Human Rights of the Economic and Social Council both in suggesting common grounds for agreement and in explaining possible sources of differences. The Unesco Committee is convinced that the members of the United Nations share common convictions on which human rights depend, but it is further convinced that those common convictions are stated in terms of different philosophic principles and on the background of divergent political and economic systems. An examination of the grounds of a bill of rights should therefore serve to reveal, on the one hand, the common principles on which the declaration rests and to anticipate, on the other hand, some of the difficulties and differences of interpretation which might otherwise delay or impede agreement concerning the fundamental rights which enter into the declaration.

---

1. Final result of the Unesco enquiry on the theoretical bases of human rights, drafted by a committee of experts on the basis of the various contributions to the enquiry.

* * *

The United Nations stands as the symbol to all of victory over those who sought to achieve tyranny through aggressive war. Since it was created to maintain the peace of mankind and, as it maintains peace, to make ever more full the lives of men and women everywhere, it is fitting that it should record its faith in freedom and democracy and its determination to safeguard their power to expand. That faith in freedom and democracy is founded on the faith in the inherent dignity of men and women. The United Nations cannot succeed in the great purposes to which it is committed unless it so acts that this dignity is given increasing recognition, and unless steps are taken to create the conditions under which this dignity may be achieved more fully and at constantly higher levels. Varied in cultures and built upon different institutions, the members of the United Nations have, nevertheless, certain great principles in common. They believe that men and women, all over the world, have the right to live a life that is free from the haunting fear of poverty and insecurity.

They believe that they should have a more complete access to the heritage, in all its aspects and dimensions, of the civilization so painfully built by human effort. They believe that science and the arts should combine to serve alike peace and the well-being, spiritual as well as material, of all men and women without discrimination of any kind. They believe that, given goodwill between nations, the power is in their hands to advance the achievement of this well-being more swiftly than in any previous age.

It is this faith, in the opinion of the UNESCO Committee, which underlies the solemn obligation of the United Nations to declare, not only to all governments, but also to their peoples, the rights which have now become the vital ends of human effort everywhere. These rights must no longer be confined to a few. They are claims which all men and women may legitimately make, in their search, not only to fulfill themselves at their best, but to be so placed in life that they are capable, at their best, of becoming in the highest sense citizens of the various communities to which they belong and of the world community, and in those communities of seeking to respect the rights of others, just as they are resolute to protect their own.

* * *

Despite the antiquity and the broad acceptance of the conception of the rights of man, and despite the long evolution of devices to protect some human rights by legal systems, the systematic proclamation of declarations of human rights is recent. The history of the philosophic discussion of human rights, of the dignity and brotherhood of man, and of his common citizenship in the great society is long: it extends beyond the narrow limits of the western tradition and its beginnings in the West as well as in the East coincide with the beginnings of philosophy. The history of declarations of human rights, on the other hand, is short and its beginnings are to be found in the West in the British Bill of Rights and the American and French Declarations of Rights formulated in the seventeenth and eighteenth centuries, although the right of the people to revolt against political oppression was very early recognized and established in China. The relation of philosophic considerations to the declarations of human rights is suggested by the differences of these two histories. The philosophic temper of the times was an indispensable background and preparation for each statement of human rights, but despite the broad agreements among the resulting statements there was no more agreement among philosophers in the eighteenth than in the twentieth century. Moreover, despite the faith in human dignity and the formula for human happiness prepared by philosophers, an implementation was needed in social and political institutions to secure human rights for men. An international declaration of human rights is involved in precisely the same problems. The philosophies of our times, notwithstanding their divergences, have deepened the faith in the dignity of man and have vastly expanded the formula for his happiness; but the differences of philosophies have led to varied and even opposed interpretations of fundamental rights and the practical import of philosophies has become more marked.

The civil and political rights which were formulated in the eighteenth century have since that time been incorporated into the constitution or the laws of almost every nation in the world. During the same period, the developments of technology and industrial advances have led to the formation of a conception of economic and social rights. The older civil and political rights have sometimes been extended to embrace these new rights. In such applications and other contexts of the newer rights, the meanings have frequently undergone modification, and indeed the two have sometimes been thought to be in conflict. Finally, as science and technology have given men greater control over nature, rights which were in the past reserved for the few have gradually been extended to the many and are now potentially open to all. This addition of new rights and the changes in the significance of old rights in the context of developing knowledge and technology presents problems as well as opportunities. Perhaps the greatest problem involved in the basic ideas which underlie a declaration of human rights is found in the conflict of ideas which have been used to relate the social responsibilities entailed in the material and social developments of the nineteenth century to the civil and political rights earlier enunciated. This conflict has even shaken the simple form of the faith in the dignity of man which was based on the confidence in progress and the advance of knowledge, for it is the source of complexities in the interpretation of liberty and equality and of their interrelations, as well as of apparent contradictions among the fundamental human rights. In like fashion, the problem of the implementation of human rights, new and old, depends on the tacit or explicit resolution of basic philosophic problems, for the rights involve assumptions concerning the relations not only of men to governments, but also of the relations of groups of men to the state and of states to one another, and in the complex of these interrelations the interdependence of rights and duties has been redefined.

Notwithstanding these difficulties, the Unesco Committee on the Philosophic Principles of the Rights of Man is convinced that the perspectives open to men, both on the planes of history and of philosophy, are wider and richer than before. The deeper the re-examination of the bases of human rights that is made, the greater are the hopes that emerge as possible. The Committee has therefore circulated to a select list of the Scholars of the world a series of questions concerning the changes of intellectual and historical circumstances between the classical declarations of human rights which stem from the eighteenth century and the bill of rights made possible by the state of ideas and the economic potentials of the present. On the basis of that inquiry, it has set down briefly, first, what seem to it some of the significant consequences of the evolution of human rights and, second, a schematic formulation of basic rights which in its opinion can and should be vindicated for all men. The history and the schematics grew out of the discussions of the Committee during its meetings in Paris from June 26 to July 2, but although they are based on a study of the replies received to the questionnaire, they do not represent the opinions of all the scholars who contributed to the symposium.

It is the conviction of the Unesco Committee that these inquiries into the intellectual bases of human rights may contribute to the work of the Commission on Human Rights in two fashions: first, by a brief indication of the places at which the discovery of common principles might remove difficulties in the way of agreement and the places at which philosophic divergences might anticipate difficulties in interpretation and, second, a more precise and detailed examination of the common principles that may be formulated and the philosophic differences that have divided men in the interpretation of those principles. The document which is here presented is an attempt to perform the first and preliminary task. The Committee is convinced that Unesco will be able to muster the scholarly resources necessary for the accomplishment of the second task.

For the purposes of present inquiry, the Committee did not explore the subtleties of interpretations of right, liberty and democracy. The members of the

Committee found it possible to agree on working definitions of these terms, reserving for later examination the fashion in which their differences of interpretation will diversify their further definition. By a right they mean a condition of living, without which, in any given historical stage of a society, men cannot give the best of themselves as active members of the community because they are deprived of the means to fulfill themselves as human beings. By liberty they mean more than only the absence of restraint. They mean also the positive organization of the social and economic conditions within which men can participate to a maximum as active members of the community and contribute to the welfare of the community at the highest level permitted by the material development of the society. This liberty can have meaning only under democratic conditions, for only in democracy is liberty set in that context of equality which makes it an opportunity for all men and not for some men only. Democratic liberty is a liberty which does not distinguish by age or sex, by race or language or creed between the rights of one man and the rights of another.

The Committee is fully aware that these working definitions are susceptible of highly diverse particularizations and that they contain, therefore, great ambiguity. But the Committee is convinced that the philosophic problem involved in a declaration of human rights is not to achieve doctrinal consensus but rather to achieve agreement concerning rights, and also concerning action in the realization and defense of rights, which may be justified on highly divergent doctrinal grounds. The Committee's discussion, therefore, of both the evolution of human rights and of the theoretic differences concerning their nature and interrelations, was intended, not to set up an intellectual structure to reduce them to a single formulation, but rather to discover the intellectual means to secure agreement concerning fundamental rights and to remove difficulties in their implementation such as might stem from intellectual differences.

I.

The fundamental human rights which were specified first and proclaimed widely at the beginnings of the modern period were rights which regulated man's relations to political and social groups and which are therefore usually referred to as *Civil and Political Rights.* They had as purpose to protect man in actions which do not derogate from the freedom or well-being of others and to assign to him the exercise of functions by which he might exert a proper influence on the institutions and laws of the state. As a result of religious movements and the development of national states, a series of freedoms were formulated more and more precisely and insistently from the Renaissance to the eighteenth century: to free man from unwarranted interference in his thought and expression, the freedom of conscience, worship, speech, assembly, association and the press.

During the seventeenth century, each of these freedoms received eloquent defense on the grounds, not only that they may be granted without danger to the peace of the state, but also that they may not be withheld without danger. Legal implementation for their protection was step by step provided by the institution of courts or the extension of the jurisdiction of existing courts, and these rights may, therefore, be associated with respect to the means of securing them, with other personal rights and with the right to justice, by which it was recognized that all men have an equal right to seek justice by appeal to law and in that appeal to be protected from summary arrest, cruel treatment and unjust punishment. As civil rights, moreover, they are closely related to the right to political action by which the function of citizens in states is defined, and the growth of democratic institutions during this period is largely an expression of the conviction men can achieve justice and the defense of their rights only by participation direct or indirect in the governments by which they are ruled.

Political rights were therefore written into instruments and institutions of government, whereas civil rights, protected from interference by governments by recourse to courts, were written into bills of rights. The right to political action within a state discussed during this period, moreover, in close conjunction with the right to rebellion or revolution by which men might set up a government in conformity with justice if the fundamental principles of justice and the basic human rights are violated in such fashion as to permit no redress by recourse to peaceful means, and also in conjunction with the right to citizenship by which men may abandon their existing citizenships and assume the citizenship of any country which is prepared to accept them as citizens. Finally, during the nineteenth century, the discussion of the right to political action made increasingly clear that it is a right which can be exercised wisely only in conjunction with the right to information by which the citizen may equip himself for the proper exercise of his political functions.

During the nineteenth century there were added to these rights another set of fundamental human rights which grew out of the recognition that to live well and freely man must have at least the means requisite for living and which was made increasingly practicable by the advances in technology and industrialization in making the means of livelihood potentially accessible to all men. These have come to be called *Economic and Social Rights*. They were first treated as sub-divisions or extensions of civil and political rights, but in the course of the last hundred years it has become apparent that they are different in kind from the older rights and that they therefore require a difference in implementation.

In their earliest form they are associated with the right to property, which in the eighteenth century was conceived by many philosophers to be the basic human right from which the others are derived, in such a fashion that even liberty and the pursuit of happiness are often treated as property rights of man. The evolution of social and economic rights depended on the discussion of the relation of the ownership and the use of property, of private and common ownership, and of private rights and public responsibility. Similarly, the right to education was early conceived to belong to all men, and the institution of public systems of education was designed to effect the realization of that right. Likewise, the right to work was treated first as a freedom consequent on the right to property and was only later implemented with legal provisions for bargaining and arbitration concerning the conditions and the rewards of work. The right to protection of health usually started in the various states from modest beginnings in pure food and drugs legislation under the provisions of police power, and slowly extended to the provision of minimum medical and dietetic services, while the end of the nineteenth century and the beginning of the twentieth century saw the growth of various forms of social security designed to embody the right to maintenance during infancy, old age, sickness and other forms of incapacity, and involuntary unemployment. Finally, there are few to deny, in the retrospect of technological advances, today, the right of all to share in the advancing gains of civilization and to have full access to the enjoyment of cultural opportunities and material improvements.

Since the increased accessibility of economic and social rights was achieved as a consequence of the advances of science and since the ideals and accomplishments of an age find their expression in art and literature, a new emphasis has been placed on Rights of the Mind: on the right to inquiry, expression and communication. Whether the purpose of communication be the expression of an idea or an emotion, the furthering of an individual or social purpose, or the formulation of an objective and scientific truth, the right is grounded both in the purpose of developing to the full the potentialities of men and in the social consequences of such communications.

II.

The evolution, extension and increase of human rights provide clear indication of their scope and of the problems which must be solved by a modern declaration of human rights. Rights which were first proclaimed effectively for only a privileged few have been extended until they may now be claimed by all. Rights which were imperfectly secured have been supplemented by rights which are essential to their realization. But in that process of extension and growth, the

significance of many basic rights has been changed. Their significance has sometimes been rendered more precise and that process has frequently led to the recognition of how far man is from the realization of his rights. The change in their
significance has frequently extended them to applications for which they were not
originally intended, sometimes with good, and sometimes with evil, effect. It has
sometimes rendered rights vague, and it has even perverted what had been conceived as rights to sources of abuse against the fundamental rights of other men.

The evolution of man's conception of his rights serves to make clear, moreover, not only the problems involved in a modern declaration of human rights,
but also the means for the solution of those problems. Human rights have become, and must remain, universal. All the rights which we have come slowly and
laboriously to recognize belong to all men everywhere without discrimination
of race, sex, language or religion. They are universal, moreover, not only because
there are no fundamental differences among men, but also because the great
society and the community of all men has become a real and effective power,
and the interdependent nature of that community is beginning at last to be recognized. This universality of the rights of man, finally, has led to the translation
into political instrumentalities of that close interdependence of rights and duties
which has long been apparent in moral analysis. But the enjoyment of rights involves, not only the acceptance by the individual of corresponding obligations to
society but it is conditioned by the material resources of the society to which he
belongs. Thus, the right to work implies the obligation to engage in work useful
to the society; the right to maintenance, education, etc. . . . can be enjoyed by
each man only in so far as the society by productive work creates the resources
out of which these rights can be assured. The problem, which the Commission
of Human Rights must resolve consequently turns on the relation of rights to
political and economic institutions and the implementation of a bill of rights
proclaimed for all men, as men and as members of the world community.

In the present world situation then, all of the rights which man has acquired
through the centuries are important to the life of man and the development of
the world community, but those which have been made possible by the most
recent advances of knowledge and technology and by the institution of the agencies of the United Nations have assumed priority over, and have affected, the
conception of the earlier rights, for the new rights have not only been added to
the list of rights, but they have made also clear the full sense of older rights and
have made them universally practicable. They make it possible to draw a list of
fundamental rights on which, the Unesco Committee on the Philosophic Principles of the Rights of Man is convinced, all men are agreed. They are rights which
should inspire individual men, nations, and international agencies to work for

their achievement and to use their full authority and power in support of them. They may be seen to be implicit in man's nature as an individual and as a member of society and to follow from the fundamental right to live.

1. THE RIGHT TO LIVE

The right to live is the condition and, as it were, the foundation of all other rights. It is the condition of other rights since it is the minimum human right. It is inseparably involved in the very existence of man. But to live is more than barely to exist, and it is therefore the right which makes specific all other rights since they mark the degree of well-being which man may achieve. All rights derive, on the one hand, from the nature of man as such and, on the other, since man depends on man, the stage of development achieved by the social and political groups in which he participates.

* * *

One group of rights is essentially connected with the provision of means for subsistence, through his own efforts or, where they are insufficient, through the resources of society.

2. THE RIGHT TO THE PROTECTION OF HEALTH

3. THE RIGHT TO WORK

Every man has the right to work, at a wage which represents a fair reward for the quantity and quality of the work done, provided the wages be always at least sufficient to provide means of subsistence and provided the hours of work be reasonable and the leisure adequate.

The right to work implies the right of the workers to participate in the collective determination of the conditions of their work, as well as the right of the workers to understand the general significance of the work done. Work cannot be considered as a commodity, and the recognition of its moral and social value is, therefore, an essential right of the workers.

No discrimination will be set up to bar anyone from access to any form of work for which he is qualified.

4. THE RIGHT TO MAINTENANCE in involuntary unemployment, infancy, old age, sickness and all other forms of incapacity.

5. <u>THE RIGHT TO PROPERTY</u>

Every man has the right to private property in so far as is necessary for his personal use and the use of his family; no other form of property is in itself a fundamental right.

* * *

Bare living, however, is not sufficient, and another group of rights supplements these, providing intellectual foundations for living well, training for the proper use of human as well as the opportunities for self-development and the advancement of the common good.

6. <u>THE RIGHT TO EDUCATION</u>

Every man has the right to a certain minimum of elementary education. That elementary education should eventually be brought to a minimum level of fundamental education available to all men, which should in turn facilitate the mutual understanding of the peoples of the world. In addition, higher education should be accessible to all who have the capacity to benefit by it, and society should select such persons by appropriate means, with due respect to the principle of equal merit and the satisfaction of legitimate aspirations on the part of the individual.

7. <u>THE RIGHT TO INFORMATION</u>

Every man, that he may play his part in human society, has the right to the fullest and most accurate information from all relevant sources.

8. <u>FREEDOM OF THOUGHT AND THE RIGHT TO FREE INQUIRY</u>

The right to live finds its most complete manifestation in the life of thought and in the various modes of artistic and scientific expression. Every man has the right to follow as he finds them compelling the consequences of his reasoning and to hold such doctrines as he judges to be true. He shall not be hindered in the pursuit of knowledge or in communicating the results of his inquiries to others in the effort to increase the sum of human knowledge.

9. <u>THE RIGHT OF SELF-EXPRESSION</u>

Even apart, from direct calculation of social utility, however, every man has the right to express himself in art and science, not only as part of his own self-fulfillment, but also as a possible contribution to the culture of his nation and time, since the highest expression of culture and the greatest utility to society frequently derive from works little esteemed by their contemporaries for aesthetic value or immediate practical use.

* * *

Finally, there is a group of rights which bear on man's participation in society and his protection from social and political injustice.

10. <u>THE RIGHT TO JUSTICE</u>

Every man has an equal right to justice. He cannot be summoned for an act which was not a legal offence at the time when it was committed. He has the right to be protected by law from illegal arrest, brutality, torture, cruel and unjust punishment and double jeopardy. In the case of legal arrest, he has the right to a speedy and public trial by due process of law.

The inviolability of domicile and correspondence is limited only in accordance with due process of law and in so far as its enjoyment may endanger the existence of society or the principles on which it is founded.

11. <u>THE RIGHT TO POLITICAL ACTION</u>

Every citizen is entitled, both by voting and by direct participation, to make his contribution to the conduct of public affairs. In pursuance of this aim, he has the right to express his ideas and to form associations for the promotion of his ideas, provided that such expressions and such associations are not incompatible with the principles of democracy or with the rights of man.

12. <u>FREEDOM OF SPEECH, ASSEMBLY, ASSOCIATION, WORSHIP AND THE PRESS</u>

As instruments, therefore, in the exercise of his right to political action, no less than as consequence of his right to self-expression, man has the right to set forth his ideas and to seek to persuade others to accept them. Society is entitled to limit the exercise of these rights only in exceptional circumstances and only in so far as their exercise might endanger the existence of the society or the principles on which it is founded.

13. <u>THE RIGHT TO CITIZENSHIP</u>

In the event that a man is not satisfied with the institutions of the nation of which he is part, he has the right to abandon his existing citizenship and to assume the citizenship of any country which is prepared to accept him as a citizen.

14. <u>THE RIGHT TO REBELLION OR REVOLUTION</u>

In the event that the government of his nation operates contrary to the fundamental principles of justice and the basic human rights in such fashion that no redress is permitted by peaceful means, man has the right to set up a government more nearly in conformity with justice and humanity.

15. <u>THE RIGHT TO SHARE IN PROGRESS</u>
Every man has the right to full access to the enjoyment of the technical and cultural achievements of civilization.

* * *

These rights, the Unesco Committee on the Philosophic Principles of Human Rights is convinced, are of fundamental importance not only to the enrichment of the human spirit but to the development of all forms of human association, including the development of national cultures and international co-operation. The Unesco Committee has attempted to indicate some of the intellectual ramifications and implications of the problem of human rights in the modern world and in the international framework of the United Nations by setting forth briefly the turns of the historical development of human rights and the broad lines of the interrelations of human rights which are consequent on that development. The Committee is particularly concerned to emphasize the dynamic character of the interrelations of human rights and the need, therefore, to explore and control the basic ideas which are in process of being fitted to new industrial and technological means for the achievement of human good.

The Committee reaffirms its conviction that a further study of the oppositions of philosophic doctrines which lead to diversities of interpretations of human rights, or which conceal fundamental principles on which agreement is possible despite these diversities, might facilitate the discussion of human rights today. It reaffirms also its further conviction that Unesco might properly take the study of these philosophic differences. Such a study should be undertaken, however, only if it is seen to contribute to the formulation and implementation of the Declaration of Human Rights which is in process of preparation by the Commission on Human Rights, for the Unesco Committee is convinced that agreement is possible concerning such a declaration and that it will constitute a basic contribution to the fullness of man's life, and to the stability and to the effectiveness of the operation of the United Nations.

Paris, July 1947
The Unesco Committee on the theoretical bases of Human Rights

Foreword and Introduction to Human Rights, Comments and Interpretations, UNESCO 1949

FOREWORD
Jacques Havet[1]

In the course of the year 1947, UNESCO has carried out an enquiry into the theoretical problems raised by the elaboration of an International Declaration of the Rights of Man. The reader will find hereafter (Appendix I)[2] the text of the explanatory statement and questionnaire, which were sent to the various persons from Member States of UNESCO asked, as individual experts, to give their views.

The texts which constitute the body of this volume were chosen among the replies which UNESCO received to this enquiry. They are an expression of the personal opinions of their authors and should not be taken as necessarily conforming to the official position of the Governments of the countries to which the authors belong.

A first group of these essays concerns the general problems of human rights, the others deal more particularly with the respect for diversity of cultures, the social implications of science, the value of objective information, the right to education and the special position of primitive and dependent peoples and prisoners.

It is fitting also to state precisely what principles were followed in choosing such texts as were retained after a selection made necessary by the copiousness of the material. The primary consideration was to secure a representative sample of the whole range of expressed opinions. In particular it was thought desirable to give an audience to the views of certain thinkers whose outlook, although stimulating, does not coincide with the conclusions which UNESCO finally drew from its consultations.

The conclusions which UNESCO drew from this enquiry are to be found hereafter (Appendix II)[3]: they were elaborated, on the basis of the many con-

---

1. For biographical information on Jacques Havet, see the chapter entitled "UNESCO in the Paradigmatic Transition" in Part I [ed.].

2. See the first text in Part II [ed.].

3. See the previous text, "The Grounds of an International Declaration of Human Rights" [ed.].

tributions received, by a Committee of Experts which brought together in July 1947 Mr. Edward H. Carr, Chairman, Mr. Richard P. McKeon, Rapporteur, and Messrs. Pierre Auger, Georges Friedmann, Harold Laski, Chung-Shu Lo, Luc Somerhausen. UNESCO's conclusions were forwarded to the United Nations Commission of Human Rights in the hope that they would help clarify its discussion and explore the ground for a constructive agreement. The same Committee agreed to the composition of the symposium as it is now presented to the public.

The Secretariat of UNESCO will be happy to receive comments about the contents of the volume as well as criticisms and replies.

INTRODUCTION
Jacques Maritain[*]

Of the tasks assigned to the United Nations Organization, one of those which could and should most nearly affect the conscience of the peoples is the drawing up of an *International Declaration of Human Rights*. The task was committed to the Economic and Social Council of the United Nations. UNESCO's part was to consult philosophers and assemble their replies. This volume is a collection of the most significant texts thus gathered in the course of UNESCO's enquiry into the philosophic bases of Human Rights.

This book then is devoted to the rational interpretation and justification of those rights of the individual which society must respect and which it is desirable for our age to strive to enumerate more fully. Many schools of thought are represented, each of which brings to the whole its particular view and justification of individual rights, leaning in various degrees towards the classical, or the revolutionary, interpretation: it is not the first time that expert witnesses have quarreled among themselves. The paradox is that such rational justifications are at once indispensable, and yet powerless to bring about agreement between minds. They are indispensable because each one of us believes instinctively in the truth, and will only assent to what he himself has recognized as true and based on reason. They are powerless to bring about a harmony of minds because they are

---

* Jacques Maritain, a French Catholic natural law philosopher and leading interpreter of Thomas Aquinas, was the French ambassador to the Vatican at the time he delivered his speech at the 1947 UNESCO General Conference in Mexico City and then later wrote the introduction to what became Human Rights: Comments and Interpretations. When his wife died in 1960, Maritain moved to a monastery in Toulouse, France, where he died in 1973 at the age of ninety.

fundamentally different, even antagonistic; and why should this surprise us? The questions they raise are difficult and the philosophic traditions to which they are related have long been divergent.

It is related that at one of the meetings of a UNESCO National Commission where Human Rights were being discussed, someone expressed astonishment that certain champions of violently opposed ideologies had agreed on a list of those rights. "Yes," they said, "we agree about the rights *but on condition that no one asks us why.*" That "why" is where the argument begins.[4]

The question of Human Rights offers us an outstanding example of the situation I attempted to outline in an address at the Second General Conference of UNESCO, from which I venture to reproduce certain passages. "How," I asked, "can we imagine an agreement of minds between men who are gathered together precisely in order to accomplish a common intellectual task, men who come from the four corners of the globe and who not only belong to different cultures and civilizations, but are of antagonistic spiritual associations and schools of thought . . . ? Because, as I said at the beginning of my speech, the goal of UNESCO is a practical goal, agreement between minds can be reached spontaneously, not on the basis of common speculative ideas, but on common practical ideas, not on the affirmation of one and the same conception of the world, of man and of knowledge, but upon the affirmation of a single body of beliefs for guidance in action. No doubt, this is little enough, but it is the last resort to intellectual agreement. It is nevertheless, enough to enable a great task to be undertaken, and it would do much to crystallize this body of common practical convictions.

I should like to note here that the word 'ideology' and the word 'principles' can be interpreted in two very different senses. I have shown that the present state of division among minds does not permit of agreement on a common *speculative ideology*, nor on common explicit principles. But, on the other hand, when we are concerned with a basic *practical* ideology and basic principles of action implicitly recognized today, in a live, even if not formulated state, by the consciousness of free peoples, we find that they constitute *grosso modo* a sort of common denominator, a sort of unwritten common law, at the point where in practice the most widely separated theoretical ideologies and mental traditions converge. To

---

4. This passage has often been misquoted in the literature on the history of human rights. Maritain refers here to a very interesting exchange that he heard about within an unspecified UNESCO National Commission. The quote itself has wrongly been taken to reflect the prevailing approach of the UNESCO Committee of Experts (in which Maritain played no part) and has even been misattributed to the UN Commission on Human Rights [ed.].

understand this, it is only necessary to make the appropriate distinction between the rational justifications involved in the spiritual dynamism of a philosophic doctrine or religious faith, and the practical conclusions which, although justified in different ways by different persons, are principles of action with a common ground of similarity for everyone. I am quite certain that my way of justifying belief in the rights of man and the ideal of liberty, equality and fraternity is the only way with a firm foundation in truth. This does not prevent me from being in agreement on these practical convictions with people who are certain that their way of justifying them, entirely different from mine or opposed to mine, in its theoretical dynamism, is equally the only way founded upon truth. If both believed in the democratic charter, a Christian and a rationalist would still give mutually incompatible justifications for their belief, if their hearts and minds and blood were involved, and they would fight each other for them. And God forbid that I should say it does not matter to know which of the two is right! It matters essentially. The fact remains that, on the practical expression of this charter, they are in agreement and can formulate together common principles of action.

Where it is a question of rational interpretation and justifications of speculation or theory, the problem of Human Rights involves the whole structure of moral and metaphysical (or anti-metaphysical) convictions held by each of us. So long as minds are not united in faith or philosophy, there will be mutual conflicts between interpretations and justifications.

In the field of practical conclusions, on the other hand, agreement on a joint declaration is possible, given an approach pragmatic rather than theoretical and co-operation in the comparison, recasting and fixing of formulae, to make them acceptable to both parties as points of convergence in practice, however opposed the theoretic viewpoints. There is nothing to prevent the achievement, in this way, of a new and wider declaration of Human Rights marking a notable stage in the unification of the world, and wherein more especially the concept exclusive to classical individualism of man as a being inherently entitled to rights and liberties for the working out of his personal destiny, and the concept exclusive to Marxism of man as a being with rights and liberties deriving from his role in the historic evolution of the community of which he is a part, would supplement and integrate each other—I mean purely pragmatically and only for the promulgation of a number of principles for action and rules of behavior. It is not reasonably possible to hope for more than this convergence in practice in the enumeration of articles jointly agreed. The reconciling of theories and a philosophic synthesis in the true sense are only conceivable after an immense amount of investigation and elucidation of fundamentals, requiring a high degree of insight, a new systematization and authoritative correction of a number of errors and confusions of thought. For that very reason, and even if it succeeded in influencing culture to any important degree, this synthesis would remain one doctrine among many, accepted by some and rejected by others, with no pretention in fact to universal dominion over the minds of men.

The very diversity of the interpretations and justifications put forward in the essays in this book is in itself an important object lesson for the reader, wherein he will find, I trust, confirmation of the considerations set out above. Is there anything surprising in systems antagonistic in theory converging in their practical conclusions? It is the usual picture which the history of moral philosophy presents to us. The phenomenon proves simply that systems of moral philosophy are the products of reflection by the intellect on ethical concepts which precede and govern them, and which of themselves display, as it were, a highly complex geology of the mind where the natural operation of spontaneous reason, pre-scientific and pre-philosophic, is at every stage conditioned by the acquisitions, the constraints, the structure and the evolution of the social group. Thus, if I may be allowed the metaphor, there is a kind of plant-like formation and growth of moral knowledge and moral feeling, in itself independent of philosophic systems and the rational justifications they propound, even though there is a secondary interaction between them and itself. Is it surprising that, while all these systems quarrel over the why and wherefore, yet in their practical conclusions they prescribe rules of behaviour which are in the main and for all practical purposes identical for a given age and culture? What is chiefly important for the moral progress of humanity is the apprehension by experience which occurs apart from systems and on a different logical basis—assisted by such systems when they awake the conscience to knowledge of itself, hampered by them when they dim the apperceptions of spontaneous reason, or when they cast suspicion on a genuine acquisition of moral experience by linking it with some error of theory or false philosophy.

Finally, it is the speculative and interpretative approach, as such, which, in the present book, will afford the reader the chief food for thought. For the texts here collected bring us the testimony of men specially well qualified to give an authoritative exposition of the main currents of contemporary thought. It is profitable to know those currents, however severely we may censure those which are not our own, and however legitimate that censure may sometimes be. Whatever school of thought we belong to, the comparison of our own ideas with those of so many distinguished minds will perfect and broaden our views on the nature and basis of Human Rights, on what enumeration of them should be attempted at our present stage in historical evolution, and on the scope—indeed on the gaps also—of the new declaration being prepared in the councils of the United Nations.

From the point of view of philosophic doctrine, it may be said, without over-simplification, that, as regards the question of Human Rights, men are today divided—as the readers of this collection will easily perceive—into two antago-nistic groups: those who to a greater or lesser extent explicitly accept, and those who to a greater or lesser extent explicitly reject "Natural Law" as the basis of those rights.

In the eyes of the first the requirements of his being endow man with certain fundamental and inalienable rights antecedent in nature, and superior, to soci-ety, and are the source whence social life itself, with the duties and rights which that implies, originates and develops. For the second school man's rights are relative to the historical development of society, and are themselves constantly variable and in a state of flux; they are a product of society itself as it advances with the forward march of history.

Such an ideological contrast is irreducible and no theoretical reconciliation is possible; it could however be lessened to some extent, insofar as it was possible for the supporters of "Natural Law" to stress that, although certain fundamental rights meet a prime necessity of that law while others meet only a secondary necessity or are merely desirable, nevertheless our knowledge of both is in all circumstances subject to slow and irregular growth, so that those rights only stand forth as acknowledged rules of conduct as moral consciousness progresses and societies evolve; and insofar as it was possible for the opponents of "Natural Law" to stress that, though many rights are seen to be conditioned on the evolu-tion of society, other more primitive rights stand out as a condition of society's very existence. However, it is by no means certain that the "fundamental rights" of the first group would always coincide with the "more primitive rights" of the second. . . .

If thereafter we adopt a practical viewpoint and concern ourselves no longer with seeking the basis and philosophic significance of Human Rights but only their statement and enumeration, we have before us an entirely different picture, where no theoretical simplification is any more in question: then, as I have ex-plained above, not only is agreement possible between the members of opposing philosophic schools, but it must be said that the operative factors in any histori-cal introduction to a joint assertion of Human Rights are less the schools of phi-losophy themselves than *currents of thought*, which are doubtless linked more or less closely to those schools, but where the principal part has been played by the lessons of experience and history and by a kind of practical apprehension, bring-ing with them a greater dynamic force and simultaneously a wider liberty rela-tively to the principles and logic of abstract systems. In consequence, it cannot be too strongly emphasized that admission of a particular category of rights is not the exclusive possession of any one school of thought: it is no more necessary to belong to the school of Rousseau to recognize the rights of the individual than it is to be a Marxist to recognize the "new rights," as they are called, economic and social rights. The gains of the collective intelligence under the influence of its several cross-currents go far beyond the disputations of the schools.

It is legitimate to suspect that the antagonism which many contemporary authors see fit to postulate between "old" and "new" Human Rights is partly artificial and derived either from the liking of theorists for ideological conflicts or more, perhaps, from the absolutist concept of Human Rights held by the philosophy—or better the rhetoric—of the 18th Century, whose after effects still in some measure give rise to misunderstandings today, and taint certain sacred formulae of the vocabulary of Human Rights. If each of these rights is in itself absolute and not susceptible of any limitation, in the same way as a divine attribute, clearly any conflict between them is insoluble. But in practice everyone sees that these rights, being human, are subject, like every other human thing, to modification and limitation. Even where rights are "inalienable," a distinction must be made between possession and exercise, the latter being subject to the modifications and limitations dictated in each instance by justice. If a criminal can justly be condemned to lose his life, it is because he has, by his crime, deprived himself, not of his right to existence, but rather of the possibility of demanding that right with justice: morally he has cut himself off from membership of the human community, as far as concerns the use of that fundamental and "inalienable" right which the penalty imposed prevents his exercising. Again, the imparting by teaching and upbringing of the heritage of human culture is a fundamental right: in practice it is subject to the physical capacity of a given society, and justice may forbid its enjoyment by all being demanded *hic et nunc*, if such enjoyment is only conceivable through the dissolution of the social body, as in the case of the slave-owning society of ancient Rome, or the feudal society of the Middle Ages; the claim nevertheless remains a legitimate goal to be achieved in time. It then remains to endeavor to change the social order in question. Incidentally, this instance shows us that at the root of the hidden urge which impels us ever to the transformation of society, there lies the fact that man *possesses* "inalienable" rights and that nevertheless he is deprived of the possibility of justly claiming to *exercise* certain of them by such inhumanities as subsist in the social structure in each age.

It is only normal that the various acknowledged rights of the individual should be mutually limitative, and in particular that economic and social rights, the rights of man as a social animal, cannot take their place in human history without some restriction upon the freedom and rights of man as an individual.

Where the difficulties and arguments begin is in the determination of the scale of values governing the exercise and concrete integration of these various rights. Here we are no longer dealing with the mere enumeration of Human Rights, but with the principle of dynamic unification whereby they are brought into play, with the tone scale, with the specific key in which different kinds of music are played on the same keyboard, music which in the event is in tune with, or harmful to, human dignity.

Conceivably the advocates of the liberal-individualist; of the Communist and of the co-operative type of society might draw up similar, even identical, lists of Human Rights. But their exercise of these rights will differ. All depends on the ultimate value whereon those rights depend and in terms of which they are integrated by mutual limitations. It is in terms of the scale of values which we thus acknowledge that we establish the means whereby, in our eyes, Human Rights, economic and social, as well as individual, shall impinge on life; it is from these different scales of values that spring mutual accusations of misunderstanding certain essential rights of the human being leveled by those for whom the mark of human dignity lies firstly and chiefly in the power to appropriate individually the gifts of nature so that each may be in a position to do freely what pleases him; by those who see it in the power to place those gifts under the collective control of the social body and thus deliver man from the treadmill of labor and gain control of history; or by those who see it in the power of bringing the gifts of nature into service for the joint attainment of an immaterial good and of the free self-determination of the person. It remains to be decided which has a true and which a distorted vision of Man.

By following this line of thought the extent and limits of the practical agreement on Human Rights so often mentioned in the pages of this Introduction would become clear. It would be understood that to go beyond a mere list or enumeration of rights and to produce a true Charter determining a common way of action, the agreement must also cover the scale of values, the key in which in their practical exercise in social life, the acknowledged rights of man must be harmonized.

Thus, we must not expect too much of an International Declaration of Human Rights. Yet does it not, above all, bear witness to what the peoples await today? The function of language has been so much perverted, the truest words have been pressed into the service of so many lies, that even the noblest and most solemn declarations could not suffice to restore to the peoples faith in Human Rights. It is the implementation of these declarations which is sought from those who subscribe to them; it is the means of securing effective respect for Human Rights from States and Governments that it is desired to guarantee. On this point I should not venture to express more than the most guarded optimism. For to reach agreement, no longer merely on the definition of Human Rights, but on arrangements for their exercise in daily life the first necessity, as I have pointed out above, would be agreement on a scale of values. For the peoples to agree on the means of securing effective respect for Human Rights, they would have to have in common, however implicitly, not necessarily the same speculative concept, but at least the same practical concept, of man and life, the same "philosophy of life," if I may for once be allowed to use the word "philosophy" in the outrageously improper sense of the popular pragmatism of today.

Does the testimony collected in this volume give grounds for hope that, despite the clash of theory, a few scanty features of such a practical ideology, sufficiently defined and resolved to be effective, are in the course of taking root in the conscience of the nations? Does it give grounds for hope that one day agreement may be reached throughout the world, not only on the enumeration of Human Rights, but also on the key values governing their exercise and on the practical criteria to be used to secure respect for them? We do know that, though the crisis of civilization which rose with this century has offered to our gaze the gravest violations of Human Rights, yet simultaneously it has led the public mind to a keener awareness of those rights, and Government propaganda to pay to them—in words—the most ringing tributes. Pending something better, a Declaration of Human Rights agreed by the nations would be a great thing in itself, a word of promise for the downcast and oppressed throughout all lands, the beginning of changes which the world requires, the first condition precedent for the later drafting of a universal Charter of civilized life.

New York, July–August 1948

PART III

THE UNESCO
HUMAN RIGHTS SURVEY:
RESPONSES, REFUSALS,
CORRESPONDENCE

Liberalism from the Ashes

A FRAGMENT OF THOUGHTS CONCERNING
THE NATURE AND THE FULFILMENT
*Arnold J. Lien**

It is not surprising that mankind, horrified by the unspeakable atrocities of recent regimes equipped with all the destructive know-how of modern science and technology, has despairingly cried out for an international bill of the rights of man, just as in the critical revolts against the tyrannies of other eras demands were launched for national or local bills of rights. For bills of rights are always monumental indictments of regimes of the past, as well as promised safeguards against the same abuses by regimes of the future.

Since rights exist only in the sphere of the relations of man to man, the occasions for asserting them arise mostly when they are threatened, restrained or suppressed. Bills of rights, therefore, never have been and probably never can be complete and definitive catalogues of the rights of man. The Declaration of Independence of 1776 mentioned specifically only a few "among these" rights. The Bill of Rights of the constitution of the United States warns that "the enumeration in the Constitution, of certain rights, shall not be construed to deny or disparage others retained by the people." The lists to be found in the Atlantic Charter and other recent documents are similarly only fragments.

Human rights are universal rights or enabling qualities of human beings *as human beings* or as individuals of the human race, attaching to the human being wherever he appears, without regard to time, place, color, sex, parentage or environment. They are really the *keystone of the dignity of man*. In their quintessence they consist basically of the one all-inclusive right or enabling quality of complete freedom to develop to their fullest possible extent every potential capacity and talent of the individual for his most effective *self-management*, security and satisfaction. In this one transcendent human right, all others are implied, or, of

---

* Arnold J. Lien was the longtime chair of political science at Washington University in St. Louis. He had served as a captain in the American Red Cross in Luxembourg during the First World War and was the author of, among others, *Privileges and Immunities of the Citizens of the United States* (1919) and *Concurring Opinion: The Privileges or Immunities Clause of the Fourteenth Amendment* (1957).

it, all others are phases, each receiving a position of prominence or an emphasis dependent upon the particular temper or trend of the times.

From the primitive to the contemporary, education (not to be confused with propaganda or indoctrination), has had as its central aim the guidance and training of the individual for the responsible and successful exercise of this right. Nowhere is there any principle of nature or religion or science or reason which assigns prenatally one man to be master and one to be slave, one to be pauper and one to be prince. Yet under one pretext or another, implemented with the necessary military, economic, religious or political force, these human rights have been wantonly disregarded and suppressed throughout the history of man by all sorts of absolutist tribal, feudal, monarchical, industrial and other dictatorial regimes.

The great political revolutions of the late eighteenth century came as an explosion of the accumulated discontent of the oppressed. The phases of human rights which had been most abused at that time were formulated into declarations and bills of rights the reverberations of which in the next century were felt around the world.

But more important than the statement of the rights of man was the new doctrine that the main purpose of every government should be to preserve these rights and guarantee them against encroachment. Universal human rights were henceforth to be accepted as basic privileges of citizens of the state and be given the full protection of all the sanctions set up by the government. No longer were they to remain merely pitiable natural rights which the individual could proclaim as sacred but for which he could offer no sanction or authority other than his own feeble assertion.

With its beginnings even before the wars at the close of the eighteenth century, but its greatest momentum attained only in the late nineteenth and early twentieth centuries, another revolutionary movement encompassed the world and transformed society from a comparatively simple agricultural one into a complex and highly industrialized one. This industrial revolution brought infinite possibilities for the elevation of the standard of living and the promotion of the welfare of men; but it also involved new opportunities for oppression and abuse. Its tempo, complexities and magnitude threatened to reduce the individual to a babe, clinging to its pick-a-back, in the woods of the giants of mass production and, periodically, mass destruction, with their billion dollar wallets.

To add still further to the bewilderment of mankind there flared up in Russia in 1917 a political revolution comparable in intensity and far-flung effects to the American and French revolutions a century earlier. Since then the earth has been ravaged by two world wars with unprecedented dimensions of costs, destruction and dislocation and with an almost incredible resurgence of old hatreds, autocratic disregard of human rights, and bestiality.

The new formulations of the rights of man in the twentieth century, as found in numerous bills of rights in recent constitutions and in the many documents growing out of the last war and the movement for international co-operation, are different from the old especially in the large emphasis placed upon the economic and social phases. The basic rights are the same; but the stresses peculiar to the new age have brought a change in emphasis from political to economic, from liberty to equality, from freedom to security.

Basically, the right of every human being as an individual of the human race remains that of complete freedom to develop to their fullest possible limit all his talents and capacities with the aim of effective self-management, security and satisfaction. Every man lives in a very complex society. With a few exceptions, every one is a member of a political unit or state. These states are on widely varying levels of economic, social, political and cultural advancement. While the basic rights must everywhere be the same, the degree to which they can be made operative and the extent to which they can be fulfilled must vary from one state to another—and continue to vary for a long time, in spite of the accelerating processes now developing through the United Nations.

The first essential is that all states accept the basic human rights as constitutional rights for their peoples and their observances as an international obligation, with the right of an ultimate appeal to some international tribunal, although it would be premature and unrealistic as yet to consider them as the privileges of citizens of a world state.

The second requirement is that these rights be gradually implemented with the goodwill and the techniques necessary for their effective operation. In many states, certain phases of these rights cannot be put into practice at once. The imperative requirement in such a case is that the state must take constructive steps at once to formulate and carry out a long-range program through which to prepare its people for the participation required of them to make the rights operative. For instance, if the people are illiterate, let them be given an *education*; if they are starving, let them be *fed*; if they are irresponsible, let them be *educated for self-discipline*.

Within each state, what every individual is entitled to first is an opportunity for the development of a sound, healthy body and mind—a *safe-guarded heritage*, adequate food, shelter and clothing, physical education, medical care, and all the other indispensables.

He must have the opportunity to get the *training and the guidance* to enable him to earn a living through productive activity and to ensure a modicum of security against old age and misfortune. He is entitled to an education to equip him with methods, techniques and information with which to work and perform his duties and to enable him to discover what his best talents and capacities are and to acquaint him with his place in and relation to society and the universe. Without these physical and intellectual foundations, the right of the individual to a free and full progress in *self-management* becomes a mere husk. He must have these basic assurances of freedom from want and fear.

Another cornerstone in the basic rights of man is the right to a status of equality with all other individuals who are citizens of the same state. This applies to every sphere of activity of the society to which the individual belongs—to the economic as much as to the political. In the *opportunities* offered and *services* rendered by organized society, he is entitled to share equally with others. Whatever freedoms are guaranteed must be available equally to all. Whatever burdens and responsibilities are assessed must be distributed equally among all. If there are resources they must just not be monopolized or exploited by the few to the disadvantage of the welfare of the many. The diversity of opportunities must be made as extensive as the diversity of talents; for the operative principle of equality leaves ample room for infinite variation.

Nor is there any conflict between the principle of equality and the principle of liberty or the several freedoms. Rather they supplement and give substance to each other. In fact, no other application of equality is as vital as that which requires the equal distribution of freedoms or liberty among all. Liberty and equality are merely two phases of the one multiple-phased all-inclusive and universal human right of *self-realization*. Other phases should, no doubt, be listed when an international bill of rights is written, but their connection with this basic one should never be lost sight of.

These human rights are rights of the individual. Within the state which guarantees them, they are balanced with a corresponding list of duties; but, quite apart from these, there are responsibilities implied in the rights themselves. No individual born to-day finds himself in an uninhabited world. His environment, consequently, immediately demands of him a sense of responsibility, first, to himself and, second, to the society in which he lives. His main law is that of self-interest; but that law can operate on many levels and, on the top level, may come very close to coincidence with the law of the common interest of all. Self-discipline and self-regulation may thus be resorted to as means of self-advancement.

If these responsibilities are not assumed by the individual and his rights are abused to the detriment of society as a whole or of other individuals, society itself (that is, all individuals acting collectively), imposes restrictions and prescribes regulations. These are intended to protect those who assume responsibilities against the derelictions of those who do not and are, in principle at least, temporary expedients to serve until the educational system can achieve a larger success in developing more effectively the universal sense of responsibility.

In a state, all institutions and organizations and individual activities are subject to the tacit or express sanction of the society as a whole. As long as private initiative and enterprise contribute to the common weal and adequately meet the needs of society, there is no occasion for collective or public action; but whenever they resort to the injurious or fall short of the standard of adequacy, society stands ready to restrain or suppress, to supplement or supersede. Thus there may be a combination of private and public or collective initiative and enterprise, as now in the majority of states, or there may be a plan in which all major enterprises are publicly or collectively owned and operated, as now in an occasional state. In either case, the people or the state is the ultimate authority on what is and what is not for the general welfare. The sense of responsibility on the part of institutions and organizations of every kind is of the same vital importance as that of individuals.

The problem of determining when a right has been abused to the detriment of others or of society as a whole must remain a difficult one, depending upon the crystallized national and world opinion of the time for principles and standards suitable to its solution. If a trial is required in a regular court and, with adequate safeguards, an ultimate appeal can be made to an international tribunal, a reasonably satisfactory solution should be possible.

The authority to suspend basic rights in the case of critical emergencies may best be placed in a small representative body in which all parties and minorities have members. The safeguards must include very severe restrictions on the duration of the suspension and a provision for ultimate appeal to an international tribunal.

Until these guarantees of individual rights have become traditional and certain, colonial peoples and minority groups of various kinds—racial, cultural, religious—will, no doubt, also have to be assured certain basic collective or group rights. These can logically take very much the same forms as those concerned with individual rights, and be made subject to the same responsibilities.

The scientists are smashing atoms to set free new energies for the advancement of human welfare. Humanists are somewhat behind in their attempt to educate all to a sense of responsibility and a social consciousness sufficient to ensure a constructive use of these energies. Education seems to be the only key that can release the creative energies of the individual for the new era. Self-interest is the force of gravity which draws individuals together. That is the force on which the new order must be built. As individuals grow in knowledge, understanding and wisdom, their perspectives will be more complete, their horizons wider and their vision clearer. Their self-interest will find itself on ever higher levels until it ultimately coincides with the common interest of all.

THE PHILOSOPHIC BASES AND MATERIAL CIRCUMSTANCES OF THE RIGHTS OF MAN
*Richard P. McKeon**

The problems faced in framing a declaration of human rights are basically philosophic. The difficulties involved in resolving them may therefore be recognized in the paradox that the resolution of practical problems involves philosophic commitments but agreement concerning actions to be taken need not presuppose philosophic agreement. The philosophers of the seventeenth and eighteenth centuries prepared the intellectual instruments by means of which bills of rights and declarations of rights were framed and, eventually, written into the constitution of most of the states of the Western World. An agreement in the promulgation of those declarations of rights, far from signifying a general agreement on a single basic philosophy, provided a framework within which divergent philosophies, religious, and even economic social and political theories might be entertained and developed. The same paradox presents difficulties of a different order in the framing of a declaration of rights for the twentieth century.

The fundamental problem is not found in compiling a list of human rights: the declarations of human rights that have been prepared by committees and groups who have undertaken the study of the problem and the declarations that have been submitted to the Commission on Human Rights are surprisingly similar, and little difficulty is encountered in the mere statement of the rights that ought to be included in the list. The differences are found rather in what is meant by these rights, and these differences of meanings depend on divergent basic assumptions, which, in turn, lend plausibility to and are justified by contradictory interpretations of the economic and social situation, and, finally, lead to opposed recommendations concerning the implementation required for a world declaration of human rights.

---

* At the time of his participation in the UNESCO survey, McKeon was serving as the powerful Dean of Humanities at the University of Chicago; he was also a member of the US delegation to UNESCO for the first three general conferences. During the 1920s, McKeon had studied in Paris with Étienne Gilson, who would also, decades later, be a member of the UNESCO Committee of Experts. For more on McKeon's biography, see the two final chapters of Part I.

These three sources of differences concerning the meanings of human rights render nugatory any agreement concerning the list of human rights, and indeed, once they are raised, make even agreement concerning the bare enumeration impossible. The faith "in fundamental human rights, in the dignity and worth of the human person, in the equal rights of men and women" which is reaffirmed in the Charter of the United Nations stands in need, if it is to be significant, of some resolution of these differences. The effectiveness of a Declaration of Human Rights, such as is urgently needed in the world today, depends precisely on (a) its clarity in formulating an ideal which will promote and encourage respect for human rights and for fundamental freedoms for all without distinction as to race, sex, language, or religion, (b) its pertinence and adaptation to the social, economic and cultural conditions of the present, and (c) its implementation in social and political agencies. These three conditions of the effectiveness of a declaration of human rights, moreover, are not independent of one another. Opposed philosophies lead to opposed interpretations of history and of the present. Opposed conceptions of historical processes and historical methods, conversely, are used to supply the criticism of, or to lend justification to, opposed philosophies. Political institutions are adapted to circumstances and also change them; they are consequences of philosophic principles as well as instruments of ideological control. The debates concerning a modern declaration of rights will turn, not on questions concerning what the rights are, but on questions of basic assumptions, actual fact, and appropriate implementation. The difficulties will be discovered in the suspicions, suggested by these differences, concerning the tangential uses that might be made of a declaration of human rights for the purpose of advancing special interests rather than establishing universal truths or promoting general welfare.

The focus of these oppositions and debates is, in part, determined by the tradition of human rights which received its classical expression in America and Western Europe in the eighteenth century and, in part, a result of changes in the circumstances and in the ideas of men since that time. The history of human rights is long, for it is possible to trace concern with them back to the Greeks and the Romans and most of the philosophic devices by which they were developed and on which they were grounded, like the doctrines of natural law and social contract, have like origins and evolutions. But the history of declarations of human rights is short.[1] The differences in those two histories may serve to

---

1. The brevity of the history of declarations of human rights justifies the treatment of the problem against the background of the classical statements of Western Europe. The problem in China, thus, is one of the constitutional movements influenced by or comparable to those of the Western World (cf. Chun-Mai Carsun Chang, "Political Structure in the Chinese Draft Constitution," *The*

separate the respects in which philosophic differences are unimportant in the resolution of practical problems from the respects in which they are of crucial importance. "Natural law" does not designate a single philosophic doctrine: it receives different definitions and developments in the philosophies of Aquinas, Hobbes, and Locke, to mention only three of the numerous natural law philosophers; and in the controversies concerning the relation of Church and State in the late Middle Ages, the doctrine of natural law was employed to defend opposed positions of papalists, imperialists, and conciliarists. The conception of natural rights, sacred and inherent in man, was written into the constitutions of the eighteenth, nineteenth and twentieth centuries, not because men had agreed on a philosophy, but because they had agreed, despite philosophic differences, on the formulation of a solution to a series of moral and political problems. It is as easy to make a case for the derivation of the conception of human rights from the philosophy of Aquinas, Suarez and Bellarmine as for its derivation from the philosophy of Locke, and it is easy to question the historical accuracy of both derivations. What is indisputable is that the declarations of human rights separated inalienable human rights which were to be protected from governmental interference from alienable rights which were delegated to the government for due compensation in the form of just and effective government.[2] The discussion of human rights has as a consequence been couched in a series of simple oppositions: "rights" have been related, or opposed, to "wrongs," to "duties," and to "laws," and the discussion of rights has been in the tradition of constitutionalism.

The use of these oppositions has become so traditional that they are accepted as inevitable or as statements of fact; and indeed they are statements of fact, but based on unnoticed philosophic assumptions which are emerging in the present discussion of human rights to revive forgotten or unexplored differences. When Mr. Ribnikar, the member of the Commission on Human Rights from Yugoslavia, expressed his conception of human rights at the first session of the Commission, 27 January–10 February, 1947, he stressed the basic differences between the economic, social, and national life of the eighteenth century and the present underlying the opposition between the ideology of individualism

---

Annals of the American Academy of Political and Social Science, vol. 243 [1946], p.67). The Islamic tradition was crucially influenced by the Western formulations (cf. Majid Khadduri, "Human Rights in Islam," ibid., p.80), and in general the problem of declarations of human rights, as distinct from their philosophic bases, have had everywhere similar constitutional evolutions.

    2. Charles H. McIlwain, "Bills of Rights," *Encyclopedia of the Social Sciences*, vol. II, pp. 544–46.

and the spirit of collectivity, and he argued that it is "obvious that this common interest is more important than the individual interest, and that man can liberate himself only when the mass of a population is free." Dr. Malik, the member of the Commission from Lebanon, on the other hand, sought human rights, during the same session, in the essence of man and found the chief problem of human rights in a new tyranny which has been rising in the last few decades, "the tyranny of the masses, which seems to have an inevitable tendency of ultimately embodying itself in what I might call the tyranny of the State." This is only one of the many conflicts developed recently from the fertile opposition of man and state which had served earlier to protect man from unwarranted infringements on his freedoms. It could be supplemented by a long list of further conflicts or by a long list of philosophic, religious, moral, economic, or social recommendations for their resolution. The problem of human rights has, in this fashion, become a philosophic problem in which differences of basic conviction make seemingly simple distinctions deceptively complex.

There are two ways in which such a problem may be treated: a philosophic solution may be sought in an agreement which resolves the basic differences, or a political frame may be sought within which agreement is possible concerning common action toward common ends and within which basic disagreements are more likely to be removed when mutual suspicions have been lessened by successful common action. The utility of a declaration of human rights depends on the possibility of separating the political from the philosophic question. The resolution of philosophic differences would require the definition of basic terms—like freedom and right—and the balance of oppositions—like tradition and novelty—which have been variously defined and variously related in the philosophic traditions of the world. There is, among the philosophies of the world, a "utopian" or ideal tradition of analysis in which "freedom" is conceived to be a power based on knowledge of the truth; and in that tradition, which on this point is shared by philosophers as different as Augustine and Marx, to express or to follow what is false is not to be free. There is also a "circumstantial" or material tradition of analysis in which freedom depends on the power of choice and the power to follow either of alternative modes of action; and in this tradition, in which philosophers as different as Aristotle or Mill might be found, freedom is found in a region of indifference, deliberation, and choice.[3] Likewise, what is revolutionary in the context of one set of philosophic assumptions is counter-revolutionary, subversive, or even traditional in another.

---

3. Cf. R. McKeon, "Discussion and Resolution in Political Conflicts," in *Ethics*, vol. 54 (1944) pp. 246–47.

The eighteenth century did not resolve these basic philosophic oppositions, but the declarations of rights which were formulated in the philosophic language of the eighteenth century did succeed in stating ideals which had a profound influence in improving the relations of men and in advancing the practice of justice. The basic problem to which the declarations of human rights were addressed was the injustice of feudal rulers and governments. They were expressions of the revolutionary movements of the century: they reserved certain inalienable rights to man and forbade governments to infringe them; they were part of a constitutional movement in which governments were conceived to depend on the consent of the governed. In like fashion, contemporary discussions of the rights of man will not resolve the basic philosophic oppositions which have continued unabated since the seventeenth century, unless philosophers, professional and lay, have discovered unexpectedly a new versatility in terminologies and assumptions or a new susceptibility to the claims of reason. But a declaration of human rights could achieve an effect on the political and social practices of the next century comparable to that of earlier bills of rights, provided it is recognized that the problem has changed. A world declaration of human rights must, like the national bills of rights, be conceived within a constitutional frame, such as the Charter of the United Nations; and the basic problem then turns not merely on the relation of men to governments but on the relation of groups of men and of states to each other. In the framework of the United Nations, it is the problem of how men with basically different philosophic convictions and religious beliefs, associated in divergent political organizations and committed to divergent economic systems can co-operate in the maintenance of peace, the promulgation of justice, and the protection of fundamental human rights. The nature of that problem is seen both in the opposed assumptions implied in efforts to resolve it and in the nature of the additions that have been made in recent years to the list of human rights.

The fundamental issue of our times is probably to be found in the opposition of two assumptions, made implicitly and explicitly in policies advocated for the determination of the relations of the nations of the world. On the one hand, it is assumed that there are several basic ideologies, probably reducible to two, which are in necessary conflict and opposition and which are dividing, or will eventually divide, mankind into two worlds until one overcomes the other. On the other hand, it is assumed that means can be found by which men of different basic convictions in philosophy, religion, political theory and economic doctrine may co-operate to common ends in a single world of shared values. The first is a solution in which peace and human rights depend on the successful inculcation of a single basic philosophy throughout the world, and the failure of efforts toward universal indoctrination in the past, even in the case of basic doctrines which seem in retrospect more attractive than the rough outlines presented by either of the opposed doctrines to one who does not share it, make it highly probable that pursuit of that solution must lead to war. The second is a solution in which the establishment of a constitution, like that of the United Nations, and of agencies, like the specialized agencies associated with the United Nations, might preserve the peace of the world by furnishing the means by which to reach agreements concerning the equitable solution of problems and the achievement of human welfare and the common good, and which, in so doing, might facilitate the advance of common understanding and basic intellectual agreement. In the pursuit of the second solution the formulation of a declaration of human rights is of basic importance and the nature of such a declaration takes its form from the assumption that it is possible to come to agreement concerning the rights of man and to implement such an agreement short of arriving at philosophic unanimity.

The change in the problem of human rights which is seen in this opposition of basic assumptions is further exemplified in new additions to the list of human rights. As human rights can no longer be formulated effectively on the simple opposition of man and state or on the assumption that freedoms and rights will be safeguarded adequately if governments can be persuaded to desist from certain actions, so too, many of the rights which have become of basic importance in the nineteenth and twentieth centuries have burst through the classical definitions and safeguards of human rights. In even so brief an enumeration as the Four Freedoms, only two—freedom of speech and expression and freedom of religion and worship—fit the frame of the earlier conception of rights or the guarantees provided for them, while two—freedom from want and freedom from fear—require a different analysis and different implementation. The treatment of problems involving rights of the latter kind during the nineteenth and early twentieth centuries is indication and symptom of the change in the basic problem of human rights, and the clarification of that difference will serve also to suggest the appropriate means for the implementation of such rights.

When rights are to be protected from the possible tyranny of governments, the problem may be solved by recognizing that certain rights are inherent in the very nature of man and by specifying the constitutional safeguards under which other rights may be delegated to the various organs of government. The rights of man are closely related to the rights of the citizen, and civil rights are both precondition and consequence of political rights. The specification of rights proper to man and the formulation of the manner in which rights proper to citizens may be exercised determines a complex relation between them, for they are, on the one hand, different in their implementation and yet, on the other hand, involved in a process of mutual delimitation which is usually expressed in the opposition of rights and duties. Civil rights are designed to guarantee the individual against arbitrary treatment: they are formulated in terms of equality before the law and the operation of due process of law; they can be defended by providing access to court decisions when they seem to be violated. Political rights are designed to relate the government to the consent of the governed: they are formulated in the institutions of government and in the conditions, such as "free elections," by which consent is expressed; they are defended only by the constitutional frame which determines the manner of their exercise. Civil rights, like freedom of conscience and freedom of speech, were justified by their early defenders on the grounds, not only that they may be granted without danger to the public peace, but also that they may not be withheld without danger. The freedoms of association, assembly, press, and communications have like grounds, and, although a limitation might be set on any such freedom by invoking the interest of *salus publica*, the general tendency seemed, until recently, to be toward the spread and universalization of such freedoms. Similarly, although the manner in which a citizen may influence the government under which he lives varies with the forms of government, the trend toward democracy seemed, until recently, universal. The change that has come into these problems in recent years is not so much due to a change in these tendencies as to the introduction of differences in the interpretation of what constitutes "freedom" and "democracy."

These changes became apparent in the discussion of rights which were not part of the eighteenth century formulations and which are not easily reduced to the formula of rights inherent in the nature of man requiring only protection from governmental interference. The problem of the new rights arose from the changed social and economic conditions due to the advance of technology and industrialization which brought fundamental and obvious rights into conflict with extensions and interpretations of "property" rights. They have been posed variously. In practical action they have been treated by legal devices, like those by which in the United States problems in labor regulations and public health were solved by making what had been rights of which individuals could not be deprived without due process of law proper subjects for the exercise of police power. They have been the occasion for political change, for legislative action, and for revolution. In abstract analysis they have seemed to some thinkers to involve a moral problem, in the need to relate rights to functions and obligations and to discover criteria and purposes for society,[4] while to others they have seemed to pose an intellectual problem, in the need to constitute a kind of knowledge which does not now exist for the resolution of the problems of the

---

4. R. H. Tawney, *The Acquisitive Society* (London, 1937), pp. 44–45, 82–83.

"public."[5] This variety of approaches, practical and theoretic, is indication of the nature of the problem and the diversity of implementation which is required for its solution. Even if it is stated in terms of the relation of man and the state, it is no longer a problem of rights of individuals reserved from interference by government or of rights by which individuals may secure proper influence on government, but rather a problem of how far opportunities to which men have a right must be secured by governmental action. The economic and social rights, which have a place in recent formulations of the rights of man—the right to work, the right to education, to social security, to recreation, cultural opportunities and a fair share of the advancing gains of civilization, and, in general, the freedom from want and the freedom from fear—all are rights which require that something be done if they are to be secured for their recipients. The promulgation of economic and social rights has therefore brought them into conflict with civil and political rights, for the planning and control essential to the former impinge on some of the freedoms of choice and action that had seemed defensible under the latter. As a consequence one of the fundamental oppositions in the discussion of human rights is between those who hold that the preservation of civil and political rights is basic even to the establishment of economic and social rights and those who hold that, unless economic and social rights are first secured, civil and political rights are an empty sham and pretense.

The means by which to secure both sets of rights, and indeed the very meanings which they assume as their interdependences are examined, present problems which would be difficult to resolve without recourse to the other aspect of our present situation and another related set of rights. The advancement of science and technology, which gave rise, as a result of changes consequent on it, to the problem of economic and social rights, has had a direct effect in the new significance that has been given to a fourth set of rights—the freedom of communication and thought. For as political rights afford a safeguard and significance to civil rights, and as economic and social rights provide means essential to the exercise of political rights, so the rights of communication and thought may prepare the resolution of differences concerning economic and social rights. The advance of science gives promise of completely transforming the conditions by which the welfare of man is secured, and the extension of information and knowledge may lead to mutual understanding and even to the removal of conflicts found in the basic assumptions of groups, cultures, and nations.

The formulation of the philosophic bases and material circumstances of human rights would be important in an effort to remove the conflicts that have

---

5. John Dewey, *The Public and its Problems* (New York, 1927), pp. 157, 166.

arisen in the conception of human rights. It is no less important to the preparation of a declaration of human rights, even though such a declaration need not await the resolution of fundamental problems, but should precede it, for the philosophic bases of human rights provide an analysis of the problem preparatory in the one case to resolution and in the other case to implementation and action. A world bill of rights is possible, if it is recognized that both the definition of the rights and progress in their achievement depend on implementation, and that implementation in the case of a world bill of rights means not merely the recognition of agencies by which to protect rights or resolve conflicts among them, but also recognition of the fact that within the constitutional frame of the United Nations, rights will have different legal implementation and different philosophic interpretation in the various sovereign nations of the Organization. What is proposed, as an immediate step, is the formulation of a Declaration of Human Rights and Fundamental Freedoms to be adopted as a General Assembly Resolution. This declaration might serve as a standard to be observed by Member States, and might be incorporated in their constitutions and legislation. Most of the Member States already possess provisions in their constitutions for civil and political rights expressed in forms that are similar even when the interpretations are highly diverse. The economic and social rights, on the other hand, have the international aspects that are already subject to the operation of the United Nations and its various agencies. Civil rights could be given an international character, only if they were assigned to the jurisdiction of a world tribunal, and political rights would be internationally effective only if the citizens of the nations of the world were made citizens of the world by a change in the structure of the United Nations. In the case of economic and social rights, on the other hand, the Security Council and the Economic and Social Council are already engaged in establishing the freedom from fear and the freedom from want, and specialized agencies like the World Health Organization, the Food and Agriculture Organization and Unesco are engaged on the problems of health and education. Finally, the problems of communication, international understanding, and the use of educational, scientific and culture instruments in the maintenance of peace are among the chief concerns of UNESCO. The promulgation of a world declaration of rights depends, as bills of rights seem always to have depended, on the existence of a broad region of interpretation within which court decisions and administrative and legislative action have worked progressively to a practical definition and within which divergent philosophies have worked to less ambiguous or conflicting theoretic bases. The declaration will not remove the sharp differences in interpretations of civil and political rights, but it will provide a ground within which they may be brought into closer approximation, if economic and social rights are established sufficiently firmly to provide a minimum welfare and security, and if freedom of communication and freedom of thought are advanced enough to contribute to universal welfare and mutual understanding. Agreement can doubtless be secured concerning the list of human rights only if an ambiguity remains both because of the absence of a uniform manner of administering them and because of the absence of a single basic philosophy, but that ambiguity is the frame within which men may move peacefully to a more uniform practice and to a universal understanding of fundamental human rights.

June 1947

RELATIONSHIP BETWEEN DIFFERENT CATEGORIES OF HUMAN RIGHTS
Quincy Wright[*]

... To assert that men are men and that all cultures have something in common is far from a formulation of rights which may protect the needs and desires of men and may secure for all the values recognized by world culture. Any such formulation encounters circumstances in which individual needs and desires conflict with one another, or with universal values, and even circumstances in which universal values conflict with one another.

Every formulation of a human right that has been suggested raises issue (1) of man vs. the group; (2) of group vs. group; (3) of group vs. the world. These issues necessarily arise in the formulation of a bill of human rights and even more in the establishment of institutions and procedures for the enforcement of such a bill. If the final interpreter of human rights is the individual, society may dissolve in anarchy. If the final interpreter is the group, world society may dissolve in international or class war. If the final interpreter is the world, lesser groups may disappear and a universal tyranny may be possible. Consideration will be given successively to these three basic dilemmas in the formulation of human rights.

---

[*] Quincy Wright was Professor of Political Science and International Law at the University of Chicago and one of the founders of the discipline of international relations. Wright served as an adviser to Justice Robert H. Jackson during the Nuremberg Trials and was the author of the monumental 1500-page *A Study of War*, published in two volumes by the University of Chicago Press in 1942.

MAN VS. THE GROUP

The issue of man vs. the group was vigorously presented in the first meeting of the United Nations Human Rights Commission in February, 1947. Accordingly to Mr. Ribnikar of Yugoslavia:

"The new conditions of the economic, social and national life of our time have tended to develop the spirit of collectivity, and the conscience, and the solidarity of the popular masses. We are more and more aware that real individual liberty can be reached only in perfect harmony between the individual and the collectivity. It becomes quite obvious that this common interest is more important than the individual interest, and that man can liberate himself only when the mass of a population is free.

"In our time the social principle comes first. If it has one purpose, it is to create conditions necessary to the fulfillment of the interest of every individual. The social ideal is the ideal of the enormous majority of the world and it is in the identity of the interest of society and of the individual. Therefore, when we desire to speak today of the rights of man, of modern men, we must not think of the social ideal or of a political ideal of another age. This ideal belongs to the past, and if it remains in some countries, it is the ideal of one class only of a society . . . ."

On the other hand, Dr. Malik of Lebanon said:

" . . . the very phrase "human rights," obviously refers to man, and by "rights" you can only mean that which belongs to the essence of man, namely, that which is not accidental, that which does not come and go with the passage of time and with the rise and fall of fads and styles and systems. It must be something belonging to man as such. We are, therefore, raising the fundamental question, what is man? And our differences will reflect faithfully the differences in our conceptions of man, namely, of ourselves. . . .

"The individual human being, you and I, today may not be in need of protection against the despotism of the individual. The day of individual dictators and tyrants may be passed. But if man is no longer in need of protection against the tyranny of kings and dictators, he is desperately in need of protection against another kind of tyranny, in my opinion equally grievous.

"There has been rising in the last few decades a new tyranny, the tyranny of the masses, which seems to have an inevitable tendency of ultimately embodying itself in what I might call the tyranny of the state. If there is any danger to fundamental human rights today, it is certainly from that direction . . .

"The real danger of the present age is that social claims are in danger of snuffing out any real personal liberty. It is not social security and responsibility that are not going to find advocates and therefore expression in our bill. It is rather the questions which relate to personal values and freedoms.

"May I express that what I ultimately mean is this. I am not setting an artificial antithesis between the individual and the State. I am asking this question. Which is for the sake of the other? Is the State for the sake of the human person or is the human person for the sake of the State? That, to me, is the ultimate question of the present day. I believe the State is for the sake of the person and therefore our Bill of Rights must express that for the sake of which everything else exists, including the States."

This debate makes it clear that in spite of the effort of the sociologists to synthesize the individual personality and group culture, the potential conflict between the individual and the group emphasized in Herbert Spencer's "Man vs. The State" has not been solved. Those who adhere to the Socialistic view expressed by Mr. Ribnikar emphasize social and economic rights such as the right to work, the right to fair conditions of work, the right to social security, the right to education, or in more general terms the rights to freedom from fear and from want. On the other hand, those who share the individualistic thesis expressed by Dr. Malik emphasize civil and procedural rights such as the rights of conscience and free speech, rights of association and property, rights of movement and choice of occupation, the right to prompt and fair trial for alleged transgressions of law, and the right to be governed by laws which do not discriminate arbitrarily—rights which contribute to the individual freedom of religion, opinion, expression, and action customarily guaranteed in the 18th century bills of rights. It is to be observed that there rights were usually expressed in universal terms, whereas the social and economic rights which have often figured in the bills of rights of 20th century constitutions usually apply only to Nationals of the state. This perhaps indicates that the economic and social rights are less susceptible of universalization than are the more individualistic rights.

Most of the international bills of rights which have been proposed by private organizations during the last few years include both of these types of rights, and it may be that the alleged incompatibility between them has been exaggerated. It is true that states which emphasize social and economic rights have frequently neglected civil and procedural rights in practice. An emphasis upon individualistic rights has also led to problems.

. . . Modern states have generally recognized the need of compromise of individual interests and social interests, and have sought to give some protection by law to both of these interests. Twentieth century Constitutions usually guarantee both of these types of rights to their citizens. They have, however, usually expressed both types of rights relatively rather than absolutely. Furthermore, they have recognized that the method of implementation of these different types of rights must be different.

Individual rights are in the main correlative to negative duties of the State, and social rights are in the main correlative to positive duties of the State. Individual rights require that the State abstain from interference with the free exercise by the individual of his capacities, while the social rights require that the state interfere with many things the individual would like to do by the collection of taxes, the exercise of police power, the regulation of economic activities, and the administration of public services. Individual rights can, therefore, in large measure be enforced by judicial action, declaring laws and administrative decrees which violate them null and void. The social rights, on the other hand, require legislative, administrative, and executive action to make and to enforce new laws. The individual rights might, therefore, be expressed in an international Bill of Rights as rules of law susceptible of judicial application, while the social rights can only be expressed as goals or principles for the guidance of national or international legislation, or of international co-operation or administrative activity. Consequently, if both types of rights are included in a common statement, it should be understood that no common mode of implementation would be possible. The international Bill of Rights would be a declaration of purposes rather than an effective rule of law.

Even in this respect, however, the differences between the two types of rights may be exaggerated. Individual rights, while primarily correlative with the state's duty of abstention, may also require positive state action in establishing and maintaining courts with adequate jurisdiction and in providing criminal legislation and administration to prevent other individuals within the community from encroaching upon these rights. The maintenance of all human rights in the modern interdependent world also requires suitable international agencies and procedures to assure that states observe both the negative and positive duties correlative with the rights.

These considerations suggest that the initial statement of human rights should be in the form of a declaration by the appropriate authorities of the world community, stating the rights but without any formal provision concerning their implementation. It should be assumed that in application the rights are to be regarded as relative to one another and that each is to be implemented by appropriate and perhaps different methods of national and international activity.

GROUP VS. GROUP

The issue of group vs. group was less discussed in the meeting of the Commission on Human Rights than was the issue of individual vs. group, but this potential conflict underlay the discussion as indicated by a statement of Mr. Mora of Uruguay:

"The traditional bills of rights have a national character. It seems to me that in the twentieth century we must emphasize the international human rights, the international rights of the man . . .

"The classic doctrine says that only states are subject to international laws. We need now to declare that man is the most important element of any kind of law, national or international."

Why did the doctrine develop that only states are subject to international law and that individuals are subject only to national law? It was not because of a socialistic opinion that the group should dominate the individual, but because of the necessity of ultimate state control of its subjects in order to protect the state from outside states.

. . . It is clear that this argument, which objects to human rights on the ground that their enforcement by world authority would qualify the freedom of the state in its international relations, is likely to prevail so long as conditions of power politics and the demand for the absolute autonomy of the national government, economy, and culture prevails. Confidence that the United Nations can assure security to all states may be a condition for the effective implementation of human rights. So long as international emergencies may develop in which state survival may depend on state unity, the state will hesitate to surrender ultimate control of the law applicable within its domain.

But in an interdependent world, security through even the most able playing of power politics may be impossible. Security may be obtainable only through collective security, and that may be obtainable only through the development of the world community. This, in turn, may imply the universal recognition and maintenance of human rights. World institutions which can give security may be impossible unless the world community develops a common culture and common standards of human rights.

The universal maintenance of human rights may create conditions in which those relations between groups may become ones of co-operation and the expectation of peace. The rules of international law, which have defined the relations of state to state, must develop to meet this new situation. The rights of states must be considered relative to the rights of individuals. Both the state and the individual must be considered as subjects of world law and the sovereignty of the state must be regarded not as absolute, but as a competence defined by that law. Such a development, however, implies that the world community is sufficiently organized and sufficiently powerful to assure the security of states under law.

GROUP VS. THE WORLD

The issue of the group vs. the world is recognized in the somewhat conflicting clauses of the United Nations Charter. On the one hand, the Charter forbids the intervention of the United Nations in matters which are essentially within the domestic jurisdiction of any state (Article 2, paragraph 7) and on the other hand, it pledges all the members to take joint and separate action in co-operation with the organization for the achievement of universal respect for, and observance of, human rights and fundamental freedoms for all without distinction as to race, sex, language, or religion (Articles 55, paragraph C; 56).

Does this mean that United Nations action to protect human rights is by the Charter placed outside the prohibited sphere of domestic jurisdiction of states? Or does it mean that the protection of human rights is at the mercy of the interpretation and exercise by each state of its domestic jurisdiction?

The resolution of the General Assembly in December, 1946, on the Indian complaint that South Africa was denying human rights to Indians within its territory, suggests the former interpretation. This interpretation is also suggested by the provision of the Nuremberg Charter sustained as a general principle of law by the Nuremberg Tribunal that "act of state" cannot protect individuals indicted for offences against the law of nations.

Experience has shown that states cannot in all circumstances be trusted to respect any standard of rights within their own territories. Barbarities against minorities have in recent years shocked the conscience of mankind. If human rights are to be respected, the United Nations must be armed with competence and with means of enforcement which will modify past conceptions of the sovereignty of the state in the world community. Clearly the law of the Charter of the United Nations which seeks to define the relation of states to the world community must develop appropriate compromises between the domestic jurisdiction of the states and the competence of the United Nations to maintain human rights. The responsibility of the state and the power of the United Nations must be so interpreted as to give assurance that every individual will enjoy human rights.

CONCLUSION

The considerations set forth in this memorandum suggest that in the drafting of an International Bill of Human Rights, absolutistic concepts of the individual, of the state, and of the world community must be abandoned. The individual and the state, though distinct, are related to one another and this relationship varies with conditions. Among these conditions is the relation of the state to other states and to the world community.

Human rights can only be defined if due consideration is given both to the original nature of man and to the contemporary standards of world civilization. Any definition of human rights can, however, be implemented as law only if the relationship of each right to the requirements of the state and to the authority of the United Nations is recognized. The functions of the state in protecting the values of the national culture, in organizing social experiments, and in maintaining national solidarity must be recognized. The functions of the United Nations in coordinating national cultures within the world culture, in organizing international co-operation for human welfare and progress, and in maintaining international and world law can develop only gradually. Human rights must be stated in terms which recognize their relativity, and the implementation of each right must develop independently and gradually as the world community develops in solidarity and organization.

ON THE DRAFT CONVENTION AND
"UNIVERSAL DECLARATION OF THE RIGHTS OF MAN"
Levi Carneiro[*]

1. The first declarations of the rights of man, proclaimed by several nations, go back to the eighteenth, or even the seventeenth century. At first, they were characteristic of the democratic regime, but are today inscribed in nearly all, if not all, modern constitutions, where they form a long and detailed section which tends to become increasingly long and detailed.

Originally, they were limited to civil and political rights; they were then extended to other, economic rights, which have also been described, rather vaguely, as social rights. In addition to rights, these declarations set forth the guarantees without which the rights cannot become effective.

It is by the extent of these guarantees that we can judge the value of the political regime of each nation. Not infrequently nationalist prejudices deprive foreigners of what are called social rights. Nor is it rare for vicissitudes of internal politics to destroy all these rights and guarantees. We also see the existence and survival of oppression, with the aid of modern automatic weapons and the resources of the public treasury, which the dictators of today always know how to exploit. Thus national declarations have proved inadequate.

---

[*] Levi Carneiro was president of the Brazilian National Commission for UNESCO in 1947 and a leading Brazilian jurist and international lawyer. He was one of the founders and first president of the Brazilian Bar Association and later served as a judge on the International Court of Justice in The Hague (1951–55).

The joint proclamation of these individual rights, made by the civilized nations, will constitute not only a perfect guarantee for man, the full expansion of his personality, in every corner of the globe; it will also be a proof of the political identity of nations, of the realization of democracy throughout the world, of the universal spread of culture. All national declarations will have a common denominator.

We must not imagine that all nations have now reached the same degree of perfection in the recognition and guarantee of the rights of man. But the joint declaration will serve as a guide to the legislators of the different countries; it will encourage the expansion and improvement, along the same lines, of national declarations, which are still incomplete or inadequate, raising then to the level which all should attain. It is necessary not merely to make good the omissions in the declaration of each country, but also to try, as far as possible, to eliminate discrepancies due to different, sometimes diametrically opposed concepts.

Relations between states are based on the assumption that the internal politics of each nation are the concern of all nations.

The international declaration will thus be a factor for democratization and international peace.

2. The international declaration of rights will also be a factor for peace, because it will be able to reconcile the two divergent, if not antagonistic, political concepts confronting each other in the world today. Although reconciliation on a world scale is quite impossible, the declaration of rights will be made by the nations sharing the same ideal. In this connection, we should stress the declarations of the Pan-American Conferences of Rio de Janeiro and Bogotá, and the report of the Inter-American Legal Commission.

In any case, whether it be regional or world-wide, the international declaration can no longer be delayed.

3. For the same reason, the international declaration must be even more far-reaching and complete than any of the national declarations at present in force.

Some will think that the international declaration should contain only rights that are uniformly recognized by all nations. If drawn up according to this criterion, the declaration would be too laconic. Moreover, it would be useless; it would be superfluous to make a joint declaration of rights which every country already recognizes and guarantees. The elementary, fundamental rights, recognized by all nations, do not need an international declaration to command respect.

When, in the middle of the war, President Roosevelt proclaimed the four fundamental rights: freedom from want and fear, freedom of speech and worship, he was thought to be going too far. Today, no one can be satisfied with the affirmation of these elementary rights. The simple rights, granted by the Charter of the United Nations, to the Economic and Social Council, of making "recommendations" in order to "promote respect for the human rights and fundamental liberties of all peoples, and to make these rights and liberties effective," no longer satisfies the demands of our contemporary legal conscience. These rights and liberties must be given a real and effective guarantee.

4. It seems to be generally admitted that a declaration of rights should be made at the same time as the Convention, the former being wider in scope, the latter containing only those rights which are recognized and guaranteed by all the nations parties to the Convention.

I am sorry not to share this view. A simultaneous declaration and Convention reduce each other's value. The declaration will be ineffective and, accordingly, complete; the Convention will be imperfect, and for this reason, operative. I prefer the declaration in the form of a convention, complete and operative.

5. Moreover, the Declaration and the Convention, in their present draft form, have important technical defects. In some points, the Convention is more detailed, and in others, the Declaration.

6. I am certain that the same procedure should now be adopted as is usually followed by international conventions.

What should be made is a declaration of rights, but a declaration inserted in a convention and completely binding in all its legal effects—a single document, therefore.

Of course, each state, when signing the Convention, will have the right to make reservations concerning clauses or declarations to which it does not immediately subscribe, and which it does not pledge itself to respect.

These reservations will gradually disappear. Little by little each state will recognize the rights which it did not recognize at the outset. It is only in this way that the Convention can become a factor of democratic progress in the world.

7. The recognition of certain fundamental rights can be demanded immediately. The existence of a democratic government can be made to depend on this recognition. It will be a requisite minimum for admission into the international community, more significant than the vague expression "nations united for peace," adopted in the United Nations Charter.

This minimum will consist of the rights concerning:

> life,
> liberty,
> work,
> education,

equality,

participation in the government of one's own country.

It is on this basis that we must establish the other, increasingly numerous and more clearly defined rights, by which progress towards democracy is made.

Each of the fundamental rights involves sub-divisions, applications and consequences which form a complete table of rights. Some of them, in particular cases, give rise to other rights, by reason of special circumstances, such as age.

The right of living implies the right to a minimum subsistence, to health, by medical and hospital treatment, the fight against disease, the free constitution and defense of the family; the right to State protection, nationality and naturalization.

Freedom implies a great number of other rights, including some of the fundamental rights mentioned above, such as the right to work and the right to participate in government. The latter becomes the right to a government chosen by universal suffrage. Freedom includes not only the four freedoms mentioned by Roosevelt; there is also liberty of conscience, thought, opinion, worship, association, residence and change of residence, freedom of information, the dissemination of information and scientific research. From the right to work, we have the right of ownership, the right to leisure, the right to share in economic advantages, and the right to fair remuneration.

All these rights demand and presuppose the right to justice and the right to resist oppression. The right to justice becomes continually more complex; it includes the right to be tried under a previous law, to trial in public, to the assistance of freely chosen counsel, to be free from all pressure; the right to hear one's judges and to be heard by them; the right to swift, sure and effective protection of all threatened or unrecognized rights. In addition to all the rights listed and defined, it is necessary to safeguard implicit rights, all those which are necessary for the exercise of each of the explicit rights, or which follow from the explicit rights or constitutional government. This is provided for in the Brazilian and the American Constitutions.

8. The Convention will go far towards codification, if we may use the expression, of international relations, by attempting to subordinate these relations to infallible, clearly-defined legal rules. This work is complex and difficult, and is being achieved gradually along the lines defined above.

However, the Convention will immediately necessitate a central body analogous to the International Labour Office to co-ordinate and supervise its execution. Later, it will involve a jurisdictional body, which might be the International Court of Justice. Finally, it will need a specific, autonomous tribunal, before which individuals may plead against States, in order to safeguard their rights.

This will be the last stage in a laborious evolution, which cannot be achieved straight away.

The course of this evolution is inevitably bound up with world political conditions, and particularly with the realization of collective security. But nothing must be done to prevent or hinder it.

COMMENTS ON THE BASIC HUMAN RIGHTS
*Arthur H. Compton**

1. The rights of the individual must be interpreted with relation to his place as part of society. As the lives of people have become more interdependent, the concept of freedom moves toward education of the individual to choose and work effectively for those things that promote the common welfare.

It is not possible to separate the rights of the individual from the objectives for which he wants to live. The goal of life assumed in the present statement may be described in terms of altruism or of self-interest. Speaking in terms of altruism, we may say that the individual desires to make the maximum contribution to human welfare, with the resulting personal satisfaction that comes from feeling that he has done his appropriate part. The alternative statement based on self-interest would be that the individual desires complete freedom for self development as a unit of organized society. Since an individual can be permitted complete freedom only in case his desires coincide with the needs of society, these two statements of human aims lead ultimately to closely similar requirements. What from the point of view of self-interest are to be considered as rights which the individual properly may ask society to supply, from the point of view of altruism become the necessities of the individual in order that he may perform his proper service to society.

We accordingly mean by human rights whatever the individual may properly expect society to supply. Some among these rights it should be possible for the state to guarantee its citizens. Others it is possible to provide only in a well or-

---

* Arthur H. Compton won the Nobel Prize in Physics in 1927 for his research on the properties of electromagnetic radiation. At the time he participated in the UNESCO human rights survey, Compton was the acting US representative to UNESCO and the chancellor of Washington University in St. Louis. During this same year (1947), Compton's eldest brother, Karl, was serving as president of MIT and his other brother, Wilson, as president of Washington State University. Arthur Compton played a leading role in the development of the atomic bomb during the Second World War as a member of the Manhattan Project.

ganized and prosperous society, and are thus to be considered not as insurable to the citizen but rather as objectives which the state will try to attain.

2. The most basic rights which society should endeavor to ensure to an individual are three: (1) the right to a *healthy life*, (2) the right to *work effectively*, (3) the right to *choose wisely* the objectives of one's efforts. Counterparts of these rights are the obligations of the individual to society to endeavor to maintain one's health, to perform effective work for society, and to choose the goals of one's efforts with due regard for the needs of society.

Health. An individual's most fundamental right is an opportunity for the development of a sound, healthy body and mind. This implies particularly a safeguarded heritage, adequate food, shelter and clothing, opportunity to share a normal family life, opportunity for necessary rest and recreation, medical care, education, exercise, and training for physical health and a wholesome mental adjustment, and an opportunity to know a valid spiritual interpretation of the universe that will supply a basis for a stably motivated life.

Work. Society owes to the individual an opportunity to earn a living through productive labor, with a reward for his labor which will insure means of living and a modicum of security against old age and misfortune. In order that his work may be most effective, he is entitled to education and training that will equip him with the necessary techniques and skills and which will enable him to discover how he can best fit himself to be a useful part of the social structure. If he is willing to do his part, society should endeavor to supply him with such work with freedom from the fear of want.

Choice. The essence of freedom is the ability to do what one wants to do. The freedom becomes complete when a person knows what courses of action are possible, knows how to make the proposed courses effective, knows what values will be attained if a proposed choice is taken, and when he prefers the choice which is in closest harmony with the needs of society. Such wise choosing implies education and training with regard to the values of life, and such familiarity with science as will make apparent what one may hope to attain. Of especial importance is familiarity with the objectives that can be attained by cooperative effort. An individual thus has the right to that type of education and discipline which will train him to want those things which are in line with the welfare of his fellows.

3. Associated with each of these rights is a right to protection. The individual has the right, for example, to expect society to protect him against needless exposure to disease, against the needless chance for an unhappy physical or mental heritage, against known untruths sponsored by the state under the guise of truth, against intentional obstruction to the growth and availability of useful

knowledge, and against indecency and the spread of hatred that will mar his mental attitude and make cooperation difficult.

4. The rights of the individual and the rights of the state are inseparable. We recognize that the only true values are those which are appreciated by individuals. The state should thus be designed to enhance individual values. It is true at the same time that society has a right to require that the goals toward which the individual works shall be in harmony with the objectives of the state itself. It is nevertheless necessary that the individual shall have the right to dissent from the official views of the state and to express this dissent, in order that the objectives of the state may be continually adjusted to the needs of its citizens. We consider the exercise of the rights of the individual as described above to be an effective means of promoting the interests of the state.

5. A balanced education seems to be the only means of enabling the individual to choose so wisely that his free action will be in accord with the best interests of society. When that condition exists, there is no interference between the complete freedom of the individual and the requirements of society. Until such education has however ensured wise choices by individuals, enforced limitation on their actions is necessary. It should be possible, nevertheless, to effect these limitations without interfering with the basic rights described above. As individuals grow in knowledge, understanding and wisdom, their perspectives will be more complete, their horizons wiser, and their visions clearer. Their self-interest will find itself on ever higher levels until ultimately it coincides with the common interest.

A WORLD BILL OF RIGHTS
Charles E. Merriam[*]

When I wrote on an international bill of rights in 1946, the project might have seemed a little nebulous. At the present time, however, the Commission on Human Rights, set up by the Economic and Social Council of the United Nations, is now and has been for many months in full swing. The Chairman of this Commission is none other than Mrs. Eleanor Roosevelt and the present paper

---

[*] Charles E. Merriam was 73 years old at the time he responded to the UNESCO human rights survey, and had been retired from the University of Chicago for seven years. He had joined the University of Chicago as its first political scientist in 1900 and had served as chairman of the Department of Political Science from 1911 until 1940. Merriam was also an anti-corruption local politician in Chicago during the first part of the twentieth century and a key adviser to Franklin D. Roosevelt during the creation and implementation of the New Deal.

is part of a series of discussions of a world bill of rights coming in first instance from the American branch of UNESCO and finally back, we trust, to the Commission on Human Rights for consideration next September. (See Annals of the American Academy, January, 1946, on "Essential Human Rights.")[6]

At the very beginning one may say: What has a world bill of rights to do particularly with physics and politics? The answer is: much; perhaps everything. For a world bill of rights provides the essential background or framework for a jural order of the world, without which neither physics nor politics can operate. The old time sphere in which physics found a home or politics found a status have been upset by revolutionary changes, some of which may be attributed to physics and some of which, equally revolutionary, spring from political relationships. Without a world bill of rights which is universally recognized and substantially enforced or applied, the future for reflection and peaceful actions is very dark.

An international bill of rights is a statement of the rights of man in our time in a world setting. There are three sets of new conditions at the root of the present problem. One of these is the development of a jural order of the world, moving in the direction of world government. Another is the new body of social, economic, and cultural forces in our time. Another is the new discoveries and role of human intelligence in human affairs, of which the new research in atomic energy is the symbol.

A further factor is, of course, that most of the elements of a world bill of rights are already embodied in the structure of the United Nations Charter. President Truman says, "The Charter is dedicated to the achievement and observance of human rights and fundamental freedoms. Unless we can obtain these objectives for all men and women everywhere—without regard to race, language or religion—we cannot have permanent peace and security." (San Francisco, June 26, 1945).

These new conditions profoundly affect any bill of rights in our day, for they are revolutionary in nature—far more revolutionary than any other world revolution. The increasing recognition of the dignity of man and the importance of

---

6. This was a special edition of the Annals of the American Academy of Political and Science published in January 1946. This publication, edited by William Draper Lewis, founder of the American Law Institute, and John R. Ellingston, featured 26 essays organized within the following sections: the international importance of human rights; an international declaration of human rights; human rights in selected areas (Roman-law countries, England and the United States, the Chinese draft constitution, Islam, the cultural tradition of Spanish America, and Latin America); the national legal protection of human rights; international procedures for protection of human rights; and future international action [ed.].

protecting him under new economic and social conditions, the events of World War II, the emergence of the atomic bomb, a mark of the revolutionary triumphs of human intelligence in social relationships—these factors are a sharp challenge to those who frame an adequate statement of the rights of man in the twentieth century. The ends of government remain unchanged in the midst of these alarms. Security, justice, order, welfare, and freedom are universal ends of political behavior, as seen through observation, experience, and reflection. But they are applied under new conditions from time to time as basic changes are made in social, economic, and cultural conditions and in political participation.

Obviously, there are many value systems other than the political—the religious, the cultural, the artistic, and a bill of rights will deal with these in the area of the governmental. But the political is not limited to the legal in the formal sense. It includes the wider range of political ideals and aspirations. Indeed, a recognition of the pluralism of values is one of the basic conditions of world order in particular. Our present task is to place the political values of human rights in their proper governmental setting as a part of the general understandings upon which world order is built.

INHERENT RIGHTS

From time immemorial, the rights of man derived from the laws of nature, from Christianity, from human experience, observation, and reflection, and have been a refuge against human might, an altar to which man might flee, a rallying cry for resistance to tyranny or oppression or against arbitrary rule. As time went on, these rights were brought together in more systematic form. They found their way into the Roman law; they flowered in the natural law when almost forgotten by governments; they became the basis of revolutionary movements against absolute despotism, the cornerstone of constitutional democracies everywhere, the foundation of twentieth-century political progress.

Again and again it has been contended that these human rights are not true "rights" and have no place or validity in governmental documents. It has been said that there never was a historical "State of Nature" in which human rights existed prior to the establishment of civil government; that alleged human rights have no efficiency without legal enforceability; and that they possess no special value for political understanding. But both reflection and experience show that these rights of man have substantial and growing value. Their foundation rests in the nature of human personality. The validity of the claims of human nature is not dependent upon the interpretation or application given by a particular agent of authority at a given time, important as this may be practically, but upon the validity of the human claim in the framework of advancing civilization. Rights are an affirmation of the value of the ends of government, an assertion of confidence in the principles upon which all political association of human beings rests in last analysis.

That rights have not yet been fully recognized or realized does not remove them from the field of the political, for politics deals with ideals as well as with realities. Ideals indeed are themselves realities. The rights of man provide the domain of faith and hope in governments, the court of appeal which is never closed, the law beyond the law and the jurists, the lawmakers, the managers, and the adjudicators. The rights of man go deeper and higher than institutional devices for interpreting or applying them. Their vitality illuminates that recurring poverty of unjust power which is the hope of freedom in all times.

The most notable statement of human rights is that of the American Declaration of Independence. "We hold these truths to be self-evident, that all mean are created equal, that they are endowed by their Creator with certain unalienable rights, that among these are life, liberty and the pursuit of happiness. That to secure these rights, governments are instituted among men, deriving their just powers from the consent of the governed," with the right of revolution as the ultimate appeal. With this we may compare the French Declaration of the Rights of Man and of the Citizen (1789) and scores of other declarations.

THE BASIC RIGHT

The basic right is the right to life—the right to the fullest and finest development of the potentialities of the human personality, in the framework of the common good. This is the root right from which all others stem. Civil rights, political rights, social and economic rights, are implements designed to make effective the foundational right of them all—the human personality with its insistent claim for life expression and expansion, for recognition of the innate dignity of man, for the realization of the possibilities of man and of his unique position in the natural, social, and moral order.

Without the understanding and recognition of this basic right, the other so-called rights lose their meaning. The attempt to escape the implications of this basic right has led might to divorce itself from right and stand out in the ugly trappings of force alone; but only as right and might are blended is there genuine authority and genuine justice in human relations. . . .

THE COROLLARY RIGHTS

On this basic right is built a long series of guarantees, protections, and safeguards, such as human equality as a prerequisite of a system of justice, respect for the human personality, equality of treatment without regard to race, creed, or sex, freedom of religion, of the press, of associating, and a long and changing series of conditions under which life may be enriched.

These may be classified roughly as follows, without insistence on the value of the classification, which is perhaps more hierarchical than logical: (1) civil rights, (2) political rights, (3) economic and social rights, (4) scientific rights.

These are all overlapping rights, all depending on the basic right of the life and growth of the human personality. They refer to certain types of situations in which the personality must function if creative development is the goal. No one of this series of rights is complete without the others. There must be coordination of social and economic rights with the political rights which guarantee and protect them. More than that, no one system alone is adequate, without a concert of the family of nations in which it must function. . . .

MEMORANDUM ON THE RIGHTS OF MAN
FOR THE COMMISSION ON HUMAN RIGHTS
OF THE UNITED NATIONS
Lewis Mumford [*]

What is a human right? It is an attempt to define an essential attribute of the human personality, to make this attribute sacred, and to give it a constitutional and juridical status.

As soon as one passes from the essential attributes of the human personality to secondary characteristics one passes out of the sphere of rights, properly defined. One may have a "right to live" but not a right to have three meals a day, since some communities may be content with two meals and some may demand six. In short, a right should only establish those characteristics without which a person is not a person, but a mere biological organism or a slave.

So far from extending the list of human rights as set forth in the eighteenth century, I would propose, rather, to limit their number and attempt to make them truly universal. Every attempt to elaborate human rights is in fact a covert effort to give a constitutional status to some special and limited human

---

[*] Lewis Mumford was a major American public intellectual and one of the most influential urbanists of the twentieth century. He was also a prominent social activist. His son Geddes died in combat during the invasion of Italy in 1944. Mumford was the architecture critic for *The New Yorker* for over thirty years and was the author of many books, including *The Study of Utopia* (1922), *Men Must Act* (1939), *Faith for Living* (1940), and his masterpiece *The City in History* (1961), which won the 1962 National Book Award for nonfiction.

enactment. The following list of rights is offered merely as an illustration of the method and scope of a new Bill of Rights.

I. Human life is sacred. The right to live shall not be abridged, except under universally acknowledged terms of law and justice. These terms shall be defined by a World Court and established by the United Nations. Positively, the right to live constitutes a claim for access to the land and the instruments of production, or to their economic equivalents.

II. The right to form a family and to propagate the race is sacred, subject only to such regulations as may be designed to protect the health and welfare of the community as a whole.

III. Every human being has the right to continued growth and development, up to the limit of his capacities. This right constitutes a claim to schooling, to access to libraries and other institutes of culture, and to association in freedom with others for the purposes of study, research, work, play, political action, or worship.

IV. Every human being, since he is born into society, has the right not only to form new associations but to withdraw from associations that do not represent his interests or further his welfare. No state shall abridge the right of two or more people to form associations, corporations, or groups, except when the purpose of such associations are contrary to human welfare, as defined by a World Court. The state may, however, require all associations, beginning with the family, to declare their existence and to abide by regulations designed to promote the common good.

V. Every human being has the right to be treated as an equal member of the human family, without respect to race, nation, class, status or country of origin. On the positive side, this constitutes a claim to travel and migrate, subject to such regulations as may be imposed by the United Nations acting on behalf of all its members.

VI. Every group and state shall have the right to self-government, on the basis of equal participation by all its adult members. This right implies freedom of opinion and speech, freedom of assembly, freedom of public criticism, and freedom to choose and remove its officers and leaders at regular elections.

Beyond Egotistic Man:
Communist, Socialist, and Social Democratic Challenges

THE RIGHTS OF MAN
E. H. Carr[*]

Article 62 of the Charter of the United Nations provides that "the Economic and Social Council. . . . may make recommendations for the purpose of promoting respect for, and observance of, human rights and fundamental freedoms for all." The fact that this task is entrusted to the Economic and Social Council suggests that the framers of the Charter intended to lay stress on economic and social rights. In coupling with the idea of human rights the phrase "fundamental freedoms" they will certainly have had in mind Franklin Roosevelt's "Four Freedoms," which by placing freedom from want and freedom from fear side by side with freedom of speech and freedom of worship forestalled any attempt to interpret the word "freedom" in a narrow legal or formal sense.

The conception of the rights of man dates historically from the 18th century when it was particularly (though not, of course, exclusively) associated with the American and French revolutions. It was expressed at that time in wholly political terms. The more modern conception of the Rights of Man may perhaps be associated (though also not exclusively) with the Russian revolution and is economic and social as much as political. It is this modern conception quite as much as the classical tradition which must be considered as having inspired this provision in the Charter. What is implied in the transition from a purely political conception of the rights of man to an economic and social conception may perhaps be illustrated by a comparison between a fundamental document of the French Revolution, the Declaration of the Rights of Man, adopted by the French

---

[*] E. H. Carr served as Chair of the UNESCO Committee of Experts and was a leading British journalist, international relations theorist, historian, and diplomat. Carr was a member of the British delegation at the Paris Peace Conference after the First World War and played a role in the creation of the League of Nations. He was the Woodrow Wilson Professor of International Politics at the University of Wales, Aberystwyth, although his forced resignation from the position (related to a scandal involving the wife of a university colleague) was dated June 30, 1947, at the exact moment the Committee of Experts was meeting in Paris. He was the author of many influential and controversial books, including *The Twenty Years' Crisis* (1939) and the fourteen-volume *A History of Soviet Russia* (1950–78).

National Assembly in 1789, and the Declaration of Rights of the Toiling and Exploited Peoples adopted by the All-Russian Congress of Soviets in January 1918.

The declaration of 1789 lays down that "men are free and equal in respect of their rights"; that "the natural and unprescriptable rights of man. . . . are liberty, property, security and resistance of oppression" that "political liberty consists in the power of doing whatever does not injure another"; that "the law is an expression of the will of the community" and that "any restriction of liberty must be in accordance with law"; and that freedom of religious opinions and "the unrestrained communication of thoughts and opinions" should be assured, subject to responsibility for any disturbances of public order.

The declaration of 1918 describes its fundamental aim as being "to suppress all exploitation of man by man, to abolish forever the division of society into classes, ruthlessly to suppress all exploitation, and to bring about the socialist organization of society in all countries." This is to be brought about by abolishing private property in land and in the means of production, by establishing workers' control of industry and by nationalizing the banks. The declaration goes on to express confidence in the Soviets as organs representing the workers and adds explicitly that "at the decisive moment in the struggle of the proletariat with its exploiters the latter can have no place in any of the organs of power."

It would be a mistake to suggest that the new conception of the rights of man supersedes the old. In the Soviet Constitution of 1936 such familiar rights as freedom of conscience, freedom of speech, and freedom of the press and public assembly are assured to the Soviet citizen in addition to such more modern rights as the right to work, the right to material security in old age or sickness, the right to education, and equality of rights irrespective of sex or race. It would, however, be equally a mistake to suppose that the new and the old can simply be put side by side without reacting mutually on each other. By whom the political rights can be exercised, and within what limits they can be exercised, will depend on the extent to which the social rights are also assured. Will the holding of certain political opinions expose the holder to social or economic discrimination? Does freedom of speech include freedom for the worker to criticize his employer or manager? Or will freedom of speech so exercised expose him to penalties? The answer clearly depends on the nature of the social system prescribed under the category of social rights.

These considerations help to make it clear that what is involved in any declaration of rights is a definition of the relation of the individual to the society in which he lives. Such a relation is necessarily twofold and mutual; in other words a declaration of rights is *ipso facto* also a declaration of obligations. The eighteenth century declaration of rights was the revolutionary protest on behalf of the individual against an over-rigid social system still exhibiting feudal features; in this historical context, therefore, the declaration was likely to be one-sided and to lay more stress on the rights of the individual against society than on his obligations to it (these were for the most part firmly rooted enough to be taken for granted).

But even so the declaration of rights of 1789 clearly presupposes acceptance by the individual of the established social order. Liberty may be curtailed by law which is "an expression of the will of the community"; and freedom of religious belief and freedom of speech are specifically made subject to "responsibility for any disturbances of public order." No bourgeois democracy has in fact ever tolerated the dissemination of opinions hostile to its fundamental tenets on any scale likely to menace its existence. Neither in Britain nor in the North American colonies was religious toleration absolute until religion had ceased to have serious political implications. The recent example of Regulation 18B in Great Britain shows that the most cherished liberties will be curtailed if their exercise is felt to be dangerous to the community. There may be significant differences of degree and of practice which can be explained in various ways. But on the issue of principle that the exercise of political freedom cannot be tolerated up to a point where it menaces the foundation of society there is no difference at all. The obligation of loyalty to the established order is implicit in any declaration of political rights. Such a declaration may be a program, an announcement of an intention, or the consecration of a policy. But if it is embodied in a constitutional or legal enactment, it will always carry with it its "escape clause," written or unwritten. The government of the day always in effect has the reserve power of withdrawing any right which is exercised in a manner which threatens the overthrow of the existing order.

The issue of the correlation of rights and obligations arises in a far acuter form when social and economic rights are in question. The correlative obligation to political rights is the mainly passive one of loyalty to the political order under which those rights are enjoyed. The correlative obligations to social and economic rights are active. If the new declaration of the rights of man is to include provisions for social services, for maintenance in childhood, in old age, in incapacity or in unemployment, it becomes clear that no society can guarantee the enjoyment of such rights unless it in turn has the right to call upon and direct the productive capacities of the individuals enjoying them. It is no accident that the biblical warning "He that doth not work neither shall he eat" has found so prominent a place in Bolshevik writings and in the Soviet Constitution. A declaration of rights which placed on society the obligation to furnish certain material goods and services to the individual citizen without placing on the individual the obligation to produce his required share of those goods and services would be a hollow sham.

The drafting of an International Declaration of the Rights of Man should, however, in my view, be preceded by an enquiry which has in it a large factual element. What rights are in fact now enjoyed, in theory and in practice, by the individual citizen, and to what rights does he or she attach the highest importance? (The answers would certainly vary from country to country.) When we have drawn up a provisional list of minimum rights which, in our view, ought to be assured to the individual, what obligations must the individual accept in order to put society in a position to accord those rights? Until we are in possession of some sort of answer, however provisional and imperfect, to these questions, any declaration that may be drafted seems likely to remain abstract and unrealizable.

The conclusions which I draw from these observations are:

(a) that any declaration of rights which would be felt to have any validity today must include social and economic as well as political rights;

(b) that no declaration of rights which does not also contain a declaration of correlative obligations could have any serious meaning;

(c) that any declaration of rights and obligations of the individual in society should at the present stage be regarded as a declaration of intention or as a standard to be aimed at rather than as an internationally binding engagement.

ON HUMAN RIGHTS
John Lewis[*]

SECTION I
It is now generally held that the conception of absolute, inherent and imprescriptible rights based on man's origins and nature and antecedent to society, is not only a myth but involves a misleading conception of the meaning of human rights.

---

[*] John Lewis was a Welsh Marxist philosopher, Unitarian minister, publisher, and prolific author. In 1947, he was the editor of the British Marxist journal *Modern Quarterly*. The most notable among his many books and polemical pamphlets include *The Case Against Pacifism* (1939), *Marxism and the Irrationalists* (1955), and the somewhat off-topic *Anthropology Made Simple* (1961), in which Lewis makes the odd claim that "an enormous number of eastern Europeans and Negroes have the exact same blood as many western Caucasoids." In 1972, Lewis was involved in a widely publicized debate with the French Marxist philosopher Louis Althusser in the pages of *Marxism Today*.

A more satisfactory approach would consider rights as based upon human needs and possibilities and the recognition by members of a society of the conditions necessary in order that they may fulfill their common ends.

The original view was appropriate to the rights demanded in the eighteenth century by the rising industrialist class; the second view, which includes what is of value in the first, arises with the broad popular demands for social justice and human betterment characteristic of the nineteenth and twentieth centuries.

1. Rights are claimed when in the course of social development a section of the community whose strength and importance is increasing finds its needs circumscribed by the restrictions and tyrannical government of a privileged class. These rights are asserted in relation to the obstacles interposed between them and the satisfaction of these needs.

In the eighteenth century this demand was reinforced by appealing to the authority of 'Nature' to a certain 'natural right' inherent in man, which could be opposed to the 'Divine right' of Kings and similar buttresses of privilege.

The assertion of these rights had the very practical aim of widening the freedoms of an important social class, especially in the economic sphere, but also in politics, where, without power, they were at a disadvantage owing to the ability of the existing government to control the economic situation. This, rather than an imaginary state of nature, is the real origin of the rights claimed, and this is their only validity.

But the challenge to such rights can come not only from the existing ruling class, whose privileges are thus diminished, but later from below. In England, America and France these demands aroused hopes and insistent claims which seriously threatened the very rights of property, at that time being with difficulty established.

When at a later period these claims are conceded under popular pressure the resulting reforms are felt by the propertied class as a diminution of their rights and a restriction of the area of liberty, a loss of the very rights formerly won. The anxiety therefore of many people today is to set a limit to the encroachment of government on individual liberty.

We see therefore that in their origin 'natural rights', while they have an appearance of being general and absolute, are really particular (defending or asserting concrete needs) and strictly relative to the occasion. They are not general rights appertaining to man as such, under all conditions and for all time.

2. The view of 'natural rights' first set forth by T. H. Green regards them as the assertion of human purposes to be fulfilled in the future rather than characteristics belonging to man as such; and so far from believing them to exist prior to society

and to require society in order that they may be effective, holds that they arise out of society and broaden with the development of society. Rights are human needs asserted in the face of social obstacles (e.g. the right to a minimum wage).

Such rights cannot be considered as permanent or remain tied to temporary conditions and sectional interests, as is the case with rights which are considered absolute. They are by their very nature constantly changing with human needs and widening opportunity. They do not look back to things as eternal and unchanging but forward to what changing circumstances require. These are rights to pursue and realize values. The supreme right to human freedom becomes then not mere absence of restraint, the detachment of the individual from all relations and bonds, but freedom to achieve things made possible (a) by the overcoming of obstacles, (b) by assuming obligations and bonds, i.e. through co-operative effort.

The historical circumstances in which the 'rights of man' were first advanced required a demand for more individual freedoms and less government interference. This has given a permanent cast to the idea of human rights, which persists, although we have long ago entered a new period in which the rights of property are not the most important and in which new functions are found for government every year. We know today, what was not clearly realized then, that society is not a social contract to secure property rights but an organism through which men pursue a common good to be then shared. We now know that rights are not invaded and lessened by social obligations and common enterprises, but are only made effective *through* acceptance of social duty and the necessity to fit into a pattern. This is well seen in the constraints willingly accepted by players in an orchestra, through which alone the achievement of a performance is possible. In such a performance the individual himself achieves self-realization not possible in the freedom of complete isolation.

3. Such rights have, as their correlative, duties. If we are to have our rights, others must accept duties; if others are to have rights we owe them duties. If we have a right to education, then our parents have the duty to see that we are educated. If we have the right to health, then society has the duty of preventing infectious disease. Rights and duties are inseparable. We have to recognize that, since the rights we claim are claimed by all, we all of us together can only obtain them through accepting a common task and seeking in co-operation a common good.

It is essential therefore to break free from a formulation of the doctrine of human rights which separates them from joint activity and which is not concerned with discovering and achieving new values. As Whitehead says, freedom is 'the practicability of purpose'; but our purposes are only made practicable by accepting certain limitations on our absolute individual freedom; in other words freedom is not escape from organization, it depends on organization. As we shall see, the needs with which man is most urgently concerned are unobtainable without the final destruction of certain long-established sectional and individual freedoms—the freedom to own slaves, for instance.

A comparison of the American Bill of Rights of the earlier period with the Economic Bill of Rights, embodied in Roosevelt's message to Congress in January 1944, is instructive. The earlier Bill thinks exclusively in terms of what fields might not be invaded by the sovereign power in the life of the individual. Thus, Article IV: "The right of the people to be secure in their persons, houses, papers and effects etc." Roosevelt's Bill on the other hand speaks of "the right to earn enough to provide adequate food, clothing and recreation."

4. The more limited aims of those earlier 'rights', however, must not obscure the fact that they had a wider significance, as indeed the above example indicates. Firstly, the commercial interests of those times were in harmony with the general interests. The freedoms demanded by a section of society increased the freedom of the whole society and the general well-being. Secondly, the individual safeguards against the invasion of their rights are of permanent value and are not to be made little of or easily given up. They are not however as indefeasible as was supposed.

As society developed, the wider aims which the masses attached to these rights and to which indeed they always pointed—life as well as liberty, the pursuit of happiness as well as the sacredness of property, were more insistently urged and came into sharp conflict with the narrower middle-class rights.

The result was that to fulfill the original rights the earlier rights had actually to be attacked. To take an example: the rights of man included the right to property; property once consisted of negro slaves as well as the land they cultivated; but the wider conception of the rights of man requires the abolition of slavery, which involves the violation of property rights. Today the more the rights of man are seen to be the right to achieve wide human ends, the more it becomes apparent that earlier rights standing in the way of wider social aims must be overridden, and are not final and absolute. This is not a mere opposition of incompatible rights, however; firstly, because the gain is infinitely greater than the loss; secondly, because there is a possible social order lying beyond the slave order and in which the welfare of workers is harmful to no other section of the community. Such an order will exclude not only slavery, but capitalism. Under capitalism the rights of workers and the interests of employers frequently conflict. The aim of social organization should be to secure an identity of self-interest and the interests of others. We achieve this in many human associations, clubs, families, colleges, musical societies, sports organizations, etc. It by no means follows, as well-intentioned people hope, that it is as easy to obtain in industry. Hard experience may show a fundamental clash of interests here, especially in fully developed capitalism. The task of finding the correct pattern of social and industrial organization within which all interests are potentially harmonious is of course a political one, which at once involves us in the controversy for and against socialism. It is unlikely that such an order can be brought into existence without the abrogation of 18th century property rights. A public water-supply is a common project, in which the good of each is identical with the good of all, and within the system no one suffers. Yet to establish the system it may have been necessary to override private pumping rights and it certainly requires limitations and invasions of private rights when it comes to laying pipes and mains, making regulations and fixing charges. All this is clear in simple cases and in principle, but not to most people in the general economic field.

SECTION II

1. Turning now to the Document proposed by UNESCO,[1] the central issue will be found to be wrongly posed. The result is not, as intended, to make a reconciliation possible. It creates an irreconcilable contradiction.

An attempt is made so to formulate two contrasting views of human rights as to show that they are really complementary, and then to unite them eclectically. (This is quite wrongly described as an example of Marxian dialectic! It is not even Hegelian). Neither view however is correctly set forth. This is because a confusion exists between the conception of 'natural rights' as the inalienable possession of man, as absolute principles which man gradually comes to recognize; and rights as goals, as arising concretely and historically as different classes rise to importance and power. This is clearly seen when the document itself refers to 'the rise of early capitalism' as giving rise to those rights, but is missed when elsewhere the same rights are spoken of as absolute and imprescriptible.

Along the path of absolute rights there is no reconciliation possible, only a hopeless conflict, a permanent antagonism of interests. On the other hand, if rights are seen as human striving for the satisfaction of needs, the whole problem becomes tractable. To exalt the needs of the rising commercial class of the 18th century into permanent rights for all time, leads straight to conflict when quite another class under quite different conditions seeks in due course its own historic aims and finds them in contradiction with the rights of its predecessors.

---

1. "Memorandum and Questionnaire Circulated by UNESCO on the Theoretical Bases of the Rights of Man": see Part II: Key Documents [ed.].

This is clearly brought out when we consider some of the formulations in greater detail.

2. i. '*political freedom by no means guaranteed economic or social freedom.*'

The freedoms sought in the 18th century, although they carried wider implications, were essentially limited. The aims sought by those mainly responsible for advancing those demands did not include the lofty ideals of Rousseau. Both in America and France, after the defeat of the main enemy of the revolutionary commercial classes and farming interests, energetic steps are taken to see that the revolution does not continue. (e.g. the 'whiff of grapeshot' of 1795). The wider freedoms do not so much arise out of the libertarian principles of 1688 as reflect the new needs of the growing working class. The *actual* rights first fought for in the 18th century were from the first inconsistent with the rights of the workers, and were felt to be so on both sides. Indeed the more the industrialist made good his rights and achieved his liberties, the more helpless and exploited the worker became. Rights and liberties meant the disappearance of old safeguards and restrictions which protected labor, the 'freeing' of the peasant from the land and the artisan from his hand loom. The 'free' wage contract between the property-less and the property owner was a leonine contract. Therefore when social reforms are at last won, it is after a hard fight with the libertarians, and at the expense of such freedoms. New freedoms are appearing, not in the least recognized as such by those who only lose when reform wins—freedom from long hours and hunger, the freedom afforded by some measure of security and so forth. Reform is at the expense of bourgeois freedom and is attacked as 'grandmotherly legislation, government interference, loss of liberty' etc.

So far is the new freedom from being a mere extension of the old that the more you have of one, the less you have of the other.

Far from being essentially the same—the one just another form of the other—the old is essentially *negative*, the right not to be interfered with; the new is *positive*, the right to overcome any obstacle, even the most sacred 'rights', which stand in the way of human welfare.

That is why today the controls which ensure that millions have a sufficiency of rations at reasonable prices and without which there would be starvation at one end of the social scale and luxury at the other seem to the privileged *nothing but* a wanton interference with their liberty.

Therefore the earlier rights, so far from being the source of the later rights, have become their main obstacle.

They must remain so if they are considered as inalienable, as absolute.

It is only when they are seen as a stage in the development of human freedom, as establishing certain important principles and pointing forward to wider freedoms, but giving place to quite different principles in a later age, that the old and the new can come to terms.

We must therefore redefine our terms by restating most men's values in the domain of economic activity, reassessing the obstacles that stand in their way and re-defining economic liberty in terms of the minimizing or removing of those obstacles.

Liberty is re-defined in terms of the dominant values of the masses who lack them and demand them. Hence the typical obstacles to their achievement of such aims become the center of attention, and the removal of such obstacles is called the achievement of liberty and the vindication of human rights.

ii. *Soviet Russia misses the phase of individual freedom but may eventually come to recognize its importance. It does call attention to 'one new right, freedom from exploitation.'*

Soviet Russia is not at all likely to accept at any time the typical laissez faire principles of liberty.

Indeed it believes that by finally repudiating such principles it attains a greater economic freedom, that of the planned economy, which can work to capacity without inevitable crises, and which is driven by a far more effective motive than that of selfishness, namely, working for a common good which all share. Nor does it lose what is of value in the old libertarian conception, for those are included, not denied, in the wider freedoms. The individual freedoms thus achieved include the freedom to work, social security, equal opportunity etc. There is no freedom that they lose in the process, the only less of freedom is to the industrialist and the kulak, whose right to employ others for their profit is taken away. The Russian citizen would say that, by excluding certain 18th century freedoms, he attains the freedoms we seek, but only partially achieve because obstructed at every turn by the relics of those freedoms, freedom of property, freedom from government interference.

3. And now what is this solitary freedom which Russia has discovered? It is freedom *from* exploitation. That is not how the Russians put it. They would say that freedom *to* exploit has been taken away. It is this cancellation of freedom which is the condition of a vast range of new freedoms, not one only.

This prohibition is not to 'wither away', nor are any of the other essential prohibitions on which Soviet liberties rest. They are the permanent condition of these liberties.

These conditions are plainly laid down in the Soviet Constitution. They are the obligation to work, the abolition of capitalism, the abrogation of the right to own land privately, and the abolition of exploitation.

Such permanent limitations of freedoms hitherto regarded as sacred seem to many indefensible, but, as Bernard Shaw says: "All civilization is based on a surrender of individual liberty in respect of totalitarian agreements to do or not to do certain fundamental things."

There is no question of any of them being withdrawn or of any opportunity being given for overthrowing them, since they are the *sine qua non* of all the liberties that matter.

4. This is what has to be seen before the question of political liberty can be considered.

A vast social change of this sort is only comparable with the very foundation of democratic government in Europe and America. On such changes we do not go back. You cannot unscramble the eggs. We do not contemplate a reversion to a slave society or to cannibalism or to feudalism or to grand monarchy. Socialism cannot contemplate the possibility of a return to capitalism. It is the one closed question, just as in the United States it is a closed question to return to subjection to the British Crown, or even to demand the right of State secession.

Until such a move forward has been completely consolidated, all freedom to agitate for a return is denied and historically has always been denied in such circumstances. The real question is whether it is the kind of change which must in the nature of things leave interests permanently conflicting because one half of an indissoluble whole can only prosper at the expense of the other. That *was* the case under Fascism, it was *not* the case when Britain expelled the Stuarts and when America broke free from Britain. In the latter two cases therefore the wounds are healed and the issue becomes a dead one. In a socialist society, it is contended, the dispossessed classes can be done without as classes. No individual within the new society suffers exploitation. Therefore the wounds can heal. The intractable are merely refusing their rights because they would prefer to deny others theirs. The Black Market operator has no real grievance. Society can get on without him. Society offers him the same chance of working for and profiting by the common good as everybody else.

Therefore the new conditions are gradually accepted, so that it finally becomes unnecessary to enforce them. But the freedom to re-open the question is never restored. It only becomes academic.

The victory of bourgeois democracy in Europe and America was in an exactly similar way achieved by the Cromwellian, the Jacobin and the Washingtonian dictatorships. This involved the forcible and final suppression of unrepresentative and tyrannical government. Every constitutional government retains the right to prevent the subversion of its constitution. Only when there is no serious danger are extremists allowed a certain latitude. This is seen in the unrepealed Sedition Laws of George III, still on occasions invoked, "to prevent the established institutions of the state from being brought into hatred and contempt," and the American Espionage Act against those who "willfully utter, print, write or publish any disloyal, profane, scurrilous or abusive language about the form of government of the United States or the Constitution."

Professor E. H. Carr has indeed pointed out that the toleration by a democracy of any movement for its overthrow can justly be regarded as implying a disbelief in democracy rather than an exceptionally fervent faith in it. Hence in liberated Europe, which unlike us in Britain and America, has known what it is to lose democracy and fall under the yoke of Fascism, the permanent exclusion of Fascism is generally accepted as essential to democracy.

Maritain concedes without hesitation the right of the State "to resist the spread of lies or calumnies; to resist the spread of ideas which have as their aim the destruction of the state and of the foundation of common life" as not only consistent with democracy but as necessary for its preservation.

In the Soviet Union they are in the same way preserving their own society, the foundations of *their* common life, and they do not regard the political measures necessary, and the final exclusion of parties and principles hostile to civilization itself, to be in any way a departure from the principles of liberty or a restriction of freedom.

SECTION III
The particular questions covered by (B) SPECIAL in the Document are really covered by what has been said above. But it may lend clarity to some of these arguments if one or two of these questions are taken up.

1. *Limitations to Freedom of Speech and Freedom of Opinion.*
Such limitations as we have already mentioned do not imply a *general* control of opinion or censorship of the press, the repression of every kind of divergence from official policy and of all criticism. It is a limited repression which does not apply at all to ordinary people. The point is that all societies ban some minorities, subversive and anti-social minorities, when the political situation is unstable or the minority a real menace. Such coercion is relaxed just so far as the danger recedes. Therefore there is unlimited discussion and criticism *within* the new society. For example, all of Mill's principles of liberty would operate, because none of these were concerned with the establishing or the overthrow of society but only with what goes on within it.

2. The new democratic order, which removes from the political, financial, industrial and civil control of all concerns and institutions an owning class, achieves and preserves a much wider measure of freedom of expression by doing so than existed *under such class rule*. The permanent exclusion of control over opinion by such elements removes the obstacles to the fullest expansion of real freedom of expression. It does not curtail the total quantity of such freedom, it increases it. 'The right to accurate information' is more fully satisfied if the power to control the sources of information is denied to capitalist groupings and if the control of broadcasting is similarly taken from the narrow and unrepresentative circles who exercise it at present.

If it is asked who then is to control the press?, the answer is: any kind of democratic association you like, but not a minority whose interests are hostile to the general welfare.

3. The existence of the *formal* right to freedom of expression which we now possess masks the absence of the *reality*.

e.g. the limitation of Marxist publishers to one half of one per cent of the paper available for books;

the immense financial resources needed to start a full-size paper;

the *proportion* of time allotted to the Left for broadcasting.

A nominal freedom, an occasional opportunity to broadcast, exonerates society from the charge of suppressing the other side.

In point of fact the overwhelming weight of counterpropaganda is calculated easily to cancel out any impression which may have been made by such nominal freedoms. Even this limited freedom only exists on sufferance. Under conditions of emergency it disappears. The right to limit freedom of expression to any extent deemed necessary is the prerogative of every liberal government in the world.

This is clearly seen in war.

It is also seen in such cases as India, Palestine etc. And the best example is de-Nazification in Germany, which in specific terms aims at "preventing Nazi propaganda in any form, and removing of Nazism from German information services and media—such as the press, radio, the theatre, and entertainment, and also from education and religion."

4. What then are *the theoretical grounds* of freedom of speech? This, with freedom of assembly, association, access to information, organization of political parties etc., is necessary if the masses of the people are to obtain and effectually to use political power to attain human goals.

'the practical extent' of such rights will be limited only by the strength of those elements which are able to resist the popular forces. Hence their extent is seriously limited in capitalist countries today. Where such elements are finally excluded from all power, the practical extent of such rights is unlimited.

'the guarantees' of such freedom are then the permanent exclusion of parties and opinions whose avowed aims are incompatible with the realization of social democracy. Only the removal of such obstacles makes the power of the people effective and enables them to fulfill the program of true democracy.

The successful utilization of political power for this end is a further guarantee that it will not be relinquished. It is an *effective* democracy, making real social progress, that endures. It is that half-democracy, which balks at obstacles and allows itself to be compelled to leave its major tasks undone, that is swept aside by reaction, because the people have no good cause to believe in it. But effective democracy is the democracy which fulfills its social and economic aims and does not step short with the achievement of formal political rights.

But the 'practical extent' of democracy must also be widened to bestow the first elements of political democracy upon those communities which do not yet possess it, the negroes of the Southern States of America, the Indians and natives of South Africa and other colonial territories, and on those communities which have been deprived of it or among which it exists in merely nominal form (Spain, Portugal, China).

Democratic rights cannot however be extended to those parties which exist to destroy it and during the War nearly succeeded in doing so. It may subsequently be found that sections of society new enjoying economic privileges intend to interpose permanent obstacles to the full attainment of social democracy. Should that happen, they will place themselves in precisely the same position, as far as social democracy is concerned, that Fascism occupies in relation to political democracy.

There can however be no limitation of the extent of democracy determined by *differences of opinion* as to *how* democratic aims are to be attained, and there must be room for all parties who pursue that aim. Limitation only comes into effect when it becomes clear that some parties or sections of opinion do not intend that it shall take place at all. The question then arises whether the barrier to all future democratic advance is to remain or be removed.

5. The more negative freedoms, such as freedom *from* want, exploitation and insecurity etc., are based on the *positive* freedoms, which the document does not emphasize because it is thinking throughout in libertarian terms.

The positive freedoms are the right to work, to health, to personal property, to justice, to full opportunity etc. These stress what men want freedom to do, the former think of freedom as protection from some invasion of man's rights.

The '*grounds*' of such positive rights are simply man's personal values, constituting what Aristotle called 'the good life'; the '*extent*' is limited only to such goods as can be shared, i.e. which all can enjoy without excluding others; its '*guarantee*' is the final removal of social privilege based on private ownership of the means of life. Its further guarantee is the perpetuation of common ownership.

SECTION IV

Conclusion. Here we show in what way opposing views of democracy and democratic rights are compatible and what forms are incompatible with the fulfilment of human aims.

1. All agree upon the validity of the original 'human rights' set forth in the 18th century. The task still remains to extend these everywhere. We are still in the position of having to defend them against violent overthrow and to restore them where they have been lost.

All are agreed that such rights have not to be diminished or cancelled or despised but on the contrary used energetically and continuously.

2. But the earlier emphasis—the 'liberal' emphasis, misses the promise of social emancipation involved in such rights. Only in our century, because economic development for the first time makes it possible, and not only possible but necessary, can *the fulfilment* of human rights be properly placed upon the agenda of reform. Hence today we stress the next development in the struggle for human rights—social democracy, the right to control the external world, economic power and natural resources for human welfare, the right to secure opportunity, health, education, cultural enjoyment, etc.

3. But just as the first period of struggle for rights was a period of conflict, which only ended with the final defeat of autocracy, so the second period also proves to be a period of struggle. This struggle itself consists of two stages:
    (a) the stage of compromise, in which social and property rights are compelled to make mutual concessions. The general result, however, is the pushing back of negative libertarian and property rights and the advance of social rights at their expense;
    (b) the stage where compromise is more difficult, because property sees its very existence threatened and social reform finds that the solution of its most urgent and desperate problems, economic security, freedom from starvation, the end of economic wars, requires a more comprehensive and complete annulment of older rights than had ever been contemplated.

This brings mankind to the same position socially, vis à vis property, as was formerly taken up politically, vis à vis autocracy. In the first case human rights could not be established without the final defeat of autocracy; in the second case human rights cannot be fulfilled without the final defeat of liberalism. In both cases it is social development loading to a new and critical situation that poses the question and makes it urgent.

4. Political advance required the removal of those parties and elements which were unquestionably bent upon the prevention of, political freedom. Today the same position holds with regard to those sections of the community whose interests unquestionably conflict with those of the community, are inconsistent with democratic purposes and therefore implacably hostile to real democracy.

As Lincoln said, "in fundamental things severe difference may destroy the community. A house divided against itself cannot stand." Lincoln referred to slavery and himself looked forward to a new birth of freedom, even if it required death as its prelude, a freedom which in his own words would lift the weight from the shoulders of all men. This is what he called the great task remaining, the unfinished work.

So, for us, history decrees that the period of concessions and compromise, as in the slave controversy where they were for long the way by which final settlement was postponed, must end.

The reason is not impatience but the plain fact that the overwhelming magnitude of the world crisis and the imminence of the perils it brings with it cannot permit us to endanger the very existence of civilization by allowing sectional interests finally to block the way to the only means of salvation. It is as though a private interest insisted on some legal right to turn off the water supply needed to extinguish a raging fire, or as if the winning of the war against Nazism were dependent upon the removal of some political influence putting its own interests before the safety of the country—a state of affairs that actually existed in more than one country.

5. All previous advance has really been *towards* democracy, we have passed through stages loading to it. We do not possess it yet. The crises can only be solved *with full democracy*, that is, with the final release of popular power to accomplish human ends. That requires the entire removal of all sectional interests whose aim it is to prevent or paralyze popular power.

6. We have discussed the 'extent' of democracy. As Professor Carr has recently pointed out, an essential of full democracy is mass participation in political, social and economic affairs. Sir Ernest Barker has described the main func-

tion of democracy to be the enlisting of the effective thought of the whole community in the operation of discussion. Our democracy is limited because the lack of effective control is based on a division of effective power, and that again on a division of ownerships and interests. Soviet democracy, because it excludes all power and interests conflicting with social aims, can and does set the whole community onto the job of running the show. Socialism needs the whole-souled co-operation of the masses. Not alone opposition but even indifference is fatal to it. "What we build," said Zhdanov, "cannot be built with passive people."

It seems likely that our own problems cannot be solved with passive people, that indifference will be fatal for us too, and that only the fulfilment of the essential conditions of full democracy will give us the freedom, the understanding, the responsibility and the power to overcome the dangers which now confront us.

7. Liberal democracy, like Communist democracy, does not in principle allow absolute liberty; on the contrary, it accepts the principle of excluding absolutely whatever in essence is hostile to and inconsistent with political democracy. There may of course be considerable difference as to what may or may not come under this ban. That does not affect the principle.

Communist democracy, which is simply social democracy fully developed, also bans whatever is fundamentally inconsistent with human rights. Here again the question whether capitalism is inconsistent with human rights is a debatable one, but that does not affect the principle that what *is* inconsistent and finally prevents their realization must go. Neither this nor any other disagreement on when and what to ban implies a rejection of the principle.

That being so, we do not on the one hand regard the liberal suppression of anti-democratic movements as a departure from principle due to pressure of circumstances, so that eventually the ban will be lifted and principle restored. Nor do we on the other hand regard communist suppression of anti-democratic tendencies as inconsistent with democracy though perhaps excusable in an emergency. On the contrary, it is allowable in principle where justified by the circumstances. Of course there will inevitably be considerable difference of opinion whether in any case the circumstances do justify such action. But even total disagreement on the latter issue implies no disagreement on the principle.

If, on the other hand it is held that to apply it at all is a surrender of principle, then we are on opposite sides of the fence. Those who seek to excuse advanced democracy on the grounds that they have only temporarily given way on principle are on very weak ground and only succeed in strengthening the case of those who sincerely believe that the very essentials of democracy have been betrayed. The advanced democracies will not go back on this issue or give any ground for believing that their action is only a temporary measure.

That is why it is necessary to secure agreement on the essential point that the basic principle is maintained by both political democrats and advanced social democrats.

TOWARDS A UNIVERSAL DECLARATION OF HUMAN RIGHTS
Harold J. Laski[*]

1. It is of the first importance, if a document of this kind is to have lasting influence and significance, to remember that the Great Declarations of the past are a quite special heritage of Western civilization, that they are deeply involved in a Protestant bourgeois tradition, which is itself an outstanding aspect of the rise of the middle class to power, and that, though their expression is universal in its form, the attempts at realization which lie behind that expression have too rarely reached below the level of the middle class. "Equality before the law" has not meant very much in the lives of the working-class in most political communities, and still less to Negroes in the Southern states of the United States. "Freedom of Association" was achieved by trade unions in Great Britain only in 1871; in France, save for a brief interval in 1848, only in 1884; in Germany only in the last years of the Bismarckian era, and then but partially; and, in a real way, in the U.S.A. only with the National Labour Relations Act of 1935; this Act itself is now in serious jeopardy in Congress. All rights proclaimed in the great documents of this character are in fact statements of aspiration, the fulfillment of which is limited by the view taken by the ruling class of any political community of its relations to the security of interests they are determined to maintain.

2. It must be remembered, further, that one of the main emphases which have underlain past Declarations of Rights has been the presumed antagonism be-

---

[*] Harold J. Laski was a British academic and a prominent member of the British Labour Party. Early in his career, he taught at McGill University in Canada and at Harvard University, eventually becoming a professor at the London School of Economics in 1926. After World War II, Laski's political influence waned and he was forced from the chairmanship of the Labour Party after a falling out with Clement Attlee, the British Prime Minister. Laski's best-known books include *A Grammar of Politics* (1925), *Liberty in the Modern State* (1930), *Democracy in Crisis* (1933), and *Reflections on the Revolution of our Time* (1943). Laski died three years after the UNESCO human rights survey, at the age of 56.

tween the freedom of the individual citizen and the authority of the government in the political community. It is not merely that the rights of the citizens have been conceived in individualist terms, and upon the political plane. There is the deeper problem that has arisen from the unconscious, or half conscious, assumption of those who wrote the great documents of the past that every addition to governmental power is a subtraction from individual freedom. Maxims like Bentham's famous "each man is the best judge of his own interest," and that "each man must count as one and not more than one" have their roots in that pattern of social organization so forcibly depicted by Adam Smith: in which, under any "simple system of natural liberty," men competing fiercely with one another in economic life are led, each of them, "by an invisible hand to promote an end which was no part of his intention," and that end, by some mysterious alchemy, is the good of the whole community. Even if it be argued, and it is at least doubtful whether it can be argued, that this liberal pattern was ever valid, it is certainly not valid today. There are vital elements in the common good which can only be achieved by action under the state-power—education, housing, public health, security against unemployment; these, at a standard acceptable to the community in an advanced society in Western civilization, cannot be achieved by any co-operation of citizens who do not exercise the authority of government. It becomes plain, on any close analysis, that so far from there being a necessary antagonism between individual freedom and governmental authority, there are areas of social life in which the second is the necessary condition of the first. No statement of rights could be relevant to the contemporary situation which ignored this fact.

3. It yet remains true that there are certain areas of life where human rights depend, in all normal circumstances, on the limitation of governmental authority. The principles underlying the writ of habeas corpus, of double jeopardy, of what the American Constitution calls "cruel and excessive punishment," are obvious examples of such areas. It is more difficult to define with any precision the limitations which ought to be placed upon governmental interference with rights such as freedom of speech, freedom of association, and freedom of religious belief; yet, on experience, limitations upon the power of government when such rights as these are involved are of profound importance. Each of these, however, is acquiring a new and intricate context in the light of social and economic, including technological, change. The nature of modern weapons, the power of wireless, any concentration of the ownership of the press or the cinema in private hands, may be as dangerous, even more dangerous, to the fulfilment of rights than when they are in the hands of a government. General principles in these areas have little meaning except in terms of their application.

4. Nor must we forget that most attempts, since the classic Declarations of Rights at the end of the eighteenth and in the first part of the nineteenth centuries, to safeguard society against the abuse of power, especially economic power, by individual citizens have been gravely unsuccessful. This is true, for example, of the Fourteenth and Fifteenth Amendments to the American Constitution. It is true also of most of the social and economic clauses of the German Constitution of 1919; Articles 121 and 151 are examples of this. It is a pretty fair historical generalization to say that no right is likely to have effective operation in any society unless the citizens of that society have a broadly equal interest in the results of its fulfilment; whereas, in Soviet Russia, private exploitation for profit has been abolished, it is, for example, immensely easier to prevent racial discrimination than it is in the United States of America, where both Negroid and Asiatic peoples have never been admitted to a status in which equal cultural opportunities obtain. The fact that the economic system permits them to be exploited for profit by American Whites is a powerful lever to persuade the latter to continue the discrimination now practiced to their own advantage.

5. There is the further difficulty that we are now in the midst of a vast world-revolution which has brought with it one of those deep crises of values, both individual and social, in which, as Thucydides pointed out over two thousand years ago (Bk.II. 82–4), men ceased to understand one another because "the meaning of words had no longer the same relation to things, but was changed by them as they thought proper." It is obvious that "democracy" does not mean the same thing to the chairman of the National Committee of the Republican Party in the United States as it does to Generalissimo Stalin; and it is equally obvious that each has a different conception of terms like *freedom* and *right*. The economic system, indeed, which the United States business man calls "free enterprise" is unrecognizable under that description by a British socialist. The nature of the state-power itself, moreover, appears quite differently to a British socialist than it does to a British Tory. Any statement of human rights would encounter inescapable problems of understanding and interpretation which would either make it so vague as to be worthless, or so composed as to be a threat to that concept of value in any particular area it appeared to reject. It is bound to be a doubtful matter whether a Declaration of Human Rights will be universally acceptable until there is a real prospect of resolving the crisis of values before which we stand. Anyone who reads the debates, three centuries ago, in the Army Council over which Cromwell presided during the English Civil Wars will see at once that, within the confines of a national community, the assurance of peace is vital to a common recognition of values and, therefore, of rights. We are, as yet, far from having attained this assurance.

6. The absence of the assurance of peace on the international plane is still more striking. However true it be that there is no government in the world today which wants war, there are governments pursuing objectives which other governments would not permit them to realize except under the compulsion of defeat in war. What one government calls "indefensible imperialist expansion" another government regards as "necessary strategic protection." The atmosphere of doubt and suspicion leads to the development of what may fairly be called "client nations" whose sovereign control of their own affairs has become a myth without the power even to edify its exponents any longer. Any discussion of human rights must involve the discussion of the rights of those nations recognized as states. For their governments exercise, in greater or lesser degree, not only direct power over their own citizens, but also indirect power over the lives of the citizens of other nations. A loan from one government to another, the limits placed on emigration and immigration, the level of a tariff, currency policy, methods and amount of taxation, all these help to make differences, which may be important, in the well-being of one nation through the decisions of another. Before our eyes is the grim fact that the shortage of coal in half a dozen countries may settle problems of life and death. Unless, moreover, we agree swiftly on the international ownership and control of *fissionable* materials essential in atomic power, it may well become true that any territory which possesses those materials will become as grave a source of contention, in which itself it is a helpless spectator, as weak countries have become, in the last three quarters of a century, in the soil of which oil has been discovered. The assurance of peace on the plane of international relationships is a vital condition for achieving reality in any formulation of human rights.

7. The swift pace of change, especially of technological change, adds to the burden of our problem. It has the two-fold result of intensifying inequalities within nations and between nations. On the evidence, there can be little doubt that one of the consequences of mass production in a highly industrialized community upon all save the exceptional worker is a conditioning to submissiveness and irresponsibility; and this is increased where dismissal, with the prospect of unemployment, is the penalty for any failure in the adaptation required by a machine-technology which is always seeking to reduce as much as possible the initiative the worker must contribute to the performance of his job. We are becoming increasingly aware that the less the initiative the job calls for in working, the less likely is it that the worker will desire to use his leisure creatively. He gets drugged, as it were, by the routine of monotonous repetition in the hours of work; and the effort to think, in the hours of leisure, becomes continually harder

save where the worker has exceptional force of character or of intelligence. The bearing of this on education is clear. It may very easily produce workers who, unless deliberate precautions are taken, cannot, in any serious way, become responsible citizens in a democratic society. The pace and character of technological change, moreover, give the rich and highly industrialized nation an immense advantage over the poor, especially the mainly agricultural nation, whenever any issue arises which involves the possibility that force may be employed in its determination. A nation which can afford to manufacture atomic bombs, and is prepared to use them, is bound to have its way against another nation which lacks the means, financial and material, necessary to their manufacture.

8. In the light of such considerations as these, any attempt by the United Nations to formulate a Declaration of Human Rights in individualist terms would quite inevitably fail. It would have little authority in those political societies which are increasingly, both in number and in range of effort, assuming the need to plan their social and economic life. It is, indeed, legitimate to go further and say that if the assumptions behind such a Declaration were individualistic, the document would be regarded as a threat to a new way of life by the defenders of historic principles which are now subject to profound challenge. Its effect would be to separate, and not to unify, the groping towards common purposes achieved through common institutions and common standards of behavior which it is the objective of such a Declaration to promote.

9. Nothing, in fact, is gained, and a great deal may be lost, unless a Declaration of this character notes the fact of important ideological differences between political societies and takes full account of their consequences in the behavior both of persons and institutions. To attempt to gloss them over would be to ignore completely the immense changes they involve in the attitude that a socialist society, on the one hand, even a society beginning to embark on socialist experiment, and a capitalist society, on the other, is likely to take to things like private property, law, both civil and criminal, the services of health and education, the possibility of living, between certain ages, without the duty to earn a living, the place of the arts—of, indeed, culture in its widest sense—in the society, the methods of communicating news and ideas, the ways in which citizens adopt a vocation in life, the conditions of promotion in the vocation adopted, and the relation of trade unionism to the process of economic production. These are examples merely. When it is remembered that the Napoleonic Code, to take an outstanding example of law-making, set out deliberately to give the largest possible rights to the enjoyment and disposal of private property, so that the owner of a piece of real property is even safeguarded against having to recompense his

tenant for improvements made by the latter; that there is, in the code, practically no protection for a contract of service; that, while usury in loans is prohibited, nothing is said of that usury which imposes excessive rents, or pays sweated wages; that trade unions and strikes are prohibited under heavy penalties, while employers are permitted to form Chambers of Commerce and their corporate agreement to enforce a lock-out of their workers is punished by the mildest of penalties; it becomes possible to understand why the French legal historian Glasson could write that "to tell the truth, the worker was pretty completely forgotten in the Code." Its character, indeed, could hardly have been better defined than by a phrase in the speech of Boissy d'Anglas, when, as rapporteur, he introduced the Constitution of the Year III to the Convention. "A country governed by property-owners," he said, "is a true civil society; one where men without property govern is in a state of nature." It is only in precision of statement that the attitude here defined differed from contemporary attitudes in Great Britain or Germany or the United States. We take the social philosophies underlying the institutions to which we are accustomed so much for granted that, as de Tocqueville insisted, we confound them with eternal and unchanging truths. We are then outraged by their denial, or even by skepticism of them. Nothing is more difficult than to keep an open mind about the ultimate principles of social organization. Yet an anthropologist who studied the habits, say, of a society in Western civilization, would frequently find that many of the 'rights' we regard as 'sacred' are not more rational than the taboos regarded with religious veneration by a savage tribe at a fairly primitive stage of social development.

10. Under circumstances such as these, the issue of a Declaration of Rights, would be a grave error of judgment unless it set out deliberately to unify, and not to separate, men in their different political societies. It must, therefore, emphasize the identities, and not the differences, in the competing social philosophies which now arouse such passionate discussion. But even then it will have little value, even as a general expression of aspirations, unless it is both concrete enough and definite enough in character to seem clearly to possess the practical merit of being capable of application by the effort of those to whom it is addressed. It must, this is to say, be a program and not a sermon. It must be a criterion of the actual practices of existing political countries, so framed that it is felt to be a living canon of their validity. No use, for instance, to argue today that such a Declaration of Human Rights must insist that only in a political society where the principle of the separation of powers is regarded as sacrosanct can citizens hope to be free; for that principle was the expression of a half-truth, no doubt an important half-truth, which had special relevance to bourgeois society

at a particular stage in its constitutional development, but has long ceased to have that relevance even in political communities where it is still venerated. The same is true of the 'right' to trial by jury; it is at least open to the gravest doubt whether the institution of a jury is the most effective way of arriving at a just verdict, and the more complex the evidence in the issue to be decided, the more doubtful it is whether the jury is a satisfactory instrument for arriving at the truth. Nor must we forget that it is as difficult to define a right as it is to define a crime. We can only say that behaviour is criminal when the law chooses to declare it so. But the law is not likely to be effective merely because it emanates from an organ of government formally competent to enact it. The experience of the United States in attempting to enforce Prohibition shows clearly that, in the absence of a government able, like the Nazi rulers of Germany, to terrorize its citizens into obedience, law is only likely to be effective when it elicits a pretty general consent to its purposes. What is true of law is true, also, of rights which at some stage require the power of law behind them if they are to be more than pious aspirations which do not affect the social behavior of men.

11. This view has special relevance to the sphere of international relations. It is significant that, between the two World Wars, no Member Nation of the League of Nations, with the partial exception of Czechoslovakia, made any serious attempt to respect the rights of those minorities within its territory it had undertaken to respect. It is significant, also, that certain states to which the League of Nations entrusted a mandate for colonial peoples did not hesitate to violate the terms upon which they had been given a mandate, without any apparent compunction. An international Declaration of Human Rights must, in this aspect, take serious account of the fate of the Kellogg-Briand Pact which was introduced with an enthusiasm only surpassed by the contempt with which it was ignored by its signatories after the outbreak of the Italo-Abyssinian War. The danger is real that a Declaration, which is written in terms too far ahead of the probable practice of governments to be expected, will deepen the mood of cynicism and disillusion which is one of the characteristics of a revolutionary age like our own. It is at least doubtful whether we can afford to risk the deepening of this mood.

12. It is difficult, moreover, to avoid the conclusion that was aptly formulated by Marx when he said that "the ruling ideas of an age are the ideas of its ruling class." From that conclusion it follows that, historically, previous Declarations of Rights have in fact been attempts to give special sanctity to rights which some given ruling class at some given time in the life of a political society it controlled felt to be of peculiar importance to the members of that class. It is no doubt true that they were often, even usually, written out in universal

form; perhaps even their claim to the status of universality gave them a power of inspiration beyond the area in which they were intended to be effective. But it remains generally true that in their application the status of universality was always reduced to a particularity made, so far as possible, to coincide with what a ruling class believed to be in its interest, or what it regarded as the necessary limits of safe concession. That has been notably the case where there has been a formal abolition of the colour-bar; there is no limit to the ingenuity of the legislation by which the agreement to confer equal rights upon non-white persons has been evaded. Nor must it be forgotten that there are many political societies in which, on the formal plane, all the rights of democracy have been conceded without altering in a serious way the fundamental principles of the society's social and economic constitution. The fear, for example, that universal suffrage would result in the use of the private property of the rich for the benefit of the poor has been largely unfulfilled; and it is notable that, even near the middle of the twentieth century, the plebiscite, in a country like Germany, with a high standard of education, powerful trade unions, and a social democratic party with a long tradition behind it, was an invaluable weapon in the hands of the Nazi dictator and his supporters. It becomes difficult, in the light of European and American history since some such time as the French Revolution, to believe either that the institutions of political democracy are permanently safe, or that human rights essential to the life of a free man will be assured of respect, if there are wide divergences of economic interest between citizens, if, to put it in a different way, the major division of any national society is between a class owning the instruments of production and another, invariably much larger, class which can live only by the sale of its labour-power. No doubt there are groups of persons intermediate between these two fundamental classes. No doubt, also, their interests are divided so as to obscure what is the essential cleavage even in capitalist democracy. But no one can seriously study the statistics of the increasing concentration of economic power in a few hands and above all the swift growth of that concentration in the United States of America—by so much the greatest industrial society in the world today—without seeing clearly that democratic institutions, and the human rights these are intended to safeguard, necessarily function within the limits of a framework imposed upon them by the purposes implicit in the relations of production which a concentration of economic power involves. The great industrial corporations of modern civilization are, effectively, empires which deal with the state-power of government in a political society very much as one sovereign deals with another. The history both of Europe and of America since the French Revolution suggests that human rights are only effective either when the power of private ownership to make the profit that is the inherent necessity of a capitalist system is satisfied, or where the political solidarity of the majority of the community is so intensely felt and so strongly organized that an attempt at the invasion of rights would be successfully resisted and lead to a re-organization of the economic foundations of a community. In the post-war world in which we find ourselves, important internal and external factors have combined to make the satisfaction of capitalist need for profit easily compatible with the realization of human rights at the level of expectation which the workers, in any well-organized trade union movement, deem adequate. The contrast between capitalist need and democratic demand has become outstanding and momentous. This contrast is one of the major reasons for the revolutionary condition of our time. No Declaration that failed to take full account of its consequences would be more than an empty body of formulae, receiving polite recognition but exercising no serious influence.

13. This is the central reason why a Declaration of Rights which aims at assisting the victory of social justice in the present crisis of values in our civilization must take account of the fact that the private ownership of at least the vital means of production makes it increasingly impossible to maintain either freedom or democracy. Economic exploration, in the measurable future, is certain to be vertical, not horizontal. We have passed the frontiers of horizontal economic expansion; even in the United States internal migration has become more difficult as free land has ceased to be available. If we are, therefore, to make the relations of production in contemporary civilization proportional to the forces of production, the need for a basic revision of the foundations of private property, as these were conceived by all, except persons of a socialist outlook, since 1789, has become imperative. Vertical expansion of production can only be obtained in a planned economy which is consciously aimed at the well-being of the whole community. Any continued reliance upon horizontal expansion, in times of private ownership, means the increasing use of the state-power to protect a privileged minority in a political community which, sooner or later, is bound to look beyond the territorial boundaries of the community both to maintain its own privileges and to satisfy the majority excluded from them. We ought to have learned this lesson from two world wars and, not least, from the implications of the history of the years between the wars. It is, for example, no use saying that there is need to recognize the right of the citizen to a secure job with adequate wages, and with reasonable leisure, if the only periods when this right has been fulfilled have been those of the two world wars. Nor is it any use proclaiming the right to adequate medical care if, first, the territorial distribution of doctors makes this unavailable to the citizen, and his standard of life does

not permit him to take advantage of medical care even if it is available; no serious study of the problem of public health can fail to arrive at the conclusion that it is insoluble unless the medical profession is organized as a national service.

14. Freedom of speech cannot be seriously said to exist in any political society (a) in the absence of economic security, and (b) where the vital means of communication—the press, for example, the radio and the cinema—are all of them departments of big business, and tending increasingly towards monopoly in each instance. Without economic security only the very exceptional citizen will speak his full mind, for fear of losing his job; there is no safeguard for his job save in a society where there is full employment; and there cannot be full employment in a capitalist society save where it is at war. A century ago, Horace Greeley could found the New York Tribune on a capital of a thousand dollars; today, the establishment of a successful daily paper requires the expenditure of millions. Even where, as in Great Britain, radio is government-owned (though in part independently controlled), unconventional opinions, in the field of religion for example, have the greatest difficulty in securing the right to be heard. It is well known that, in most countries, if the cinema is primarily a source of profit through entertainment, its second objective is propaganda in favor of the *status quo*: and far too little means exist for utilizing it either as an instrument of social criticism or as one of the most promising aids to the process of education.

15. Freedom of speech is, in fact, largely a function of economic power; even more so is the right to freedom of association, especially in the context of industry. The right to strike, for example, is, of necessity, severely limited in any vital area of a complex economic community. A government is compelled to intervene wherever a strike endangers food, or health, communications or transport. If the services which provide these goods are privately owned, the inevitable result is that government intervention, save in the most exceptional circumstances, renders the power of the strike, as a weapon of effective protection for the worker, largely null and void.

16. Even political freedom, such as the right to organize a political party with a view to winning governmental power by constitutional action, or the right of the individual citizen to exercise the franchise, are largely functions of economic power. Groups in Great Britain which preached socialist principles were incapable of serious political action until they secured the support, and therefore the funds, of the great trade unions; without independent political action, their authority in the economic sphere was threatened by doctrines of the English Common Law which they could only get changed by legislative action. There

are wide areas of Europe in which a free election has, in fact, never been known; as there is a number of states in the United States of America where the Negro dare not exercise his vote and the 'poor white' is excluded from the register of voters by the imposition of a poll-tax which he has not the ability to pay.

17. If we make the assumption that a political society is only likely to seek through its government to secure social justice for its citizens, historical experience suggests that social justice depends upon the acceptance of two inescapable principles. The first is that each citizen must be recognized to have an equal claim upon the resources of the community; the second is that, where there is differentiation in response to that claim, it must be possible to show, to the satisfaction of those differentiated against, as well as of those in whose favour the differentiation is made, that the decision to make it does in fact lead to an increase in the resources of the community, and that this, in its turn, results in an increase in the standard of well-being for each individual citizen.

18. If we look at modern civilization in terms such as these, it is obvious that human rights are not likely to be realized on any adequate scale if any class enjoys special privileges, which may be defined as the receipt of an income from the effort of others without the performance of a function regarded by the community as an addition to its welfare. It is not likely to be realized in any political society where the operations of government are confined to external defense and internal order, together with the provision of a postal service and the provision of such other public services as it would not be profitable for private persons to undertake. Nor can human rights be made effective in the absence of an educational system which makes possible the full use by the citizen of his instructed judgment, and in the absence of his systematic and continuous access to truthful news about the world surrounding him.

19. None of these conditions is likely to be fulfilled unless citizens have an equal interest in the results of the social processes of the community to which they belong, and those processes in our own day must be regarded as not less vital in their international than in their national aspects. None of them is likely to mean very much in communities which are economically, socially, or politically backward, unless the effort to bring them forward is an organized international responsibility. None of them is likely to mean very much, either, unless the rights of minorities who are distinguished from the majority of a national community by their colour, or race, or religious creed have the assurance of international protection. But that assurance means the existence of an international organization to give protection; and the protection then depends upon the agreement

of national communities that the authority of an international organization, in those realms where the incidence of government action in one rational community reaches beyond its boundaries, has primacy over the authority of the national government. Our situation, in a word, requires a world-order to which the primary allegiance of the individual citizen must be given.

20. It follows from this, first, that the relations of production require fundamental revision if human rights are to be satisfied at a level which offers the prospect of peaceful development. It follows, second, that the era when the national state could claim the right to sovereignty, in order that its government should be bound by no will save its own, draws swiftly to its close. An International Declaration of Human Rights which was based on these premises and built upon these conclusions, to which men and women all over the world might look for a program of action, would be a valuable stimulus to the recognition of the need for reforms, any long denial of which is likely to result in violent revolution here, to violent counter revolution there, and perhaps, even more grimly, to international conflict which may easily assume the character of a global civil war. To provide the appropriate inspiration, such a Declaration would have to be both bold in its general character and concrete in its detailed conduct. It would have to take account rather of the possibilities which are struggling to be born than of the traditions that are dying before our eyes. It would be better to have no Declaration than one that was half-hearted and lacking in precision, or one which sought an uneasy compromise between irreconcilable principles of social action. A Declaration such as is proposed would do more harm than good unless it was issued in the confident expectation that the members of the United Nations gave to it an unquestionable faith and respect. An age like our own, which has seen the impotence of the League of Nations, the contemptuous disregard of the Kellogg-Briand Pact and the cynical violation of international law and customs, and has lived under the barbarous tyranny of régimes which made torture and wholesale murder the sanctions of their policy, cannot afford another failure of so supreme a significance as this failure would mean. They have no right to offer hope to mankind who are not prepared to organize the essential conditions without which it has no prospect of being fulfilled. The next betrayal by statesmen of what the common man regards as the basis of his self-respect as a human being will be the prelude to a disaster this civilization is unlikely to survive.

THE RIGHTS OF MAN IN LIBERALISM, SOCIALISM AND COMMUNISM
Serge I. Hessen[*]

I agree with you that the unity of the world depends to a great extent on whether it would be possible to elaborate a "common set of ideas and principles," including a "common formulation of the rights of man." Hence the importance of effecting a reconciliation between the two opposite conceptions of the rights of man—the Liberal and the Communist—in a higher synthesis. The circle of minor Slavonic States bordering on the USSR is especially interested in this reconciliation. All Slavonic nations naturally wish to be rather a bridge between the West and the East than a zone of division between them. May the following reflections contribute to this important task.

* * *

. . . If democracy is an equilibrium between the principles of equality, liberty and solidarity, which in their turn are but a social transcription of Christian love, does it not follow that democracy is rather an absolute ideal of the "State of Law," and not merely an historical stage in its realization? The majority of the democratic liberals see, indeed, in the democratic State the last word in political progress, and even many socialists share, to some extent, the same opinion. These "liberal socialists" conceive socialism as being the fulfilment of democracy and not its opposite. The question is, what does this fulfilment mean. Is there any new conception of the rights of liberty in the socialist idea of the State, or is the Socialist State nothing but a new technique for making effective the same rights of positive liberty which wore already proclaimed by the democratic State, but, owing to the economic structure of capitalist society, were to remain in it sheer slogans?

Expressing the claims of Socialism in terms of the "rights of man," we could conveniently distinguish between two or even three kinds of such rights. To the first belong such rights as "right to a job," the "right to education," the "right to a human existence." For many Socialists the exercise of those rights of positive liberty is the very essence of Socialism. In his "Précis du Socialisme," published

---

[*]   Serge I. Hessen was a Russian professor of philosophy who completed his doctoral dissertation on causality and transcendental empiricism at Heidelberg in 1910 under the noted neo-Kantian Heinrich Rickert. He taught at the Universities of Leningrad and Tomsk in the Soviet Union, the Russian Free University at Prague, and at the University of Lodz in Poland. He was the author of *The Philosophical Bases of Education* (1923) and *The Theory of Liberal Socialism* (1927). He died in 1950 at the age of 63.

in 1892, Benoît Malon advocated the creation of a ministry of social insurance as the chief aim of a Socialist State. He asserted that the realization of a comprehensive system of social insurance was not possible under a capitalist economy. Fifty years later Sir W. Beveridge, the author of a comprehensive system of social insurance, came to the same conclusion. Though avoiding the term Socialism and disapproving, even of the policy of thorough nationalization, he advocates what he calls "national planning" as the only means of ensuring full employment, without which the whole plan of social insurance would be unworkable. There is only a slight difference between the modern Fabian view and the standpoint of F. D. Roosevelt and "New Dealers" like W. Lilienthal and H. Wallace, for all their denial of "planned economy" and their emphasizing of the vital necessity for preserving private initiative and enterprise. It is the view of consistent democratic (or "new") Liberalism which, being free from any capitalist doctrinarism, has an open mind and the courage to experiment with a view to making the rights ensuring the dignity of man effective.

Only one step further in the some direction and we reach the attitude of the British Labour Party. Though explicitly socialist in its policy, it is free from any socialist doctrinarism and sees in planned economy and nationalization merely the technical means, the efficiency of which has to be proved in each particular case. The real aim of both is full employment, the raising of the purchasing power of the working class (the "vertical" expansion of the market), the raising of the efficiency of industry, all these and similar other aims being regarded as indispensable conditions for making the rights of positive liberty effective. While proving the case of nationalization by the necessity of fighting monopolistic economic power in private hands, as something dangerous to the progress and even the preservation of democracy, liberal Socialists are on the other hand no less careful to avoid the concentration of economic and political power in the hands of an omnipotent government. In this respect they seem to share the view of the "anarchist" Proudhon and the liberal Lord Acton that "absolute power corrupts absolutely." Their Socialism is firmly rooted in the idea of liberty, just as the liberalism of the consistent democrats in transgressing the limits of mere freedom.

The rights of positive liberty being closely connected with the negative freedoms, these latter are no less an objective of liberal Socialism than are the former. While agreeing with the argument of all the enemies of capitalism that civil freedoms are under capitalism a privilege of the well-to-do, Liberal Socialism will make them really universal and will not do away with them because of their worthlessness for the poor. If monopolistic tendencies in the publishing industry, especially in the daily press, make freedom of opinion more and more illusory, the right course is not to entrust the government with the monopoly of the press, but to break every monopoly in this sphere and to re-organize the press in such way as to ensure for everybody the "right to impartial information." This "freedom from lies and from partiality," applying not only to the readers of newspapers but also to radio listeners, is but one example of the changes which the old negative freedoms undergo under the complicated conditions of monopolistic capitalism. The socialization of the press has nothing to do with the clumsy nationalization which transfers the monopoly from the private firms to the government, but is rather an intricate technique, specially adapted to the solution of this complicated problem. According to liberal Socialism there is no single universal technique of socialization, such as nationalization, municipalization or syndicalization. The devices of socialization are as manifold as are the rights of negative and positive liberties. These are the only fundamental ends, to which all the devices of socialization are but more or less suitable means.

Yet even this conception of thoroughly liberal Socialism has its own logic, which leads it far beyond the idea of the Democratic State. The model of the latter is, as we have seen, the insurance association. Co-operation in it is limited to the distribution of the risk among a possibly wider circle of associates, as was really the case in all the schemes of unemployment insurance devised in the capitalistic democracies. Yet after the more *distribution* of the risk comes necessarily, as a further step, the *fighting* of the real causes of the risk, as practiced indeed by all insurance companies, e.g., in fostering the fire-proof buildings, etc. If the risk which is the subject of the insurance grows, as it really does in the case of unemployment, the necessity of fighting the causes of it becomes more acute. The insurance association must then extend its scope by including among its functions the organizing of the production and consumption of its members on the lines of a planned economy. The consumers-producers co-operative thus becomes the model of the Socialist State.

This brings us to the second group of rights of man involved in the Socialist doctrine, often described as "economic rights" or as the rights of man as producer and consumer. The object of all these rights is what may be fairly called "freedom from exploitation." The right of the employed worker not to be exploited by the owner of the enterprise was formulated by many influential socialists of the past century as the "right to the full product of one's labor." This formula, being a crude simplification of the Marxian theory of the surplus value, has been abandoned by the majority of Marxists themselves and replaced by a less definite but a more realistic one: "the right not to be treated as a more commodity." The rich experience of the daily struggle of the trades unions against exploitation has filled this genuine Marxian definition of exploitation ("treatment of labor as a mere commodity," cf. Vol. I of "Capital") with concrete meaning, drawn directly from life. Many special workers' or "producers' rights" have been drawn from that fundamental principle of rights. The more important of these special producers' rights are the right to a fairly paid job,[2] the right to a fair wage, the right to leisure, the right to healthy and secure conditions of work, the right to decent homes, the right (for women workers) to equal pay for equal work done, etc.

It is obvious that all these rights are subject to further individualization, e.g. the "fair wage" is dependent on the financial situation of the enterprise and the productivity of the work; the "leisure" and the working day depend on the branch of industry, the kind of work, and the age and sex of the worker; the term "decent home" includes communication and shopping facilities, etc. It is the proper function of the trades unions to see that the adjustment of the worker's right not to be exploited in relation to the concrete situation is fair in every individual case, and that leads us to a further group of producers' rights without which the right to be treated as a human being, not as a commodity, could never be carried out effectively. The second fundamental right of man as a producer is the right to associate in free unions independent of any political or economic authority. This right involves such special rights as the right of collective bargaining, the right of unions to associate in regional, national and international organizations, the right to the free choice of a union, the right to strike, etc. All those special rights are also subject to an often minute individualization, which may be very different in different concrete situations.

Yet apart from producers' rights, the "economic rights" also include the rights of the consumer. The latter has likewise a claim not to be exploited. In its abstract form this claim was often expressed as the right of the consumer to his full share in the profit. But now even the must orthodox adherents of the "Co-operative Commonwealth" see that the exploitation of the consumer cannot be identified with the surplus price extorted from him by the owner of commodities. It is rather as manifold and many-sided as is the exploitation of the worker, and includes analogous special rights. The most important of these consumers' rights are: the right to a fair price, the right to a free choice of commodities, the right to saving freely one's income (the two latter making what is often called "freedom of consumption"), etc., as well as the right of the consumer to associate in free unions and the special rights involved in that freedom of consumers' co-

---

2. This producers' right to a "fairly paid job" coincides only partly with the previously analyzed "every man's right to work." The accent is laid here on mass unemployment as an inducement to exploitation. "Full employment" means "a state of things in which there are always more jobs looking for people than people looking for jobs" (G.D.H. Cole), as against the normal capitalist state of things, when "for every two jobs available there are three candidates looking for them."

operatives (the right to associate in regional, national and international unions, their right to possess their own enterprises, the right of the consumer to a free choice of his co-operative, etc.).

One could argue that most of the above-mentioned economic rights already characterize the democratic State, and secondly that they are rather incompatible with the State as many socialists conceive it. The right to associate in free trades unions or co-operatives, their right to form regional and national organizations, etc., are indeed acknowledged rights in all democratic States; on the other hand there are many Socialists who doubt whether the right to strike, or the right to the free choice of a union or the freedom of consumption and of saving would be compatible with the principles of a socialist economy. As regards the first argument, it is true that in respect, also, of the "economic" rights of man the democratic State anticipates a good deal of what the socialist State aims to realize when fully developed. Many of the economic rights quoted are really directly involved in the general rights of negative and positive liberty. Thus the right to association in free trades unions or co-operatives is a direct consequence of freedom of association, and the right to a fairly paid job is, as we have seen, only a variety of the "right to work" already included in the democratic Constitution of 1793. In the socialist State however (1) they derive from the more comprehensible principle of the right of man to be treated in economic life as a human being, not merely as a commodity, and (2) all the manifold rights involved in this freedom from exploitation are to be developed to their possible extent and protected, by means of planned economy, from all capitalist prejudice.

Does this method really ensure man's economic rights and does it not rather endanger the freedom both of producer and consumer, as the liberal critics of Socialism insist? Take for instance the right to strike or the right to the free choice of a job, or, on the other hand, the right to save as one will. Will all these rights be upheld within a Socialist State? All adherents of Liberal Socialism agree that they ought to be maintained, and can be ensured in a planned economy. After the admirable argumentation of Barbara Wooton, there is no need to insist on this. Of course they have to be readjusted to the new conditions, because all special rights, as we have seen, get their concrete meaning from the historical situation which they have to shape. In a Socialist State aiming at the utmost realization of the workers' rights and ensuring for the trades unions wide legal possibilities for a fair settling of their disputes with the management, the "right to strike" has necessarily a meaning other than when the strike was the only means of extorting from the reluctant capitalist owner fairer conditions of work. It ceases to be a normal weapon of a class struggle and becomes, as H. Laski points out, the *ultima ratio* of the trades unions' freedom which can only be used by the official trades union authorities in the extreme cases where the freedom is endangered, similarly to the "right to rebellion" or the "right of resistance to oppression" included in the Declaration of Rights of 1789. If, as A. Beyan points out, "in a Socialist society everybody should have a right to a job, but no man should have a right to a particular job," it does not mean that the free choice of a job will there be more limited than under Capitalism, when for so many people looking for a job this right was a meaningless phrase. However, the "right to a free choice of a job" has in Socialist society a real meaning as a safeguard against the compulsory direction of labor that a liberal Socialist abhors no less than the fiercest critics of Socialism. At the stage of the Absolutist State in which the freedom of work was proclaimed first, its real meaning was different; it meant the abolition of the feudal guild and the class privileges which prohibited the majority of people from doing various productive jobs. And the same can be said about the "right to save." This right will be fully maintained in the Socialist society, though it will not involve "the right to invest as one pleases." In the last decades of Capitalism this latter right has become practically a privilege for the few and rather the greatest danger for the savings of many.

I have not yet mentioned such economic rights as the right of the workers, as well as the consumers (and users), to the control of industry. Many friends and critics of Socialism, conceiving it first and foremost as "self-government in industry" or as "industrial democracy," have considered these rights to be the very essence of Socialism. Socialism was for them the abolition of the very relation of the "employer" to the "wage-earner" (of what French syndicalists call "salariat"), and the suppression of this relation of subordination by that of co-partnership and co-ordination. I do not believe that there are at present many Socialists or even syndicalists who would still maintain this view. For Liberal Socialism at any rate "the right of producers and of consumers to the control of industry" means hardly more than the partnership of the representatives of the workers and users in the exercise of some of the functions of the management of single factories and concerns, as well as in the regional, national and international organs of the planned economy. There can be no "right" of a single worker or consumer to elect the management of the factory, as in a democratic State organization, though the producers' co-operative may be one of the many various forms of enterprise in the Socialist society. If the right to workers' control means more than what is included in the right not to be exploited (i.e. not to be treated as a mere commodity) and the special rights the general principle may imply, its real meaning, together with that of the right to consumers' control, can be nothing but the demand that the national economy be planned in a democratic way, from below, and not in a bureaucratic way from above. The model of a Socialist State is, indeed, as I have already pointed out, the co-operative association based on co-partnership in a common task and fellowship in the common work, and not the office that was the model of the absolutist State, nor the liberal joint-stock company, nor even the mere insurance co-operative, the model of the modern democratic State. Nevertheless, all these postulates concerning the structure of the Socialist society cannot be conceived of in terms of the rights of man, and overstep the limits of our inquiry.

And how is it with the third kind of rights, associated with what may be called communism rather than Socialism? The general principle of these rights may be stated as "the right to satisfy freely one's needs"; that would be a fair transcription, in terms of rights, of the classical Communist slogan "To everybody according to his needs." In spite of the theoretical up-to-dateness of the "economy of plenty," I shall not discuss here the Communist principle of rights in its maximalist version, based on the supposition of an economy of absolute plenty, knowing no scarcity at all and therefore being no longer economy but rather an omnipotent technology. The more so as such a utopian view excludes not only the notion of economic goods or "commodities" but also the notion of any rights, as it is rightly inherent in the Marxian theory of the withering away of State and Law in Communist society.

We shall rather confine ourselves to the conception of a relative Communism, claiming to satisfy only some definite, more or less elementary needs of each individual. Then, according to the needs selected to be freely satisfied, the Communist principle of rights will involve a number of special rights, e.g. the right to three decent meals a day, the right to decent shelter, the right to decent clothing, etc. The difference between this Communist conception and the Socialist conception referred to above would be two-fold. First, Socialism is anxious to guarantee everybody the right to a fairly paid job, as well as to a decent minimum for the unemployed, old aged, and disabled who cannot fulfill their wish to work; the guaranteed minimum is thought of rather as an incentive to fair work, and not to idleness—in the sense of the slogan "To everybody according to his work." Communism, on the other hand, claims to guarantee everybody the satisfaction of his elementary needs quite independently from his work. Thus it would be but fair to say that the Communist principle of rights involves "the right to idleness," not only the right to leisure as under Socialism. I wonder whether it would be easy to find a moral as well as a social basis for such a paradoxical right.

The second point of difference would be that Communism guarantees the satisfying of one's needs in kind and not in money, thus limiting the freedom of consumption which belongs, as we have seen, to the most cherished rights in the Socialist conception. One could even be induced to assert, as Bernard Shaw admirably did, that the very essence of Communism consists in the free distribu-

tion of some commodities or services to everybody, thus excluding those commodities and services from the exchange market. A park or a beach open to all, a
road that can be used freely by everybody without turnpikes and toll-collectors,
and a free water supply are elementary examples of such "communism." The
realization of rights both to education and to health already implies at present,
in many democratic States with a capitalist economy, a good deal of communism in this relative sense. Not only are the services of teachers and masters
distributed free to every child "according to his needs," but text and copy-books,
paper, pens and pencils, etc., sometimes even milk or other foods—are also thus
distributed. The same applies to the health service scheme recently introduced
in England, everybody receiving freely "according to his needs" the services of
doctors and nurses, as well as all prescribed medicines, eye-glasses, etc. Why not
replace the fare-collectors in the buses and tramways by another mode of financing these public services? Why not include the costs of the power supply for the
home consumption in local expenditure, as is more and more becoming the case
with water supply? Why not distribute to the schoolchildren work- and sports-
clothes as well as daily meals? The boundaries of this "communistic sector" of
satisfying one's needs are obviously moving.

The more elementary and the more standardized the needs are, the more
"ripe" they are to be included in the communistic sector. And one need not be a
Communist in the present political sense of the term to forecast a state of things
where everybody will have his elementary needs satisfied by the free distribution of a minimum of commodities and services indispensable for a decent life.
For instance, according to E. Mounier (cf. his "Manifeste du personnalisme"),
this enlarged "communistic sector" guaranteeing to everybody his right to have
all his elementary needs satisfied free may be to a large extent financed by the
compulsory work of the youth during the 12–13 months after he leaves school.
The youth would take over the most automatic, dull work, not qualified as
a permanent job because of its depersonalizing character. Yet, as it lasts some
months only, it can so be organized that it would have a great educational value.
To the right of everybody to have his elementary standardized needs freely satisfied would thus correspond the duty for everybody to share, on the eve of his
adult life, in the exercise of the standardized automatic work indispensable to
the community.

Communism in the relative sense of the term is, therefore, not the alternative
to liberal Socialism, but rather its constituent. It is not a higher and more distant
ideal than that of Socialism, but only a technique of the realization of the rights
of man, a technique that was already first applied at the beginning of the modern
State, when the toll-collectors on the highroads and bridges were removed and

replaced by other methods of financing public services. The enlarging of the "communistic sector" of satisfying the needs of the public is therefore a question not of principle but of calculation. Its natural limit is the freedom of consumption, which it ought not to be allowed to endanger by eliminating money through supply in kind. For to everybody who attaches value to the rights of man freedom of consumption is incomparably higher than the doubtful right to idleness.

We have seen that the Communist principle "To everybody according to his needs" begins to play an increasing part in Liberal Socialism. In doing so, it ceases to be a principle and becomes the mere technique of a fulfilment of the rights of man and his liberty in modern industrial society. Would it not be permissible, to say that an analogous development characterizes economic and political progress in the Soviet Union, only that the development here goes in an opposite direction—from the Communist principle first exposing all liberal "rights" and "freedoms" as either sham in capitalist or unnecessary in communist society, to a progressively greater acknowledgment of them as an indispensable technique of the building up of Socialism as the first stage in the realization of an integral Communism?

The first years of the Bolshevik Revolution had not only an heroic but undoubtedly also an eschatological character. The Communism they tried to realize was later justly called a "War-Communism." But then the great majority of the average members of the Lenin Party and many of its leaders shared the belief that they would see in their own lifetime the implementation of the Communist principle. Such measures as the closing of the shops, the abolition of the market, the general rationing of all commodities, free school attendance and sometimes free transport, the practical elimination of money through rationed products and services in kind, all these and other analogous measures, later declared to be mere emergency measures, were then believed, both by friends and enemies of the Soviet Government, to be genuine steps in the realization of true Communism. By introducing audaciously the NEP (New Economic Policy) and declaring that the road to Communism was a very long one, that it implied many transitional stages and many, many years of strained work, Lenin gave the *first decisive* blow to what may be called Communist doctrinairism.

This doctrinairism, filled with genuine enthusiasm for the great task of the social Revolution, was an excellent explosive, very effective for the purpose of a radical upheaval of all traditional institutions and old ways of life. It was an admirable expression of a hope and a powerful weapon in the struggle. But it could contribute nothing to a positive program to build up a new social order. With its maximalist, both revolutionary and utopian, attitude it was rather an obstacle to those who were willing to stop fighting and try to embark on the positive work of building, even if only to make a later fight more successful.

Let us remember the chief features of that utopian conception of the Communist society. In his last book, written on the very eve of the Revolution, Lenin himself gave it classical expression. He emphasized here the identity of the Communist ideal with that of Anarchism. The point of division between Communism and Anarchism, says Lenin, is not the conception of the ideal society, which is just the same, but exclusively that of the way leading to the ideal. Anarchists limit themselves to the destruction of all kinds of power—political, economic, religious. They believe that the mere destruction of the existing power machine would suffice to realize their ideal. Communists, on the contrary, think that the masses of the working people under the leadership of their political party must first conquer the State authority in order to destroy the economic power of the capitalists. This task will be completed during the transitional period of the "proletarian dictatorship." After the destruction of the economic power of the "propertied" classes and the abolition of the natural divisions between classes the process of the "withering away" of the State will necessarily begin. With the State, both its weapons for enforcing the obedience of the exploited—Law and Religion—are also doomed. According to Engels, their place will be in museums, "by the side of the stone axe and the spinning wheel." For the State, Religion and Law are nothing else but instruments of class rule. They have no other function to fulfill.

State, Law and Religion form the most immediate layer of the so-called "ideological superstructure," which is a "reflection in the minds of men" of the "economic basis," the primordial reality of all social and historical life. Law is not only the most immediate, i.e. the nearest to the basic layer of the ideological superstructure, but it even permeates the economic basis itself. Marx used to distinguish between what he called *Produktionsweise* and *Produktionsverhält-nisse*. By the former ("methods of production") he meant a certain combination of "productive forces" (*Produktionskräfte*), i.e., of natural energies, raw materials, tools of work, manpower, all this being the technical aspect of the process of production. This aspect concerns the attitude of men to nature, while the "relations of production" mean the social relations amongst men which arise on the base of the former. These relations are the relations of power, and they find their expression in the so-called rights, especially in the rights of property, possession, succession, and paternal rights, and in such legal relations as marriage, servitude, serfdom, the relation of wage-earner to employer, etc. Law and rights are, therefore, a necessary constituent of the economy, the essence of which are "relations of production," i.e. the relations of the power between men. The so-called economic laws imply a good many social laws, which are historically changing. They formulate in the last resort changing relations between men, and not constant relations between things, this latter, "fetishistic" conception being a fundamental error in classical political economy. Through that legal constituent economy differs from more technology, what is economically profitable being different from what is technically perfect. As the Law, with all the "rights" it implies, withers away in the ideal Communist society, the economy will coalesce with technology, and considerations of profitableness will no longer handicap the application of what is technically the best. To use the terms of Saint-Simon, whose influence was decisive on this point of Marxian doctrine, "the power of men over men will be superseded by the power of united mankind over nature." For this very reason Russian Communists aimed, in the early stage of the Soviet State, at eliminating political economy, as an exclusively bourgeois science, and substituting for it the pure technical "science of the work organization."

The belief that the liberation of technology from the bondage of profitableness would bring about the state of absolute plenty strengthened the suspicious attitude towards the Law as a more instrument of class rule. Even after the conquest of power this attitude remained for a long time unchanged, law being regarded as the mere command of the rulers, and not as an agent limiting their arbitrary power. Very effective for the upheaval of the old bourgeois law, such an attitude could not foster respect for any new law. As a matter of fact it was, indeed, responsible for many shortcomings in what has been called "revolutionary legality" or "proletarian dictatorship."

But it would be an unfair misrepresentation to label this revolutionary attitude in Marxian Communism "totalitarian tyranny." It is true, indeed, that both fascism and nazism see in the law, like Marxism, nothing else but the instrument of power, the mere command of the rulers denying that the individual has any rights independent of State authority. Without subscribing to economic materialism, they also maintain that spiritual life (knowledge, art, morality) is but the ideological superstructure of a harder social reality where the decisive factors are force and power. What idealistic philosophers call the "universal validity" of spiritual values (truth, beauty, goodness, justice) is nothing else but a mere fact of social acknowledgement; something is being acknowledged in a social group, as true or good or beautiful, first and foremost because of its utility in the existence of the group, its inner coherence and its external power. This sociological point of view may be common to Marxism and fascism, and it is, indeed, shared by some other trends of a doubtlessly liberal character (e.g. the doctrines of E. Durkheim and L. Duguit). But while the essence of fascism and nazism is their imperial or racial particularism, fiercely denying such sentimental ideas as humanity, the most essential feature of Marxism is its universalism, whereby it advances beyond its sociological starting-point.

Marxian universalism goes far deeper than its slogan of proletarian internationalism. It manifests itself first and foremost in the conception of the ideal Communist society. While state, law and religion are doomed to wither away, science, art and morality will become what until now they only pretended to be—the pure expression of truth, beauty and goodness themselves. Until now, in societies divided into antagonistic classes, science, art and morality belonged to the ideological superstructure. They expressed the interests of propertied classes and were instruments of class rule. But after all class divisions, and with them all particular class interests, are abolished, they will become autonomous. Not only men, but science, art and morality will be freed from all exploitation. They have been mere tools in the class struggle; they will become expressions of pure humanity. This is the deeper meaning of Engels' well-known formula that Communism "will mean a jump from the kingdom of necessity into the kingdom of freedom." It means, indeed, a breach in the original conception of economic materialism itself. As in the ideal Communist society there will be no "economy" (i.e. power relations among men, limiting the application of technology), there will obviously be no more economic "basis" "reflecting itself in men's consciousness" as its "ideological superstructure." Instead of only "reflecting" real economic relations, the spirit of man will be free in its search of truth, in its expression of beauty, in its relations with other men which will be relations of sympathy and mutual aid and not of everlasting struggle for power. Through technology as applied science, the spirit of man will freely mold its relations to nature, so that science will shape the methods of production, and not instead be shaped by them through the medium of the "relations of production." The individual, instead of being molded by authorities according to a given social pattern, will realize himself as a free personality. He will freely follow the appeal of truth, beauty and justice, being attracted by their intrinsic value (what the real meaning of their "universal validity" is) and not forced to conform to what is acknowledged by this or that social group as true or fair.

In the perspective of this humanistic and idealistic breach in the doctrine of Marxism, we can better understand the deep gulf between Marxian Communism and totalitarianism. It is true that Marx and his most orthodox followers did see in the law nothing else but the instrument of class rule, and that fascists likewise saw in the law but the command of the rulers. Yet Marx despised the law because he dreamed of a state of things in which men would obey, not the arbitrary rules of men, but either the necessity of nature (in order to over-ride it) or the inner voice of conscience. He shared with the anarchists their ideal of a society based on sympathy, equity and mutual aid, not on rivalry, struggle and rights. For all rights mean delimitation of the spheres of possession, and they are of no use where the motive of possession has yielded to that of creation. Even granted that this contempt for law in favour of a higher morality has in practice all too often turned out to be arbitrariness (according to the proverb that the better is the enemy of the good), it is something very different from the cynical and arrogant treatment of law as the mere instrument of a deified authority.

It has often been pointed out that there is a flagrant contradiction in the Marxian doctrine between the anarchistic ideal of an almost unlimited freedom of spiritual life and the complete lack of economic liberty. The liberty of cultural activities, say the critics of Communism, can not exist without economic liberty, just as the development of fascism has taught us that private initiative, praised by fascism as the best means to the prosperity and the power of the State, cannot co-exist with total lack of any political and cultural freedom. However strong this argument of the indivisibility of liberty may be as regards fascism, it does not affect Communism at all. In the view of Marx as well as of Lenin, Communism does not suppress economic or political liberty, but abolishing Economy and State makes these liberties purposeless. There is no contradiction in thought. The triumph of liberty is complete, because after the substitution of Morality for Law and of Technology for State and Economy man's whole life will be spiritualized. There is also no contradiction as regards the period of transition. For the period of "the dictatorship of the proletariat," as is openly acknowledged, all liberties will be suppressed and all rights suspended.

However consistent and noble in its final aim this doctrine of the withering away of State and Law may have been, it was decidedly hostile to the very idea of the rights of man and of the liberties of the individual. Very effective as weapon of destruction, it was unable to provide a program for constructive work. The dialectical gap between the anarchistic liberty of its ideal and the denial of individual freedoms during the dictatorial period of transition could only be widened by the consistently negative interpretation of Marx's theory. As up to now, and even in the transitional period, the whole ideological superstructure even science, art and morality are nothing else but the reflection in the consciousness of men of real class relations, the social revolution giving the whole power to a new class, hitherto eliminated from a share in it, must necessarily involve a totally new ideology. On the ruins of obsolete bourgeois science, philosophy, art and morality an entirely new superstructure must arise, no less opposed to the old than is the new proletarian State and its socialized economy to the bourgeois State and the capitalist economy. The new ideology will hardly pay any regard to bourgeois cultural tradition, save that it may draw profit from its disparate elements, just as people often use the bricks and stones of a ruined building for a new one. The only exception will be the highly socialized technology of capitalist industry, but it too will soon be superseded by proletarian technology.

Of all the Communist leaders, Trotsky seems to have represented this point of view the most consistently. His conception of the permanent revolution was quite intransigent in regard to liberal tradition. He fought not only western capitalist democracy, but everything that could be called democracy either in the Communist Party or in the Soviet Trades Unions. He conceived the proletarian dictatorship on purely military lines: labor mobilized, trades unions entirely subjected to the government, and the Party hierarchically organized from above. And in his opposition to the bourgeois tradition he went so far as to try in a special pamphlet ("Voprosy byta," Moscow, 1924) to outline the picture of a new everyday life from birth to death, substituting for the old individualist way of life and for obsolete religious symbols totally new ones, collectivist and proletarian. In Soviet educational theory it was the time of the radical upheaval of tradition and of various attempts to build something totally new on the ruins of the old. The most radical of all these attempts was the theory of the "withering away of the school" in Communist society. It was tried on a large scale at the beginning of the new constructive period inaugurated by Stalin with the first Five Year Plan, and was soon rightly exposed as a belated manifestation of "Trotskyist leftism."

Stalin's "building up of Socialism in one country" (though this country was one-sixth of the globe) means a decisive break with the radical Communist conception. Not that Stalin has lost faith in the ideal of an integral Communism or ceased to be a revolutionary fighter. During World War II he revealed himself, indeed, as a great organizer of victory. But to become such an organizer he has to substitute positive constructive work for mere revolutionary struggle. The final ideal had to be replaced by the realities of life. The industrialization of the country and the rationalization of industry and agriculture, on the basis of modern technology and without enslaving the country to foreign capital, have been declared to be the most urgent priorities. "From everybody according to his abilities, and to everybody according to his work" was the slogan of this constructive socialism, which laid stress on production—not on consumption, as Communism had done in its principle: "To everybody according to his needs."

A great deal of courage, perseverance, sagacity and patience was required in order to change the attitude of the average Communist, who could not help seeing the advent of Communism in the Five Year Plan. How many Communists took the industrialization and the rationalization of industry for the "withering away" of everything—profitableness, market, money—by which economy differs from mere technology! How many of them saw in the collectivization of the farms not the means of raising the productivity of farming through rationalization and mechanization, but the achievement of the Communist ideal! The first great blow to this obsolete attitude was Stalin's "ton points," published on the eve of 1933. They introduced into the new state-owned industry the principles of business calculation and the responsibility of the management. Instead of thoroughly nationalized industry being regarded as a gigantic common pool, single enterprises received "business autonomy," property rights having been defined. The fostering of consumers' and producers' co-operatives was a further step towards introducing into the unified economy the principle of pluralism. The paying of the members of kolkhozes according to the size of the family was superseded by pay according to the number of working days and the efficiency of the work. The property of the kolkhozes and of the other co-operatives was declared inviolable, and the land-marks delimiting their land irremovable.

Inviolable were also declared to be the contrasts between enterprises, whether nationalized or co-operative, which more and more often led to the payment of damages. Rationing and payment in kind were each year progressively superseded by money wages, even in the kolkhozes. When in 1937 rationing was definitely abolished (to be reintroduced as an emergency measure during the war) the Communist press rightly praised this as the triumph of Socialist reconstruction work.

It would be overstepping the limits of our subject to enumerate here all the ways in which present Soviet Socialism differs from the original Communist ideal. We have mentioned some of them merely to show that the building up of a Socialist economy (according to Marx and Lenin there is no such thing as a Communist economy) meant the reintroducing, though on new lines, not only of market, money, profit, even credit and interest, but also of Law and Rights, Marx's theory that Law and Rights are a necessary constituent of economy, its formative element, proved true once more. The triumph of this process of the consolidation of the legal framework of the new Soviet society was the Stalin Constitution of 1937. Officially labeled as both socialistic and democratic, it enumerates, among the rights guaranteed by it to all citizens of the Union, the right to work ("and to be paid according to its quantity and quality") and to rest ("forty-hour week, yearly leave and other leisure facilities") the right to old-age pensions and insurance against illness and infirmity, the right to education (ensured by "a system of scholarships"), and the right of women to equal treatment and special privileges in cases of maternity. Beside these democratic rights to positive liberty, the Stalin Constitution emphasizes (as an "inalienable right of every citizen") the equality of all citizens without any racial discrimination in economic, political and cultural life, as well as the rights to negative liberty: freedom of religion (and of atheism), freedom of speech and press, and freedom of assembly and meetings, even of "processions and demonstrations." A special article guarantees all citizens of the Union the right of association, i.e. the freedom of all kinds of organization (professional, co-operative, sporting, cultural), with the exception that political organization remains the monopoly of the Communist Party. Further articles guarantee the inviolability of the person, his dwelling and his correspondence. And as regards the right of property, the Constitution guarantees, besides the property rights of state and co-operative organizations, the right of "individual property of citizens" ("on their work-earned income and their savings, house," etc.), as well as "the right of inheritance to such property."

As regards the rights of positive liberty, the Soviet list of these rights seems not to differ substantially from that of Liberal Socialism. The right of the worker not to be exploited, though not formulated especially, is implied in many paragraphs of the whole of Section I of the Stalin Constitution. The analogous right of the consumer is not mentioned, obviously because the authors of the Soviet Constitution did not pre-suppose the possibility of the consumer's exploitation by enterprises managed by public bodies and co-operatives. However, the freedom of co-operatives and their unions is guaranteed by the Constitution, as well as the freedom of trades unions. The more their practical independence of the government grows, the more will the trades unions' freedom become a real guarantee against possible exploitation, even though the right to strike is not mentioned in the Constitution, obviously on the ground that in a socialized economy there can be no conflict between workers and management which could not be settled fairly without such detrimental measures. While labelling all idleness as the exploitation of fellow-citizens, the authors of the Soviet Constitution proclaim work to be "a duty and a matter of honour for every citizen." They would obviously resist every attempt to establish "the right to idleness," and I do not think that their attitude would differ much from the attitude of the Western Socialists, provided that the housewife's work were acknowledged as socially useful. The opposite view, popular in Communist circles in the first years of the Revolution, has long ago been exposed as "leftist prejudice."

As regards the negative freedoms, the freedom of private enterprise finds, of course, no place in the Soviet Constitution, though small individual enterprises "based on the personal work of the owner and excluding the exploitation of labor," are allowed in both agriculture and trade. The development of the artisan co-operatives makes the use of the freedom of small enterprise more and more important. It is well known that in Slavonic and East European countries Communist parties, rather on the advice of their Soviet friends, went a good deal further in enlarging the freedom of small enterprise. While the freedom of saving (though, of course, not of investment), is specially mentioned in the Constitution, the Government paying high interest on State bonds, freedom of consumption is implied in repeated declarations by the Soviet Government that rationing is but an emergency measure which will be abolished as soon as the rise of production permits.

The acknowledgement of the freedoms of negative liberty as necessary attributes of a Socialist State can be real only on the basis of the security of Law. Indeed, according to Stalin, there can be no real building up of Socialism without the "atmosphere of security." "We need the security of Law now more than ever," declared Stalin in his speech on the Constitution.

We thus see that the more the anarchist idea of the withering away of State and Law ceases to be actual, the more its place is taken by the conception of the rights of men, of negative freedoms and of the security of Law, one presuming the other. It is false to think that the withering away of State and Law would mean the growth of the security of Law and the Rights of Man. Rather the reverse; the fading away of the anarchist ideal has been the indispensable condition for the understanding of the part Law plays in social life, and for the changing of the negative attitude to the Law into the positive one. To yield a complex of concrete rights and freedoms the idea of Liberty, at first abstract and negative, defying historical reality, ought to descend from its absoluteness into the very depths of reality, ought to begin to permeate it and to shape it in a constructive effort. It ought to become clear that liberty, including liberty from exploitation, can not be achieved at once, at one stroke, but is rather a long process of liberation.

The building up of Socialism demands the security of Law, the negative freedoms and the Rights of Man, and demands Democracy, just as it demands the appropriation of bourgeois technology and even of such institutions of traditional economy as market, money, credit, banking, profit and interest. Of course, in a Socialist society all these institutions receive another meaning, being liberated from their servitude to private profit and private power. It is not only technology that is freed from the limitations to which it is subject under the yoke of capitalist profit-hunting, but also the economy, not combining here with technology and democracy becomes the people's real rule. It is Stalin's great merit to have understood this and, still more, to have had the courage and perseverance to carry it into effect.

The task was facilitated by the fact that Marx himself had rather a similar constructive approach to historical tradition. Indeed, his approach was a negation of the bourgeois tradition, but this negation was not exclusively destructive; it was, to use the terms of Hegel, not *Vernichtung*, but *Aufhebung*, i.e. a kind of negation in which only the limitations of a principle are denied, its essence being "saved" and raised to a higher level of development. We have seen that according to Marx spiritual culture (morality, science and art) will cease, in the classless society, to be mere "ideology" and will become the realization of values having universal, not only class, validity. We have then spoken of a breach in Marx's economic materialism. There are many places in Marx's writings where this breach seems to be enlarged, e.g. in the explaining of the past. Marx often points out that in the epochs of feudalism or capitalism there were periods where the feudal class, and later the class of the bourgeoisie, really did fulfill social functions useful and even indispensable for the community as a whole. Being a part of society, it represented society as a whole, just as according to Hegel's philosophy of history each "historic nation" had its optimum stage of development when it was embodying humanity as a whole or when, speaking in Hegel's own terms, the "national spirit" was coalescing with the "world spirit." There was a time when the feudal baron was really an organizer of the economy of his serfs, being also their protector against numerous robbers and pirates. He provided his tenants with tools of work, cattle, and grain, supplied them with products in times of bad harvest, etc. The justice administered by the baron was based on customary law that was not a mere command of the rulers, but was largely acknowledged as fair. Art and philosophy flourished, they possessed an intrinsic value far transcending their class origin. The same can be said about the bourgeoisie in the XVII and XVIIIth Centuries. At this time the class of feudal landlords had already ceased to play any substantial part in the economy of society. The important social functions it used to fulfill had been taken over by other classes and factors. It kept only its privileges. Thus the "spirit of the wholeness" had abandoned it. Its philosophy and literature, lacking any elements of universal validity, had degenerated into a retrograde ideology, a vindication of narrow class interest. The place of the degenerate feudal class was taken by the bourgeoisie, which began to represent the interests of the whole of society. Even granted that the postulates the bourgeoisie fought for in the XVIIth and XVIIIth Centuries did express its class interests, they were welcomed and approved as just and right by an overwhelming majority in all classes of the nation, because of their universal character, transcending narrow class interests. And this could happen, because the "third estate" was more and more becoming "everything," yet legally remaining, as formerly, "nothing" (in the famous words of Sieyes). This ascendant and revolutionary period of the capitalist class was the time of its prime. Most, and the best of, spiritual culture at this period was of bourgeois origin, and favored the economic and politic interests of the bourgeoisie. But over and above that, science, philosophy, literature and art, even the conceptions of Goodness and Justice, of Law and State, rooted as they were in the aspirations of the capitalist class, had a universal value transcending mere class interest. Indeed, they revealed and expressed truth, justice and beauty themselves, being far more than the mere reflection of class interest in the brains of men.

In publishing his "Communist Manifesto" (1849) Marx firmly believed that the capitalist class had already fulfilled its historical calling and from being formerly a creative class of society, was more and more becoming a parasitic one. Its real functions of adventure and discoveries, of management and organization were more being taken over by proletariat, which from a nought was becoming everything. Thus the spiritual activity of the bourgeoisie was losing its freshness and originality of thought, its universal validity, and degenerating into a narrow ideology, defending class privileges and challenging every attempt at social change. Contemporary political economy and the theory of Malthus were, according to Marx, typical instances of such ideology. On the other hand, the proletarian ideology, though deeply rooted in the economic interests of the working class, was far more than mere ideology. As the proletariat becomes the representative of the interests of the community as a whole, its ideology becomes the revelation of truth itself. It becomes exact science the more so in that the working class will hold this privilege of representing the whole of society not temporarily, as it was the case with the bourgeoisie or the feudal class, but for ever, because its victory means the abolition of all class divisions through the merging of all the remnants of other classes into the classless community of the working people. We see, therefore, that the breach in economic materialism, originally thought of but for the remote future, has also been widened gradually for the present and even for the past. In one of his last letters in the late eighties, Fr. Engels went so far as to maintain that the spiritual superstructure evolves its own logic and, by reflecting the "relations of production," does for its part influence the economic basis. That the role of ideology in shaping economic relations is especially great in the period of transition is one of the chief points of Leninism as interpreted by Stalin. It is closely connected with the new, affirmative attitude towards historical tradition. According to it, there are in what has been created by the bourgeoisie, and even in the epoch of feudalism, elements of imperishable value. Their validity is not limited to a class, but is universal and human. Indeed, this tradition was deeply rooted in the social class relations of the time.

But those class relations did not create those spiritual values as a mere reflection in the minds of men. They only limited the development of science and technology, of philosophy and art; they have too often lessened their discoveries and deformed their achievements. While building up Socialism, Communists ought not to reject the cultural tradition of the bourgeois or even of the feudal past, but should only disentangle it from its class limitations. They must free it from its deformation, but also appropriate in it what was great and true.

Even if these briefly outlined philosophical consequences of the new constructive attitude are not yet explicitly acknowledged by Russian Marxists, held in check by the attitude of the revolutionary approach, the practical issues have been formulated clearly and unmistakably by both the most authoritative leaders of Russian Communism. "To be a Communist," Lenin said shortly before his illness in 1922, "means to enrich one's mind with all the values humanity has created in the past." And ten years later Stalin expressed the same thought in the suggestive words: "The Proletariat is not a tramp without parentage and kinship. On the contrary, it is the proper heir of whatever great and valuable has been produced in the entire past history of mankind." From 1933 onward the appropriation of tradition in Soviet Russia has made considerable progress. It began with the appropriation of technology, but was soon enlarged to include education, literature, art, and even political and military tradition.

What kind of tradition was it? That of Byzantine Moscow or the tradition of Peter the Great, the tradition of the West European civilization? Undoubtedly the latter, all the Russian Marxists being essentially "Westerners" ("zapadniki"), notwithstanding their Eurasian achievements (consisting in the expounding of Western civilization) and their Slavonic policy, imposed on them by the latest historical developments. Yet one of the greatest ingredients of the European tradition has been undoubtedly the idea of the Rights of Man. We have, therefore, every reason to expect that further progress in the appropriation of the European tradition, being but the other side of the building up of Socialism in the Soviet Union, will include a growing realization of the Rights of Man, and thus contribute to the synthesis we all are aiming at—provided, of course, that this progress will not be checked by armaments and the fear of a new war.

COMPARISON OF SOVIET AND WESTERN DEMOCRATIC PRINCIPLES, WITH SPECIAL REFERENCE TO HUMAN RIGHTS

John Somerville[*]

. . . The differences between the Soviet and western democratic conceptions are not of principle, but rather of area and method of implementation. On both sides the basic philosophic writings and constitutional documents stress the principle of human rights, that is, that people have inalienable rights in virtue of the fact that they are human beings, irrespective of differences of race, colour, sex or social background. On both sides this stress derives in large part from a common historical source: the general idea of the brotherhood of man, which is, of course, quite old, and the special philosophic and political developments in seventeenth century British and eighteenth century American and French society which produced concrete manifestations of such great historical importance in the area of human rights.

The contrast between the western democratic tradition, and the younger Soviet conception, as it has developed so far, can be traced along two lines: area and method. Put briefly, this contrast night be formulated as follows. As to area, the primary emphasis of the western democratic tradition has so far been on political rights, while the primary Soviet emphasis so far has been on social rights, that is on factors connected with race, colour and sex in relation to such areas as employment, health care and education. As to method of implementation, the primary emphasis of the western democratic tradition has been on giving individuals freedom from government interference, while the primary Soviet emphasis has been on government planning.

Two important points should here be noted. First, those different emphases are not necessarily contradictory, but may be viewed as supplementary. They may well be regarded as different phases or stages in the growth of the democratic principle. Men and women the world over have for centuries needed freedom from arbitrary governmental action in the sphere of political rights.

---

[*] John Somerville was an American philosopher and leading Sovietologist. During the time of the UNESCO survey he was a professor of philosophy at Hunter College of the City University of New York (CUNY). After living in the Soviet Union during the late 1930s, he wrote *Soviet Philosophy* (1946), an early study of Soviet ideology based on original sources. In the 1950s, he testified to the US Congress as a non-Communist expert on Marxist-Leninist philosophy during the controversial anti-Communist investigations. After retiring from academia, Somerville became a peace and anti-nuclear activist and the founder of the group International Philosophers for the Prevention of Nuclear Omnicide (IPPNO).

But they have also needed freedom from arbitrary personal or group action on account of race, colour or sex in the sphere of social rights. Moreover, history has amply demonstrated that a given culture or society may have a strong tradition of individual political rights functioning for generations or even centuries, without this tradition, important and valuable as it is in itself, resulting in the attainment of widespread social rights in respect to differences of race, colour, sex, or social background. The hope of mankind really lies in reaching that condition wherein people everywhere will possess both political freedom from arbitrary government action and social freedom in relation to the means of physical and mental development. Put in other terms, our hope should be that Soviet society, as it grows, will extend its conception of human rights more and more to the political sphere, and that western society will extend its conception of human rights more and more to the social sphere. Philosophic analysis lends strength to this hope by pointing out that there is nothing intrinsic to either conception which would prevent this further growth. The two conceptions may be regarded as emphasizing different aspects of the same principle.

A second point, connected with the preceding, and likewise important to note, is that the choice of emphasis in each case was hardly accidental. Historical analysis shows that it was dictated largely by the concrete, pressing problems of time and place. When the Soviet regime came to power, it was confronted by these basic problems, among others: mass illiteracy (around 76%), totally inadequate health care, semi-starvation of millions, chronic widespread economic insecurity, and a system of aggravated race discrimination inherited from the Tsarist regime, not to speak of the ravages and tensions of protracted Civil War and armed foreign intervention.

In terms of calm historical reflection, it is perhaps not surprising that this regime, in the thirty years it has so far existed, should have concentrated on the area of social problems. In the language of human rights, as expressed in the Soviet Constitution, this concentration resulted in an emphasis on such conceptions as the right to continuous employment, implemented by state planning and collective ownership of the means of production, the right to education at all levels free from financial, race, colour, and sex barriers, the right to health protection, implemented by a government budgeted national health service, and protection of the newly extended rights of women and of ethnic minorities by strict legal enforcement. Whatever the political sins of the Soviet regime, it should be said to its credit that it has made more progress in the area of these social problems in the course of one generation than the preceding Tsarist regime made in centuries. Instead of about 24% literacy, there is now about 81%. Health care, economic security, the position of women and of ethnic minorities have improved concomitantly.

Historical analysis will also show that the choice of emphasis of the western nations in the area of human rights was far from accidental. While it is impossible to present any adequate historical survey within the limits of this brief report, we can, in a broad view, recognize that the key problem of the western peoples was largely political in the sense that, they were historically prepared to take great progressive steps, and to solve their basic problems in new and more fruitful ways if they could but free themselves free the restrictive interference of governments which were largely feudal in orientation. This they succeeded in doing, and one of the priceless results has been the western tradition of political rights and liberties. In other words, the western situation was one in which, if the people were let alone, they could advance, and in which government activity presented itself largely as a hindrance. On the other hand, the Russian situation was incomparably worse. Government action, nationally co-ordinated, presented itself largely as a necessity. While there were certainly other factors operative in the whole historical situation, this pragmatic factor, arising out of the concrete needs in each case, should perhaps be given emphasis.

. . . On our side, I think we might best utilize and strengthen the existing basis of co-operation by concentrating on the area of agreement rather than on the differences (this should also be done on the other side). To bear fruit, this process must not confine itself to abstract intellectual recognition at the higher administrative levels. It must find a congenial place in the general educational effort. The predominant pattern of effort in most western nations so far has unfortunately been to emphasize differences rather than agreements, and to concentrate upon what we might recognize as sins and mistakes rather than upon what we might recognize as virtues and achievements. Frequently, in contrasting the western democracies with the Soviet system, what we really contrast is our ideals with their shortcomings, forgetting that they also have ideals and we also have shortcomings. Thus, many of us refuse to recognize, let alone emphasize that, in their view, their social principles represent a development of the democratic idea, that they look upon their system as a type of democracy, with differences from contemporary western patterns, but organically connected with the same source, and dedicated to the same ends.

. . . There is, of course, one social system which is explicitly excluded from membership in the U.N.—Fascism, or its German version, Nazism. We cannot help but see sound philosophic reasons for this exclusion: the Fascist and Nazi philosophies emphatically reject, in principle itself, and not simply by any partial deficiency of practice, the very conceptions we have been discussing; the whole idea of the brotherhood of man, the proposition that human beings have equal and inalienable rights irrespective of race, colour or sex, the philosophical and historical developments of the seventeenth and eighteenth century democratic Enlightenment. Thus they proudly teach, not only doctrines of racial superiority, but the doctrine that the values of war are superior to those of peace, that aggressive warfare represents the highest form of personal and national conduct. There is an obvious barrier in principle to co-operation with such a system for the purpose of maintaining peace and promoting democratic values. Fortunately, there is no such barrier in the case of the Soviet Union. In spite of these facts, there is still a wide-spread tendency to couple the Soviet and Nazi-Fascist systems, as if they were built upon an identical set of values, and were dedicated in their philosophies to the same ends. If this tendency is not overcome through proper educational effort, the road to co-operation will remain blocked in the public mind, and the possibility of utilizing the actual basis of co-operation will go by default.

THE CONCEPTION OF THE RIGHTS OF MAN IN THE U.S.S.R. BASED ON OFFICIAL DOCUMENTS
*Boris Tchechko**

INTRODUCTION

The Memorandum on the Rights of Man produced by the Philosophy Section of UNESCO gives, in succinct form, a general survey which is extremely fertile in analytical and constructive ideas; it is most satisfactory to have available such a valuable work of guidance, giving an adequate treatment of one of the greatest problems of contemporary civilization.

---

* Not much is known about Boris Tchechko's biography, except for the fact that he was a Soviet law professor specifically commissioned by the UNESCO Secretariat to write an analysis of human rights from a Soviet perspective. His study was received by UNESCO on May 15, 1947 and it focuses, as Tchechko puts it, "on [the] evolution of the Rights of Man as they were understood, absorbed, transformed, and finally crystallized in the Constitution of the U.S.S.R., 1936." Interestingly, Tchechko's contribution figures in an obscure book of short stories published in 1951 by the English Vorticist Wyndham Lewis entitled *Rotting Hill*, in which a character, who had just purchased *Human Rights: Comments and Interpretations* (called "the Unesco book, Human Rights"), discusses Tchechko's study on a train to Oxford with a student. During a debate about rights, individualism, and socialism, the character says to the student, "You talk as Boris Tchechko writes," to which the student responds, "That's an insult! . . . Perhaps you don't know it but that's an insult! Tchechko's an agent of the U.S. government. I have never read such dirty tripe as his. That would be the kind of phony expert they would get to explain the 'Russian point of view' to people."

As a preliminary to the endeavour to arrive at a higher synthesis by the comparison of certain guiding ideas or even different conceptions of life, it is advisable that the premises of the problem should be stated as precisely as possible. In this connection, it seems to us that the true starting-point of Marxist-Leninist philosophy has not been made sufficiently evident.

In particular, it seems to us inaccurate, both historically and ideologically, to present Marxism as a sort of light coming from the East and to consider the West, on the other hand, almost as the natural guardian of the so-called "Western" spiritual and ethical values.

The links which attach Marx and Engels to the great English intellectuals, such as Francis Bacon, Hobbes and Locke, with his theory of experience, and to the French Encyclopedists, are so well-known that it is unnecessary to dwell on them. The contributions of Kant and Hegel, often in conflict with one another, must also be mentioned; last but not least, the system of dialectical materialis could scarcely have been conceived without the ancient foundations laid in Aristotle's "Universalia in re" and Plato's "Dialogues."

The right way to reach the higher synthesis we are seeking to establish in the light of ideas and facts which can be verified in history, is perhaps to realize the full and entire inter-dependence of the ideas of East and West—even from the ill-defined and debatable standpoint of geographical demarcation—instead of accepting the rather rough and ready contrast between East and West, based on the once-famous phrase of Rudyard Kipling "East is East and West is West."

The country of the Incas should properly be considered as the original home of State Socialism, as is proved in an extremely interesting work, not yet published, written by a professor at the Catholic University in Paris, N. Jean Pouzyna (following the parallels drawn between Campanella's "City of the Sun" and Thomas More's "Utopia").

Furthermore, at one time, both Egypt and China experienced a fully developed system of state control.

In short, it seems to us difficult, if not actually misleading, to try to contrast Marxism with Liberal Capitalism as the concepts of East and West respectively.

In view of the close inter-relationship of the ideas and concepts of every continent and every race, we have to regard those ideas and concepts as stages in the general development of the world as an economic entity.

THE 1936 CONSTITUTION OF THE U.S.S.R.
On such a view of the relentless stages in the economic evolution of mankind and the associated Rights of Man, the 1936 Constitution of the U.S.S.R., rightly called the "Stalin" Constitution, not only constitutes one of the most

decisive stages in the advance of the ideas of the democratic emancipation of man, but also—and this is of vital importance—sets man as a worker in ideal political, social and economic conditions, and gives him facilities for work and intellectual life.

Following the decision of the Seventh Congress of the Soviets of the U.S.S.R., the Commission on the Constitution, under the chairmanship of Stalin, submitted its report.

THE RIGHT TO WORK

The first principle is contained in Article 118 of the 1936 Constitution, the text of which is given below[3]; it is the right to live, not in the abstract, but the right to live in conditions suitable for the healthy functioning of any human organism, with its need to breathe, to drink, to eat and to create, leading to the right to regular employment paid according to the quantity and quality of labor.

Article 118 can (and indeed must) be regarded as the King-pin of the whole Soviet system, since the right to work is ensured by the *Socialist organization of the national economy* with its Five-Year Plans.

INDIVIDUAL LIBERTY

The second guiding principle is that of individual liberty within the social and economic machine, the whole mechanism of which is designed to achieve a single purpose: to give man, in his creative aspect, the opportunity to express himself in every field of human activity (Articles 124 to 128).

EQUALITY

The third principle   that of equality in all branches of economic, political, cultural, social and public life is included in Article 123 which has the force of an indefeasible law.

Returning to that cornerstone of the Constitution, Article 118 read in conjunction with Article 119, 120 and 121, which are dependent on it, we quote an article from the newspaper "Pravda" of 16 October 1936, which gives an admi-

---

3. "Citizens of the U.S.S.R. have the right to work, i.e. they have the right to secure employment, remunerated according to the quantity and quality of their work.

The right to work is guaranteed by the socialist organization of the national economy, the continual development of the productive forces of Soviet society, the removal of the risk of economic crises and the abolition of unemployment."

Connected and derivative problems are dealt with elsewhere, such as the right to leisure and the right to education, which are treated in Articles 119 (1946) and 120, respectively.

rable statement of the feelings of all citizens of the U.S.S.R.: "the right to work! the right to education! the right to leisure! the vast majority of men living in the world look upon these words as the expression of a cherished dream, not yet to be realized; for Soviet citizens, however, these are natural self-evident rights."

In the endeavour to achieve a higher synthesis, legal authorities have proposed to confer an additional personal guarantee on all Soviet citizens by proposed legislation under the general provisions of Article 118—the right to institute judicial proceedings against any Soviet organization which, with vacant posts, refuses without sufficient reason to engage the individual concerned. . . .

THE NEW DEMOCRATIC CIVILIZATION
The fact that the U.S.S.R. is ruled by all its adult citizens, without any form of discrimination, so that all its inhabitants are included in a vast network of collective organizations in accordance with the principles of the new political economy as embodied in practice in the Five-Year Plans; the fact that a systematic philosophy and a new code of behaviour based on a fresh ethical conception of the relations of man to the universe and his duties towards his fellows has been created—all these factors led Mr. Sidney Webb to the conclusion that: "we seem to be concerned with something more important than a Constitution—with a new civilization";[4] that, in fact, is the subsidiary title of his work. . . .

Mr. Somerville,[5] a sagacious observer, remarks that the conception of democratic government, as understood in the U.S.S.R., is not restricted to the normal institutions of government, but, on the contrary, gives rise to higher bodies formed by all the economic and social institutions. . . .

SOVIET ETHICS
Soviet man is convinced that "in a classless society, everyone leads a higher life from the moral standpoint, because the existing social and economic institutions do not compel men to exploit one another."[6] A Soviet philosopher[7] has written: "What is important to society becomes important to the individual, without thereby losing its social importance—this is demonstrated in the vigour of individual aspirations and energy."

---

4. Stalin, "Moscow," 1932, pp. 347 et seq.

5. Op. cit. p. 47.

6. John Somerville "Soviet Philosophy," *New York*, 1946, pp. 90 et seq.

7. An article by M. Rubinstein in the Russian newspaper "Under the Banner of Marxism," *Moscow* 1943, No. 9–10.

There is but a step from such a concept to the acceptance of the principle of socialism—from each according to his means, to each according to his labor.

Soviet man is convinced of the superiority of socialist economy, because that economy necessarily excludes the possibility of war and economic crises.[8] The figures which are quoted as representing the direct and indirect losses due to the two world wars, have not been prepared and checked with the requisite care, and the approximate estimates drawn from various sources should be considered subject to reserve; for various reasons, a total figure of 600 milliard dollars (200 for the first world war, and 400 for the second) is, in our opinion, the cost nearly accurate.

It is impossible to estimate, even approximately, the cost of periodical economic crises; the origins of such crises are as debatable as they are ill-defined, ranging from the effect of the sun's radiation on the weather, and consequently upon the crops, through the psychological explanation of crisis cycles, involving the forces of production, distribution and consumption, properly so-called, to the explanation provided by M. Stalin:[9] "Economic crises in capitalist countries—where capitalist private ownership of the means of production is in direct conflict with the social character of the productive process and the nature of the productive forces—are an illustration of the clash between relationships in production and the nature of the productive forces, and of the conflict in which they are engaged. . . . The socialist economy of the U.S.S.R.—where communal ownership of the means of Production is perfectly suited to the social character of the productive process, and where there are, consequently, no economic crises or wastage of the forces of production—is an example of the perfect adjustment of relationships in production to the nature of the productive forces."

Soviet man realizes that, under a capitalist system, the "normal reserve of unemployed workers" is inevitable, as Marx said; this opinion is strengthened by the admission of the late Lord Keynes, an authority on financial matters recognized throughout the world, that some degree of unemployment, called cyclical unemployment, is an inevitable consequence of technical development.

The Soviet system of ethics not merely proclaims the equal rights of men and women, but endeavors to protect women, mothers and children, so that woman's natural function shall not be to her disadvantage. In the U.S.S.R., a woman does not have to choose between her desire to have a home or a career; the two are perfectly complementary (Article 122). . . .

(Translated from French)

---

8. Articles 1–12 of 1936 Constitution.
9. *History of the Communist Party in the U.S.S.R.*, Moscow 1930, p. 115.

HUMAN RIGHTS IN THE WORLD TODAY
*Luc Somerhausen**

. . . Apart from any question of the relative values of different political systems, the problem is essentially to determine:

(a) Whether the rights proclaimed have so far been fully and effectively attained;
(b) Whether there are new rights which should be proclaimed;
(c) Whether the attainment of the old and new rights is compatible with the maintenance of the present forms of social organization.

On point (a) it appears indisputable and mainly undisputed that under the present economic organization of society, human rights have not been fully attained. Whether it be the right to own property, the right to personal freedom, the right of personal security, freedom of association or freedom of the press, it is found that apart from the limitations on all rights arising from legal enactments freely agreed to or grudgingly acquiesced in, such rights are limited as a consequence of the system of ownership in force, in which the profit motive and hence the exploitation of man by man is involved. It is symptomatic that all that has been said in the last century and more particularly in our day on the subject of human dignity, was stated by Marx, notably in his famous theory of alienation: society, he said, may be defined as the consubstantiality of man and nature, man must be able to produce freely, to enjoy the fruit of his own work and to live in fellowship with other men and in harmony with himself.

Of this basic analysis we still retain today the concept of the precarious nature and the relative ineffectiveness of declarations of right which have in mind only "man, the egoist" as he exists in a society based on the profit motive, man at odds with the community, "turned in on himself, solely preoccupied with his personal interests and obedient to his private whims."

Without underestimating the importance of declarations and formulations of human rights, it must be admitted that in contemporary society the strongest links between men are not the rights and duties to which appeal is commonly made, but material requirements, private needs and interests, the preservation of their property and of their individualism.

It may also be said that, wherever there has been conflict between material

---

* Luc Somerhausen, a member of the UNESCO Committee of Experts, was a Belgian journalist and communist and former Nacht und Nebel prisoner of the German concentration camp Esterwegen, where he established with other prisoners a Masonic lodge they called Loge Liberté chérie. A longtime analyst and functionary for the Belgian Senate, Somerhausen was the author of *L'humanisme agissant de Karl Marx* (1946).

interests and human rights, the letter have been sacrificed either overtly or indirectly. Freedom of the Press, which is mentioned in the memorandum is a typical case. It is hardly necessary to re-emphasize the precarious nature of the principles of equality of freedom, of assembly or association.

It may thus be said that up to now there has been and still is a number of restrictions of varying severity on the full exercise of those human rights proclaimed as long ago as 1776.

(b) Not Soviet constitutional theory or practice, but the whole trend of modern thought has led to recognition of the need for distinguishing between political and economic human rights. It is a socialist platitude to say that no true human independence will exist until the individual's economic and social as well as his civil and political rights shall have been proclaimed. To put it another way, it may be said that traditional human rights will not become a reality until they have been completed by a social organization which will make it possible for man to protect himself against exploitation.

It is purposeless to say that man is entitled to respect for his personality and to freedom in its development, if at the same time those essential rights are not proclaimed which in fact enable man to achieve the development of his personality and to secure respect for his dignity. This was the spirit behind the French Constitution of 1946, when it proclaimed the right to work, with the right to strike involved in it, the right to leisure, the right to proper conditions of work and to joint management, the right to health, the right to culture, the right to society's help where anyone is unfit for work, etc.

(c) It must be conceded with regret that in those areas where democratic effort has been directed towards political rights, the social and economic rights of man are still not recognized.

It is worth stressing that, as developments tend to ensure the progress of economic democracy, there may be noted, even in Western Europe, attempts to limit certain rights once insisted on as essential. For instance, one can hardly fail to be struck by the reasoning of a French politician of advanced views, who said that in nationalized undertakings the substitution of public for private ownership must involve a modification of the workers' rights. Under pretense that the further we advance along the path to economic democracy, the more inconceivable becomes the idea of industrial conflict, many people in the West have come (for quite a different purpose, of course) to recommend the ideological conceptions which they disapprove of in the U.S.S.R., where one notes that the new social conditions have completely overthrown the old concept of human rights.

Obviously assent cannot lightly be given to the establishment of relative scales of human rights varying with the social legislation or economic evolution (or revolution) achieved. New human rights, like the old ones, will have meaning only in so far as the conditions necessary to their free exercise will be insured and secured.

It is quite otherwise as regards the question of deciding whether the values prevailing in a democracy should not be reassessed and the principal place be given to certain human rights which in the past have been denied or undervalued. However, in our opinion, the best course would be to proclaim equal rights while simultaneously evolving means to secure respect for them.

To sum up, it is our view, in opposition to that generally held, that the course of history is today tending to a more or less perfect synthesis between individualism and collectivism. A more difficult matter is to ascertain the norm on which can be based the proclamation of rights implying a direct curtailment of the right to own property.

Our views can best be summed up in Jaurès's general statement of human rights:

"We must ensure the fullness and the universality of the rights of the individual. No human being at any stage must be left outside. None must be exposed to the risk of being the proxy or tool of another. None must be deprived of positive means to work in liberty without servile dependence on anyone at all."

Brussels, 15 June 1947
(Translated from French)

DECLARATION ON THE RIGHTS OF MAN
*Hyman Levy**

These notes are concerned only with the problem of bridging the gap between "western" and "Marxist" approaches to this question.

1. A formulation of Human Rights along the lines suggested by the Memorandum sent out,[10] will find universal acceptance only if it is formulated in such wide and general terms as to make it possible for, say the USSR and the USA, to

---

* Hyman Levy was a mathematician and philosopher of science who was Professor of Mathematics and Dean of the Royal College of Science at Imperial College at the time of the UNESCO human rights survey. His scientific specialties were numerical methods, differential equations, finite difference equations, and statistics. Levy joined the British Communist Party in 1931 but was expelled from the Party in 1958 after criticizing the persecution of Jewish intellectuals in the Soviet Union in his book *Jews and the National Question* (1957).

10. UNESCO/Phil/1/1947 [ed.].

interpret the formulation in different if not actually opposite ways. It will therefore mean so many things that it will be meaningless in practice.

2. No marxist would think of accepting a broad formulation by itself. He would hold that what is formulated cannot be divorced from the method and the means for realizing it in practice. This is presumably out of the question for UNESCO to do, for obvious reasons. This is presumably what lies at the root of the USSR's aloofness to UNESCO, and there is no way of bridging that particular gap in the simple way of expressing abstract ethical principles in a political and social vacuum; that is, without it being directly linked up with a social dynamical plan to implement them.

3. When they were formulated in the 18th Century as principles they could then become a rallying point for action, for the development of a policy to change social conditions and so to make these principles into something approximating to a physical reality; and this was so because the conditions were such that people did indeed believe that they themselves were actually denied these freedoms in practice. The situation today is quite different. In the non-marxist countries people "believe" *they* have most of these freedoms and the equivalent of these rights, but they do not "believe" that this is the case in the marxist countries. And conversely. Hence a pronouncement will inevitably be regarded by one or another of the groups as "propaganda" either against themselves—if that group thinks you do not believe that their members have that freedom or right—or against the other, if it thinks that you believe it has. All of this is of course a reflection of the division of the world into two social systems.

4. It is no use however taking a *non possumus* attitude to all this. Something can be done, and I believe it could be done in the following way:

a. It is a mistake to try to set out a system of human rights as such.

b. It is necessary to go one step back and ask what are the physical and material conditions that may make the emergence of these rights in practice a real possibility.

c. To deal with such things in full would lead UNESCO into the realm of controversy from which it would presumably like to steer clear. Nevertheless, I think it might be possible to set out a statement not of the *Rights of Man*, but of the *Needs of Man*, both personal and social, with particular stress on the material aspects of the problem. It could then be followed by a statement that once these needs are in being they would drag in their train ethical ideas and ethical practice that would make it possible to set out in due course a statement of the Rights of Man with which all peoples would agree.

UNTITLED
Ture Nerman*

With the unfortunately very limited view on the various detailed questions of the world politics inevitable for all men and especially every citizen of a small country, I have no competence to answer UNESCO's questions, which are founded on facts, wisely detailed and therefore very stimulating.

UNESCO's memorandum seems to me a splendid basis for considerations. It points out that the questions have reference to human rights today, not in an abstract timelessness, and it gives a good guidance to the history of those rights, where the appreciation has changed with the historical development after man's freedom of movement/discoveries, inventions, techniques of traffic etc. and in different periods have been emphasized freedom of conscience or worship, freedom of speech and opinion, political, social, and economical freedom. The memorandum also properly points out, how in hard times the freedom of the individual has been limited in interest of solidarity. UNESCO now tries to fix the postulates for and the ways to an, in spite of all, common ethical wavelength for all men.

The question is the most elementary important of all, today and always. I answer in all modesty:

To get a common wavelength will be extremely difficult as long as economically, socially, politically and culturally we live in different centuries contemporaneously. In interest of self-support every people or group is forced to argue its own special view, i.e. especially emphasize for instance the political or the economical side of human rights. And still we must at least try to get a smallest common denominator, try to get so close that to begin with at least the most receptive can be reached by the voice from the other wavelengths.

We have one thing in common: the need of balance, and with that the elementary wish to escape fear of all kinds. Freedom from fear ingeniously was put in center by the authors of the Atlantic Charter. As men we have two stationary poles, stationary as long as there are men living: the individual and the human race, the ego and humanity. Between them emerge and disappear in the course of history several formations: tribes, classes, empires of various kinds. Today the state is the

---

* Ture Nerman was one of the founders of the Swedish Communist Party after splitting from the Social Democratic Party over the Russian Revolution. Nerman was a major anti-Nazi propagandist in officially neutral Sweden during the Second World War. During the time of the UNESCO human rights survey, he was a Social Democrat member of the Swedish parliament (he had left the Communist Party and rejoined the Social Democrats in 1939). Nerman was the author of historical studies of Marxism, biographies (including one of Joe Hill, the Swedish-American labor activist executed by firing squad in a Utah state prison in 1915), and several volumes of poetry.

strongest historical factor, historically well-founded but not everlasting, subject to changes and destruction. Today the state—in the decay or transformation of an economic system and with that of a political system—compelled by its own need, its own want to stick together, oppresses man both as individual /state-slavery/ and as a race /decay of internationalism and humanity/.

We can and may see all of this historically and so understand it. But in order to get a step further, i.e. make new history, not only soulless drift away, we must also give a critical declaration of value and raise precise ethical claims.

I do not believe in any possibility to unite in wavelength before the economic development has reached an international order in broad outline, i.e. the states have been subordinated to humanity. Till that time the wars between peoples and classes will have possibilities to go on, that are produced by the existing relative anarchy. Till that time the different parts unyielding will maintain their view on human rights according to their position and its needs. We, that contrary to Russia, Asia, and Africa have passed a bourgeois period of history with thereby created needs of individual freedom, in broad outline will claim human rights as they are summed up in the American Declaration of independence 1776 and the French Déclaration des droits de l'homme 1789 and later lined out by the liberalism of the 19th century completed more or less with recognition of solidarity claims of socialism. In times of destruction of the bourgeois society and in face of the danger of a totalitarian [illegible] / whatever be its economic and social type/ the side of freedom must be emphasized together with the side of solidarity. . . .

CONTRIBUTION TO DISCUSSION ON DECLARATION OF HUMAN RIGHTS
R. Palme Dutt[*]

. . . It is desirable that the problem should be thus set out in specific terms as a current immediate problem, the fulfilment of a specific task for a specific purpose at a specific time, viz., the elaboration of a useful and agreed Declaration of Human Rights to be adopted by the United Nations in the world situation of

---

[*] R. (Rajani) Palme Dutt was an Indo-Swedish journalist and political radical who was raised in Britain. Palme Dutt was a longtime member and theorist of the British Communist Party and editor of *Labour Monthly* until his death in 1974. Palme Dutt was a hardline supporter of the Soviet Union and of Stalin. He was noted—and reviled by many—for his 1956 "spots on the sun" speech, in which he defended Stalin to British communists by arguing that, like the sun, Stalin (a source of life) also had his spots.

1947–48. The alternative method of endeavouring to search among rival philosophical conceptions for some absolute, eternal and universally valid conception of Human Rights, irrespective of time or place or conditions, is likely to prove fruitless and give rise to interminable controversy, owing to the question being wrongly posed. The search for such an absolute and timeless conception of Human Rights would be like the search for the Philosopher's Stone. It would be equivalent to substituting dogma for a scientific approach.

. . . As the introductory memorandum and questionnaire opening this discussion has correctly pointed out, the conception of Human Rights has developed under certain historical conditions, has changed with changing conditions, and is still developing. Originating in the modern era in the fight against monarchist and feudal domination and doctrines of human inequality, it has advanced and deepened through two centuries of social experience, theory and practice. Just as the ancient Greek conception of democracy ignored the slave majority of the population on whose subjection and labours it reposed, the eighteenth century and early nineteenth century conceptions of liberty and human rights, concentrating on the fight against the old forms of monarchical and feudal oppression, did not yet clearly see the new forms of class domination which were arising and paid less attention to the problems of economic and social inequality and domination, the relations of private property and freedom, and commercial expansion and domination of weaker and less developed nations. In the second half of the nineteenth century, and especially in the twentieth century, with the development of capitalist concentration and imperialism, and with the advance of the working class movement and of the national liberation movements in the colonial countries, these problems have come increasingly to the forefront and have found their formulation, and the programme and policies put forward for their solution, in the theory and practice of socialism or communism, carrying forward and extending in new forms the liberating aims of the earlier English, American and French Revolutions.

. . . Today in the countries of the United Nations there are different stages of democratic development and of social change. These are reflected in differing social and political conceptions, within the common framework of recognition of democratic aims. The newer conceptions of human freedom associated with socialism or communism are not yet universally accepted in the countries of the United Nations. They are ardently contested by the adherents of the older individualistic doctrines associated with private property. There is sharp conflict and controversy between opposing social and political conceptions, which in fact reflects the conflict of classes. This conflict in the realm of ideas and social and political institutions expresses itself also in the attitude to particular questions of human rights. What the property-owner may feel to be tyranny, the worker may feel to be the essential conditions for his liberation. This conflict in the realm of ideas cannot be resolved in the realm of ideas alone, before it is resolved in the real world; that is, until the conflict of classes is finally resolved. Until then, this conflict is necessary and inevitable and an integral part of the process of democratic development. Accordingly in the present stage of transition it would be idle to demand as yet a single universally accepted and all-embracing social and political theory of the United Nations. What we need to search for is the greatest measure of common ground for democratic and progressive advance.

. . . We should reject at the outset all attempts at a dogmatic, absolute, abstract, universally valid and super-historical definition of the Rights of Man, which would only conceal the attempt to impose a particular social conception of a particular social section at a particular stage of development as an eternal law.

There can be no abstract definition of human rights in isolation from the social organization within which those rights are realised and which can alone make possible their realisation. Every assertion of human rights is in fact a demand for an organisation of society which will realise those rights.

Similarly, there can be no abstract definition of the Rights of Man as the rights of an imaginary non-existent individual in isolation. What is under consideration is always the rights of men and women in society, with all the obligations which the given form of social organisation imposes for the realisation of those rights.

Further, there can be no abstract definition of human rights in isolation from the material conditions which are necessary for the fulfilment of those rights.

These considerations mean that in discussing human rights we need always to take into account the form of social organisation, the stage of economic and social development and its possibilities, and the fact that rights change with changing social conditions.

. . . A reasoned social and historical approach, the recognition that any formulation of human rights must in fact be governed by the given stage of economic, social and political development, does not mean that we must therefore sink into a morass of relativistic scepticism, in which all conceptions and political formulations are regarded as equally valid and justified on the basis of a given social organisation. The rejection of any final, absolute, unchanging standard of human rights does not mean that we therefore surrender any basis of judgment and cannot distinguish between conceptions or institutions which are historically progressive and those which are historically reactionary. . . .

ECONOMIC AND SOCIAL RIGHTS

It is evident that all abstract formal rights of democratic citizenship, of liberty, equality and self-government, are in practice dependent for their effective fulfilment on the basic and primary economic and social rights, or material conditions, which alone can make possible their fulfilment. Nevertheless, it is precisely in this sphere that the divergences arising from different economic and social structures are most marked, and that there is consequently the widest room for controversy in the definition and interpretation of these rights.

The older types of democratic theory were concerned almost exclusively with the formal abstract political rights of democratic government, and of the relations of the individual and the state, and only to a very limited extent with economic and social rights or the organisation of civil society. This corresponded to the historical development of democratic theory as first arising as the expression of a propertied class which was politically disenfranchised or debarred from participation in government, but materially secure, and which consequently in the field of economic rights was mainly concerned to ensure the protection of the rights of private property and of the sanctity of contracts, the limitation of taxation and the removal of restrictions on trade and commerce. This is the old classic type of liberal democratic theory which still survives, and which condemns all social organisation and state intervention in the economic sphere as a "totalitarian" invasion of individual rights.

In proportion, however, as the democratic movement drew into conscious activity the masses of the people, and democratic theory developed as the theory expressing the interests of the majority of the people, specifically of the working class and unprivileged sections, who were materially insecure, and who required indispensable material conditions in order to be able to exercise effective political rights, just as they fought for political rights in order to improve their material conditions, so the conception of economic and social rights has come to the forefront as an integral part of modern democratic theory. The conception has found expression in the demand for such rights as the right to work or maintenance, the right to social security, the right to protection of conditions of labour and leisure, and the right to minimum provision for health, education and culture.

The eighteenth century American Declaration of Independence set out the "inalienable rights" of man as comprised in "life, liberty and the pursuit of happiness" without further precise definition in the economic and social field.

The Declaration of Rights of the French Revolution, drawn up in 1789, and prefixed to the Constitution of 1791, defined the "natural and imprescriptible rights of man" as "liberty, security and resistance of oppression," and further laid down the "right to property" as "inviolable and sacred," and the principle that taxation should be "divided equally among the members of the community according to their abilities."

The Declaration prefixed to the French Revolutionary Constitution of 1793 defined the right of property as the right of the individual to enjoy the fruits of his labour, and limited it as subject to the superior right of public necessity; added the right to freedom of choice of occupation; and further added the right to work or public maintenance, and the right to education as a public provision. Here we see the beginning of a more radical conception of social and economic rights.

As against these, if we take the example of the most modern advanced definition of social and economic rights, as laid down in a socialist constitution, we shall find it in the Constitution of the U.S.S.R. This lays down, in the Chapter on "The Fundamental Rights and Duties of Citizens":

Right to Work, i.e. "the right to guaranteed employment and payment for work in accordance with its quantity and quality."

Right to Rest and Leisure: reduction of the working day, annual vacations with pay, provision of sanatoria, rest homes and clubs.

Right to Maintenance in old age and in case of sickness or loss of capacity to work: social insurance at state expense, free medical service, etc.

Right to Education: universal compulsory elementary education, free higher education with state scholarships, etc.

It is evident that the full provision of these rights assumes the foundation of a socialist organisation of society.

There is room for discussion and interchange of views as to the extent of basic economic and social rights which should be laid down for inclusion in a Declaration of Human Rights to be adopted by the United Nations at the present stage. The following may be suggested as a minimum basis which should receive general recognition:

Right to Work: guaranteed employment in a society organised for full employment, with adequate maintenance in the event of interruption of full employment; protection of working conditions.

Right to Leisure: limitation of working hours, annual paid holidays, and provision for sports and cultural recreation.

Right to Social Security through fully developed social insurance, with provision for old age, sickness, accident, or loss of the breadwinner.

Right to Health, through a free state health service, with adequate health provision.

Right to Education, through a universal free state education service, with provision for the endowment of research and for adult education. . . .

12th May 1947

ECONOMIC AND SOCIAL RIGHTS OF MAN
Maurice Dobb[*]

Clearly, the notion of a declaration of rights which shall hold true of all times and conditions is too abstract to be tenable in this age, which is more conscious than its forbears of the historically-relative character of social and economic problems. Problems, needs, rights and duties only have a meaning within the framework of a particular set of social institutions and social relations: institutions and relations which are subject to historical change, and in the contemporary world are continually changing before our eyes. Yet declarations of rights can have a function in summarising the aspirations of progressively minded persons in a given age, confronted with the given situation and a given group of problems: as pointers to the direction in which efforts at social advance must be turned.

Foremost among the requirements of any new society must be the attainment of full employment. This is nowadays a commonplace. But it has not always been so; and there are even some today who resist its attainment, or if they accept the end will not accept the means. Until recently unemployment was considered to be either an inevitable accompaniment of a so-called "free society" or even a desirable reserve without which a capitalist economy would lack a vital instrument of flexibility and of discipline. It is of interest in this connection that the 1936 Constitution of the U.S.S.R. included as the first among its "basic rights of citizens" "the right to work" (ARTICLE 118).

Secondly, there is the need for guaranteeing a certain minimum subsistence for all, sufficient to banish poverty and want. This has two aspects. First is the guarantee through a comprehensive system of social security against loss of earning-power from any of the risks to which the wage-earner is prone: risks arising from accident, sickness or old age. Second is a guarantee of certain minimum terms and conditions of employment: a prohibition of any contract of employment which fails to secure a certain minimum standard of earnings. This is not only a matter of aspirations: it is a matter also of attainment; while the

---

[*] Maurice Dobb was one of the leading Marxist economists of the twentieth century and a professor of economics at Cambridge University. Under Dobb's leadership, Cambridge became the central node in Britain for the development of Marxist thought, communist political activism, and support for the Soviet Union. His students included Amartya Sen, Eric Hobsbawm, and Kim Philby, who later became a Soviet double agent within British intelligence. Dobb founded the Communist Party Historians Group with other leading British Marxist intellectuals such as E.P. Thompson and Christopher Hill. The many books he authored include *Russian Economic Development since the Revolution* (1928), *Soviet Economic Development Since 1917* (1948), and *Welfare Economics and the Economics of Socialism* (1969).

standard that is regarded as the minimum standard—as "a living wage"—is itself subject to change from one generation to the next and varies with the level of social and historical development in different parts of the world. Over large parts of the world any desirable minimum standard is at present unattainable (even with radical alterations in the distribution of income) owing to the low level of productivity per man hour. Here the practical realisation of this "right" requires a planned development of these regions as a prior condition (development which is systematically integrated under public auspices over a wide area, and not left to *laissez-faire*; and preferably development that is financially assisted from outside, provided that undesirable political conditions are not attached to such assistance).

Thirdly, it is necessary that rights of assembly and of organisation should be guaranteed to all employed persons: moreover, that this right of organisation should be made actual by extension of the right to all representative workers' organisations to negotiate regarding the terms of their employment and to be represented on bodies responsible for controlling the conditions of work. It is manifestly inconsistent with the dignity of man that labour should be regarded (as hitherto) as a mere hired factor of production, excluded from any voice in the conduct of industrial policy.

Fourthly, it is necessary that employment and access to the means of livelihood should be unrestricted by any considerations of race, creed, opinion or membership of any legal organisation.

It can reasonably be held that ownership of the means of production (including land) by private individuals on such a scale as to imply that independent access to these means of production is barred for a substantial section of the community represents an infringement of the economic rights of man in any full sense of the term. Where ownership of land and productive equipment is concentrated in the hands of a class, the remainder of the community is deprived of the possibility of a livelihood except as hired servants to the former: a situation which involves a substantial inequality of rights *de facto*, and in an important sense involves a deprivation of freedom for the class of non-owners. Such an interpretation of human rights is, of course, incapable of being reconciled with Capitalism as an economic system. In a more modified form, however, this interpretation could be held to debar the existence of privately-owned monopolies which dominate whole industries and control the production and sale of essentials of human existence or essential raw materials and requisites of production, and which are accordingly in a position to dictate their terms to private consumers or to other producers.

Rights in a Sacred Universe

PHILOSOPHICAL EXAMINATION OF HUMAN RIGHTS
Jacques Maritain[1]

1. The effects of the historic evolution of humanity and of the ever more universal crises of the modern world, coupled with the advance—be it never so precarious—of moral consciousness and reflection, have resulted in men apprehending today more clearly than heretofore, though still very imperfectly, a certain number of practical truths about their life together, on which they can reach agreement, but which, in the thought of the different groups, derive, according to types of mind, philosophic and religious traditions, areas of civilization and historical experience, from widely different, and even absolutely opposed, theoretical concepts. Though it would probably not be easy, it would be possible to arrive at a joint statement of these *practical conclusions*, or in other words, of the various rights recognized as pertaining to the human being as an individual and a social animal. But it would be quite useless to seek for a common *rational justification* of those practical conclusions and rights. That way lies the danger either of seeking to impose an arbitrary dogmatism, or of finding the way barred at once by irreconcilable divisions. While it seems eminently desirable to formulate a universal Declaration of Human Rights which might be, as it were, the preface to a moral Charter of the civilized world, it appears obvious that, for the purposes of that Declaration, *practical* agreement is possible, but *theoretical* agreement impossible, between mind and mind.

2. Now that these basic truths have been made clear, I have less hesitation in saying that as a philosopher I am concerned with the principles as much as, and more than, with the conclusions, and with the rational justification of Human Rights as much as, and more than, with a more or less effective practical agreement thereon. In embarking on the question of that rational justification, I am fully aware that, viewing things from a certain philosophic standpoint, which is for me the true one, I cannot hope for the agreement of those who hold to other philosophic principles.

---

1. For biographical information on Jacques Maritain, see the section entitled "Foreword and Introduction to *Human Rights, Comments and Interpretations*, UNESCO 1949" in Part II [ed.].

I disagree with the view that the 18th Century's concept of Human Rights was an extension to the individual of the idea of the Divine Right of Kings or of the indefeasible rights which God granted to the Church. I should be more inclined to say that that concept ultimately traces its ancestry from the long history of the idea of natural law and of the law of nations evolved by the ancient world and the Middle Ages, and more immediately springs from the one-sided distortion and rationalistic petrifaction which those ideas, to their great despite, have undergone since the time of Grotius and the birth of a mechanistic ratiocination. Thus there arose the fatal misconception of natural law—which is interior to the creature and precedes any explicit expression—as a *written* code to be proclaimed to all, whereof every just law would be a copy and which would decide *a priori* every detail of the norms of human conduct on lines claiming to be dictated by Nature and Reason, but in fact arbitrary and artificial. Moreover, the end of the matter was that the individual was deified and all the rights to which he was deemed entitled were looked on as the absolute and unlimited rights of a god.

To my mind, any attempt at rational justification of the idea of Human Rights, as of the idea of right in general, requires that we rediscover in its true metaphysical connotations, in its realistic dynamism and in its humble dependence on nature and experience, that concept of the natural law which was defaced by the rationalism of the 18th Century. We then understand how an ideal order, with its roots in the nature of man and of human society, can impose moral requirements universally valid in the world of experience, of history and of facts, and can lay down, alike for the conscience and for the written law, the permanent principle and the primal and universal norms of right and duty.

3. Simultaneously we understand how the natural law calls for completion, according to the needs of time and circumstance, by the contingent dispositions of human law; how the human group's awareness of the obligations and rights implicit in the natural law itself evolves slowly and painfully in step with the evolution of the group, and despite all errors and confusions yet definitely advances throughout history along a path of enrichment and revelation which has no end. Here we see the immense influence of economic and social conditioning and, in particular, the importance for the men of today of the new viewpoints and new problems, transcending liberal or bourgeois individualism and touching the social values of human life, which are being brought to birth by the crises and catastrophes of the capitalist economy and the emergence into history of the proletariat.

No Declaration of Human Rights will ever be exhaustive and final. It will ever go hand-in-hand with the state of moral consciousness and civilization at a given moment in history. And it is for that reason that even after the major victory achieved at the end of the 18th Century by the first written statement of those rights, it remains thereafter a principal interest of humanity that such Declarations should be renewed from century to century.

4. Lastly, a reasonable concept of natural law allows us to understand the intrinsic differences distinguishing natural law as such, the law of rations, and positive legislation. We then see that any Declaration of Human Rights necessarily involves a concatenation of rights differing in degree, of which some meet an absolute requirement of the natural law, such as the right to existence or the right to profess, without interference by the State, the religion one believes true (liberty of conscience), others responding to a need of the law of nations, based on natural law, but modified in application by human law and the requirements of "common use" or the common good, such as the right to own property or the right to work,—others again meeting an aspiration or desire of the natural law confirmed by positive law, but with the limitations required by the common good, such as the liberty of the press or more generally liberty of expression, freedom of exposition, and freedom of association. These last types of liberty cannot be erected into absolute rights, but constitute rights (conditioned by the common good) which any society which has attained a condition of political justice is required to recognize. It is modern liberalism's misfortune to have made that distinction impossible for itself, and thus to have been obliged either to contradict itself or to have recourse to hypocrisy, in order to limit the practical exercise of rights which it has confused with the fundamental natural rights and which theoretically it proclaimed as absolute and sacrosanct.

5. The concept of natural law has been so much abused, so much pulled about, distorted, or hypertrophied that it is hardly surprising if, in our age, many minds declare themselves weary of the whole idea. Yet they must admit that since Hippias and Alcidamas, the history of Human Rights and the history of the natural law[2] are one, and that the discredit into which positivism for a period brought the concept of natural law inevitably involved similar discredit for the concept of Human Rights.

Certainly, as Mr. Laserson wrote recently, "The doctrines of natural law must not be confused with natural law itself. The doctrines of natural law, like any other political and legal doctrines, may propound various arguments or theories in order to substantiate or justify natural law, but the overthrow of these theories cannot signify the overthrow of natural law itself, just as the overthrow of some

---

2. Cf. Heinrich A. Rommen, *Die Ewige Wiederkehr des Naturrechts*, (Leipzig, Hegner, 1936); Eng. Transl. *The Natural Law*, Herder, St. Louis, 1947.

theory or philosophy of law does not lead to the overthrow of law itself. The victory of juridical positivism in the 19th Century over the doctrine of natural law did not signify the death of natural law itself, but only the victory of the conservative historical school over the revolutionary rationalistic school, called for by the general historical conditions in the first part of the 19th Century. The best proof of this is the fact that at the end of that century the so-called 'Renaissance of natural law' was proclaimed."

It remains true that a positivist philosophy based on observed facts alone, or an idealistic or materialistic philosophy of absolute Immanence is powerless to establish the existence of rights inhering by nature in the human being, antecedent and superior to written laws and agreements between governments, which the civil community is required, not to *grant*, but to *recognize* and enforce as universally valid, and whose abolition or infringement no consideration of social utility can even for a moment authorize. Such a concept cannot logically seem other than a superstition to these philosophies. It is valid and rationally defensible only if the rule of nature as an aggregate of facts and events includes and invents a rule of nature in the form of Being transcending facts and events, and itself based on an Absolute greater than this world. If there be no God, the only reasonable policy is that "the end justifies the means"; and, to create a society where man shall finally enjoy his full rights, it is today permissible to violate any right of any man if this be necessary for the purpose in hand. It is an irony stained with blood to think that, for the revolutionary proletariat, the atheist ideology is a heritage from the most "bourgeois" representatives of the bourgeoisie, who, after calling on the God of the Deists that they might base their own demands on the natural law, rejected that God and the God of the Christians alike when they were come to power and sought to free the all-embracing exercise of proprietary rights from the shackles of the natural law, and to close their ears to the cry of the poor.

6. I think that two further general remarks are necessary. Firstly the family group is, under the natural law, anterior to the civil society and to the State. It would thus be important in a Declaration of Rights to indicate precisely the rights and liberties deriving under this head and which human law does no more than acknowledge.

Secondly, if it be true that the foundations of Human Rights lie in the natural law, which is at once the basis of duties and of rights—these two concepts being correlative—it becomes apparent that a Declaration of Rights should normally be rounded off by a Declaration of man's obligations and responsibilities towards the communities of which he is a part, notably the family group, the civil society and the international community.

In particular, it would be important to bring into the light the obligations incumbent on the conscience of the members of a society of free men, and the right of that society to take suitable steps—through accepted institutions for the guarantee of justice and rights—to protect liberty against those who seek to use it in order to destroy it. The question was put in a form which we shall long remember by the activities of those who, before the second World War, became the propaganda tools of racialist and fascist perversion, to disrupt the democracies from within and to arouse among men the blind desire to deliver themselves from liberty itself.

7. On the enumeration and formulation of rights which logically follows, I take the liberty of referring the reader, for a fuller exposition of my ideas than I can give here, to the outline in my small book on "Les Droits de l'Homme et la Loi Naturelle" (Paris, Paul Hartmann), where I tried in particular to show the need of complementing the declarations of the 18th Century by a statement of the rights of man, not only as a human and a civic personality, but also as a social personality (a part of the process of production and consumption), and especially of his rights as a worker.

I would point out, too, that many valuable suggestions and lines of thought may be found in Georges Gurvitch's essay, *The Declaration of Social Rights* (New York, Ed. de la Maison française, 1944).

Finally, on the special question of freedom of the press and of the means for the dissemination of thought, it seems to me impossible to deal with this fully without reference to the work of the *Committee on the Freedom of the Press*, which in the United States has during the last few years investigated exhaustively all aspects of the problem and of which I had the honour to be one of the foreign members.

Rome, June 1947
(Translated from French)

SOME REFLECTIONS ON THE RIGHTS OF MAN
Pierre Teilhard de Chardin[*]

As first expressed, in 1789, the Rights of Man were mainly an assertion of the desire for individual independence. "All for the individual within Society," implying that the "human species" was created in order to expand and culminate in a multiplicity of units which would each, in isolation, reach their maximum development. This would seem to have been the principal concern and ideal of the 18th century humanitarians.

Since then, owing to the importance assumed in the world by collective phenomena, the fundamentals of the problem have changed considerably. There is now no longer any room for doubt. For numerous convergent reasons (rapid increase in ethnic, economic, political and psychic ties), the human individual is finally drawn into an irresistible process directed towards the establishment on earth of an inter-dependent organo-psychic system. Whether we like it or not, humanity is collectivizing, "totalizing" itself, under the influence of physical and spiritual forces of a world-wide nature. Hence the new conflict, which is taking place in every human heart, between the human unit, who is ever more conscious of his individual value, and his social ties, which become ever more exacting.

On reflection, we realize that this conflict is only apparent. We now see that the human being is biologically not self-sufficient. In other words, it is not by self-isolation (as one might have thought), but by *proper* association with all other human beings that the individual can hope to achieve full development of his *person*, full development of energy and movement and full development of consciousness, particularly as each of us cannot become complete "reflections" (i.e. "men") except by reflecting ourselves in and taking reflections from other human beings. Collectivization and individuation (not autonomous, but personal) are

---

[*] Pierre Teilhard de Chardin was a French Jesuit philosopher and paleontologist who won the Legion of Honor for courage as a stretcher-bearer during the First World War. Teilhard participated in major excavations around the world, particularly in China, where he was on the team that discovered Peking Man's skull. Teilhard was also a prolific writer who attempted, over many publications, to develop a unified philosophy that combined science with religion. Because of this, his writings and teaching were regularly subject to censure by the Church, which banned many of his books, forbade him to teach at the Collège de France, and ordered his writings removed from libraries and bookstores. Although he died in 1955, Teilhard's writings were still subject to Church sanction into the 1960s, when Pope John XXIII issued a *monitum* (warning) against them. This *monitum* was reaffirmed by the Vatican in 1981. Teilhard's best-known works include *Le Phénomène Humain* (1955; written between 1938 and 1940) and *L'Énergie Humaine* (1962; written between 1931 and 1939).

therefore not two contradictory movements. The whole difficulty is to regulate the phenomenon in such a way that human totalization is carried out, not under the influence of an external mechanizing compression, but through inner harmonization and sympathy.

From this point of view it becomes immediately apparent that the object of a new definition of the Rights of Man must be no longer, as hitherto, to secure the greatest possible independence for the human unit in society, but to lay down the conditions under which the inevitable "totalization" of humanity is to take place, in such a way as not to destroy, but to enhance in each of us, I will not say independence, but—what is quite a different thing—the incommunicable uniqueness of the being within us.

The problem is to cease organizing the world for the benefit, and in terms of the isolated individual, and to direct all our efforts toward the complete development ("personalization") of the individual, by wisely integrating him within the unified group, which must one day become the organic and psychic culminating point of humanity.

When thus restated in terms of an operation with two variables (progressive, inter-dependent adjustment of the two processes of collectivization and personalization), the question of the Rights of Man does not admit of any simple or general answer.

At the least we can say that any solution envisaged must satisfy the following three conditions:

(1) Within a Humanity that is in process of collective organization, the individual is no longer entitled to remain inactive, i.e. to refrain from developing himself to the greatest possible extent; because on his perfection depends the perfection of all the others around him.

(2) Society must, in its own interest, *tend* to create around the individuals it comprises the most favorable environment for the full physical and psychical development of what is most original in each of these individuals. This is admittedly a commonplace proposition, but the ways in which it is to be applied cannot be laid down uniformly for all cases, since cases vary according to the educational level and the potentialities for progress in the various human units to be organized.

(3) Whatever be the measures taken in this direction, one capital principle must be stated and constantly observed. This is that in no case, and for no purpose, must the collective forces be in a position to compel the individual to distort or falsify himself (as he would do if he accepted as true what he saw to be false, i.e. if he lied to himself). If it is to be legitimate, any limitation or direction applied to the independence of the human unit by group force can only be

applied *in conformity with* the free and inner structure of that unit. Otherwise a fundamental discord would be introduced into the very heart of the collective human body . . .

Each human being has an absolute duty to work and personalize himself.

Each human being has a relative right to be placed in the best possible conditions for personalization.

Each human being within the social organism has an absolute right not to be distorted by outward coercion, but to be integrated within the organism by inward persuasion, i.e. in conformity with his aptitudes and personal aspirations.

These three points must be made explicit and guaranteed in any new Charter of Humanity.

(Translated from the French)

GRAMMATICAL ANALYSIS OF THE RIGHTS OF MAN
Marcel de Corte[*]

A right, in the *concrete* sense of the word, the only sense that is valid in social and political philosophy, is the expression of an imperative: *to have a right to.* It is too obvious indeed, as has often been reported, that a theoretical and abstract right, indiscriminately granted to all men in a homogeneous manner, does not constitute a guarantee but rather a bonus to oppression: whatever right I receive to choose my job freely, without submitting to the requirements of any professional organization whatsoever, that right is void for me if the "labor market" is saturated with similar rights; whatever right I receive to vote in the community where I live, if the elections place me in the minority, I must submit to the law of the majority, etc. . . . If we now decide to reduce or even do away with this undeniable disadvantage of a theoretical right, it is important to rebuild society from the ground up, through a meticulous and precise technique that will descend to the smallest individual differentiations in order to reduce them, which

---

[*] Marcel de Corte was a professor of philosophy at the University of Liège in Belgium at the time of the UNESCO human rights survey. De Corte was a conservative thinker, Belgian royalist, and strong supporter of Christian-right political parties. Across a range of works, de Corte criticized many ideas and movements he believed to be derived from the French Revolution, including egalitarianism, social progress, and socialism and communism. His books include *Essay on the End of Civilization* (1949), *Where Did My Country Go?* (1951), *Man Against Himself* (1962), and *The Mind at Risk of Death* (1969). This piece was translated from the French by Romana Iorga.

will make the social order resemble the one that governs artificial communities built from scratch by human artifice, such as barracks or prisons.

It therefore seems impossible to us to list all the rights that will serve as an indirect object to the expression *to have a right*, because these rights will always be theoretical and, therefore, oppressive in some way, as long as the *real* subject of the verb has not been strictly determined. If one considers the subject to be the *I* or, simply put, the individual, that will lead—because this *I* lives in society with other *I*'s—to individual differences that will have to be removed in order to save the abstract amplitude of rights. If, on the other hand, we believe that the subject is man in general, then it is only too easy to answer that man in general has no concrete existence and that one has to exist in order to have a right.

Are we then in the presence of an unsolvable problem?

We do not think so. Each individual *I* actually possesses a certain *radically concretized* structure, which has been given the vague title of "human nature." It is while possessing this radically concretized structure *that I have a right to something*. My right here is no longer an abstract, uniform right, separated from myself, frozen in the timelessness of a concept and inclined to all the oppressive deformations. My right is a concrete and living right, which is rooted in me or is, more accurately, part of me. My right cannot take shape outside myself nor, a fortiori, be removed without me disappearing as a living being. Here the blurry cloud that envelops the term *nature* begins to dissipate. My primordial right is the *right to life*, not the life of the body or the life of the mind, but life in the most ordinary sense of the word, which holds the root of all the possible kinds of life and that is guided by the commandment: thou shalt not kill. But it is clear that I did not give this life to myself: it comes to me from my parents. I have a *right to a family* that is not a mere abstract entity or a simple aggregate of disparate beings but a living reality, diffusing life and whose life must be respected like my life itself. In addition, my life expresses itself outwardly: in some way, I "profess" my life, which grows and develops according to my vocation. By externalizing my life, I meet other lives, similar or different, that express themselves like mine and with which I enter into a relationship of living proximity all around me. I have the *right to a concrete framework of life* in which I can forge effective and living relationships with my peers. We shall call this framework *profession*, if it gathers similar beings, and *region*, if it brings together different beings. Finally, I have the right to recognize and worship God, who gave me this concrete individual and social life. I have the *right to join a religion*. My family, the concrete framework of my life, and my religion are all parts of my life and they *spill beyond* it. All this is rooted in my life, but flowers and yields fruit in a way that is relatively independent, beyond my life. The right *to* a family, *to* a profession, *to* a region, *to* a religion, develops somehow into a right *of* the family, *of* the profession, *of* the region, *of* the religion, *which is absolutely correlative with the first* and without which the first would be futile. If the family, the profession, the region, the religion are banned, it is the very foundation of my life that is affected. Therefore, I have a right to have all of this protected, because if it is protected, then it is my life that is protected. Thus, my right to life, which is fundamental, naturally extends into a right of living communities. The right of what we have called, along with the philosophers, "human nature," is simultaneously a right *of* natural communities.

All the other rights seem to us measured, regulated, and nuanced upon these fundamental rights. Do I, for example, have the right to property in a similarly absolute manner as in the previous cases? We do not think so. The right to property is only required to the extent that it favors the flourishing of fundamental rights. Do I have the political right to vote? The response is identical. The same goes for the right to strike, the right to opinion, etc. . . . The radical rights that are at the same time the rights of the concrete communities of daily life regulate all the others. In other words, there is an objective *hierarchy* of rights, which resolves conflicts between the various requirements whose manifestations are related to the here and now and without which all of the rights together would constitute nothing but a chaotic mass. The dilemma is clear here: either hierarchy or anarchy.

As for the question "*who* will safeguard and regulate the fundamental rights?"—it is not subject to *any* theoretical solution that is valid once and for all in time or in space. There is not any and there cannot be any government, caretaker, or regulator of rights that is "the best" *in and of itself.* The best government is *relative* to the maintenance of the rights of natural communities, because it is made for the *concrete* common good of their members. Monarchy, aristocracy, democracy, are here indifferent in and of themselves. As with that which is concrete, it is only the historical experience of these different regimes that can settle the debate. Just as the art of medicine does not treat illness but rather the ill, the art of government does not apply to abstract entities but to the prosperity of concrete societies. It is its *success*, more or less constant given the precariousness of human affairs, that justifies its form. Apart from this healthy pragmatism, all discussion in the absolute is only nonsense. The *essential* thing is that government, whether elected or not, monarchic or popular, or an intermediate between the two, should always keep the rights of natural communities, without which human life would be a meaningless word, *present* before it. It is therefore required that these rights be *represented*. It matters little how, provided that they are. Again, only experience can give a perspective here.

SOME FUNDAMENTAL IDEAS FOR THE UNITED NATIONS' DECLARATION OF THE RIGHTS OF MAN

Pedro Troncoso Sánchez[*]

The Declaration of the Rights of Man that is being considered should be based on the fundamental axioms below:

1. That between man and other living beings there is not a simple difference in terms of level or species, but a more profound and radical difference, which comes from the presence in humans of the higher realities of the spirit.

2. That on earth human existence has a final purpose where it finds Happiness, the fulfillment of the spirit through access to values of religion, morals, aesthetics, and knowledge.

3. That, in consequence, the final purposes of man are not exclusively material and economic—as has been claimed, thus lowering man to the condition of animals—but are essentially different purposes such as goodness, justice, religion, science, and art, which outweigh physical and economic purposes, which only constituting auxiliary means for the other purposes.

4. That all men, without distinction of race or sex, possess, in principle, the same material and spiritual qualities and identical opportunities to develop these qualities.

5. That what we understand as freedom should not be the power to do or not do something when the will is animated only by the primary natural appetites of enjoyment, possession, and domination that derive from organic life but, rather, when the will finds its guide or its source in the moral values and the other spiritual values.

6. That, consequently, the true regime of freedom is one that encourages and facilitates in human beings the advent and implementation of spiritual values and that opposes the invasion of the area where these values are realized by the primary appetites.

7. That the ultimate purpose of education is the development of the indi-

---

[*] Pedro Troncoso Sánchez was a diplomat, law professor, and jurist from the Dominican Republic. During his diplomatic career, he served as the Dominican ambassador to Argentina, Mexico, the Vatican, and Italy. In 1947, at the time of the UNESCO human rights survey, he was both professor of law at the University of Santo Domingo and president of the Supreme Court of the Dominican Republic. Later in his career he served variously as president of the University of Santo Domingo, Minister of Education, president of the Academy of History, and president of the Academy of Sciences. His books include *Philosophical Sketches* (1932), *The Judge's Mission* (1948), and *Positions of Principle in Dominican Political History* (1967). This piece was translated from the French by Romana Iorga.

vidual's spiritual possibilities even before the development of his natural possibilities, in preparation for the realization of properly human purposes on the personal and social front.

8. That education, being the only path that leads to freedom, consitutes the first of the rights of man and the first among the duties of States.

9. That freedom being the ultimate purpose of education, the individual must be free to act only to the extent to which he is educated.

10. That the firmest and most certain foundation for social progress is the improvement of the individual through education, and not the exercise of power or the application of an imposed social work plan.

11. That, to be profitable, the exercise of individual freedoms in a given society should vary in direct proportion to the average level of culture.

12. That it is as harmful and reprehensible to prevent those who, being good, are entitled to act freely, as it is to allow those who, being bad, have no right to direct their own actions or those of others.

13. That the realization of values is primarily the responsibility of individuals and secondly of the State, with the exception of Justice and Order, which can only be achieved within a community. Consequently, in this respect, on the one hand, society is made for the individual, and on the other, the individual is made for society.

14. That necessarily, all the blood, sweat, and tears shed by humanity during the last world war must result, above all, in a greater reality of the rights of man. Otherwise, the sacrifice of humanity will have been in vain.

15. That the main purpose of the State is to ensure Justice and Order, the necessary conditions for the fulfillment by individuals of their proper purpose, which is access to the life of the mind, that is, freedom.

16. That in fact Justice and Social Order constitute the necessary environment for individuals to do good, think, know and live without fear, work, rest, play, earn a fair wage, own property, believe and feel without restrictions, teach and learn, create beauty and enjoy it, express their thoughts, respect each other in their bodies, their honor, and their dignity, care for their health, insure themselves against disability, protect their families, and exercise all the other individual freedoms. That all these human rights are also at the same time duties of society towards the individual.

17. That the need to educate populations is important and urgent in our time, because States and men have appropriated to themselves the means of domination without relation to their moral progress.

18. That in every home, every school, every university, in newspapers, in books, in entertainment, in radio broadcasts, and, in general, in all aspects of

popular education, anything that could raise selfishly national sentiments and prejudice against other peoples and other races should be avoided wherever possible.

19. That at the same time, at all levels and in all aspects of education, we must seek to form an international moral conscience, which, existing in each individual, could serve to build a peaceful, orderly, and just community of peoples.

20. That for no reason of system, necessity, or convenience of the international community, must one ever infringe the sacred and unalterable right to self-determination of independent and sovereign peoples.

21. That, on the contrary, we should develop the ideas and stimulate the feelings that can elicit a sense of justice among the new generations of major countries that would lead them to consider it a crime to impose their will on other countries for any reason whatsoever.

22. That, in order to destroy racial prejudice and racist ideologies, we must develop in schools and in universities the research and teaching of ethnology, of sociology, and of history that is objective and free of all prejudice.

23. That in schools we should describe wars as essentially a set of actions that generate pain, misery, and death and from which no one emerges victorious.

24. That in the field of education, the United Nations should give the highest priority to the moral rehabilitation of those who participated in the last war, because it is a supreme necessity.

25. That we must educate the international moral conscience so that it will sincerely and spontaneously repudiate all recourse to arms, even in pursuit of the most obvious and most legitimate rights, except in the case of of defense against aggression, and to accustom it to resort to methods of conciliation, arbitration, and international justice, so long as there are reputable courts and organizations to resolve the disputes that arise between people and governments, just as we usually present ourselves before our national courts to resolve the disputes of civil life.

Ciudad Trujillo, June 30, 1947

The Universal Declaration of Human Duties

A LETTER ADDRESSED TO THE DIRECTOR-GENERAL
OF UNESCO
*Mahatma Gandhi**

> Bhangi Colony,
> New Delhi.
> 25 May 1947

Dear Dr. Julian Huxley,

As I am constantly on the move, I never get my post in time. But for your letter to Pandit Nehru in which you referred to your letter to me, I might have missed your letter. But I see that you have given your addressees ample time to enable them to give their replies. I am writing this in a moving train. It will be typed tomorrow when I reach Delhi.

I am afraid I can't give you anything approaching your minimum. That I have no time for the effort is true enough. But what is truer is that I am a poor reader of literature past or present much as I should like to read some of its gems. Living a stormy life since my early youth, I had no leisure to do the necessary reading.

I learnt from my illiterate but wise mother that all rights to be deserved and preserved came from duty well done. Thus the very right to live accrues to us, only when we do the duty of citizenship of the world. From this one fundamental statement, perhaps it is easy enough to define the duties of Man and Woman and correlate every right to some corresponding duty to be first performed. Every other right can be shown to be a usurpation hardly worth fighting for.

---

* In case Albert Einstein was right, and "[g]enerations to come, it may well be, will scarce believe that such a man as this one ever in flesh and blood walked upon this Earth," Mahatma Gandhi was the leader of the independence movement in British-ruled India. Trained as a barrister at the Inner Temple in London, Gandhi agitated for civil rights in South Africa before returning to India to take up the cause of independence using techniques of civil disobedience and nonviolence. Gandhi was 77 years old when he wrote this letter to Julian Huxley, less than three months before India gained independence from the British Empire. On January 30, 1948, during the chaos that followed partition, Gandhi was assassinated by a Hindu nationalist.

Yours sincerely,
M. K. GANDHI

Dr. Julian S. Huxley,
Director-General, Unesco,
Paris

HUMAN RIGHTS IN THE CHINESE TRADITION
Chung-Shu Lo[*]

Before considering the general principles, I would like to point out that the problem of human rights was seldom discussed by Chinese thinkers of the past, at least in the same way as it was in the West. There was no open declaration of human rights in China, either by individual thinkers or by political constitutions, until this conception was introduced from the West. In fact, the early translators of Western political philosophy found it difficult to arrive at a Chinese equivalent for the term "rights." The term we use to translate "rights" now is two words "Chuan Li," which literally means "Power and Interest" and which, I believe, was first coined by a Japanese writer on Western Public Law in 1868, and later adopted by Chinese writers. This of course does not mean that the Chinese never claimed human rights or enjoyed the basic rights of man. In fact, the idea of human rights developed very early in China, and the right of the people to revolt against oppressive rulers was very early established. "Revolution" is not regarded as a dangerous word to use, but as a word to which high ideals are attached, and it was constantly used to indicate a justifiable claim by the people to overthrow bad rulers; the Will of the People is even considered to be the Will of Heaven. In the "Book of History," an old Chinese classic, it is stated: "Heaven sees as our people see; Heaven hears as our people hear. Heaven is compassion-

---

[*] Chung-Shu Lo was a professor of philosophy at West China Union University in Chengdu during the 1940s, but not much is known about his early or later career. He apparently earned a B.Litt. from Oxford University in 1939 and spent considerable periods of time in Britain and on the European continent. He was a strong advocate for "East-West" cultural exchanges and in 1947 was working as a consultant for UNESCO in Paris. On behalf of UNESCO, Lo wrote to General Jan Smuts, Prime Minister of South Africa, in June 1947, enclosing the Phil/1/1947 documents and asking him to respond. In his substantive refusal letter to Lo, Smuts argues that any declaration of rights should be tested against the standards of logical positivism in order to avoid "pitfalls in language which have led to endless philosophical puzzles and insoluble problems" (Smuts papers, National Archives of South Africa, Vol. 84, no. 101).

ate toward the people. What the people desire, Heaven will be found to bring about." A ruler has a duty to Heaven to take care of the interests of his people. In loving his people, the ruler follows the Will of Heaven. So it says in the same book: "Heaven loves the people; and the Sovereign must obey Heaven." When the ruler no longer rules for the welfare of the people, it is the right of the people to revolt against him and dethrone him. When the last ruler Chieh (1818–1766 B.C.) of the Hsia Dynasty (2205–1766 B.C.) was cruel and oppressive to his people, and became a tyrant, "Tang" started a revolution and overthrew the Hsia Dynasty. He felt it was his duty to follow the call of Heaven, which meant obeying exactly the Will of the people to dethrone the bad ruler and to establish the new dynasty of Shang (1766–1122 B.C.) When the last ruler of this dynasty "Tsou" (1154–1122 B.C.) became a tyrant and even exceeded in wickedness the last ruler "Chieh" of the former dynasty, he was executed in a revolution led by King Wu (1122 B.C.) who founded the Chou Dynasty, which in turn lasted over 800 years (1122–296 B.C.) . . . The right to revolt was repeatedly expressed in Chinese history, which consisted of a sequence of setting up and overthrowing dynasties. A great Confucianist, Mencius (372–289 B.C.), strongly maintained that a government should work for the Will of the people. He said: "People are of primary importance. The state is of less importance. The sovereign is of least importance."

. . . The basic ethical concept of Chinese social political relations is the fulfilment of the duty to one's neighbour, rather than the claiming of rights. The idea of mutual obligations is regarded as the fundamental teaching of Confucianism. The five basic social relations described by Confucius and his followers are the relations between (1) ruler and subjects, (2) parents and children, (3) husband and wife, (4) elder and younger brother and (5) friend and friend.

Instead of claiming rights, Chinese ethical teaching emphasized the sympathetic attitude of regarding all one's fellow men as having the same desires, and therefore the same rights, as one would like to enjoy oneself. By the fulfilment of mutual obligations the infringement of the rights of the individual should be prevented. So far as the relation between the individual and state is concerned, the moral code is stated thus: "The people are the root of the country. When the root is firm, the country will be at peace." In the old days, only the ruling class, or people who would be expected to become part of the ruling class, got the classical education; the mass of the people were not taught to claim their rights. It was the ruling class or would-be ruling class who were constantly taught to look upon the interest of the people as the primary responsibility of the government. The sovereign as well as the officials were taught to regard themselves as the parents or guardians of the people, and to protect their people as they would their own children. If it was not always the practice of actual politics, it was at least the basic principle of Chinese political thought. The weakness of this doctrine is that the welfare of the people depends so much on the goodwill of the ruling class, who are much inclined to fail in their duties and to exploit the people. This explains the constant revolutions in Chinese history. It is, however, interesting to compare the different approach to the problem of human rights by the Chinese with the theories of human rights developed in the West by thinkers of the 17th and 18th centuries.

Let me state now what I regard to be the basic claims, the principles from which all human rights may be derived for all the people of the Modern World. A declaration on the Rights of Man for the entire world should be brief yet clear, broad yet concise, fundamental yet elastic, so that it may be interpreted to suit the needs of peoples in different circumstances. For this reason, I lay down here only three basic claims, valid for every person in the world, namely: (1) the right to live, (2) the right to self—expression and (3) the right to enjoyment.

(1) *The right to live*

The right to live seems to be such a natural thing, yet it is neither properly recognized nor universally enjoyed by all the people. The world is big enough for everybody to live in, yet many are deprived of a proper dwelling place. The natural resources of the earth, used according to the scientific knowledge at our disposal, should provide plentifully for all the people to live comfortably, yet natural resources are wasted in many ways and are not made accessible to all those who need them. Each individual should be allowed to have his proper share in society as well as to make his proper contribution to it, and no individual should be allowed to have more than his share or to live idly at the expense of others.

(2) *The right to self-expression*

We want not only to live, but also to live with the sense of dignity and self-reliance. We are social beings. Each individual naturally considers that he has a proper place in society. In order to contribute fully to the society, each individual should have the fullest degree of self-expression. Social progress depends on each individual's freedom of expression. The right of national groups to self-determination is also a form of self-expression.

(3) *The right to enjoyment*

By "enjoyment," I refer to the inner aspect of the life of the individual. Our life should be not only materially adequate and socially free but also inwardly enjoyable. That there is an inner aspect of life is undeniable. "Enjoyments" are of different kinds, but they are all connected with the inner life of the individual. The mental satisfaction of the inner life leads to peace of mind, and the peace of mind of the individual is a necessary condition of the peace of the world. The elementary right to enjoyment is to a life free from drudgery; it means that each should have an adequate amount of leisure and also be able to make good use of that leisure. No one should be constantly overweighed either by work or by social activities. He should have the opportunity to refresh himself and enjoy life. Other forms of enjoyment are aesthetic, intellectual, cultural and religious. Although not everyone can find enjoyment in the mystical experiences of religion, religion is a form of enjoyment for the inner life of many, which should not be repudiated by alleging it to be mere superstition. There should be religious toleration not only for all religions but also for atheism. Each should enjoy the right of giving the greatest satisfaction to his emotion and intellect without interfering with what others treasure most in their inner life.

The three basic claims of human rights stated above, namely, the right to live, the right to self-expression and the right to enjoyment, can, I believe, cover all the fundamental rights that a modern man should enjoy. The right to live is on the biological and economic level. The right to self-expression is on the social and political level. The right to enjoyment is on the aesthetic and spiritual level. When man can enjoy the rights at all levels, he attains a full life. It is time for all the nations and each individual in the world to be conscious of the following conditions, namely (1) that the world is an organic whole, so we should work in co-operation to improve the individual lives of people as a whole; (2) that each individual is an end in himself, and all social institutions are the means to develop each individual as fully as possible; (3) that each individual or national group should respect the rights of others to the same degree as we treasure our own; and (4) that each, by making the most of himself, can at the same time contribute best to the world at large.

1 June 1947

REFLECTIONS ON HUMAN RIGHTS
*Kurt Riezler**

I. The natural law, in its original conception, was intended to include both rights and duties. The exclusive emphasis on the Rights of Man belongs to the eighteenth century. In our own time, a considerable change of feeling has occurred. Modern man seems to be willing to admit that rights are conditional on duties.

This change of feeling is obvious with respect to property rights. A natural right of doing with one's property whatever one pleases can no longer be claimed. Social legislation interfering in the ways a man runs his factory is supported by public feeling everywhere. The rights of property imply duties.

II. Hence it seems that any modern formulation of a bill of natural rights should be supplemented by a bill of duties. Any formulation, however, of these obligations of man encounters difficulties far greater than the formulation of a Bill of Rights. If we assume that the principle of natural law should be respected by, or find an expression in, positive law, any formulation of such obligations will provide the actual power-holder not only with the moral excuses and the intellectual tools but also with the legal instruments to disregard the Rights of Man. It is he who decides whether the obligations have been respected.

III. There is only one such obligation, the legal recognition of which may do no harm (though perhaps not much good either). It is everybody's duty to recognize the human rights of his fellow citizen. This would mean, in practice, that whoever advocates the disregarding or abolishing of these rights loses the moral claim to, and the legal protection of, his own human rights.

IV. If, however, these duties of man should be duties towards the "public welfare" [or] the "Society," and the state and rights are made conditional on the fulfilment of these duties, the duties will uproot the rights. The rights will wither away. Whoever is in a position to interpret the *salus publica* or to act in the name of "Society" or "state" can use the allegedly unfulfilled duties to shove aside the rights.

---

* Kurt Riezler was a German diplomat, academic administrator, and philosopher. He was the closest adviser to Theobald von Bethmann-Hollweg, chancellor of the German Empire, both leading up to and throughout the First World War. After the war, he played a role in the drafting of the Weimar Constitution and was later appointed rector of the University of Frankfurt during the time when the Institute for Social Research was attracting scholars such as Herbert Marcuse to the university. Because his wife was Jewish, Riezler was forced out of the university by the Nazis in 1933; he later emigrated to the United States, taking up a professorship at the New School for Social Research. In 1947, when he contributed to the UNESCO human rights survey, he was a visiting professor at the University of Chicago.

V. A bill of duties of the citizens towards the state would require as its counterpart a formulation of the duties of the "sovereign" state towards the citizen. However, though the state can compel the citizen, the citizen cannot compel the state to respect these duties.

Hence the possibility that a government transgresses the rights or fails in its duties would logically require not only a right, but a duty, of rebellion or revolution on the side of the citizen—a thing completely empty under modern technological conditions. As this right and duty of revolution can be misused, the state will again have a right and the duty to suppress such revolutions. That means the theoretical justification of civil war by natural law.

VI. Conclusion: Any bill of rights that makes the rights conditional on duties towards society or the state, however strong its emphasis on human dignity, freedom, God, or whatever else, can be accepted by any kind of totalitarian leader. He will enforce the duties while disregarding the rights.

Hence a bill of rights would better be restricted to rights, i. e. to those rights which as minimum conditions, however insufficient, of human freedom any state or society can respect and protect—these are the old civil liberties. Any addition, be it of economic rights, be it of duties, means in practice weakening the civil rights and their hold on the human mind.

REPLY TO THE QUESTIONNAIRE ON THE RIGHTS OF MAN
Inocenc Arnošt Bláha[*]

The idea of the Rights of Man is basically the humanitarian creed and has its roots in stoic philosophy, in stoicism's concept of natural right, based on the metaphysical proposition that every human soul is a part of the divine World Soul, and all human intelligence is part of the general Divine Intelligence, so that all men are accordingly Sons of God and therefore equal by nature. This concept of natural rights was received and restated with more precision in mod-

---

[*] Inocenc Arnošt Bláha was one of the founders of the discipline of sociology in Czechoslovakia. He established the sociology department at Masaryk University in Brno in 1921 and was a professor there at the time of the UNESCO human rights survey. Bláha had studied with Émile Durkheim in Paris and was credited with creating a distinct "Brno school of sociology." During the German occupation of Czechoslovakia, all universities were closed. Unfortunately, although they were reestablished in 1945, the new communist regime eliminated Masaryk's sociology department in 1948 and Bláha was forced to retire in 1950. He died in 1960, several years before the sociology department he had founded was restored.

ern times by Grotius, Locke, Althusius, Montesquieu, Rousseau, etc. and had a powerful reforming influence in the spheres of political rights, penal law (Proffendorf, Thomasius, Baccuria), health (the nature treatment of F. Quesnay), economics (the postulate of "natural economic freedom" by Adam Smith and others), education (Ratke, Comanius, Pestalozzi), ethics (Hutcheson, Shaftesbury and others), religion (natural religion; B.B. Vico, Locke, Tindal and others) and finally the theory of cognition (Truth is the daughter of Experience and not of Authority).

All this can be summed up as the humanisation of social institutions. This idea found further powerful support in the development of Science, particularly biology, psychology and sociology. The theory of Evolution has helped philosophy and ethics towards a new assessment of the worth and meaning of life; the penetrating analyses of psychology have shown what miracles the human soul can perform through its own creative power, above all when it is securely based on moral principles; in the light of sociology each human life is seen as a great co-operative enterprise owing a vast debt to society for its material and spiritual comfort.

In addition, particularly since the Renaissance, and also with the help of Science the humanisation of the individual has proceeded parallel with the advancement of scientific knowledge and has gone forward simultaneously. Individualism originally meant the emancipation of the individual from all social oppression (particularly by Church and State). Its gaze is now directed inwards in the sense of the maxim: "Man should not only refuse to be oppressed by external constraints, but should also not oppress anything human within himself." At the same time this individualism is becoming gradually socialised in the sense that there is a social link between all individual lives.

Thus the humanitarian idea indicates on the one hand the ever-increasing and progressively more perfect humanisation of social institutions, and on the other the humanisation of the individual in the sense of the full development of the personality in relation to society. This humanising process, working sometimes from below, through the individual, and sometimes from above, through social institutions, found formal expression when the humanised, i.e. democratised State, proclaimed in the XVIIIth century (French and American revolutions) the Rights of Man, whence sprang logically the rights of peoples, linguistic, social and economic rights (right to work, right to a minimum standard of life) and finally the rights of women and children.

At the same time the humanitarian ideal grows not only more extensive but more intensive. It thrusts its roots deep in the soil whence it sprang by accenting the worth and dignity of the human soul as the power creating all other values; of its eternal worth (immortality) whence it derives a certain metaphysical (almost religious) sanctification; for as T.G. Masaryk said, the eternal can never be indifferent to eternity. Another sign of the "intensification" of this humanitarian ideal, which has been evolving gradually since the Renaissance and the Reformation, is that whereas it was originally stated in the great century of philosophy—in too purely intellectual a form, it is now acquiring a certain element of feeling in that its basis is becoming love of one's neighbour; in a word, it is becoming more ethical and more social.

This then is a general outline of the process in its most important features. It did not develop at the same rate everywhere, either extensively or intensively. The manner and tempo of its development were conditioned by the degree of cultural evolution of the different nations, by differences in their social systems, by their degree of internal cohesion, and by a number of external factors (particularly geographical and social; the nature of their environment).

Paris, 13 June 1947

MEMORANDUM ON THE RIGHTS OF MAN
*Hubert Frère**

1. The Memorandum in question here is so exactly thought out and written that it barely lends itself to discussion. One is simply surprised that it contains no repeated allusion to the notion of *duty*, a notion that is classically correlated with that of right, not, however, in truth, in the same person, as we summarily pretend in moral treatises, but rather, according to Ch. Renouvier's fairer view, in the person with respect to whom the first person has any rights. Because it is always with respect to someone else that we have a right, and in that other person, that right is automatically transformed into a duty towards the person who holds the right. That's why there is room, in a *Declaration* relative to *the Rights of Man,* for mentioning the beings with respect to whom man has rights and to require of them, consequently, symmetrical obligations. Not, however, without

---

*At the time of the UNESCO human rights survey, Hubert Frère was a professor of philosophy at the University of Mons in Belgium. Not much is known about his biography except that he was an active member in the 1940s of the Belgium Teaching League, an organization in francophone Belgium dedicated to preserving secular and public education. In 1946, Frère published a document in this context entitled "The Secular Moral Ideal." This piece was translated from the French by Romana Iorga.

emphasizing that some rights are transformed into duties towards oneself within each man, just as a business executive may have debts towards his own company.

However, through a very natural and quasi-instinctive requirement of mutual benefit, it is not possible to impose duties on someone without admitting in return that he has the same basic rights and, possibly, the same special rights as do the person or persons towards whom he has these duties. This is why it is true, according to the overly hurried assertion of moral treatises, that whoever claims rights for himself must logically assume symmetrical duties; failing that, he would be establishing himself as the beneficiary of a privilege that is insulting to others.

2. The fact is that the concept of rights is indissolubly linked to that of *human dignity*, and that the latter belongs by definition to every human being . . . worthy of that title; on the premise that no man can, as a Man, claim for himself rights that he would refuse to another . . . worthy of that name.

But what is this dignity? Essentially, it is the eminent quality that characterizes Man due to the fact that, having acquired or conquered the mental virtues that radically distinguish him from "other animals," he has ipso facto established himself in a new "kingdom" in relation to the zoological one and one that is manifestly superior to the three previous "natural kingdoms": the mineral, the vegetable (which feeds on the mineral), and the animal (which feeds on the vegetable and on itself); not, however, without retaining strong ties with the three pre-human "kingdoms" in the direct and indirect satisfaction of his physical "needs" as well as in his sleep, where he turns into a "stump," and in death, where he turns into "dust."

Thus, all man's dignity resides in this portion of his "nature," through which he judges over the animal, the vegetable, and the mineral, the entirety of this portion consisting of several psychological factors: free and insatiable curiosity, abstract intelligence, rational thought, the sublimation of emotions, imagination, the direct and symbolic use of tools, the appetite for risk, willpower, all of these "miraculously" served by the hand, and the vocal larynx; man's long physical and psychological childhood, the social division of labor. And to the extent to which a human being, zoologically speaking, tends, in all of his activities, even the animal ones, to give precedence to these factors over the other portion of his "nature," he acquires and conquers human dignity, thus carrying the rights that belong to Man because of this dignity, all of which flow from the *respect* due to this dignity, and he arouses in all beings who claim the same rights—including himself, of course—symmetrical duties towards himself and towards his peers, all of which are duties of *respect* for his dignity.

Note: One could rightly call mankind the collection of psychological factors that are proper to Man and which, by an automatic culmination of their harmoniously combined interplay, produce *culture* in the Western sense of the word, and the *civilization* that suits its needs.

3. Moralists have been accustomed, since Em. Kant, to call a *moral person* every being in whom humanity triumphs under an enlightened will, whether he is otherwise zoologically human or not, whether individual or collective. This is why a State may or may not be a moral Person, just like a "pure spirit," a church, a business, a cultural association, a club, etc. And this is also why the Rights of Man, with their symmetrical Duties, automatically belong and fall to these beings to the exact extent that they have achieved human dignity. In short, a declaration of the Rights of Man must be conceived in terms of Rights and Duties that are valid, generally speaking, for any moral person.

We must, of course, also discuss individual and collective human entities that are morally deficient. Because while a child, a barely evolved native, or a more or less backward human group is still far from being a moral Person, they are nonetheless potential or pending moral People; and while rogues and hardened "villains," as well as "lost causes" of all kinds, individual or collective, may be forever denied access to full human dignity, they nevertheless bear the physical traits and some of the moral traits of man and of human groups; therefore, all of these groups are too directly reminiscent of humanity not to arouse in the minds of authentic men the thought that, despite their definitive or provisional moral deficit, they do have rights related to the Rights of Man.

And, moreover, what man and what group of men absolutely deserve the title of humans? Even the very best, be that an individual or a community, always manifests some moral deficit. Therefore, while legislating for moral People, a Declaration of the Rights of Man must remember that every man and group of men is always morally very imperfect.

Note: One could very justly give the title of *Man* not only to every zoologically human being that displays the characteristics of the moral Person but also to all organized groups of such beings that manifest some dignity. Because moral dignity is very naturally transmitted from the human individual to the non-chaotic communities that he constitutes in the first degree (human groups), the second degree (groups of groups), the third degree, and so on, and it is even transmitted to the products of the properly human activities of every man or group of men—the works that are constitutive of civilizations and cultures—and to all the products of their activities, no matter what they may be.

4. Some might argue that, in view of the economic, political, and social upheavals that have occurred in the world in the last century, a Declaration of the Rights of Man in 1950 could have just about nothing in common anymore with

those of the eighteenth and nineteenth centuries. But that would be wrong. For, even as the epistemologist positions himself in the perspective of a final universal truth, so must the ethicist consider the Rights of Man from the angle of eternity. Not as a theoretical failing, but because the very concept of the Rights of Man implies a mental stance that is not relative to time or the environment, but is absolute. At least in principle. We are talking here about ideal rights, not effective rights. And even the very concessions that, at some point in the Declaration in question, are demanded by human imperfection must remain somewhat ideal.

None of this is absurd or laughable, given the dialectical relativity of the human condition. On the contrary. Mankind resembles a traveler dealing with unknown regions, which his eye cannot penetrate. In the same way that with the help of its historians, mankind is willing to look both proudly and sorrowfully at the tortuous, but clearly progressive, path traveled by its civilizations and culture; so with the help of its ethicists, mankind has the duty to turn its eyes sometimes to the horizon opposite to that from which it arose, which it dismisses with no thought of turning back, in order to contemplate, with faith and hope, the moving and consoling promises that it places in that horizon and wants to see there.

However, this absolutism does not, in principle, condemn any reference to the factors that today particularly threaten the rigorous Rights of Man: secret weapons, financial concentrations, ideological totalitarianisms whether police-based or plan-based, or partisan propagandas. But such a reference can emerge in the contrast that must be drawn, as has been said, between the ideal and the reality. . . .

May 5, 1947

UNTITLED
M. Nicolay[*]

53 Speekaert Avenue
Woluwe St. Lambert, Belgium, July 30, 1947

Mr. Director-General,
The Brussels newspaper "Le Peuple" has published, in its July 27 and 28, 1947, issue, the text of "A New Declaration of the Rights of Man" (a Unesco Draft).
I read this document with great interest. I also hope that its publication,

---

[*] Nothing more is known of "Mr. Nicolay" except for what is contained in this response sent to UNESCO in July 1947. This piece was translated from the French by Romana Iorga.

which should be generalized, will be followed, on the part of its readers, by useful reflections and remarks that can benefit the committee charged by your organization with collating and summarizing the briefs that have been submitted to you. As for myself, I take the liberty to submit to you the following ideas:

1. *The Right to Work*. If this chapter involves the idea, expressed elsewhere in the text, to give every man sufficient leisure, wouldn't it be better to emphasize, first of all, the concept specified above?

It is not enough for a man to have leisure. He must know how to draw its full benefits. Why? To educate himself above all; to understand better the purpose of life so that he can become better, more human; and finally to create, in mutual understanding, the universal society towards which evolution tends, a society that should be founded on the idea of unconditional solidarity if we want peace to finally reign between men and peoples.

Thus the right to leisure, derived from the right to work, takes on a predominant importance; and this should, in my opinion, be emphasized by an appropriate text.

2. Would it not have been appropriate, moreover, to include in the New Declaration a sentence highlighting the need for the internationalization of all rights, because they will not be efficient unless they are exercised on a global scale?

3. *The declaration of duties*. I fear that the mere declaration of rights will remain inoperative if it is not accompanied by a declaration of duties.

This truth, for it is a truth for those who have experience, among which I count myself, should be considered with all the attention it deserves.

The rights mentioned in the draft are ones that we never stop claiming! They are legitimate in principle, and should we dare to pretend that they do not become excessive when we realize—how many millions of times have I myself done this?—that their recipients too often neglect their duties towards the community?

In that case, a declaration of duties must be developed, I think, one that will form an essential complement to the declaration of rights. A century ago, the philosopher Renouvrier already said this. People did not listen. Yet he was right.

The second without the first can only, for that matter, in the present state of mind that is too often dominated by an unhealthy selfishness, accentuate the imbalance from which the world is dying. Moreover, does not Nature give us the example of balance through the rhythm of its manifestations?

I no longer know which wise man it was who wrote, "The centripetal and centrifugal forces, depending naturally on each other, are necessary to one another, so that both of them may live. If one were stopped, the action of the other would immediately become self-destructive."

Rights (the centripetal force) and duties (the centrifugal force) must therefore go hand in hand. This is my humble opinion.

Please accept, Mr. Director-General, the assurance of my highest consideration.

(Signed) Mr. Nicolay.
Honorary Director of the Ministry of Labor and Social Welfare

The Technological Society of the Future

SCIENCE AND THE RIGHTS OF MAN
W. Albert Noyes, Jr.[*]

If the advent of gunpowder to Western Europe had much to do with the disappearance of the feudal system and the French Revolution which culminated in the Napoleonic Wars showed the way for the inclusion of science in making war felt by whole populations, it is evident that recent scientific advances have almost completed a cycle in which science may prove to be one of the chief factors in the enslavement of mankind. Because of his importance in warfare the scientist can no longer be considered as a free and independent individual and whether he likes it or not, he is tied to the military destinies of the various countries. The Rights of Man and the rights of the scientist have become, therefore, inextricably entangled. The struggle of the scientist to maintain his freedom of action has an important bearing on the struggle of mankind for prosperity and happiness.

Modern means of transportation have caused an inter-relationship between the various nations of the world which formerly did not exist. No longer is it possible to look disinterestedly upon diseases in the far corners of the world. For the same reason that centers of poverty and of social disturbance have been potential sources of trouble within one country, these phenomena anywhere in the world constitute threats for those portions of humanity which now enjoy high standards of living. It may even be that extravagance in the use of natural resources by one nation would be of such vital concern to other nations that threats to world peace would be involved. We have hardly made a beginning in conserving our natural resources for the national good. We are a long way from looking on natural resources as assets which must be conserved for the good of the world. The implied threat to certain Rights of Man considered heretofore

---

[*] W. Albert Noyes, Jr. was a professor of chemistry at the University of Rochester at the time of the UNESCO human rights survey. Noyes served in the First World War in Europe as a radio operator and performed research for the US government during the Second World War, as head of the Office of Scientific Research and Development's Chemical Warfare and Smoke Division. His academic specialty was photochemistry, for which he was awarded the 1954 Priestley Medal (an award his father, W. Albert Noyes, Sr., had also won in 1935).

as fundamental in a society made of individualists is so obvious as not to need detailed comment.

The foregoing paragraphs present humanity in general and scientists in particular with a very real dilemma.

The conflict between nationalistic aspirations and the real need for a broader outlook is not one which can be resolved in a few months or years. It is evident, however, that certain rights of scientists and consequently certain Rights of Man will necessarily be curtailed for the common good. The really important question is whether this curtailment will lead to such a decrease in happiness and to such an invasion of privacy that life would cease to have any real meaning. Freedom to travel, to impart information, and even to engage in certain forms of livelihood will be so intertwined with the political sphere that the greatest caution must be exercised in plotting a course for the future.

The first duty of the scientist is to ensure that the black spots in the world, where poverty and disease are all too common, are eradicated. This necessarily implies more universal scientific education together with the imposition of certain laws restricting freedom of personal action as regards matters pertaining to health and the use of natural resources. It is difficult but possible to carry these steps forward without at the same time invading the most important Rights of Man as understood in the enlightened countries of western Europe and the Western Hemisphere, but inevitably material progress will run counter to certain deep-seated prejudices, arising partly from religion, in large fractions of the earth's population. The social and political implications of what we usually term progress are so vast that it is difficult at this time to make any sweeping generalizations concerning the future. There are differences of religion and of political ideologies which will always exist. Such differences should be encouraged, for each culture can contribute its bit to the happiness of mankind. The question arises mainly as to whether these differences can be prevented from leading to war, because war is the main instrument in the destruction of the Rights of Man.

Scientific training is supposed to lead to the cultivation of an objective attitude, one which permits judgement of matters on their merits without the incorporation of prejudice. Scientists by no means always carry this objective attitude into their discussions of political matters, but the scientific type of mind should be adaptable to social problems. Perhaps the greatest contribution the scientist can make in preserving the Rights of Man is to educate the world into a free discussion of all matters without personal animosity. Such an ideal cannot be reached overnight. The intolerance of the true scientist toward errors in fact and errors in logic must be tempered by a real tolerance toward varying basic postulates in the social sphere. Ultimate truth is difficult to reach in the physical sciences. It may never be attained in the science of human relationships.

It is vital for the future of the world that intense animosities and hatreds be allayed. This cannot be done solely by social and psychological studies. Good nourishment and congenial surroundings are essential if persons are to divorce their inner feelings from immediate problems. The immediate objective of the politician should be to avoid war at all costs, and the immediate objective of the scientist should be to ensure that all levels of society in all nations are freed from economic anxiety. If this is done, then given a long enough period of peace, the Rights of Man can gradually be worked out, and a code of ethics evolved which will fit the human race into a scientific world. The Rights of Man will have to be redefined, but we are confident that they can be redefined in such a way that the elements essential to human happiness are preserved.

Rochester, 23 April 1947

THE RIGHTS OF MAN AND
THE FACTS OF THE HUMAN SITUATION
*Aldous Huxley**

The increasing pressure of population upon resources and the waging, threat of, and unremitting preparation for total war—these are, at the present time, the most formidable enemies to liberty.

(1) About three quarters of the 2.2 billion inhabitants of our planet do not have enough to eat. By the end of the present century world population will have increased (if we manage to avoid catastrophe in the interval) to about 3.3 billions. Meanwhile, over vast areas of the earth's surface, soil erosion is rapidly diminishing the fertility of mankind's four billion acres of productive land. Moreover, in those countries where industrialism is most highly developed, mineral resources

---

* Aldous Huxley was the younger brother of Julian Huxley, director-general of UNESCO during the human rights survey. The Huxleys were a prominent family: Aldous and Julian's grandfather was T. H. Huxley, Darwin's "bulldog"; their brother Andrew would win the Nobel Prize in Medicine in 1963; and they were related to the English poet and critic Matthew Arnold through their mother. Huxley was a writer and author of many works of fictions, including *Brave New World* (1936), generally considered one of greatest novels ever published in English. In 1937, he emigrated to the United States, where he experimented with Indian mysticism, Hollywood screenwriting, and the psychedelic drug LSD. He died in 1963 on the same day that the US President, John F. Kennedy, was assassinated.

are running low, or have been completely exhausted—and this at a time when a rising population demands an ever increasing quantity of consumer goods and when improved technology is in a position to supply that demand.

Heavy pressure of population upon resources threatens liberty in several ways. Individuals have to work harder and longer to earn a poorer living. At the same time the economic situation of the community as a whole is so precarious that small mishaps, such as untoward weather conditions, may result in serious breakdowns. There can be little or no personal liberty in the midst of social chaos; and where social chaos is reduced to order by the intervention of a powerful centralized executive, there is a grave risk of totalitarianism. Because of the mounting pressure of population upon resources, the twentieth century has become the golden age of centralized government and dictatorship, and has witnessed the wholesale revival of slavery, which has been imposed upon political heretics, conquered populations and prisoners of war. Throughout the nineteenth century the New World provided cheap food for the teeming masses of the Old World and free land for the victims of oppression. Today the New World holds a large and growing population, there is no free land and over the vast areas, the much abused soil is losing its fertility. The New World still produces a large exportable surplus. Whether, fifty years from now, it will still have a surplus, with which to feed the three billions inhabiting the Old World seems doubtful.

It should be added, at this point, that while the population of the planet as a whole is rapidly increasing, the population of certain extremely overpopulated areas in Western Europe is stationary and will shortly start to decline. The fact that, by 1970, France and Great Britain will each have lost about four million inhabitants, while Russia will have added about seventy-five millions to its present population, is bound to raise political problems, which it will require consummate statesmanship to resolve. But political problems are not the only ones that will arise. In Western Europe the reduction in the quantity of population is destined, it would seem, to be accompanied by a deterioration (owing to the infertility of the more gifted members of the community) of its quality. In the light of existing trends, Sir Cyril Burt foresees that, by the end of the present century, the average intelligence of the British population will have declined by five IQ points. How far personal liberty, group co-operation and local and professional self-government— the three factors which constitute the essence of any genuine democracy—are compatible with the qualitative deterioration of the population remains to be seen.

(2) By destroying accumulated wealth and the sources of future production, total war has sharply increased the pressure of existing populations upon their resources and has thereby sharply curtailed the liberties of vast numbers of men and women, belonging not only to the vanquished nations, but also to those

which were supposed to be victorious. At the same time the fear of, and busy preparation for, another total war in the near future is everywhere resulting in an ever greater concentration of political and economic power. Bitter experience has proved that no individual or group of individuals is fit to be entrusted with great powers for long periods of time. The socialist rulers of welfare states may imagine that they and their successors will be immune to the corrupting influence of the enormous powers which total war and mounting population pressure have forced upon them; but there is, unfortunately, no reason to suppose that they will prove to be exceptions to the general rule. The abuse of power can be avoided only by limiting the amount and duration of the authority entrusted to any person, group or class. But so long as we are menaced by total war and mounting population pressures, it seems very unlikely that we shall get anything but a steadily increasing concentration of power in the hands of the ruling political bosses and their bureaucratic managers. Meanwhile conscription, or military servitude, is almost everywhere imposed upon the masses. This means in practice that, at any moment, a man may be deprived of his constitutional liberties and subjected to martial law. Recent history has shown that even socialist rulers are ready to resort to this device for coercing persons engaged in inconvenient strikes. It is virtually certain that, at the present time, no government actually desires war. But it is also probable that many governments would be reluctant to give up all preparations for war; for such preparations justify them in maintaining conscription as an instrument of control and coercion. And we may add that universal disarmament, if it should ever be achieved, would not necessarily mean the end of conscription. Compulsory service to the States will probably persist in some other than military form—as a scheme for the "training of youth," for example, or as a "labor draft." To a highly centralized government the advantages arising from the power to regiment and coerce its subjects are too great to be lightly sacrificed.

(3) A constitutional Bill of Rights, whose principles are applied in specific legislation, can certainly do something to protect the masses of ordinary, unprivileged men and women against the few who, through wealth or hierarchical position, effectively wield power over the majority. But prevention is always better than cure. Mere paper restrictions, designed to curb the abuse of a power already concentrated in a few hands, are but the mitigations of an existing evil. Personal liberty can be made secure only by abolishing the evil altogether. Unesco is engaged at present in facilitating the task of mitigation; but it is in the fortunate position of being able to proceed, if it so desires, to the incomparably more important task of prevention, of the radical removal of the present impediments to liberty. This is primarily an affair for the scientific section of the Organization. For the problem of relieving the pressure of population upon resources is

primarily a problem in pure and applied science, while the problem of total war is (among other things, of course) a problem in ethics for scientific workers as individuals and as members of professional organizations.

To provide all of the 2.2 billion persons at present inhabiting the planet with a nutritionally adequate diet, it would be necessary to double the existing food supply. It will take years, by conventional methods, to achieve this goal and by that time the population will be, not two billions, but more than three—and malnutrition will be very nearly as serious and as widespread as it is today.

Every industrial nation spends huge sums on research into the techniques of mass destruction. Thus, two billion dollars went into the production of the atomic bomb and many hundreds of millions more are at present being spent upon research into rockets, jet planes, the dissemination of pneumonic plague and the wholesale destruction of food plants. If comparable amounts of money and scientific ability could be devoted to the problem of producing foodstuffs artificially, it seems likely enough that methods would quickly be found for providing the half-starved millions of Europe and Asia with an adequate diet. The synthesis of chlorophyll, for example, might be, for the later twentieth century, the equivalent of what the exploitation of the empty lands of the New World was for the nineteenth. It would reduce the pressure of population upon resources and thereby remove one of the principal reasons for highly centralized, totalitarian control of individual lives.

The prosperity of an industrialized society is proportionate to the rapidity with which it squanders its irreplaceable natural capital. Over large areas of the earth's surface, easily available deposits of useful minerals have already been exhausted, or are running low, with the increase in population and the progressive improvement in industrial techniques, the drain upon the planet's remaining resources is bound to be accelerated.

Useful minerals are very unevenly distributed. Some countries are exceedingly rich in these natural resources, others lack them completely. When a powerful nation possesses a natural monopoly in some indispensable mineral, it is thereby enabled to increase its already formidable influence over its less fortunate neighbours. Where a weak nation finds itself blessed, or cursed, with a natural monopoly its stronger neighbours are tempted to acts of aggression or "peaceful penetration." Scientific workers have it in their power to postpone the day of planetary bankruptcy and to mitigate the political dangers inherent in the existence of natural monopolies. What is needed is a new Manhattan Project, under international auspices, for the development of universally available surrogates for the unevenly distributed and soon-to-be-exhausted minerals, on which our industrial civilization depends for its very existence—e.g., wind power and sun power to take the place of power produced by coal, petroleum and that most dangerous of all fuels, uranium; glass and plastics as substitutes, wherever possible, for such metals as copper, tin, nickel and zinc. A project of this kind would be valuable in several ways. It would shift our industrial civilization on to a foundation more permanent than that accelerating exploitation of wasting assets, on which it rests at present; it would break those natural monopolies which are a standing temptation to war; and finally it would make possible an extension of personal liberty and a reduction of the powers wielded by the ruling minority.

We now come to the ethical problems confronting scientific workers as individuals and as members of professional organizations. Whatever may have been the wishes of the inventors and technicians involved, applied science has in fact resulted in the creation of monopolistic industries, controlled by private capitalists or centralized national governments. It has led to the concentration of economic power, strengthened the hands of the few against the many and increased the destructiveness of war. Applied science in the service, first, of big business and then of government has made possible the modern totalitarian state. And applied science in the service of war departments and foreign offices has begotten the flame thrower, the rocket, saturation bombing and the gas chamber, and is now in process of perfecting methods for roasting whole populations by atomic explosions and for killing the survivors by means of man-made leukemia and artificially disseminated plague. The time has surely come when scientific workers must consider, individually and collectively, the ethical problem of "right livelihood." How far is a man justified in following a course of professional action which, though involving no immediate wrong-doing, results in social consequences which are manifestly undesirable or downright evil? Specifically, how far is it right for the scientist or technologist to participate in work, the outcome of which will be to increase the concentration of power in the hands of the ruling minority and to provide soldiers with the means for the wholesale extermination of civilians? Up to the present applied science has been, to a great extent, at the service of monopoly, oligarchy and nationalism. But there is nothing in the nature of science or technology which makes it inevitable that this should be so. Professionally speaking, it would be just as easy for the scientific worker to serve the cause of peace as of war, of personal liberty, voluntary co-operation and self-government, as of monopolistic statism or capitalism, universal regimentation and dictatorship. The difficulties are not technical; they lie in the realms of philosophy and morals, of value judgments and the will that acts upon those judgments.

June 1947

THE RIGHTS OF MAN: A BIOLOGICAL APPROACH
Ralph W. Gerard[*]

Science and Technology have revolutionized the material existence of man and are revolutionizing his mental existence. Scientists are the autocatalysts of social evolution, acting on and reacted upon by the society so as to produce accelerating change. Science has created the present milieu *in* which men must live and interact and it is creating new view–points as to *how* men must live and interact. Biology, especially, dealing with organisms—with systems composed of individual units integrated into a community which is an effective whole—has much to say of the forces operating in such communities of individuals, of the freedoms, duties, controls that must be present, and of regular trends in these over the enormous span of organic evolution. Its findings seem equally valid for the community of cell entities in the individual complex animal or the community of animal entities in the individual complex society. And they seem equally valid (if less complete) for the human as for the sub–human animal. Science views man primarily in his natural setting—discarding the supernatural as a source of knowledge—and would approach the problem of human rights and duties as a special case of the problem of part and whole, as best exemplified by living organisms.

The central problem of man in society is that of outlining the territory of the individual within the larger territory of the group. Were society simply a mosaic of the completely separate territories of its members or, conversely, were men equal and random occupants of a homogeneous group territory, this problem would not exist. It must, however, remain true, from the very nature of an organism, that the individual man, an entity in his own right, and the communal man, a part of the community, exist simultaneously. This is the inescapable dichotomy: each man (and his neighbour) is a complete whole, dedicated to self-survival and in basic competition with other men; but each man (with his neighbour) is a component unit of a larger whole, the society, and dedicated to group-survival by basic co-operation with other men in the group. Of course, this duality is repeated with varying emphasis at many levels—individual and family, family and community, member and minority group, political party and political unit, state and nation, nation and world state. And, of course, territory is not a spatial unit

---

[*] Ralph W. Gerard was a professor of physiology at the University of Chicago at the time of the UNESCO human rights survey. Gerard was a child prodigy who entered the University of Chicago at age 15, earning his PhD at age 21 and an MD at age 25. Gerard conducted research on the human nervous system and the links between physiology and human behavior. Later in his career, he played a role in the development of the new University of California, Irvine, serving as dean of the Graduate Division and then as vice-chancellor of the university.

nor a single entity; it is the surrounding in which the individual (unit) exercises dominant control of his environment, and its extent is different for different aspects—physical, biological, psychological, sociological, legal.

. . . Man, immersed in a group culture and largely served by his fellows, is enabled to differentiate and to fulfill latent capacities. He becomes more than anthropoid; but also less, for he would survive poorly on his own. As organisms surrendered immortality, but gained more effective living—perhaps even self-consciousness—when single cells banded into multicellular units, so man must lose and gain freedoms as he forms a society. He must accept group restrictions in gratifying his primitive urges, he is not free to take what he can by force; but he receives from the group new urges and means of gratifying them; he comes to possess language and is free to think with its aid.

Man's rights and duties, then, cannot be absolute but remain always relative to his milieu. As some privileges are attained, others must be surrendered. Whether a particular exchange is desirable depends on the value assigned to each freedom, and this is again largely determined by the culture. Indeed, in an important sense, the most complete freedom is enjoyed by the person (or group) most completely moulded to the prevailing culture. A "free-falling" object is fulfilling its "destiny" without hindrance by conflicting forces. A man is free to the extent that he is permitted to satisfy, or attempt to satisfy, felt needs; and his rights are therefore a composite of the desires stimulated in a society and the restrictions placed upon gratifying them. Until chickens were domesticated and pots turned, no right to a chicken in every pot could come into question. Before language developed sufficiently to stimulate and communicate abstract thought, freedom of speech was no problem; it was neither present nor desired.

To the extent that man's social environment expands, so can the many individual territories do so without undue pressure. But compression as well as expansion occurs and boundary problems are inevitable. The "rights of man" are attempts to define the territory of the individual (or the small group) vis-à-vis his neighbours and the larger group. They can never be absolute and they must not too long remain fixed by any codification. For man in society evolves and territories are not merely relative but are also varying. The acute problems arise in each period only in regard to the growing points. The right of every man to breathe is not now in question, because it is universally assumed to exist. The right of every man to a plot on Mars is not now in question, because it is universally assumed not to exist. But what would happen if invention enable some entrepreneur to meter air (as toilet facilities have become metered) or to import Martian uranium? Indeed, in the pre-atomic-fission era uranium was more a nuisance than a prize; as was petroleum before the internal combustion engine.

Changes in the society altered the values of these materials and so created a new set of problems as to rights. As newspapers, radio and other mass media have developed, so have arisen problems of freedom of communication; as men have cohered, on the basis of specialization, into groups with special interests or beliefs, so have arisen problems of the right to a job or to strike, the right to worship or to scoff, the right to conform or to revolt. This may all be pointed up in the field of health. . . . Health is not only individual, it is also public; and public health measures are accepted with relatively little demur by individuals. (When a considerable interest group is involved, however, as with farm butter as against vegetable oleomargarine, this is not so.)

. . . A final word from biology on the problem of enforcement and of power. Man as an individual has certain urges, which insensibly pass into desires, habits, customary privileges, recognized interests, legal rights. Man as a member of a group accepts certain controls, habits, customary responsibilities, recognized obligations, legal duties. Rights and duties become codified in laws, which is useful, and crystallized in them, which is disastrous. For change continues and codes must yield or break. The continuous growth of vertebrates seems to be a better device than the spasmodic moultings of insects. When tensions become great enough, the weakest element gives. With rigid social systems, this usually means revolution and brute mechanical force. With less rigidity, multiple small changes occur and the power is exerted by "persuasion" via communication.

It is striking that in biological evolution certain general trends are evident. Cells in organisms and organisms in groups tend to greater cohesiveness and interdependence. Co-operation increases relative to conflict. The influence of the whole on the unit is enhanced relative to that of the unit on the whole. And the integrating forces shift from an emphasis on mechanical control to ever greater use of communicative control, via nerve and hormone. A rigid unadaptable species remains stagnant and is superseded in evolution; a highly specialized one is most easily wiped out by a change in conditions. Evolutionary mechanisms operate on the group even more than on the individual. It is a violence to demonstrable truth to say that the organism exists for the cell or the group for the individual, just as it is to say that the cell exists for the organism or the individual for the group.

Society is a form of epi-organism, and social evolution cannot violate general laws of biological evolution, however unique it may be in particulars. The biologist cannot supply details of what present human rights should be. He can say:

1. Rights are relative to the society. Minimal ones will be universal, others valid only in very special cultures.

2. Some rights must be abrogated as new ones are demanded. Which will be valued more in each case depends on the group culture.

3. Greater dependence of the individual on the group is in the line of evolution. Altruism is growing relative to selfishness, and control is being exercised relatively ever more by suasion, as compared to force.

4. Any doctrine which regards man only as an individual or only as a unit in a group is necessarily false. The duality of man, as an individual whole *and* as a social unit, is inescapable. The extremes of eudemonism and utilitarianism, individualism and collectivism, anarchism and totalitarianism, laissez faire and absolute economic socialism are untenable. The rights of man involve rights of the individual (or small group) as against other individuals (or groups) or the whole society—which implies duties of them to him—and rights of the whole (or small group) as against the individual (or group)—which implies duties of him to it.

5. The particular codification of rights at any time will be imperfect and rapidly become less good. With any formulation should be included provisions for mandatory re-examination and reformulation at appropriate intervals.

June 1947

RIGHTS AND DUTIES CONCERNING CREATIVE EXPRESSION, IN PARTICULAR IN SCIENCE
Johannes M. Burgers [*]

. . . . 1. There shall be freedom of creative expression, except in so far as harm thereby may be done to other people, or irresponsible or weak people may be seduced to acts which are harmful to themselves or to others. Restrictions for this purpose can be made only by constitutional authorities in consultation with and under the guidance of representative scientific and educational opinion, and must be subjected to periodic revision.

---

[*] Johannes M. Burgers was a Dutch physicist and leading authority on fluid dynamics. At the time of the UNESCO human rights survey, he was a professor of aerodynamics and hydrodynamics at the Technical University of Delft. Burgers was active in international professional networks and was one of the founders of the International Union of Theoretical and Applied Mechanics in 1946. In 1955, he moved to the United States to become a professor at the University of Maryland. In 1965, Burgers published *Experience and Conceptual Activity*, a study "based on the writings of Alfred North Whitehead" that develops the idea that human values should have the same status as causal relationships in the physical sciences.

2. The community has the duty of setting aside from its funds means for developing the creative abilities of its gifted members.

3. The part played by science in modern society makes possible and at the same time puts upon us the obligation of international co-operation, as well as of looking into the future in the interest of coming generations.

The community has the duty of setting aside from its funds means for elaborate scientific research, as a means for alleviating wants of mankind, for the development of mankind, and for the pursuit of truth.

The community at the same time has the duty of providing men and women with education and information preparing them for co-operation and citizenship in a society largely influenced by science.

4. When scientific work leads to the possibility of technical applications or of other measures of importance for, or affecting in any way, the whole of mankind, such applications or measures should come under the sponsorship of international bodies, deriving their status and power from international authority. Such sponsorship may include supervision, control, direction or exploitation (example: atomic energy).

5. There shall be freedom of scientific intercourse and publication, and free access to all published material, independently of the way in which scientific work is financed.

No secrecy restrictions may be put upon scientific research or its publication for competitive purposes, either by private companies or by nations. Secrecy deemed necessary for defense purposes can be enforced only by international authority, in consultation with and under the guidance of representative scientific opinion, and must be subjected to periodic revision.

6. Every scientific worker is responsible for what he publishes and for the form in which he publishes it.

Every scientific worker has the duty to contribute towards the understanding of the implications of science and the possibilities afforded by it.

7. Every scientific worker has the duty to insist upon the necessity of considering the social and moral obligations of science; and to exert his influence against the misuse of science.

Scientific workers must have the right to consider and investigate the way in which applications of their work are brought into society and affect the people concerned (or mankind as a whole); and to make known the results and conclusions to which their researches in this respect have led.

8. Scientific organizations may bring forward claims for the protection of nature, which must be taken in full consideration by international and national authorities and can obtain priority over proposals for exploitation.

COMMENTS

A number of points in the "Memorandum" submitted by UNESCO[1] under "Problèmes particuliers" referred to the possibilities of creative work. The most important are : "8. Freedom of expression (including freedom of the writer and the artist)." "12. Freedom of scientific and philosophic enquiry and publication." Points 5, 6, 21 and several others more or less touch upon closely related matters.

In view of the principle that the ultimate object of human life is to aim at truth in as full a sense as possible, and in view of the fact that conception requires personal freedom as well as stimulation and criticism derived from intercourse with other free minds, social organization should guarantee the freedoms mentioned in 8 and 12. Every definite curtailment of these freedoms can develop into obstructions of the road towards truth.

Nevertheless the following points require attention;

(a) Every expression of what a man or a woman or a group of people believes to be true, is subject to the limitations of the mind which framed the expression, and to misunderstanding, to unexpected reactions and even to misuse by other people.

(b) The realization of an artistic conception or the pursuit of scientific work may require means far surpassing the possibilities of individuals and of small groups of interested persons, so that it must be decided whether material support can be granted out of the general fund of richness which the community has at its disposal.

(c) Creative work, in particular in science, gives power; hence the central problem of modern society: who shall decide about the application of this power?

Certain rules must be framed to cope with these matters.

The greatest difficulties are involved in the problem of power. They are particularly enhanced by the fact that human society has a tendency to develop into competing organizations. Technical advance, leading to extremely efficient means for communication as well as for influencing opinions and instinctive tendencies in men and women, have led to an enormous rise in power and size of such organizations, at the same time reducing their number. The consequence is that the struggles between the remaining bodies take an increasingly fierce character and menace the whole world with destruction; while inside each group the freedom for individual play of mind and individual choice in action becomes less and less.

---

1. "Memorandum and Questionnaire Circulated by UNESCO on the Theoretical Bases of the Rights of Man": see Part II: Key Documents [ed.].

The consequence of this development is that scientific workers become bound to machinery set up for competition or for fighting and lose the power over the results of their work. The situation can make it impossible for them to discontinue this work, even when it takes a direction they would feel strongly opposed to. The further consequence is the growing enforcement of secrecy on scientific research and its results, which has now even been laid down in legislative form in some countries.

The impetus of political development is extremely strong at present. At the same time the interconnection of all social relations and the extreme complication of present day human affairs make it extremely difficult to obtain a proper view of one's obligations, the more so as scientific workers are accustomed to analyze a situation, and to focus their attention mainly on some detail they can treat with exactness. This makes them less apt to come to synthesizing pictures; whenever they try they are conscious of their limitations.

The only way to work against the outbreak of a life-and-death struggle between the now existing (or developing) centers of power, must be found in openness and fearlessness of mind, and in strengthening the urge for attaining and expressing truth existing in individuals and in independent groups. Only by the free and open contest of opinions formed in as many minds and in as diverse minds as possible, can the danger be evaded that our society runs into directions which will bring an end to all creativeness, either by ruining the world or by curtailing the free operation of personal responsibility and moral consciousness.

The introduction of legal secrecy restrictions into science brings extreme dangers:

to our personal attitude of mind;

to the development of science as pursuit of truth;

to adequate and ethically justified application of science;

as a legal principle which will have destructive and far reaching consequences for our civic rights;

and as a cause of distrust and suspicion between groups and nations which ought to come to co-operation.

These dangers are so imminent at present that any dangers involved in free communication of discoveries in what is now the forefront of scientific advance, must be risked, rather than that "secrets" should be guarded for fear of misuse, by competing groups. Similarly there should be no restrictions upon the discussion of political questions and theories. The world apparently stands before great changes, the outcome of which cannot be seen; we must accept our part in it with the firm faith that honesty and intelligence have a value in themselves. In view of what is coming it is unwise to make reciprocity in this respect a matter of principle; one party at least must start in the right direction.

The freedom of publicly communicating their discoveries for all scientific workers entails the duty to give attention to what comes out of the applications of their work and to the conditions of the world in which they are working. They must devote part of their time to help the public to understand the meaning and importance of scientific findings; they must give advice in those cases where their work influences social relations or where new applications become possible; they must make investigations concerning these matters and make known their results and views. The positions in which they are working should afford them the necessary freedom for this.

Delft, 7 May 1947

Universal Human Rights in a Colonial World

THE RIGHTS OF MAN AND THE ISLAMIC TRADITION
Humayun Kabir[*]

The first and most significant consideration in framing any charter of human rights to-day is that it must be on a global scale. In the past, there have been many civilizations but never one world civilization. Two different conceptions of human rights could and sometimes did subsist side by side and because of lack of communication, could even be unaware of one another. To-day such a state of affairs is unimaginable. Whatever happens in one corner of the globe has an almost immediate repercussion on other parts. Days of closed systems of divergent civilizations and, therefore, of divergent conceptions of human rights are gone for good.

The second consideration is that not only must there be uniformity between countries but also uniformity within countries. It the past, civilization and culture were often the concern of a section or a class within the country. It was only these classes who had any rights. As the systems of civilization were more or less self-contained and closed, the dispossessed classes within the country reconciled themselves to their fate. In many cases they were unaware that any system other than that to which they had been born was at all possible. There were, no doubt, revolutionary changes in human affairs from time to time. More often than not, these changes occurred when two divergent cultures or world outlooks met. To-day the situation is entirely different. The continuous condensation of space and time is bringing different regions of the world more and more into contact and compelling, through comparison of conditions in different areas, a movement towards uniformity within the country itself. A charter of human rights to-day must therefore be based on the recognition of the equal claims of all individuals within one common world.

---

[*] Humayun Kabir was recommended to Julian Huxley in a letter of April 1947 by the distinguished Indian philosopher Sarvepalli Radhakrishnan, then Spalding Professor of Eastern Religion and Ethics at Oxford (who himself had refused to participate in the UNESCO human rights survey). Kabir was a Bengali intellectual and writer who was serving in India's Ministry of Education in 1947. Kabir was one of the original drafters of UNESCO's influential *The Race Question* in 1950. Later in his career, Kabir served as India's minister of education under two prime ministers.

It is necessary to emphasize this because of one fundamental flaw in the western conception of human rights. Whatever be the theory, in practice they often applied only to Europeans and sometimes to only some among the Europeans. In fact, the western conception has to a large extent receded from the theory and practice of democracy set up by early Islam, which did succeed in overcoming the distinction of race and color to an extent experienced neither before nor since. It is against the background of a compelling movement towards uniformity that we have to examine the different existing conceptions of human rights.

. . . The problem of the 20th century is to reconcile the conflicting claims of liberty and security. A new charter of human rights must secure to each individual, irrespective of race, creed, color or sex, the minimum requirements for a bare human existence, viz.:

(a) the food and clothing necessary for maintaining the individual in complete health and effectiveness;

(b) the housing necessary not only from the point of view of protection against the weather but also from that of allowing him space for relaxation and enjoyment of leisure;

(c) the education necessary for developing the latent faculties and enabling the individual to function as an effective member of society;

(d) the medical and sanitary services necessary for checking and curing disease and for ensuring the health of the individual and the community.

These are the four basic rights on the enjoyment of which all other rights depend. It will be noticed that they appertain to the security rather than the liberty of the individual. This is only a recognition of the fact that liberty is essentially a social concept and has no significance outside society. On the other hand, society itself is based on the need for security and therefore the demands of security must take precedence over the demands of liberty in respect of the minimum human needs.

The totalitarian systems have enriched our conception of human rights to the extent that they have compelled recognition of this fact. Their error seems to be that they have drawn no limit to the precedence of security over liberty for the individual. Both theory and experience, however, indicate that, once the basic minimum of security is reached, human beings place greater value on the rights and claims associated with the concept of liberty. Freedom of conscience or worship may be meaningless for a person whose mental faculties are restricted to the existing superstitions of his environment, but the moment he has attained some intellectual consciousness, he attaches the greatest value to the right of freedom of thought. Similarly, once the basic requirements of food, clothing and housing have been met, the individual is willing *to forego the claims to their extension* and even accept some diminution in them for the sake of rights like freedom of speech or assembly.

To sum up. The modern charter of human rights must secure to all individuals in all communities and countries a basic minimum of human requirements in respect of food, clothing, housing, education and sanitary services. Since this cannot be done without planning and control, the rights of the individual must be subordinated to the community to the extent required for securing these claims. Once, however, the basic minimum has been assured, the individual must be at liberty to press for other claims without check or interference from state or society.

The crux of the problem is, however, to determine (a) what constitutes the minimum human requirements in respect of security and (b) the degree of control and interference by the State necessary to secure these basic standards. On both these points there is room for wide divergence of opinion, and any formulation of human rights would be wrecked unless the difference can be overcome or methods found to resolve them without conflict or violence. From this is derived the decisive importance of political democracy. The community as a whole must decide both what constitutes the human requirements and what degree of control and authority may vest in the State to secure them. It is true that political democracy loses much of its significance without economic and social freedom. A residue of liberty even then exists and there are hopes for its further expansion. Without political democracy the very possibility of social and economic democracy is destroyed. Political democracy is therefore the basis on which alone the structure of full human rights can be raised.

. . . Similarly in the relation between the group and the world as a whole, it must be the world which determines both the content of the four fundamental requirements and the method necessary to secure them. In all other matters and subject to the over-riding authority of the world as a unit to preserve the fundamental rights, each group or community should be free to pursue such policy as it may desire for realizing the values it considers highest.

The implication of this is the creation of a world authority—democratically based on the will of all groups and individuals of the world—to ensure the achievement of the fundamental human rights. The lessons of history also point the same way. As already stated, right is itself a social concept and requires the creation of some authority within whose orbit individuals may enjoy it. Science is making the world into one through constant improvements in methods of contact and communication. This is breaking down the barriers of separate authority and of separate systems of rights. The corollary to a world charter of human rights is therefore the creation of some world authority.

Unfortunately, there seems no immediate prospect for the setting up of such a world authority. The demand for uniformity of rights cannot however wait, for within the same system there is no room for different standards. What can be done is to define the minimum human requirements in respect of the four basic rights mentioned above and ask for an agreement of all States to accept and enforce then. There must also be a similar agreement as to the degree of interference with individual liberty permissible for the purpose of securing those ends. Thus, the rights to food and clothing involve the obligation to work, but there must obviously be some limit to the hours of such work, or to the class of persons called upon to perform such work. A world charter should therefore confine itself to the definition of the content of the four fundamental human rights and the degree of control and interference permitted to the State for securing them.

New Delhi, 1 May 1947

THE RIGHTS OF PRIMITIVE PEOPLES
A. P. Elkin[*]

I.

INTRODUCTION

In this contribution, I confine myself to man in primitive society, drawing in particular on my knowledge of, and work amongst and for, non-self-governing peoples, usually referred to as primitive peoples, in Australia and the adjacent islands of the South-West and South Pacific.

To say that the principles of the Atlantic Charter can and must be applied to such peoples, does not mean, however, that governing and mandatory powers should at once divest themselves of all responsibility for, or interest in, their

---

[*] A. P. Elkin was one of two anthropologists to participate in the UNESCO human rights survey (the other being Melville Herskovits; see his "Statement on Human Rights," which appears later in Part III). Elkin was an Australian Anglican clergyman and a professor of anthropology at the University of Sydney in 1947. He exercised wide-ranging control and influence over the development of anthropology in the country. He advised the national government on Aboriginal affairs, edited the journal *Oceania* for fifty years, and played an active role on the Australian National Research Council. Elkin was an advocate for Australian Aborigines who nevertheless believed that assimilation to majority society was the best strategy for the country's native populations. Among his more notable publications are *The Australian Aborigines: How to Understand Them* (1938), *Citizenship for the Aborigines* (1944), and *Aboriginal Men of High Degree* (1946).

colonial or mandated native peoples and leave them to themselves. To do so, after having interfered in, controlled, and allowed interference with, the latter's indigenous way of life, would make their "last state worse than the first." What is meant is (i) that such sovereign powers will administer native peoples only until such times as the latter become self-dependent economically and politically, and (ii) that the policy of such administrations will include such educational, health, economic, cultural, legal and political measures, that this aim of self-dependence and self-direction in relation to the peoples of the world, will be reached in the shortest possible time.

This time-condition is required lest representatives of the administering power—officials, employers or missionaries—should rationalize the *status quo* of subjection on political, economic and educational aspects of life, as a necessary stage which must be retained for an indefinitely long period, until the native peoples are ready, *in the opinion of the governing power, to take even one step out of tutelage.* In actual fact, this present, or pre-war, condition suits the "invaders" or "intruders" economic interests. To keep a people as permanent apprentices or wards, and therefore as cheap labor, and to justify this compulsory employment as necessary training for civilization and citizenship, constitute a convenient situation, especially if the implication be overlooked that the particular trainees will never realize that citizenship and are not expected to do so. Perhaps a later generation will, so it may be argued, but unless radical changes are made in the systems of employment, government and education, this will never occur.

Those immediately concerned are seldom perturbed by this poor prospect. Even well-intentioned missionaries still echo glibly the fallacy that Papuans or other ethnic groups are child races, who must be treated as such and who may grow up intellectually and emotionally, but not yet.

In both these cases, native peoples are deprived of their rights as human beings, simply on the grounds of belonging to a culture different from ours and less complicated industrially and financially. They must, however, adapt themselves to this new situation, for it is backed by force—the administration. And this they do by consciously assuming the role of an inferior, by being perpetual apprentices in our occupations, and by being child-like to satisfy our vanity. In themselves, and with reference to their own cultures and societies, as anthropologists can testify, they are not stupid, inferior or childish.

Another argument advanced for keeping primitive peoples in tutelage from generation to generation, is that a stone-age people cannot advance to the steel-age in a generation, for it took Europe so many centuries. The fallacy is obvious; peoples of primitive cultures have not to invent the many steps between the two ages. Their task is to adapt themselves to the present age, that is, to the twentieth-century environment as it is in, and spreads from, Europe, Asia and America. This they have the intelligence to do, and to do quickly. But they need now the education which will enable them to understand their problem and task. Given education and literacy, and experience gained by their own representatives visiting, and observing the conditions of life in, those countries from which ideas and practices are brought to their own country, their grasp of the situation will deepen, their intelligence will advance, and they will build up a working adaptation.

They have, moreover, a right as human beings to be allowed to do this. But that is not all. "Civilized" powers and peoples have disturbed and confused native peoples' ways of life, upset their adjustment to their environments, and indeed, changed the very environments. Therefore, primitive peoples have a right to receive from the civilized world assistance in understanding, and making new adjustments to, the changes in their environment, changes resulting from civilization and its bearers.

II.

RIGHTS OF PRIMITIVE MAN

(1) *Primitive and Civilized Man, alike Human Beings.*

. . . *A basic Right of primitive man today is the Right to be considered a human being in the same manner and degree as civilized man.* He is part of the same international complex of relationships, possesses the same fundamental needs, and has the same potentialities of intelligence. The differences are those of history and of cultural environment and heritage.

(2) *The Right to his own Pattern of Civilization and Personality.*

. . . *A second basic Right of primitive man, which can be recognized today, is the Right to be civilized according to the pattern which he will develop*—to each separate people its own pattern—but fitting into the general pattern of human values and rights on the world-scale, with its economic and cultural relationships. This is, of course, the right to freedom of self-determination in the cultural and religious spheres and in the sphere of personality development.

(3) *The Right to Education in Civilization.*

. . . If the basic right of free personality development within a people's own pattern of civilization is to be respected, the institutions and methods of education introduced and used amongst a primitive people must not be instruments of imposed propaganda, but must possess two fundamental aims. These are: first, the development of an appreciation by a people of its own cultural background and of the individual's relation to it, and an understanding or, at least, an awareness of the cultural changes resulting from contact with civilization; and, second, the opening of the door, on approved educational principles, to world thought, science, technical achievement, literature and religion, to be used and built into their own changing culture as they find possible.

That is, *in the third place, primitive peoples have a Right to benefit from the civilized world's advances in both the method and content of education, conceived of in the widest sense.* This Right derives from, and must be subservient to, their second basic Right.

(4) *The Right to Community Land.*

. . . Deprivation of land or external interference with the use of it, has religious, moral and psychological as well as economic effects. It undermines communal life and its sanctions, leaves the individual adrift, and leads to unbalanced personality development.

. . . It is clear, therefore, that a *Basic Right of Primitive Man, as a human being, both as an individual and as a community, is the Right to retain his land with its many-sided associations and meanings.* That is, all administering powers should guarantee their primitive peoples the permanent use of their land. As the First Point of the Atlantic Charter reads: The powers concerned "seek no aggrandizement, territorial or other."

(5) *The Right to Economic Development.*

. . . To use the words of the Fourth Point of the Atlantic Charter, the products of their lands and labor should ensure them "access, on equal terms, to the trade and to the raw materials of the world which are needed for their economic prosperity."

Therefore, *Primitive Man, though his community be non-self-governing, has today a Right to the full use of the products of his land and labor and to take his place in the exchange of world products.*

(6) *The Right to the Disposal of one's own Labor.*

. . . Seeing the effects of the conditions which have arisen in Aboriginal Australia, and under the Indenture labour system in the Southwest Pacific, and admitting that native peoples are human beings with a right to their own way of life and to the use of the lands to which they are bound in the several ways mentioned in the preamble to the Fifth Right, it follows that:

Primitive Man has a Right, as a Human Being and a Social Personality, to the free control and disposal of his own labour power, and should not be deprived of this by invasion, by force, by deceit, or by abuse of his unavoidable ignorance of the terms and conditions of employment which he is asked or persuaded to accept.

(7) *Primitive Woman's Right to a Secure Sexual and Related Social and Economic Position.*

. . . In the frontier or marginal regions of intrusive settlement and administration, the "invaders" or immigrants consist for the greater part of males. It is only after many years, when conditions have become safe and more comfortable that, apart from a very few brave and devoted women, wives and families of their own ethnic group settle with them. In the meantime, however, the male settlers have not all remained continent. Through force, prestige, payment, economic pressure, or the attraction of the novel, they have obtained sexual partners, either in prostitution or concubinage. Such cohabitation is seldom sanctioned by any contract, or even ritual, which they or their kith and kin would acknowledge, or which they themselves would regard as binding, if they left the country or decided later to marry one of their own "color."

From their point of view the position seems simple, but it is very different as far as the native women are concerned. Very few of these are recognized in their own society as prostitutes to be hired or sold. They have their place as potential wives and mothers in the native system of reciprocal bonds between clans, families and other social groups. They are important links, and their betrothal and marriage set in operation series of mutual gifts and services and other forms of behaviour, on which the maintenance of social and economic activity and of social cohesion depends. But the "permanent" and even temporary liaisons of women with white men disturb and partly disrupt the normal working of the social system. As a result, some betrothals cannot be fulfilled, and apart from the resulting dissatisfaction and sense of deprivation, the several social, economic and ceremonial bonds which should have been forged between the groups concerned, fail to materialize. In this way damage is done to the community—damage which is not repaired by the gifts which the women may be able to obtain and distribute to their relations. In these liaisons, the woman and, of course, the non-native man with whom she cohabits, remain outside the native social structure, and the gifts do not require an exchange of effort or gifts on the part of her relations, as would occur in native marriages.

The woman also runs the risk of finding no place, psychological or marital, in the structure if she is discarded by her non-native *de facto* husband, or is no longer wanted as a prostitute by non-natives. She may, indeed, have to become a prostitute in the village to which she returns, or else seek a haven on a Mission. The degree of social insecurity or ostracism which such a woman incurs varies from society to society. The non-native man, however, can drop her, and she has no redress. In other words, she has legally no rights in this matter.

. . . Thus, through the woman, an attack is made, though not designed, on the spirit, and on the very existence, of the tribe. Her position as a social or tribal personality is not considered; she is just thoughtlessly regarded as an individual of sexual possibilities, with no need for social security for her life. The disposal or use of her person, her body, is not considered in relation either to her society's rights or to her own as a human being and a woman.

. . . Finally, we see inherent in these conditions of contact in marginal regions that *Primitive Woman has a Right to a secure sex position with its related social and economic role in her own society, that this role is essential to the latter's existence, and that neither she nor her society should be deprived of her role by prostitution, concubinage or any temporary and non-legalized form of sexual liaison with men of the dominant and intruding group.*

(8) *The Mixed-Blood Minority Group's Right to the* Rights of the Society of which it forms part.

. . . The real difficulty is that in this Pacific and Australian region, the mixed-blood is culturally and socially a "half-caste." When brought up, as is common, in some degree of association with non-natives, he finds it difficult to fit in satisfactorily to the natives' way of life; but he also realizes that he is not acceptable to the non-native society. To members of the latter, he is just a native, and any attempt on his part to rise in social and cultural life is met with strong prejudice. Consequently, he is a misfit, and lacks a social personality. It is only as the mixed-bloods in a region increase in numbers to such an extent that they intermarry and form "in-groups" of their own, that some degree of personal integration can be attained. In relation, however, to the dominant community, the mixed-bloods' attitudes and patterns of behaviour—partly native and partly European—can be irritating, the result of their realizing their outcaste position.

. . . The obvious fact in Australia and in the Islands is the growth of the mixed-blood group, struggling for economic, social and cultural rights, and in time demanding to be freed from discrimination. To prevent or to tide over this stage, mixed-blood minority groups must be given the content, not merely the formal pronouncement, of political, legal, economic, social, cultural and religious rights as part of the total community.

In other words, *Mixed-Blood Minority Groups are entitled to, and should be accorded, a Right to the rights acknowledged in the Society of which they form a part, and to be freed from "race" discrimination.*

(9) *The Right of Justice.*

. . . In the relations of the representatives of an administering or possessing people with a non-literate indigenous people the maintenance of justice is likely to be supplanted by what is considered good for the latter, and, at best, by a considerate and sincere paternalism. This is usually considered unavoidable, especially when, as in Melanesia, there is no strong centralized native political system, through which "indirect rule" can be instituted" It means, however, the *imposition* of rules of behaviour in social, economic, and even religious spheres.

But regulations governing community behaviour are not likely to be considered just unless both they, and the sanctions enforcing them, are self-imposed either on the basis of established custom or of legislative measures, or at least are understood and accepted as fair in the circumstances. What usually happens in the contact situation, however, is that the orders are obeyed and the sanctions accepted because they are the fiat of the Administration or Government, which has the physical force to back its fiats. Alternatively, they may be accepted and followed because the local administrative officers are respected.

Such administration may be for the good of the native people, but this is not necessarily an acknowledgement that the latter possess fundamental human rights.

. . . This process of "conquering rule" under forms of Justice requires constant watchful examination, and replacement by forms germane to native ways of maintaining equitable relations between individuals, and between individuals and the total community. There are such forms. In addition, a new content must be given to the forms to meet the problems arising from contact and the process of civilizing. By education, by showing respect to Primitive Man as a Human Being of intelligence, who possesses Rights of the same order as Civilized Man, and by willingness to co-operate with him, a solution of the problem of Justice will be obtained.

To put the matter briefly: *Primitive Man in the Contact situation and in non-self-governing conditions has a Right to contribute to the constitution, content and working of the forms through which Justice is sought and administered.*

(10) *The Right to Political Self-Determination*

. . . It is often overlooked that there are always some members of a native people who are quite unaware of their subordinate position, resent it, and occasionally become vocal about it. This comes as a shock to well-intentioned administrators, but is taken as proof by many employers and caste-conscious settlers of the natives' treacherous or ungrateful character. Moreover, if a limited but subordinate share in the policy making and administration be given to educated natives, they are apt to be irritated by this limitation, and to resent openly the policy and its implementation, just because it is, at least in the last resort, imposed.

. . . On grounds of expediency, therefore, the problem of political self-determination and self-government of native peoples needs to be tackled quickly. Moreover, this time-condition is important and even fundamental. To withhold a Right from a people because they are not considered ready for it by the governing power, or because the time is not considered convenient for granting it, is an infringement of the Right. Steps therefore should be taken to prepare both parties for association in government and administration, and to make this effective on a basis of equality and self-determination in the shortest possible time.

This is, *primitive peoples have a fundamental community Right to political self-determination. Where this has been taken from them, it should be returned in a form, worked out with their co-operation, to meet the present circumstances of contact with the civilized world.*

(11) *The Community's and Individual's Right to Freedom of Religious Beliefs and Practices.*

The religious beliefs and practices of any people are part of its equipment for providing moral and social sanctions, for dealing with the contingent and for furnishing grounds of certainty and hope in the face of apparently unsolved problems of life and death. In other words, religion is a mechanism of adaptation to the total environment—social and geographical, past present and future, seen and unseen, known and unknown. Since, however, this total environment varies for each particular people, its means of adaptation, including religion, must be its own, worked out in its own history. Thus, in spite of its universal aspects, religion appears only in "national" or "tribal" forms, interrelated with the other institutions and with the total way of life of each particular nation or tribe. This fact underlies the conflicts of religions in the past. Those conflicts have not been simply concerned with different dogmas or rituals, but also with political, economic and social differences and ambitions. The religious dogma provided the inspiring symbol on which the various interrelated motives and urges were centered. This is true also of the religious conflicts within Christendom; and even in the cases of denominational conflicts within one national boundary, motives besides those connected with doctrinal or ritual differences operate, for example, the struggle for political or administrative power, and the carry-over from earlier national and territorial divisions.

In other words, religion is not an independent cultural trait, with only incidental influence on, or relation to, other cultural traits. Likewise, it is not wholly a matter of individual relationship between the believer and the supernatural object of his belief. Indeed, except in an age of sophistication and cultural breakdown, religion is very much more a matter of cultural heritage than individual decision, for what is at stake is not simply individual salvation, but national or tribal continuity.

. . . Amongst a primitive people, however, the part played by religious and magical beliefs and institutions in the functioning of society is so vital and complex, that hastily to undermine the former, as by conversion of individuals, is to jeopardize the whole social structure. Moreover, the individuals, so converted by, and attracted to, the new and foreign religion, are not aware of the social effects of the change in their beliefs and in their attitudes to accepted customs. It is also doubtful whether the adults of the community as a whole realize these consequences, though they may be puzzled by the conversions and may resent them. The implication is that in much "successful" missionary activity, the right of a primitive people to determine the content and course of its culture is not respected. Indeed, comparatively few Christian missionaries in the past have been concerned with the principle of freedom in religion. Urged on by the injunction "to preach the Gospel to every creature," to baptise, and so save them from eternal damnation, they have paid little or no respect to the cults of the people whom they sought to convert. In particular, they have shown little appreciation of the functional role of those cults in community life. Moreover, they have urged on individuals a creed derived from a western cultural and social context, without advising them that only after a long period could this creed, with its implications for social relationships, and the native way of life be adjusted to each other. In short, the native adherents were not aware of the social effects of accepting the introduced creed. Generally speaking, too, the missionaries were also unaware of this, although they did deliberately attack some social and moral customs. They also took pride in the convert who remained steadfast, in spite of a conflict of loyalties, to the missionary and to the new creed on the one hand, and to the traditional beliefs and social practices on the other hand.

In addition, too, the missionaries in most primitive regions had behind them the prestige, authority and force of the European administration. It is, therefore, doubtful whether the natives' conversion was based on freedom of choice amongst alternatives, seeing that they were ignorant of the implications of their decision, and that they could not be unmindful of the authority attached to the missionaries.

On the other hand, it must be remembered that missionaries have seldom been the only, or the first, contacts which the natives had with western civilization. Traders, planters, recruiters and administrative officers were, and are, also its representatives. And if the economic and administrative interference has been, and will be, allowed, it is difficult to argue against the presence and work of missionaries in the South and South-west Pacific. In the first place, Christianity is an integral and historic element in western civilization, and as native peoples are to be brought into closer relationship with that civilization, they should see it as a whole, and understand its sanctions and ideals. In the second place, about half of the native peoples are adherents of various Missions, and many of them are keen Christian missionaries, who will in time work out an adjustment of Christianity and native life. Moreover, the contact situation as a whole has resulted in much disintegration of native moral and social sanctions and loss of spiritual beliefs. It is, therefore, reasonable to present other religious sanctions and beliefs, especially those which are part and parcel of the invading culture and of the civilization to which, in the modern world, they must become adjusted.

. . . To sum up: In the contact position of Civilized Administering Peoples and Primitive Peoples, the Right to Freedom of Religious Belief and Practice is inherent in a People's Right to Cultural Self-determination, provided that the individual's Right to life and health is not infringed. With regard to this proviso, no Administration will permit any rites, even though associated with religion, which are repugnant to the enlightened conscience of mankind, such as head-hunting, cannibalism, human sacrifice, exposure of the dead in villages and prostitution. The Right of the community or people as a whole to self-determination and existence must be weighed against the Right of the individual to freedom of choice in what he regards as his personal benefit or salvation.

In the contact position, the Right to Freedom of Religious Belief and Practice is a communal as well as an individual Right, and attacking the former through the latter may lead to disintegration of the community, and not to religious progress.

In the contact position as it is, the native peoples have a Right to understand the religious element in western civilization, but to have it presented to them without any suggestion of compulsion or material inducement, and without implied or associated condemnation of their indigenous beliefs and sanctions. With education and understanding of the differences, they will make their decision. Whether this be to modify or to condemn the latter or to blend the old and new, or to reject the new, its value will depend on the understanding of the individual and community implications with which it is made, for religion is a social institution and not merely an individual satisfaction.

Therefore, in the present-day contact situation, a *Primitive Man both as a Community and as an Individual, has a Right, inherent in that of cultural Self-Determination, to Freedom of Religious Belief and Practice. This involves both respect for indigenous beliefs and sanctions, and the "free" presentation of the religion of the dominant and invading culture.*

(12) *The Right to Health of Body, Mind and Spirit.*

The contact of Europeans with peoples of primitive culture in the South and Southwest Pacific and in Australia, has had several disastrous effects. New diseases have been introduced against which no immunity existed. The taking of natives from their own environment to work in another quite different one, has taken its toll. The decrease of the village food-producing and reproductive powers through over-recruitment has had debilitating and depopulating effects in some regions, which are only very slowly, if ever, overcome by closing the latter to recruiting. The diet-scale and health on some plantations and stations have been far from satisfactory. And finally, many natives in the islands died during the early and desperate stages of the Japanese War from dietary deficiencies and disregard of other health measures.

In spite, therefore, of the devoted work of missionaries during the past fifty years, and of a limited amount of health services conducted by the Administrations, the native peoples' health has not, speaking generally, gained from the coming of the European.

This does not mean that their health was perfect in pre-white days; for example, malaria and deficiency diseases took their toll. But it is only in recent years that civilized man has begun to admit that *Primitive Man has a Right to Physical Health.* This admission, however, implies a heavy responsibility, namely, expensive surveys of diseases and of diet and the gathering of vital statistics amongst primitive peoples, especially amongst those to whom civilization owes much by way of reparation for the damage to health and population wrought since contact began.

The illness developed by Primitive Man out of the contact-situation, has not only been physical in nature. It has also affected his mental and spiritual adjustment. The success of Government officers, of missionaries and of employers in attracting the younger generation away from traditional sanctions and ways of life and even from the villages and camps to live in foreign ways, has caused much mental distress and conflict in the elders. Often, too, the "younger" become disillusioned after they reach middle-age and realize that they have not been, and are not likely to be, admitted to the Europeans' way of life, except in an inferior degree and in a separate caste. They see that they are used, and at best, patronized. The resulting so-called inferiority complexes are manifested in attitudes which are described as cheeky or dangerous, and which did result, in the war in the Islands, in a few cases of betrayal. Actually they are symptoms of contact-illness, physiological in nature. Moreover, as seen in the introduction, primitive peoples are too often compelled by circumstances to play an inferior or child-like and subservient role, which they despise. Unfortunately, this can become an accepted habit and prevent that progress in arts and crafts of which they are capable. In other words, they become mentally dull. In the long run, of course, this does not pay the invading and employing group.

No group, however, whether dominant or not, has a right to cause psychological illness or mental backwardness in another group, any more than one individual would be granted a right so to afflict another. On the contrary, every people has a *Right to Mental Health and Development.* The corollary to this is that the administering Power must remove the causes of such mental illness and retardation, and provide such educational and economic opportunity that Primitive Man's ability will be fully developed.

. . . Thus, as we see him in the contact-situation, *Primitive Man has a Right to Physical, Mental and Spiritual Health, in short, to a fit and good life. While admitting this as a fundamental human Right for the members of a society, within that society, we see that in the contact-situation, it takes on the aspect of just reparation, which it is the duty of the administering Power to pay.*

III.

CONCLUSION AND SUMMARY

The question of Human Rights is one of the relationship of the individual to his fellows within a community, and of community to community. Fundamentally, the individual is a social personality, and his rights are an integral part of his place and role in his society and in its external relationships. Apart from the society he would have no rights. But, because his personality is socially conditioned, his rights are not co-terminous with his desires, but can only exist in so far as they do not impinge upon the rights of the rest of the community. The basic necessity is the living together. Consequently, the community must have rights as against the individual, but in the interest of all its members. In the larger world of contact, too, it must have rights admitted by other communities or powers, so that its members will have a social and cultural continuum; for without this, they could not become social personalities.

The form and content, however, of both communal and individual rights vary in the different situations and conditions of a community's history, including its contacts with other peoples. Human rights therefore have to be reviewed from time to time both as to form and content, lest they become so abstract and generalized as to be meaningless in actual human relations. Thus the propositions that an individual, as a human being, has a right to his life, to the free disposal of his physical and intellectual powers, and to as much food as he needs, especially if he has earned the means for obtaining this—may seem fundamental and enduring rights. But when a community is in jeopardy, through war or food shortage, these rights give place to the right of the community to persist, even at the expense of the individual.

And this aspect of relativity applies to all human rights, for they arise out of, and are conditioned by, the necessity of communal life, the mould and nurturer of personality. But this communal living implies mutual respect, which in turn demands a *modus vivendi*—a complex of rights and duties arising from a common source, the former mutually accepted, and the latter generally acknowledged, and socially enforced. This *modus vivendi*, however, must change as the generations change, as knowledge and contacts increase, and as aspirations become more complex.

Human rights, therefore, have no content unless they are related intimately and causally to the actual community situation. For example, the change of a country's basic economy from agriculture to manufacture deprives the farmers of their previous rights and security, for these can no longer be guaranteed, while decades may pass before fresh content and, indeed, form can be given to the 'rights' of the individual, now a factory hand, for many issues are involved. So too, the Melanesian had his *modus vivendi*, with its rights and duties, in his village—gardening—fishing—clan-organized social organizations. But contact with the bearers of civilization has disrupted this system, and a modified complex of rights and duties has to be evolved, which accepts the intrusion of western civilization, non-natives, central and regional administration as distinct from village and clan systems, new ideas of law, of morality and of religion, employment, trade, "half-castes" and so on.

It is in the light of this context in the South and South-west Pacific and in Australia, that this series of twelve rights, each preceded by a preamble, suggesting its causal context, is here presented.

These, like all rights, can be guaranteed only by the communities and administrations concerned,—and that in three ways: (i) By positive legislative or administrative action designed to ensure some or all of them. (ii) By legislative or administrative action of a negative or protective kind, prohibiting under penalty interference with the individual in certain spheres of activity. (iii) By officially doing nothing, except being a latent court of appeal, and leaving the individuals free to determine their own behavior within the limits set by the positive and negative action mentioned, that is, without damaging the rights of others. The effectiveness of these methods however, in the contact position, depends on the development of supporting public opinion amongst both the native and nonnative elements in the population. The existence of the legislation, regulations and courts help in this regard, provided that the natives are encouraged and educated to use their rights and to perform the correlated duties. Otherwise rights, policies and regulations remain a dead letter, interred quietly by those non-natives who desire the *status quo*. Fortunately, the moral pressure of an informed and enlightened world-conscience, through international groups and organizations, or administering powers, can do much to make these rights effective in the culture-contact situation and amongst non-self-governing peoples.

Only a careful analysis of the position in each region could determine whether the twelve rights suggested here, are of wider application. Possibly they contain principles which could be applied in most contact and minority-group situations, though their content and application might need to be considerably varied.

June 1947

HUMAN FREEDOMS AND HINDU THINKING
S. V. Puntambekar[*]

The proper study of mankind is man. There is something more in man than is apparent in his ordinary consciousness and behaviour under a given system of environment, something which frames ideals and values of life. There is in him a finer spiritual presence which makes him dissatisfied with merely earthly pursuits. The ordinary condition of man is not his ultimate being. He has in him a deeper self, call it soul or spirit. In each being dwells a light and inspiration which no power can extinguish, which is benign and tolerant, and which is the real man. It is our business to discover him, protect him and see that he is utilized for his own and humanity's welfare. It is the nature of this man to search for the true, the good and the beautiful in life, to esteem them properly and to strive for them continuously.

Then we must note that there is also an incalculable element in the human will and an endless complexity of human nature. No system, no order, no law can satisfy the deep and potential demands of a great personality, be they religious, political, social or educational. Men are often endowed with great potential energy and creative power which cannot be encased within the bounds of old formulas and doctrines. No fixed discipline can suit the developing possibilities of new human manifestations in the psychological, ethical or spiritual fields. No system can satisfy the growing needs of a dynamic personality. There always

---

[*] As with Humayun Kabir, S. V. Puntambekar was recommended to Julian Huxley in an April 1947 letter by the Indian philosopher Sarvepalli Radhakrishnan. Puntambekar was an Indian political scientist and Hindu nationalist who played an important role in the development of the discipline of political science in India, both before and after independence from the British Empire. He was a strong critic of a secular state, agreeing, instead, with Gandhi, that "there are no politics without religion. Politics bereft of religion are a death trap because they kill the soul." At the time of the UNESCO human rights survey, Puntambeker was a professor of history and political science at the Hindu University in Benares and the president of the Indian Political Science Association. Earlier in his career, Puntambekar had been a supporter of Mussolini and had published an article in 1927 calling for the establishment of what he called a "democracy dictatorship" in India.

remains something unthought of and unrealized in the system. Hence we want freedom for man in the shape of human freedoms.

There is always a tendency for new values and new ideals to arise in human life. No ready formulas end systems can satisfy the needs and visions of great thinkers and of all peoples and periods. Freedom is necessary because authority is not creative. Freedom gives full scope to developing personality and creates conditions for its growth. No uniformity or conformity or comprehension of all aspects of life will be helpful. The present centralization of all authority, its bureaucracy and party dictatorship, its complexity and standardization, leave little scope for independent thought and development, for initiative and choice.

. . . Can we be aware of a call for national freedom and for human freedom, when we are so rigid, inflexible, fanatic and exclusive in our political, religious, cultural and socio-economic outlook? Not having succeeded in disposing our rules and system on all countries and continents, some of us still harbour feelings of superiority and hatred, coercion and dominance against our neighbors.

Therefore first let us "be men," and then lay down the contents, qualities and inter-relations of human freedoms. We must respect humanity and personality, tolerate our differences end others' ways of internal and external group behavior, and combine to serve one another in calamities and in great undertakings.

To talk of human rights in India is no doubt very necessary and desirable, but hardly possible in view of the socio-cultural and religio-political complexes which are so predominant today. There are no human beings in the world of today, but only religious men, racial men, caste men or group men. Our intelligentsia and masses are mad after racial privileges, religion bigotry and social exclusiveness. In short we are engaged in a silent war of extermination of opposite groups. Our classes and communities think in terms of conquest and subjugation, not of common association and citizenship. There is at present a continuous war of groups and communities, of rulers and ruled, in our body politic and body social, from which all conception of humanity and tolerance, all notion of humility and respect, have disappeared. Bigotry, intolerance and exclusiveness sit enthroned in their stead.

The world is mad today. It runs after destruction and despotism, world conquest and world order, world loot and world dispossession. The enormous hatred generated against human life and achievements has left no sense of humanity or human love in the world politics of today. But shall we renounce "being men" first and always? What we want is freedom from want and war, from fear and frustration in life. We also went freedom from an all-absorbing conception of the state, the community and the church coercing individuals to particular and ordered ways of life. Along with this we desire freedom of thought and expression of movement and association, of education and of expansion in the mental and moral spheres. In any defined and ordered plan for living, we must have the right of non-violent resistance and autonomy, in order to develop our ideas of the good human life.

For this purpose we shall have to give up some of the superstitions of material science and limited reason, which make man too much this-worldly, and introduce higher spiritual aims and values for mankind. Then on that basis we shall have to organize our social life in all its aspects. We want not only the material conditions of a happy life but also the spiritual virtues of a good life. Man's freedom is being destroyed by the demands of economic technocracy, political bureaucracy and religious idiosyncrasy.

Great thinkers like Manu and Buddha have laid emphasis on what should be *assurances* necessary for man and what should be the *virtues* possessed by man. They have propounded a code as it were of *ten essential human freedoms* and *controls* or *virtues* necessary for good life. They are not only basic, but more comprehensive in their scope than those mentioned by any other modern thinkers. They emphasize *five freedoms* or *social assurances* and five *individual possessions* or *virtues*. The five social freedoms are (1) freedom from violence (Ahimsa), (2) freedom from want (Asteya), (3) freedom from exploitation (Aparigraha), (4) freedom from violation or dishonor (Avyabhichara) and (5) freedom from early death and disease (Armitatva and Arogya). The five individual possessions or virtues are (1) absence of intolerance (Akrodha), (2) compassion or fellow feeling (Bhutadaya, Adroha), (3) knowledge (Jnana, vidya), (4) freedom of thought and conscience (Satya, Sunrta) and (5) freedom from fear and frustration or despair (Pravrtti, Abhaya, Dhrti).

Human freedoms require as counterparts human virtues or controls. To think in teams of freedoms without corresponding virtues would lead to a lop-sided view of life and a stagnation or even a deterioration of personality, and also to chaos and conflict in society. This two-sidedness of human life, its freedoms and virtues or controls, its assurances and possessions must be understood and established in any scheme for the welfare of man, society and humanity. Alone, the right to life, liberty and property or pursuit of happiness is not sufficient; neither, alone, is the assurance of liberty, equality and fraternity. Human freedoms and virtues must be more definite and more comprehensive if they are to help the physical, mental and spiritual development of man and humanity.

In order to prevent this open and latent warfare of mutual extermination, national and international, we must create and develop a new man or citizen assured and possessed of these *tenfold freedoms* and *virtues* which are the fundamental values of human life, and conduct. Otherwise our freedoms will fail in their objects and in their mission to save man and his mental and moral culture from the impending disaster with which the whole human civilization is now threatened by the lethal weapons of science and the inhuman robots of despotic and coercive powers and their ideologies and creeds.

We in India also want freedom from foreign rule and civil warfare. Foreign rule is a damnable thing. This land has suffered from it for hundreds of years. We must condemn it, whether old or new. We must have self-rule in our country under one representative, responsible and centralized system. Then alone we shall survive.

I know that men who are devoted to and dominated by rigid ideas of cultures and religions cannot feel the call of national or human freedom. But we cannot give up higher objectives and aspirations for their sake and their prejudices.

THE RIGHTS OF DEPENDENT PEOPLES
Leonard Barnes[*]

... The general picture of a colony, is of a territory where economic subordination entails political disability; where political disability may bring with it severe restrictions upon civil liberty and an exceptional widening of the legal meaning at the word "sedition" (such restrictions being at their most severe when the metropolitan authorities regard the native culture as backward or inferior); and where official anxiety about sedition and allied offences leads to judicial and police practices which in the metropolitan country would be regarded as unusually harsh.

The consequence is that the subject peoples as a whole, and particularly their more cultivated and better educated representatives, exhibit to a marked degree the frustrations and the corruptions of impotence. For it should not be forgotten that, true as it may be that absolute power corrupts absolutely, the psychological effects of absolute powerlessness are no less damaging.

---

[*] Leonard Barnes was a British academic, government adviser, and anti-colonialist writer. After serving in the First World War, where he was a highly decorated solider (receiving the Military Cross), Barnes studied at Oxford University. After serving briefly in the Foreign Service, Barnes went to South Africa, where he worked as a farmer and journalist. He returned to Britain in 1932 to begin a long academic career. In 1947, Barnes was appointed director of what later became the Department of Social and Administrative Studies at Oxford. He was the author of many books on South Africa, race relations, and educational policy, including *Caliban in Africa: An Impression of Colour Madness* (1931), *The New Boer War* (1932), *Empire or Democracy?* (1939), and *African Renaissance* (1969).

Formulations of human rights naturally tend to reflect the major frustrations of those who make them. If a right, declared and claimed, is to be more than an empty aspiration, if it is to serve as "a working conception and effective instrument," it will express the natural demands of dissatisfied groups and of the have-nots of the social order. Liberty is the cry of the bond, equality the cry of the victim of discrimination, fraternity the cry of the outcast, progress and humanity are the cry of those whom their fellows use as means instead of respecting as ends, full employment is the cry of the worker whose daily job or lack of job stunts his soul and mocks his capabilities, social planning is the cry of those who are trampled underfoot when privilege and power strive to make the world safe for themselves. That is why declarations of the rights of man are strong allies of social progress, at least when they are first promulgated. For social progress *is* reorganization in the interests of the unprivileged.

Hence it might be predicted that when colonial peoples set about drafting a Bill of Rights their claims will tally generally with those of depressed and disabled groups everywhere, but will also show a special distribution of emphasis corresponding to the special character of colonial disabilities. And in fact, wherever colonial discontent achieves articulate form, it shows a keen awareness both of the fundamental significance of an equity-less economy, with its necessary corollary of political subordination, and of the organic connection between these and the denials of civil liberty common in colonial territories. It is, further, ready enough to subscribe to the traditional democratic slogans of liberty, equality, and fraternity, partly because colonial peoples have wide experience of being used as means to other people's ends, and partly because such slogans are handy for embarrassing the metropolitan authorities.

But all these diverse sentiments and attitudes are given a particular colouring, they wear a particular livery, distinctive of colonial experience. This colour, this livery, is the claim to equal rights with citizens of the metropolis, the protest against a discrimination that appears, to those on whom it falls, to be as arbitrary as it is comprehensive.

For this reason progressive movements among colonial peoples tend to assume a nationalist and liberationist form. They are liberationist because their awakening political consciousness sees the established constitutional ties with the metropolis as emblems of foreign domination. They are nationalist because separate nationhood is the repository of state power, and without state power at their disposal the liberationists can neither sever their political and economic dependence on the metropolis nor take over the administrative functions of the metropolis after the severance has been made.

We should, therefore, see the colonial peoples both as aggregations of individuals repressed and thwarted by specific forms of disprivilege, and as emergent nations struggling to attain equal status with the so-called independent countries in point of sovereignty and international recognition. The claim—we emphasize this—is to formal equality of status. It is not to material equality of function. Nor is it necessarily to full national sovereignty in the classical signification of the term. Colonial peoples object to limitations of sovereignty when they are fastened on them from without, and appear as badges of inferiority. They might well accept limitations, provided they could do so of their own choice in the interests of effective international organization, and provided they were assured that the majority of other free countries were genuinely making the same acceptance.

Such is the position of the dependent peoples, and such are their needs or rights. The needs cannot be satisfied by legislative enactment, nor can the rights be guaranteed by constitutional charter. Attempts to give the force of unalterable law to the claims of particular groups or communities have often been made. But since no legislators can bind their successors for ever, the attempts prove in the end either fruitless or superfluous.

For the hope of seeing their claims acknowledged in practice the colonial peoples must rely on the establishment and maintenance of certain broad politico-economic conditions inside and outside their own countries. Of such conditions perhaps the most indispensable are:—

(a) an international system of co-operative peace and defense, without which the security and integrity of small countries tend to be merely nominal;

(b) social planning of the lend-lease type, under which the colonies could draw on the richer countries for capital needed for colonial development, without surrendering the equity in that development, and without creating such vested interests in the colonies themselves as may impede the growth of popular responsibility in either the economic or the political field;

(c) a working system of political and economic organization both in the metropolitan countries and in the colonies, such that social power and responsibility may be given the widest possible distribution; as education in the colonies widens the compass of popular responsibility, so political advances should extend the opportunities for its exercise;

(d) full employment both in the metropolitan countries and in the colonies; and this not merely in the sense of a productive job of some kind for every man and woman able and willing to take it, but also in the ampler sense of work offering scope for the highest skill that each individual, in the given social conditions, is capable of developing.

Human Rights as History and Practice

THE FUTURE OF LIBERALISM
Benedetto Croce[*]

Declarations of Rights (of the *natural and inalienable rights of man*, to quote the French Declaration of 1789) are all based upon a theory which criticism on many sides has succeeded in destroying: namely, the theory of natural right, which had its own particular grounds during the 16th, 17th and 18th centuries, but which has become philosophically and historically quite untenable. Nor can we argue from the moral character of such rights, for morality recognizes no rights which are not, at the same time, duties, and no authority but itself—this is not a natural fact but the first spiritual principle.

This, moreover, is already implied in the report you have sent me, when it says that these rights vary *historically*; thereby abandoning the logical basis of those rights regarded as universal rights of man, and reducing them to, at most, the rights of *man in history*. That is to say, rights accepted as such for men of a particular time. Thus, they are not eternal claims but simply historical facts, manifestations of the needs of such and such an ago and an attempt to satisfy those needs. As an historical fact the Declaration of 1789 had its importance, since it expresses a general agreement which had developed under European culture and civilization of the 18th century (the Age of Reason, of Enlightenment, etc.) concerning the certain urgent need of a political reform of European society (including European society in America).

---

[*] Benedetto Croce was 81 years old, and nearing the end of his remarkable life, when he contributed to the UNESCO human rights survey. Croce came from a wealthy family that suffered a terrible tragedy in 1883, when he was 17: an earthquake struck the village of Casamicciola where the family was vacationing, killing his parents and only sister and burying Croce in the rubble. Croce, who barely survived, later inherited his family's fortune and used it to support a lifetime of learning, contemplation, and writing. He eventually became Italy's most influential intellectual and one of the most important philosophers of the first half of the twentieth century. Although he initially supported Mussolini, he soon became a strong critic of the Fascist regime, drafting the public "Manifesto of the Anti-Fascist Intellectuals" in 1925. After the Second World War, Croce served in various governmental roles. Among his most important works are *Aesthetic* (1902), *Philosophy of the Practical: Economic and Ethic* (1908), and *What is Living and What is Dead of the Philosophy of Hegel* (1915).

Today, however, it is no longer possible to realize the purpose of the Declaration, whether of rights or of historical needs, for it is precisely that agreement on the subject which is lacking and which Unesco desires to promote. Agreement, it is obvious, is lacking in the two most important currents of world opinion: the liberal current and the authoritarian-totalitarian current. And indeed that disagreement, though moderated in its expression, may be discerned in the report I have before me.

Will this agreement be obtained? And by what means? By the reinvigoration of the current of liberalism, whose moral superiority, power of thought and persuasion and whose political wisdom and prudence will prevail over the other current? Or will it be through a new world war which will bring victory to one or the other side, according to the fortunes of war, the course of events or Divine Providence? And would the immortal current of liberalism emerge from its opposite, should the latter be temporarily victorious?

I assume that Unesco reckons with the first alternative or hypothesis and I need not tell you that, for my part, I am heart and soul in favor of this endeavour for which each of us is bound to work with all his energies and for which I myself have been working for nearly 25 years in Italy and also further afield.

If that is so, however, a working organization such as that you invite me to and in which representatives of all currents, especially the two most directly opposed, will participate with the same rights, cannot possibly proclaim in the form of a Declaration of Rights, a declaration of common political action, an agreement which has no existence, but which must, on the contrary, be the ultimate outcome of opposed and convergent efforts. That is the point to be carefully considered, for it is the *weak point*.

Nor do I even see how it would be possible to formulate any half-way or compromise declaration which would not prove either empty or arbitrary. It may be that you and your colleagues, when you get to work, will discover the futility and the impossibility of it and even, if you will allow me to say so, the danger of causing readers to smile at the ingenuousness of men who have conceived and formulated such a Declaration.

In my opinion, there is only one useful form of practical work for Unesco to do: namely, a formal, public and international debate on the necessary principles underlying human dignity and civilization. In such a debate I do not doubt that the force of logic, culture, doctrine and the possibility of fundamental agreement would secure the triumph of free minds over the adherents of autocracy and totalitarianism, who are still reduced to reiterating the same slogans and the same sophistries to catch the public ear. Once that debate was held, it would no doubt be possible to formulate a declaration of certain historical and contemporary rights and needs in some such short form as the Ten Commandments or, if it were to include details, at somewhat greater length.

Naples, 15 April 1947
(Translated from Italian)

REFLECTIONS ON SOME DECLARATIONS OF THE RIGHTS OF MAN
*Jean Haesaert**

The Memorandum on Human Rights dated 27 March 1947 brings out, clearly and completely, the difficulties in the way of any general Declaration today. Having as its object "to reconcile by some means the various divergent or opposing formulations now in existence," it must be not only "sufficiently definite to have real significance both as an inspiration and as a guide to practice," but also "sufficiently general and flexible to apply to all men, and to be capable of modification to suit peoples at different stages of social and political development while yet retaining significance for them and their aspirations." Is not this what is called squaring the circle?

Moreover, all the declarations which have played a part in modern history, from the 1776 *Declaration of Independence* down to the Fourth French Republic's declaration of rights in 1946, have stumbled, *mutatis mutandis*, against similar difficulties. Their authors were unable, more particularly, to solve the technical problem before them, a problem which the Memorandum has very properly stressed on the present occasion.

I am not speaking of the obscurities, misconceptions and contradictions which these documents reveal. Discussion of the documents, which generally began in an atmosphere of enthusiasm, more often resulted in votes dictated by exhaustion, in which such peccadilloes were passed over. There are more serious shortcomings than these, and they represent real professional mistakes.

---

* Jean Haesaert was a Belgian legal scholar, lawyer, and judge who was a professor at Ghent University at the time of the UNESCO human rights survey. Haesaert had wide academic and intellectual interests, having published on art history, religion, and educational policy earlier in his life. He also played a role in the development of the sociology of law in Belgium. Haesaert was a strong critic of natural law theories and abstract conceptions of law more generally, describing the interest in natural law (and perhaps human rights) as a "temporary disease." His works include *The Foundation of Natural Law* (1933), *The Theory of Law* (1935), and *A General Theory of Law* (1948).

I would mention the following:

1. These proclamations quickly dated. They were overtaken by events and their effects betrayed the intentions of those who drafted them. Freedom of labour in the United States of America opened the way to strikes which imperiled victory and are even today prejudicing a return to normalcy. The freedom of the trade-unions has been marshaled against the State. The freedom of the press has become the perquisite of a few magnates who, whatever one may say, make and unmake opinion. Adjustments have everywhere been necessary: the 116,000,000 working days which they lost in 1946 will perhaps lead the Americans to revise the *National Labor Relations Act* and to forbid collective abandonment of work.

. . . . Other provisions in the declarations have remained a dead letter. Equality has been reduced to the narrow civic equality that we know so well. Political equality has barely begun and economic equality is not considered. Resistance to oppression is hunted down wherever it appears, but oppression itself is flourishing, thanks to the crises which pursue us, and it threatens rights the possessors of which have no means of defending themselves.

These facts are sufficient proof that all the work so far done has been ineffective. It has been ineffective because no realism, no sense of law and no professional skill were brought to bear upon it.

(a) In the first place, the authors of these declarations were fired by a political passion which was still hot, or had barely cooled, and concentrated their attention upon their own special position and the times in which they lived. The Virginia *Bill of Rights* (1776) is steeped in a pioneering spirit, which was itself fed by religious fervour. The principles of 1789 reflect the revolt of the Third Estate. Those of 1793 reveal the mind of the pure revolutionaries who viewed with suspicion the encroachments of authority. The Belgian Constitution of 1831 was a reaction against the Dutch regime, while the preamble of the 1946 declaration reflects not only the 1940 psychosis but the "arrival" of the masses and their contradictory aspirations, bent as they are upon both freedom and planning.

These turbulent improvisers, with their blind concentration upon themselves, did not stop to think that a charter applies to generations to come and that, although the latter may in a general way converge in the long run, their physiognomies and structures differ. This difference produces so many surprises that it would be better, on this subject, not to commit the future in matters of detail. It is hopeless, in any case, to attempt to do so; tomorrow will have no hesitation in releasing itself from to-day, and the new rebels can resort to unforeseen stratagems to evade precautions taken by earlier stabilizers. What is to be done? The answer is that the rules laid down must apply to factors that are constant. I do no[t] mean that they should crumble away in abstractions. They must remain positive, but be elastic enough to absorb change. Charters should contain only what is essential. The rest is matter for the law, for regulations and above all for jurisprudence.

Under laws and regulations there is room for second thoughts, relaxations, adaptations and resistance to abuses. In the face of this constant give-and-take between rights and their limitation, no document could succeed in drawing a demarcation line which would cover all possible cases. It requires the intelligent intervention of the man who is able to weigh all the decisive factors and imponderabilia. The important thing is therefore to establish this office of arbitrator, and to establish it in such a way that it will be effective. This is the surest means of guaranteeing that the principle will remain constant through all the vicissitudes of history and that it will be protected against malicious attacks.

The general framework of this arrangement—the drafting of the principle and the setting up of a judicial body—must therefore be sufficiently wide to command all circumstances. A standard, therefore, is likely to be preferable to a rule.

The standard is commonly known to be a form of directive. It is a compromise between the need of a right to be secured and its need to develop. It indicates, in a general way, what the legislator wants to achieve. It develops according both to the subject-matter of the standard and the rank of the legislator; the development is greater in regard to the principle than in regard to the ways in which that principle is applied; it is greater for the constitution-maker than for the ordinary lawgiver. Articles 1 and 6 of the Soviet Penal Code, as well as Article 1 of the Soviet Civil Code, are classic examples of a standard; and there are several examples in American law, especially the *due process of law* so constantly invoked.

In the case we are considering, the subject-matter represents the very basis of social life and the legislator is represented by the member of a constituent assembly. The expansion of the formula must therefore be as wide as possible, though it must not cease to be a guide; to state, as in 1848, that the Republic is based on . . . . . "public order" has no practical significance.

(b) Moreover, on the occasion of each fresh social change, the new masters have advanced their own ideals by clothing them with the name of rights. This procedure reduces the charter to the level of a program, or even of an electoral platform; it becomes no more than a catalogue of claims, ill-assorted and impassioned; additions or deletions are made as feeling dictates. The authority of the charter is thereby undermined.

The Constitution of 1789 mentions, in somewhat of a jumble, liberty, equality, property, security, resistance against oppression, the right to take part in drawing up laws and to occupy public positions, individual freedom, freedom of opinion, and the right to fix, vote and control taxation. The Constitution of 23 June 1793, more social in character, adds not only the right of assembly, but freedom of work, culture and trade, the right to public assistance and the right of petition. The Belgian Constitution, which had the benefit of considerable recent experience and approached the matter more soberly, suppressed the right of resistance to oppression, circumscribed the right of petition and introduced the inviolability of domicile, the free use of languages, the inviolability of correspondence and the right of association. The 1946 Declaration incorporated the principles of 1789 as a whole and frenziedly added, with a stroke of the pen, the right of asylum, the right to work, the right to trades union activity, the right to strike, the right to the collective fixing of working conditions, the right to the management of enterprises and to the nationalization of the most important of them, the right to the development of the individual and the family, and the right to health, material security, rest, recreation and culture. It then surpassed itself by guaranteeing the same rights to all men and women in the French Union. At which, the lawyer, the economist and the sociologist are left breathless and aghast.

These declarations seem therefore to have been mere intellectual excursions. They take no account of ways and means; for them, everything has been achieved once the formula has been drawn up in more or less clear-cut terms. No matter what trouble it causes; no matter what the state of society is, or what means are available for putting the principles into practice; all this, to these visionaries, is trifling detail. The right to work and to manage enterprises is established, no matter whether the economy perishes as a result; when finances are exhausted, the right to leisure is proclaimed; every individual receives the right to vote, even if he cannot read and write. Circumstances, however, will not be jostled, hard facts remain hard facts. Society has its traditions, and demography its laws; economics exercises its sway, and even geography has not lost all influence. And all the while the historical situation proffers or withholds a chance, as the case may be.

2. These documents do not emphasize sufficiently that there can only be rights when they are accompanied by corresponding duties. Philosophers have always been careful to make this clear. Indeed, the *National Catholic Welfare Conference*, on 1 February last, began by defining man's duties, to fulfill which, it said, he receives certain rights. This is pushing matters too far, but it does emphasize a relationship between rights and duties in the absence of which rights alone constitute a public danger. Admittedly some declarations—for example,

those of 1789 (Article 4) and 1793 (Article 6)—acknowledge this condition; others ignore it; but none gives it its due prominence.

The result has been that disorder which is now familiar to all and the discredit which has overtaken the vaunted individualism in these declarations.

3. The technical needs of legislation also demand a structural relationship which allows some to exact and compels others to fulfill this requirement. They presuppose sanctions where the obligation is evaded. Liberty and equality may be established, but fraternity is elusive. To state in a charter, as the Americans did in 1776, that man has the right to seek happiness is to confuse terms, and to talk philosophy instead of legal regulations. It is idle to claim the right to progress or to health. Health is normally a natural gift, and progress is in the hands of fate, which walks like the blind and makes signs like the deaf

Conclusion. In the case of every single State, declarations have proved, owing to the shortcomings we have described, incapable of adjusting themselves to social evolution. If we were to make the same mistakes on the international level, these would inevitably, and even more pronouncedly, produce the same results. A common formula must therefore be restricted to principles, in their widest possible application; for the rest, each State must translate them, as need be, into the legal measures which seem most indicated. But the formula will in any case provide for the establishment within each community of a jurisdictional organ to apply the law in question, i.e. to pass from the general standard to the rule deriving therefrom, and from the rule to the particular case.

Nowhere less than here does the rule suffice to prescribe conduct or settle a conflict; it is a mere instrument, and in order to be effective requires a man who can apply it discriminatingly. He alone can assess the actual situation properly and arrive at a suitable decision in full knowledge of the facts and according to a proper procedure. Since he will be a professional, he will have no difficulty in avoiding those technical mistakes which have made the declarations so vulnerable.

An international organization cannot do more than this if it is not to run the risk of achieving something that is not only useless but dangerous.

The universal declaration would be confined to the following paragraphs:

I. Man has an indefeasible right to the respect and development of his physical and moral personality, to the extent that these are compatible with the essential needs and the potentialities of collective life; and he assumes responsibilities corresponding to those rights.

II. The law of a country decides, where necessary, how these principles are to be applied, and provides the sanctions required to ensure their effective application.

III. A special and independent court will, in each State, alone be competent in this matter. It may refuse to apply any measure that is contrary to the principles enunciated in Article I, whatever be the authority that has taken such a measure. Appeals will be heard before an International Court of Justice.

Brussels, 29 April 1947
(Translated from French)

TOWARD A BILL OF RIGHTS FOR THE UNITED NATIONS
F. S. C. Northrop [*]

A Bill of Rights for all the nations cannot be based solely upon the traditional values and ideological assumptions of any one of the nations. If it is to capture the aspirations and ideals of all the peoples of the world, it must be rooted in at least some of the accepted institutions and social doctrines of each and every people.

The usual approach to the Bill of Rights or to the establishment of any other cultural value ignores the foregoing principle. It is usual, for example, to assume that the traditional modern French and Anglo-American concept of freedom and its attendant Bill of Rights exhausts the meaning of the concept. Precisely this assumption operates when anyone proposes to extend the governmental forms of the United States of America to a United States of Europe or a United States of the World. Such proposals have always left their recipients cold.

Yet the reason for such a reaction is surely not far to seek. The classical French and Anglo-American concept of freedom, which its Bill of Rights is designed to achieve, is conceived for the most part in, or after the analogy of, purely political terms. Freedom consists both politically, economically and even religiously in being left alone. Although this is perhaps somewhat of an exaggeration,

---

[*] In 1947, at the time of the UNESCO human rights survey, F. S. C. Northrop had just been appointed Sterling Professor of Philosophy and Law at Yale University, where he was also Master of Silliman College. Northrop was involved in international academic and intellectual circles at the highest levels, counting many prominent scientists, politicians, and artists among his close friends and colleagues. In 1946, his most influential book was published, *The Meeting of East and West: An Inquiry Concerning World Understanding*, a work that was discussed closely among the UNESCO Committee of Experts at its meeting in Paris in June 1947. Correspondence shows that Northrop played a role in securing an American publisher (Columbia University Press) for *Human Rights: Comments and Interpretations*. Northrop retired from Yale in the 1960s and died in 1992 at age 98.

Emerson's dictum that the best government is the minimum government tends, according to this conception, to hold. Furthermore, the economic freedom to have the work necessary to maintain even a minimum livelihood tends to be left to chance, as a mere by-product of the individual actions of men or groups who operate independently. Similarly, psychological freedom of the sentiments, the emotions and the passions, which the Spanish and Latin Americans cherish, is hardly even recognized as existing. And often in the religious field, because of a freedom to believe any faith, there tends to arise a culture in which people have no deep-going convictions about anything. In short, the price of a society rooted in the traditional modern Bill of Rights has tended to be a culture of laissez faire businessmen's values, with all the other values and aspirations of mankind left anemic and spiritually and ideologically unsustained.

A Bill of Rights written in terms of the contemporary Russians' values and ideology would have virtues and demerits different in content but similar in its neglect of the values of other cultures. The same would be true of a Bill of Rights grounded in Spanish or Latin-American values. For the latter Bill of Rights, the price which others would have to pay would tend to be a social system which escapes social anarchy at the cost either of monarchy or military dictatorship. A Bill of Rights formulated in terms of Oriental values would illustrate the same general thesis, as the difficulties of the contemporary Orient clearly indicate.

But to become aware thus of the inadequacies of a Bill of Rights defined in terms of the traditional values and ideology of any one of the nations or cultures of the world is to find the clue to the construction of an adequate Bill of Rights for a United Nations. The values and ideology of each nation or culture throughout the world must be determined and brought out into the open in terms of their basic assumptions. The existence of these different values and ideals must be frankly and honestly faced and admitted. In fact, the basic premise of this new Bill of Rights must be the right of any people to a world so organized socially that at least some of their values and ideals can have expression. A true Bill of Rights must guarantee a world in which there can be many ideologies, not merely one ideology. In short, the foundation of an adequate Bill of Rights must be conceived not solely in terms of political freedom but in terms of a plurality of cultural values.

More, however, is necessary. A designation of the diverse ideologies of the peoples of the world shows not merely that they differ but also that certain of them contradict one another. The latter is the case with respect to the ideologies of the present Western democracies and communistic Russia. Here we reach the real heart of the difficulty: An adequate Bill of Rights must guarantee the type of world in which there can be many ideologies; yet not even a catholic Bill of

Rights can support a contradiction. For contradictories cannot be embraced. This means that an adequate Bill of Rights must both guarantee a world with a plurality of differing values and guarantee also a procedure by means of which peoples and nations can and must pass beyond their present ideologies when these ideologies are so mutually contradictory, as to threaten the peace of the world.

Unless this second guarantee is provided, a recognition and fostering of the existent ideological pluralism of our world will generate war rather than peace and destroy rather than create a united world. This follows because contradictories anywhere, if not transcended, destroy one another.

The prescription for guaranteeing a transcendence of the contradictory and conflicting valuations and social ideals of certain existent peoples and cultures of the world should be clear: obviously one must go beneath the traditional ideologies to the considerations and methods which lead people anywhere to an ideology.

No conception of human values, no economic, political or religious ideology, as the history of human civilization clearly shows, comes *a priori*, perfect in every detail, God-given from heaven. Even the founding fathers of the United States and even Karl Marx were mortal men and not a perfect God. And being mortal men, they envisaged Utopia as the lessons of history and the finite empirical knowledge at their disposal at the time permitted them to envisage it. Thus at best they got facets of the truth, but not every facet.

Analysis shows that the basic assumptions of the political and economic Utopia of classical modern French and Anglo-American democracy are those for the most part of pro-Kantian British empirical modern philosophy. It is equally well known that the philosophical assumptions of contemporary communistic Russia are those of Karl Marx. Nor did the latter philosophical assumptions spring, with complete originality, into the mind of Karl Marx directly from the perfect omniscience of God. The philosophy of Karl Marx is a composite of contributions of his human historical predecessors, namely, Hegel, Feuerbach and the French socialists.

Nor were the contributions of the British empirical philosophers to the modern French and Anglo-American conception of human values and its Bill of Rights, or the contributions of Hegel, Feuerbach, the French socialists and Marx to the communistic Russian conception of a Bill of Rights as expressed in the Russian Constitution of 1936, mere philosophical speculations. Both sets of philosophical premises brought forward empirical, scientifically verifiable information in their support. This means that the philosophical premises at the basis of the diverse human values and ideologies of the peoples of the world are in part at least scientifically testable premises. Consequently, ideological conflicts are issues which can be discussed in the light of empirical and scientific evidence and treated by means of the methods of scientific inquiry. It follows, therefore, that any Bill of Rights which will guarantee effectively the processes for transcending the inescapable contradictory and conflicting ideologies of the contemporary world must prescribe freedom of scientific inquiry and of philosophical investigation of the underlying problem to which the existent diverse, and in some cases contradictory, ideologies are different answers.

An adequate Bill of Rights, therefore, must possess two basic guarantees: (1) The guarantee of a world in which all the differing ideologies of the world gain expression, each one in part at least. (2) The guarantee of the freedom for, and the establishment of the scientific and philosophical inquiry into the basic premises of human and social ideologies necessary to provide the means for transcending and resolving the ideological conflicts of the contemporary world.

The minimum foundation for a Bill of Rights is a political philosophy which is both a philosophy of all the world's cultures and a philosophy of science. For unless this Bill of Rights is grounded in a philosophy of all the world's cultures, the first guarantee will not be met, and unless it is also grounded in a philosophy of science, the second guarantee will not be insured. Recent inquiry shows that such a scientifically verifiable, truly international political philosophy is already at hand.

June 1947

THE RIGHTS OF MAN
Peter Skov[*]

In endeavoring to complete the code of the Rights of Man, we cannot start from the philosophical first fruits of the eighteenth century. Natural right has lost its authority. The classical expression "natural, sacred, and inalienable rights" has no meaning for us. There can be no innate right, since all rights are conventional and the result of a social determinism whose causes vary with circumstances and

---

[*] Peter Skov was a Danish jurist and diplomat who studied law at the University of Copenhagen, graduating in 1907. While at the university, Skov was a founding member of the famous discussion group "Ekliptika," which included many future Danish leaders of society, politicians, and scientists, including Niels Bohr, who would win the Nobel Prize in Physics in 1922. During his diplomatic career, Skov served as a government minister, head of the minorities section of the League of Nations, and Danish ambassador to the Soviet Union, Turkey, Czechoslovakia, and Poland.

often elude us. Our political principles must be founded on practical considerations; our task is to formulate principles expressing the vital interests which all
the members of society have in common and which are in consequence also the
interests of society itself—if not of the state.

However, if our point of view differs from that of the authors of the first
historic declarations, we cannot do better than inspire ourselves with their intentions and with their way of thinking, the precise and logical way of the eighteenth century.

Nowadays, political ideas are confused and contradictory. It would be tempt-
ing to draw up an endless list of specific rights in the hope of being thus able to
solve the political and social problems of our time. Such a work would be diffuse
and would lack logical cohesion and conviction. The thinkers of the eighteenth
century proved their political acumen by formulating declarations all of whose
articles hold together because they were inspired by the same concern. Their
formula was brief and luminously clear. A natural right was, in their opinion,
a right whose justice was obvious to the common sense of every thinking man.
We must try and follow their example as best we can. A declaration lacking in
clearness and terseness would fail to command acceptance.

Formulae of a conditional character have no value. The distinguishing mark
of imprescriptible rights is precisely that they are unconditional and absolute;
they never yield to other opposed rights; they are by their nature so vital that any
other rights must give way to them.

Once it is admitted that in certain cases those rights are not applicable, the
caprices of interpretation can always invalidate them. Declarations which seek
to establish rights in circumstances contingent upon the future merely express
pious wishes. But the Rights of Man must have binding force, otherwise they
lose all value. The only restriction upon natural rights is that, if the entire system
of law disappears in circumstances of absolute necessity natural rights inevitably
share the collapse. But such circumstances—war or revolution, for instance—
must be considered as temporary and, as soon as ever the reign of law is restored,
the Rights of Man will form an indispensable part of it. New articles may be
added, but none may be taken away. Historical experience and philosophic judgment deny eternity to any institution or principle. But the popular conscience
expresses its unshakable belief in a moral or legal principle by declaring it to be
perpetual and absolute: this means only that no other principle worthy to take
its place, or to limit it, can be imagined, just as no other political or social order
can be deemed acceptable without its inclusion.

The authors of the first declarations were concerned with the protection of
individuals against the abuses of authority; the independence and freedom

of the citizen had to be guaranteed in every possible way. Historical experience had shown that abuses due to coercion by the State we re more to be feared than any threats from other individuals or groups. The State alone could justify its acts of violence by using "reasons of State" or moral considerations as their pretext. That experience, which deeply impressed the thinkers of the Revolution, has lost none of its validity today—as recent examples remind us. Nevertheless our age has a tendency to stress particularly the dangers to individual liberty from all sorts of economic and other groups. The appeal against such dangers is to the authority of State. Because democracies have successfully checked the danger of abuse by public authority, we forget that the wider the Government's sphere of action becomes, the greater is this danger.

The historic declarations of the Rights of Man aimed at setting precise limits to governmental authority and at creating a "State of Right." We, too, have good reasons to concentrate on this point and not to allow ourselves to be diverted by other far more complicated problems. The Rights of Man are the very foundations of public order and determine the relations between the citizens and the Government. The protection assured to individuals against public authority should also extend to relations between the members of society, but, in that case, the delimitation of the rights and duties of each individual is far more complex, since the circumstances which may arise are much more varied. It is evident that rights which must be respected by the state itself cannot be transgressed with impunity either by individuals or by groups of individuals. The task of regulating them is entrusted to civil legislation.

The historic declarations were negative: they aimed at curtailing the exercise of authority, whereas, nowadays, we seek to set up positive obligations incumbent upon the State. This is much to be desired when the interests of the individual are in obvious harmony with those of the State, for example, in establishing the rights to education and the right to health services; it is in the interests of the State that its citizens should be well educated and healthy in body and mind. In these cases, the right does not imply any extension of the coercive power of the State, except in a few cases (compulsory school attendance, compulsory inoculation, etc.).

It would probably do more harm than good to introduce into the enumeration of the Rights of Man principles for determining the complicated relations between the State and individuals and intermediate groups. These relations are of too complex a nature to be summed up in an absolute principle. If, for example, the right to strike were to be admitted, it would be necessary to ensure that this right was only exercised in conformity with the will of the members of the professional union.

The new French Constitution has rightly laid down that the right to strike should be recognized only within the limits prescribed by the law. It is a right which is not easily expressed in an absolute formula.

Always bearing in mind that a natural right must be one that is to be commended by its simplicity and justice, we should avoid introducing into the declaration formulae which are too vague to be put into practice. For example, the so-called right to freedom from fear (as set forth in the Atlantic Charter), is not a right in the true sense of the word. In order to put it into practice, we should need an international organization which we are still far from achieving. As a step in this direction, a clause might be introduced prohibiting aggression. This, however, would not be a right, but an obligation. The clause would be of a fairly precise nature, but it remains to be seen whether anything would be gained by introducing into the declaration prohibitions the observance of which might be difficult to enforce.

On the other hand, the rights of members of a racial or religious minority to liberties indispensable to their intellectual and cultural life are sufficiently precise to be incorporated in a world declaration. It must not be forgotten, however, that these rights could only be enforceable if an international authority were made responsible for ensuring respect for them by refractory states.

There is no doubt that one of the most important points to be considered in revising the declaration is that it should be completed in such a way as to meet the needs of international solidarity in our time. If the Rights of Man today are particularly exposed to infringements by governments, the reason is to be found in the frequency of wars and the constant fear of fresh aggression. There is little hope of securing universal respect for the Rights of Man unless we can safeguard peace. It is, therefore, perfectly logical to introduce the formula of these rights into a document of universal validity, in order that the observance of such rights may be safeguarded by an international body. Experience, however, has shown that these rights are never fully respected unless all the individuals, the people, of a nation take it upon themselves to ensure that their government does so respect them.

This applies equally to international life. It is to be feared that a world organization, composed exclusively of representatives of the various governments, would not concern itself overmuch with safeguarding the rights of the individual. Yet it is particularly important that the peoples should feel that the world organization is defending their rights against their national governments. Nothing would strengthen the authority of such an organization so much as a conviction on the part of oppressed peoples that they had only to appeal to it for oppression to cease. Accordingly, individuals whose fundamental rights are violated should be given every opportunity to sue their government. It would even be desirable to enable peoples, in one way or another, to exert pressure on international bodies with a view to ensuring the observance of these rights. Otherwise it is to be feared that the international protection of the Rights of Man may remain a dead letter. It is the business of nations which enjoy full civic and political liberty to see that less fortunate nations are not ill-treated. If they do not assume this responsibility, it is to be feared that their own liberty may soon be threatened.

AMENDED PROJECT FOR A DECLARATION OF THE RIGHTS OF PERSONS AND COLLECTIVITIES
(Published Following A Survey Undertaken By The Magazine "Esprit," 1945)
Emmanuel Mounier[*]

The undersigned States recognize the authority over individuals and societies of a certain number of rights attached to the existence of the human community, deriving neither from the individual, nor from the state, possessing a dual root:

1) The good of persons;

2) Life and its normal development in the heart of the natural communities in which those persons are placed: families, nations, geographical or linguistic groupings, working communities, groups based on affinities or beliefs.

The goal of every society is the implementation of the best methods of raising everyone to free choice, responsible action, and consensual community.

The proper function of the State is to actively assist both the independence of individuals and the life of communities; the first, against the ever-threatening tyranny of groups; the second, against the ever- recurring anarchy of individuals. An organization independent of the States is empowered to judge the abuses of State power and to resolve without appeal the conflicts they cause. It defines State crimes.

I. INDIVIDUAL RIGHTS

1) Personal responsibility, actual or perceived, is the foundation of individual rights. These rights are the physical and moral integrity of the individual and

---

[*] Emmanuel Mounier was a French essayist, philosopher, and publisher, and the leader of the French Personalist movement, which was critical of both communism and capitalism. He founded the journal *Esprit* in 1932, in which he published many essays from a personalist perspective. His works include *The Communitarian and Personalist Revolution* (1934), *From Capitalist to Human Ownership* (1936), *The Personalist Manifesto* (1936), *The North African Awakening* (1948), and *The Little Fear of the Twentieth Century* (1948). Mounier died in 1950 at 44 years of age. This piece was translated from the French by Romana Iorga.

freedom in its various forms: of association, labor, leisure, security, and equality before the law.

2) Men, unequal in their talents and their functions, are all equal, regardless of their ability, race, class or sex, in front of these fundamental rights. No special law may be promulgated based on one of these factors.

3) Every human being has the right to his physical and moral integrity. Apart from measures foreseen under criminal Law, one can impose upon him neither systematic violence, nor degrading treatment or mutilation motivated by his lack of physical or mental integrity, nor any form of pressure on his will, even in the name of the best interests of society.

4) Every human being has the right to health and to the preventive and curative medical care and treatment that it requires.

5) In return, the individual is accountable to the community for the power that he represents. No one has the right to mutilate or kill himself, unless it is in an interest superior to his own.

6) The spiritual integrity of an individual cannot be compromised by methods of suggestion or propaganda, emanating from either the State or private powers, when these methods are likely to exert an unacceptable pressure on the individual will and when individuals are denied the methods of effective defense while confronting them.

7) Human beings are free in their movements, their words, their writings, or their actions, insofar as those do not violate this Declaration or the laws enacted in harmony with this Declaration. Freedom in its various forms must serve the personal dignity of each individual and the good of all. It is inalienable and bears responsibility for them.

8) Private life and the home are inviolable. Every human being has the right to go, to stay, to leave, without being arrested or detained, except according to procedures set by law. No home may be entered except according to a law or an order emanating from a public authority, and only for the person and the object expressly designated in the document ordering the visit. The interference of public bodies in private life must be reduced to the necessary minimum.

9) Nobody shall be prosecuted, accused, arrested or detained, except in cases determined by law and only according to the forms it has prescribed. No one can be detained for more than eight days without appearing before a judge asked to rule on the legality of the arrest. Any other act exercised against an individual or against a community is arbitrary and null. The victim of such acts shall be entitled to seek redress in the courts, and those responsible must be punished.

10) Everyone is presumed innocent until he has been proven guilty. Any rigor that is not necessary to secure his person must be severely suppressed by law. No

individual shall be punished except under a law established prior to the offense. No one may be punished twice for the same offense. Enforcing laws retroactively or cumulatively is a State crime.

11) Penalties must be proportionate to the offense, cautionary, and, as much as possible, reformative of the culprit.

12) Everyone is free to speak, write, print and publish thoughts, opinions and information, except in cases, determined by law, when that freedom is abused, in particular in accordance with article 6.

13) No one may be harassed for expressing opinions or beliefs in matters of religion or philosophy, to the extent that they do not offend the rights guaranteed by this Declaration.

14) Freedom of education stems from the two previous articles. It is exercised subject to guarantees of competence, morality, and civic education determined by law and controlled by the State. It can only be limited by institutions that guarantee its spirit even in the act of restricting its implementation. Elementary education shall be compulsory. Entry into higher forms of education will be resolved according to merit.

15) The citizens of the same State have the right, across its territory, to assemble freely, without weapons, without unauthorized uniforms, meeting police rules and in accordance with article 6. This article is particularly applicable to non- adversarial campaign meetings and large marches.

16) The citizens of the same State have the right, across its territory, to associate for study, for the development and the defense of their common interests according to the combinations they prefer. These associations may be authorized to receive as ordinary members foreigners residing in the national territory of their jurisdiction. International associations that do not threaten the State structure are authorized. Any coalition that is likely to endanger the guarantees of article 6 may be banned.

17) Every individual shall have the right to work, that is to say, the right to receive guaranteed employment with fair remuneration for his work, both in quantity and quality.[1] The State guarantees this right.

18) Work is not a commodity and can not be treated as such. Every worker has the right to the minimum of resources required for him and his family to lead a life worthy of a human being.

19) The worker is free to join the union of his choice or not to join any. He is entitled to the collective determination of working conditions, to occupational protection, to respect for his qualifications, and to the technical and social train-

---

1. We have used the formula of the Soviet Constitution as a basis for this article.

ing necessary to allow him to become closely involved with the duties of leadership and management in the workplace.

20) Everyone has the right to the necessary leisure to relax physically and educate himself spiritually according to his free choice.

21) Everyone has the right to security. Whether infirm or incurable, he is entitled to a social function compatible with his diminished capacity. If the diminishment of his capacity is absolute, both he and his minor children become the responsibility of the community.

22) The law must be equal for all, whether it rewards or punishes, whether it protects or restrains.

23) All men are eligible for all positions, jobs and public services, without any distinction except that of their capacities and moral values.

24) All contributions are distributed among all, in accordance with each person's means and so as not to interfere with those goods that are indispensable to personal and family life. Decided by the sole needs of general usefulness, these contributions are subject to public scrutiny.

25) A woman may not be treated in any way as a lesser person. The law guarantees her a dignified status equivalent to that of man in her public and private life. The civil status of a married woman can be modified by the marriage contract to the extent necessary for the administration of individual and common goods.

26) Children are protected by social legislation in their physical, intellectual and moral development.

II. COMMUNITY RIGHTS

27) There exist natural communities. Originating outside the State, they can be neither identified by nor subjugated to the State. Their spontaneous powers limit State power. They should be represented as such to the State.

28) The first of these communities is the family. The State protects it like any and every other member. Family expenses must be taken into account for the remuneration of labor and during the establishment of public services.

29) The nation has an absolute right to the independence of its culture, its language, and its spiritual life, but not to unconditional political sovereignty. It must protect, within the limits of its cohesion, the regional, ethnic, linguistic or religious groups within it.

30) Economic communities and work communities are based on the services they render, not on acquired privilege nor the power of money. They do not serve primarily the State's profit, production, or power, but rather the needs of free consumption, under conditions that respect the dignity of workers and the development of entrepreneurship.

31) Economic power can only belong to workers of all kinds. Economic profit must recompense workers, according to the requirements of articles 18 and 19, before it is used to reimburse lost capital.

32) The hierarchy of functions must be ensured so that it does not give rise to a separation of classes.

33) The human community is the usufructuary of all the riches of the universe. In a general organization, every nation has the right to receive its fair share. Every worker has the right to emigrate, to the extent possible, to a place where his sustenance can be better or his work more productive.

34) Everyone has the right to personal property in the vital space necessary for the individual to constitute an environment of freedom and autonomy, provided that such possession is neither a means of oppression nor a means of spoliation of another's legitimate fruit of labor.

35) Everyone has the right to pass on to his children the goods of the family defined within these limits. These limits are those of the right to inheritance.

36) As the custodian of the public good, the State must ensure these guarantees. It may act against persons or communities whose possessions violate the provisions of article 33 or threaten its authority. It can declare expropriation because of public need or the forfeiture of the owner; in the first case, the expropriation shall be subject to prior and just compensation.

37) There is a natural international community, a community of peoples and nations whose legal translation is a society of States. It implies an interracial community. A freely organized federation is the normal mode of uniting the members of the international community.

III. STATE RIGHTS

38) The State is a power committed to the guarantee of the common political good, to the external defense of a nation or a group of nations, and to the co-ordination of individual and collective activities in its geographical jurisdiction.

39) The power of the State is limited by the spontaneous powers of natural societies defined under section II. It is subject to the supreme authority of the Declaration, particularly with respect to fundamental freedoms. It should be regulated by a constitution and the organization of a constitutional review.

40) The consent of the nation to State authority must be guaranteed by a full, sincere, and effective representation of opinions, situations, and interests. In all public elections, the vote is mandatory and guaranteed against any pressure from the State or private individuals.

41) A separation of the various powers of the State is necessary for its proper functioning and the guarantee of rights. It must include in particular the inde-

pendence of the judiciary, which should, through its recruitment and its structures, remain a living expression of the nation.

42) A police force is required for the function of the State. It must neither create an autonomous body within the State, nor enter areas other than those that are the strict responsibility of the State.

43) It is oppression when one of the requirements of the Declaration is violated by the state. A Supreme Court, in which tenured judges will mingle with the delegates of all the living elites of the nation, will be charged to arbitrate any application and delimitation of the Constitution.

(published in the May 1945 issue of "Esprit")

NOTE REGARDING THE PROPOSED "DECLARATION OF THE RIGHTS OF MAN"
Maurice Webb[*]

The reference in the Preamble to the United Nations Charter to "Fundamental human rights" is, perhaps, unfortunate. The term has no defined meaning. It can easily give rise to expectations unlikely to be realized and is likely to afford still another subject for fierce examination when a definition is attempted.

Man in isolation has no rights. Robinson Crusoe on his island could have no rights before the arrival of Man Friday against whom rights could be enforced or who would willingly concede them.

Rights imply absence of rights, or curtailed rights, or rights resisted. There must be another person to limit or deny, to concede or uphold. The Divine Right of Kings implied the presence of subjects to submit, or to revolt.

Human rights, then, can exist only where there is community: they have to be asserted, claimed, conceded, maintained, in a community relationship. The nature and extent of rights is determined by the form of the community in which alone they can exist. The rights of the person are determined by the form of the

---

[*] Maurice Webb was an English educational reformer, journalist, and social analyst who was a conscientious objector during the First World War. After the war, he served for a short period as secretary of the London Vegetarian Society, following which he emigrated with his family to South Africa. A strong opponent of racial segregation, Webb was one of the cofounders and leading researchers and advisers of the South African Institute of Race Relations and authored many books and studies under its auspices, including *The Indian in South Africa: Towards a Solution of Conflict* (1944) and *In Quest of South Africa* (1945). He died in 1966.

society of which he is a member (e.g., the right to own property would not exist in a completely socialist state; it would be a primary right in a capitalist state).

An attempt to formulate a Declaration of the Rights of Man is, therefore, in effect, an attempt to formulate a uniform pattern of human society, a formidable task. It is questionable whether there is within the United Nations at the present time sufficient unity to make agreement as to a social form possible, even if such agreement were itself desirable.

Human rights, being inextricably bound up with social structure, it is important to remember that any internationally accepted Bill of Human Rights would tend towards rigidity in social structure, to retard change and experiment in social patterns.

On the assumption that we do not yet know the last word on social structure and that it is desirable for the form of human society to continue to change and to develop, any attempted Declaration of human rights should be restricted to a minimum: leaving the largest possible scope for variation.

We seek, then, not an ultimate goal, not a declaration of all those rights that we may think desirable, but rather a minimum statement covering what we think to be the very least human rights that any State, whatever its form, should concede to its people. We seek not the end, but a means: a foundation on which other varied rights and freedoms, in different social settings, may be built.

Such minimum rights, I suggest, are these:

(1) The right of worship, individual and collective (Religious Freedom).

(2) The right of the person. (Freedom from arbitrary arrest or detention, the principle of Habeas Corpus).

(3) The right to own property. No confiscation or dispossession without process of law.

(4) The right of access to courts of justice and equal justice as between person and person.

(5) The right of free speech, assembly, publication, specifically the right to criticize and oppose a particular government or form of government.

(6) The right of opportunity in respect of education, employment, participation in the processes of government free from discrimination solely on grounds of sex, racial origin, nationality, membership of a minority or specially designated group.

To anyone whose mind has been influenced by the thought and ideals of Nineteenth Century Europe these six "Rights" are elementary, it would be impossible to subscribe to less. Yet in formulating them we are made immediately aware that they are unacceptable on theoretic grounds in many parts of the world; and that even if they are theoretically acceptable they are not capable of immediate or even early attainment in many countries including our own.

We are at once faced with the question whether we are justified in putting forward proposals for a Declaration of the Rights of Man that are not possible of attainment, at least within reasonably early time, in our own society. We find ourselves left with a Declaration which while being elementary to some, would be a statement of a distant goal for others, would be rejected by many.

Nevertheless, I think that we should formulate at least these six points not so much as a Declaration of Human Rights "to which all countries should be asked to adhere" (to quote Sir Hartley Shawcross, speaking in the United Nations Assembly), but rather as a declaration of faith for some of us, for the information of others.

On analysis the re-affirmation of fundamental human rights contained in the Preamble to the United Nations Charter does not help us. It may indeed prove a considerable hindrance in giving rise to bitter fruitless dispute. There is more hope to be found in the determination expressed a little later in the same Preamble "to promote social progress and better standards of life in larger freedom." This does not so obviously invite precise definition. The terms can more readily remain general and vague. But all the same if effect were given to this undertaking, made by all the member Nations of the United Nations, conscientiously, over a period of time, it might be that a generally acceptable Declaration of the Rights of Man would presently begin to come into view.

Maurice Webb
Members of the Executive Committee of
S.A. INSTITUTE OF RACE RELATIONS
P.O.BOX 97, JOHANNESBURG,
SOUTH AFRICA

Durban, May 17, 1947

THE RIGHTS OF MAN
John Macmurray[*]

I am at a loss to know what contribution I can usefully make to the effort to draft a statement on the rights of man without more knowledge of the procedure which is proposed. As a student of moral and social theory, I should be ready to discuss the traditional theories, and to criticise their philosophical bases and assumptions; and if ever UNESCO should decide to publish a symposium of views on such topics I should be glad to take part. But I doubt whether this is the time to indulge in the luxury of abstract theory, and I propose to restrain myself for the present.

It seems better that I should consider the matter from the practical stand-point, in the light of the function of UNO and the purpose that can be served by any attempt to draft a statement of human rights under its auspices at the present juncture. Statements of the rights of Man have hitherto been drawn up, for the most part, in relation to a real or supposed conflict between the individual and the State of which it is a citizen. Their function has been to set limits to the right of the State to interfere with the lives of its subjects. Consequently, the theory of rights has grown up and has been debated as part of the theory of the State, conceived as determining the relations between human beings on the one hand, and the governments to which they owe allegiance on the other.

For UNESCO this approach is insufficient and unsuitable. The question of human rights is now raised from the international standpoint. Its discussion has a new function, not to find a way to mediate between the individual and his own government, but rather to achieve uniformity between governments in their treatment of their own subjects; and equally an agreed position as of right for *any* individual in relation to any government with which he may have to do, whether it be his own or a foreign government. Any statement drafted

---

[*] John Macmurray was a Scottish philosopher who, at the time of the UNESCO human rights survey, held the chair in Moral Philosophy at the University of Edinburgh; before that, from 1928 to 1944, he had served as the Grote Professor of the Philosophy of Mind and Logic at University College London. During the First World War, he had been seriously wounded in battle in France. As a philosopher, Macmurray focused on broad questions of the self, agency, and the role of philosophy in public life, interests that set him apart from mainstream debates in the discipline. For this reason, his works have been largely ignored in the history of twentieth- century philosophy. His most important works, which grew out of the Gifford Lectures he delivered at the University of Glasgow in 1953 to 1954, are *The Self as Agent* (1957) and *Persons in Relation* (1961). Macmurray was asked by Havet to join the UNESCO Committee of Experts, but refused. Upon his retirement in 1958, Macmurray became a Quaker; he died in 1976.

by or on behalf of UNESCO on the Rights of Man should, in my opinion, be conditioned by this unique purpose; and theoretical discussion directed to this end should begin with a clear recognition of the difference which the new frame of reference must make. It might be a good thing to take the position of an airman forced by accident to make a landing in the territory of a foreign State, as defining the *locus* of the question.

The major question in debate in the philosophy of rights—whether there are natural rights which inhere in the individual prior to their recognition by society, or whether all rights are conferred by society—becomes from this point of view purely academic. For the purpose is to get universal agreement that certain rights *should* be accepted as normal human rights; and secondly, to persuade all States to incorporate these rights in their own constitutional or legal system.

One other point seems to me to call for consideration before the procedure is determined. The idea of the Rights of Man is traditionally bound up with the rise and development of liberalism and liberal democracy. There is therefore a danger that it should be suspect, particularly in the Soviet Union, as an ideological weapon in an anti-communist struggle. It is clearly important that precautions should be taken to prevent this; and the question how this is to be done is a difficult and important one. Perhaps it might even be better to avoid the title "Rights of Man," as being too closely associated historically with a particular theory of government, and to secure the substance of what is intended under some other and more neutral title.

I suggest that the various rights to be discussed might be divided into two classes: those fundamental rights on which general agreement in principle is already achieved or is likely to be easily obtained, and secondly, other rights which are likely to prove more controversial. Every effort should be made to get the first section accepted by all the Great Powers as soon as possible; and it should be compiled with this in view. The remaining right would compose a list of varying importance, on which discussion could be initiated. Items from this list might be transferred to the first section when it seemed likely that general support would be forthcoming for an effort to get them incorporated in the legal system of the member states of UNO.

It might be possible to begin the drafting of this first section by including all rights which are common to the constitutions of USSR, USA, and France, and to the constitutional law of Great Britain; to this might be added any rights already incorporated in international law, and any others arising clearly from the Atlantic Charter and the constitution of UNO, and which might reasonably be expected to find general approval.

These are the points which seem to me to require consideration and decision right at the beginning, as determining the procedure which should be adopted. Until they have been dealt with, I think it would not be desirable to go further. I have therefore limited my contribution to their statement, and have reserved any views I may have on the substantial issues which are not matters of procedure to a more suitable occasion.

UNTITLED
Julius Moór[*]

1. It is clear that by adopting the idea of evolution we can no longer consider the rights of man, the way the old theory of natural rights did, as inalienable rights inherent in human nature. Just as man does not bring into the world along with his birth the contents of his spiritual life, his culture, that is to say, everything that makes him human, since the elements of this culture are brought to him mainly by society; in the same way, society, in its turn, may establish—differently depending on time and location—the rights given to its members, and therefore can assume the right to necessarily limit human freedom, which was never a given for primitive man, since freedom is the result of a long moral and intellectual evolution of mankind.

For even though the rights of man will not let themselves be reduced to the philosophy of natural law, they nevertheless have a solid foundation in the moral conscience of humanity, which, during its evolution, claims more and more the recognition of equal human dignity. The rights of man are the consequences of this moral concept, whose most sublime manifestation was the teaching of Jesus Christ.

2. Among the most fundamental rights of man are those that should be called human freedoms: personal liberty, freedom of press, freedom of thought, freedom of religion, freedom of association and assembly, etc. These ensure that

---

[*] Julius (Gyula) Moór was a Hungarian jurist, academic, and member of Parliament. At the time of the UNESCO human rights survey, he was a professor at the Institute for Economic and Legal Studies at the Pázmány Péter Catholic University in Budapest, where he had been rector until 1946. Besides serving in the Hungarian Parliament, Moór had also been president of the Hungarian Academy of Sciences. In 1948, a year after submitting his response on human rights to UNESCO, Moór gave a speech to the Hungarian Parliament that was strongly critical of the imminent Communist takeover of the country. As a result, he was ousted from Parliament, forced to resign from the university, and expelled from the Academy of Sciences. He died in 1950. This piece was translated from the French by Romana Iorga.

man organizes his life according to his will and realizes his ideal of happiness according to his own design, provided he uses means that do not harm others and do not violate legal provisions.

Also important are the political rights that ensure the individual's ability to influence the direction of the life of the State: the right to vote, the right to hold public office, etc. These also constitute the indispensable conditions of human dignity, because they enable man to move from the state of a passive object of power to that of an active subject.

Finally, social and economic rights: rights to an existence consistent with human dignity, to work, to fair labor compensation, to public assistance in case of need, etc., also resulting from the recognition of human dignity. Certainly, everyone has to provide for the needs of his own existence, nevertheless, human fairness requires the support of the community for the benefit of those in need, whether as a result of the prevailing economic system, or, consequently, as a result of their weakness.

3. The three groups of human rights listed above are intimately connected with one another, so that political rights presuppose the existence of human liberties, while social and economic rights presuppose the existence of political rights and human freedoms. Indeed, the social and economic rights of the people should have a solid foundation in case they are deprived of political rights or power is held by one man or by a privileged minority, since political privileges usually include economic privileges and political power always disposes of sufficient means to cut back the economic rights of individuals.

The authoritarian systems of modern times represented this view that the economic welfare of the people and, therefore, man's right to existence are better guaranteed by a dictatorship than a democracy based on equal rights. The practice of fascist systems provided an eloquent rebuff to this concept.

The fact that the system of the U.S.S.R. assigns more importance to the consolidation of the economic well-being of its citizens than to political freedoms, while in Western democracies political freedoms have a leading role, seems to contrast Eastern and Western conceptions of human rights. However, the opposition between these two systems is starting to fade: firstly, because the U.S.S.R.'s new 1936 constitution inserts in the code the greatest part of the principles of political democracy in the Western sense, and secondly, because in his message to Congress on January 11, 1945, President Roosevelt proclaimed social rights in a new "Bill of rights," which broadly accord with the rights specified in articles 118–122 of the 1936 constitution of the U.S.S.R.

The line of evolution seems then to evolve neither toward a strong restriction of the human freedoms and political rights proclaimed in the eighteenth century nor toward the substitution thereof by economic and social rights advocated by Marxist systems. It is more likely that we progress toward a synthesis of two trends, which will be facilitated by the well-being created by the technological progress of mankind. Indeed, it is quite simple and easy to guarantee human freedoms and political rights; this is only a question of organization and adaptation to the life of the State. However, it is more difficult to guarantee the social and economic rights of individuals, because such an effort requires a thriving economy in order for the State to be able to provide its citizens an existence worthy of man.

We can hope from now on that, parallel with the progress of culture, technology, and economic life, there will be a gradual evolution of human rights, which will unite in a harmonious blend of the Eastern and Western conceptions that appear today so irreconcilable. It goes without saying that this process involves planned organization. But planning does not necessarily diminish freedom, since freedom implies order and succumbs to anarchy. One can well imagine that planned organization that provides social rights will be based on respect for human freedoms and political rights.

UNTITLED
L. Horváth[*]

What, in the world to-day, are the theoretical grounds, the practical extent, and the efficient guarantees of specific rights or freedoms, such as:

1. Freedom of conscience or worship (a) for individuals, (b) for organised religious groups; 2. Freedom of speech (the right to free speech) and freedom of opinion; 3. Freedom of assembly; 4. Freedom of association and freedom for consequent action (the right to strike); 5. Freedom of movement (a) within (b) across national boundaries (c) freedom to leave one nation for another; 6. Freedom of communications and the right to accurate information (a) within (b) across national boundaries (freedom of the press, etc.); 7. Political freedom and equality (a) for organised political parties (b) for individuals in the exercise of the franchise (the right to vote); 8. Freedom of expression (including freedom of the writer and the artist); 9. Freedom and equality of economic, social and educational opportu-

---

[*] Nothing more is known of L. Horváth except that he (or she) indicated that he/she was a "Dr." from Hungary. Horváth's name does not appear on any of the lists prepared by Huxley or Havet, but it is known that Huxley sent the Phil/1/1947 documents to government officials in Hungary, asking them to forward them on to anyone who could usefully contribute to the inquiry.

nity; 10. Freedom of opportunity for the pursuit of the good life; 11. Freedom of teaching; 12. Freedom of scientific and philosophic inquiry and publication; 13. The right to work and not to work; the right to leisure; 14. Freedom and equality of access to the means of subsistence (a) for individuals (b) for nations; 15. Freedom from fear (the right to protection); 16. Freedom from want (economic rights: the right to economic security and to a basic level of material well-being); 17. Freedom from exploitation and oppression (social rights); 18. The right to justice; 19. Freedom from preventible disease (the right to health); 20. The right to property; 21. The rights and freedoms of minorities (a) racial (b) political (c) religious (d) cultural or linguistic, including the right to self-determination; 22. The rights and freedoms of politically dependent (non-self-governing) peoples; 23. The rights of nations in relation (a) to each other (b) to existing or possible international or supra-national organisations; 24. The rights of women, of children, of the disabled and of the aged; 25. Other rights and freedoms?

A.

I.

1. First I intend to treat the theoretical grounds of Human Rights and Freedoms.

2. I think that it would be preferable not only to treat the historically developed Human Rights themselves but the search for their theoretical grounds in general.

First I mean to look for the new ruling ideas of mankind to which the majority of people seems to consent to-day and which are apt to serve as the origins of a Code of Human Rights. In the following I wish to outline the fundamental Human Rights and Freedoms without which apparently there can be no basis for an estimation of a concrete formulation of the relation of man to the Universe and to his fellowmen. After that I shall enumerate the already formulated Human Rights as having been published during the last years in relation to the respective fundamental rights and freedoms. At the same time I will try to derive some farther Human rights and Freedoms out of these generally formulated principles without wanting to consider them to be a complete or definitive enumeration of the Human Rights.

3. According to the present conception of Human Rights and Freedoms it need not be emphasized that we cannot declare such everlasting rights—as the school of Natural Rights did,—being convinced of the great possibilities of human Evolution and of the today impossibility of the restriction of man's claims for Freedom. But we must look possibly far into the future by codifying, and consider the whole of the humanity hoping for the realization of the "One World."

II.

1. The rise of the concept of Human Rights was caused by perception of the understanding, of the human personality as being a thing of worth and in concept the very worthiest reality of the things on this earth. Human life is to be defended even if it is bodily and mentally defective.

2. A further cognition was that we are equal in the fundamental conditions of our human existence. In the interval between birth and death we all must have the same chances of life limited only by caprice of Nature. There is no social barrier, caste system, or isolation to prevent Nature in producing uniformly geniuses and degenerates, people with perfect or defective morality, artists and people who are not appreciative in the arts in the families of the poorest and richest. Thus the man is not only a valuable reality, but every man personally is the potential bearer of the same value. The marshal stick is met only in the service-kit of the common soldier, but there is the laurel wreath of artists and scientists and the signmark of saints in every cradle.

3. Despite the fact that we are humanly the same, there are differences. We think differently about ourselves and of the Universe. We learned the name of our mother in a different tongue and we speak of our country at different frontiers. Our skin may differ from that of our northern and southern neighbours and in every respect differ from those living at the farthest end of earth and also from our respective brothers. These differences, which have caused much struggle and contempt between man and man have taught man, after religious, national and civil wars, that there are differences (racial, sex, language, religion), which belong to the substance of man, which are to be taken into consideration in the evaluation of our personality and which are to be appreciated.

4. These three basic cognitions: the consciousness of the valuable substance of human life, the recognition of human equality and the convaluation of the differences in man's allocation and basic rules of thinking have been expanded with a negativum to be emphasized especially that is with scientific uncertainty of the transcendental role of man. It is a scientifically free and non attack-provocative to state that this is the soil of man, but that also can be stated scientifically that the grave does not receive the substance of man.

5. These considerations in themselves would leave man indifferent in relation to the man, if there were not in force a power which perhaps cannot be defined with a universal terminology. This derived from the fact that man is "soon politician" and had developed there that he not only lives in society but that he is not even indifferent towards the either man, in the same way as human society means more and more the entire world one feels more and more community with one another. We are not only concerned with each other under

the influence of purposefulness and of economic forces but the fact that we recognize a value in man brings forth the desirability of the recognition of these values as a categorical imperative to be understood in a more generalized way. Man does not fool himself well in the perspective of "homo homini lupus," he feels that he commits something against something if he abstains from, that he should see a value to be recognised also in the other man. Whether we call this force love, sociality or anything else is not important. The emphasis is on that man starts seeing responsibility for his fellow-man living in the other parts of the world. Today communities give up part of their bread so that people from other countries should be eased in their distress. According to me practicability and economic political point of view is not enough explanation of same.

III.

1. The above ideas perhaps are now not in effect in the entire world, still they are to be considered as such norms, which can be considered as acceptable for a starting point. Our ruling political and social ideas can also conditionize an agreement on same. Taking a historical example, the three slogans of the French Revolution: "Liberté. Egalité. Fraternité" express already the understanding in this consciousness. Liberty expresses on the one hand the independence of man as wishing to free himself from the feeling of binding to transcendentalism, on the other hand it deducts from the substantial equality of man, that no one is justified to suppress the other. Equality is to a certain extent the prerecognition of Liberty as mentioned above. Fraternity is joy and pledge coming from the recognition of human equality, unnoticeably it is the second highest command of Christ and that is: Love thy neighbor as thyself as if you wish to say it is the categoric imperative of values.

2. Democracy, humanity, sociality, individualism, all precondition an understanding of the above principles. Examining the theoretical principles of the Human Rights I believe, it would be not only logically incorrect to deduct Human Rights from these political concepts, but it would seem aimless to choose as a starting point concepts differing both as to practicability and theory.

IV.

1. From the above cognitions a few more emphatically recognizable Human Rights and Freedoms become evident, emphasis on which can be a directive from the point of view of further examination. Notwithstanding the following, classifications cannot be considered as a rigid system and we have recognized the fact that some Human Rights could be grouped according to other points of view.

2. From the recognition that there is no more valuable earthly existence, furthermore from that recognition that human individuals are in principle the same as far as personalities are concerned (on the bases of the transcendentalistic scientific uncertainty) every man is justified to dispose of himself. According to my opinion, this is the most basic Human Right: *the Freedom of Human self-determination.* This includes in itself: freedom of life (in its extreme limits the right of suicide, and the wish for the abolition of death penalty); the freedom of religion (1. W. USSR); the freedom of movement (5, W.); the freedom of occupational selection (R); freedom of work undertaking (W.R.); the freedom of release from the binding of a state (5, 25.); freedom of mate selection (25); freedom of scientific and philosophic enquiry and publication (12); the freedom of work and not to work (13); freedom of sale (W); the freedom of silence (R.); freedom from coerced nutrition, and from the forced taking of medicaments (W.); the freedom of passive resistance; strike (4.), (satisgraha) [the writer is likely meaning to refer to "satyagraha" (ed.)] (25.); the freedom as to choice of apparel on clothing (25); the freedom from any recruiting against one's conscience (W.).[2]

The enumeration is naturally not complete, I just ventured to mention as to what Human Freedoms can be derived from the ideas derived from the theoretical treatment of Human Rights.

2. From the above mentioned conditions, comes also an other great grouping of Human Rights. The *right to Human Dignity.* This is more comprehensive and therefore precedes the freedom of self-determination, still as a Human Right I mention it in second place as compared with the absolute characteristic of the self-determinational freedom. The self-determinational freedom claims only the endurance of the use of freedom, the right the human dignity requires already a determined attitude on the part of every man, from groups of men, communities or state sovereignty.[3]

Grouped here is the right to life without fear (15 A.C.), right to health (19), which in certain extent includes the right to proper living (10, 14), clothing (R.), living quarters (R.), medical help (R. W. USSR), the right to maintain the already acquired citizenship (25.); right to teaching (11.); right to free time (13. R.); right to economic security (16. A. C.); right against exploitation and suppression (17.); the right against misappropriation of technical achievements (25.); the right against power derived from technical centralisation (25); the

---

2. The numbers in brackets refer to the sign of the title; W. The contributions of Wells to the Declaration of Human Rights (1934); USSR. The constitution of USSR (1936); R. The message of President Roosevelt to the Congress in 14.1.1942.

3. The author uses the number 2 twice in this list (ed.).

right for protection against personal perjury (W.); the right to liberty from physical punishment (W.). According to my opinion it is included here also the right to exemption from war as an activity injuring in principle human dignity, as a right to peace as affecting the individual.

3. Also the *right to justice* comes from equality (18.)

This includes the right to equality before the law court (R.), the right to exemption from unjust inflection (W.); the right to social, economical and educational equality (9.); the right to things acquired by a lawful way and the right to property (20); right to free criticism (W.); the right to feminine equality (USSR, UNO, 24.).

4. In the fourth group we can include the *right to human free cooperation*.

These are derived principally from right of self-determination (the common self-determination of many people) and from human dignity. If many agree commonly to cooperation there is no basis, without the examining the contexture, according to which impediment of scene would be justified without infringement of the human dignity and self-determination. Naturally cooperation for such purposes which infringes the prospering of above mentioned more basic Human Rights can be avoided by the means of the sanctions of same.

Thus accordingly principally grouping and association for war would be abandoned, (as for instance the demand for disarmament as a Human Right affecting the individual).

There is included in the right of human free cooperation: right to free speech (2. W.); right to communication and right to press (3.); right to scientific and philosophic enquiry and publication (12); right to assembly (3); right to union (W.); right to vote (7); right to street demonstration (USSR).

There is much danger for corruption in connection with the right of free cooperation as for instance by means of freedom of speech such propaganda can be developed which reflects Human culture, yet the conditioning would not be in conformity with human dignity, that the majority of people would not discover the misrepresentation with the right to free speech and would not make itself independent of this or at least they should not occur such minds by the right of the freedom of speech, who convince one of the incorrectness of the defective propaganda. However, if the majority of people would detour from the right path although admitting and respecting the freedom of speech, there is no intellectual basis dependence on which we could conditionize that not we make a mistake.

5. One could regulate rights affecting not every man, but only certain men, or groupings of man as special Human Rights.

Thus rights concerning Women, children, invalids, disabled, aged (24); the rights of politically dependent peoples (22), and special rights affecting nations (22). The inclusion of same in the scope of Human Rights would be justified not so much by logical but by practical points of view. Special rights pertaining to women should be conceived out of the Human Rights to health, rest, feminine equality, human dignity as a special feminine dignity, the right to assurance against inability to work, childbirth, etc. However, it would be more correct to regulate these separately that as when collected accessibly and specially defined emphasis should be given.

6. I did not treat the above mentioned Human Rights merely from a point of view of [a systematic] experiment but I think, if the above mentioned course of Human Rights is not correct, before the construction of the codex of Human Rights to deduct from the conceptions of historically developed Human Rights, to the contexture of their origin and after the general examination of the correctness and generally accepted substance of same, starting out from these and other things worthy of consideration to build up the Charter of Human Rights.

B.

1. The third question of my study is: what are the efficient guarantees of specific rights and freedoms.

2. Above all it is to be considered that Human Rights and Freedoms as I had mentioned above are different in conception. They are partly absolutely conceived and these demand only the toleration that the individual should live with these rights. Such are freedoms of self-determinations. As for instance on the basis of the freedom of free movement I cannot expect of anybody to promote my free movement, but I can demand it of everyone not to determine my movements. On the basis of the freedom of the release from the status of citizenship of one country I cannot demand that a state should accept me as its citizen, but I can demand that the state to which I belong should release me. In the grouping of the Human Rights however individual man has a right to such an objective protective position, the creation and maintenance of which is the duty of certain states or directly of entire humanity, in the last analysis always that of entire humanity. As for instance the right of life without fear the respective states should be obliged to guarantee, for the nations it should be guaranteed internationally. To organize and later to guarantee the right to proper living is likewise the task and duty of states and the United Nations.

3. The declaration of Human Rights would therefore in itself not be enough. Before we state a Human Right we first have to guarantee its conditions. Before we announce rights to proper living of those unable to work we have to create those assurance organizations which make it possible for these to live properly. The 55

para. of UNO before the announcement that 55 par. (c) they will promote the universal respect and appreciation of Human Right and Freedom states (55 para. (a)) that the UNO will promote the higher stand of life, the complete work opportunity, as well as the conditions of economic and social progress and development.

These questions are such detailed questions, the detailed treatment of which cannot belong to the present study.

4. The respective question of sanctions however means that by the existence of special conditions what guarantees that Human Rights are truly effective living rights. What can guarantee that the administration and legislation of certain states should not be able to exceed the limits of the internationally accepted Human Rights.

5. This question according to my opinion demands concise study of cooperative experts, however it should not seem as act of immodesty if I venture to outline a conception. The Human Rights conceived by UNO should be accepted into the constitutions of every state as specially defined basic rights. The law regulations possibly conceived without consideration of same, should be previously considered constitutionally invalid, lex perfecta. On the occasion of the application of such an unappropriate law-regulation—as well as for judgment of any kind of insulting attitude concerning Human Rights—an international court should be organised which in effect make a final statement as to the invalidity of a law regulation, or would apply according to proper criminal procedure against those who infringe Human Rights. It is a detailed question but I mention it, that according to my opinion, an international law court of this kind should be organised in every state despite the veto, the declaration of the invalidity of a law-legislation of the international court, would wish detour from same the human right, the question would be decided by referendum. And in as much the majority opinion expressed in the secret vote would also wish to detour from some accepted Human Right the comity dealing with the Human Rights of the UNO should be convened and would be decided internationally as to whether it is necessary to revise Human Rights and Freedoms. If Human Rights would modify so, then they should be included in this modified form in the constitution of the respective states.

6. I know this regulation means a lot of difficulty but I believe that whatever realisation of the Human Rights affecting the entire world of necessity goes with great difficulty.

The problem of sanctions should be decided upon because without the assurance of same the declaration of Human Rights would only be a dream as to a happier future. The function of international courts seemingly would restrict sovereignty of certain states, according to me this is just a supposition, because every state would restrict itself by this means, as well as in other international agreements. The restrictions of these kind would not be a deterring factor for humanity. I much rather expect from the functioning of international courts the development of the belief of mankind as belonging to one world; the cognition of same that every citizen of the world guards the individual rights of every man, and development of that responsibility that we are all responsible for the infringements of Human Rights no matter in what part of the Earth it may take place.

RESPONSE TO THE QUESTIONNAIRE AND MEMORANDUM ON THE RIGHTS OF MAN
Alfred Weber[*]

1. Human Rights have both an absolute and a relative character. They are absolute in their spiritual foundation and relative in their precise and concrete expression, a function of their historical and geographical location.

2. The very idea of Human Rights was born in the West. This idea is based on the concept of a natural right common to all men, a concept that comes from the Roman Stoics and was taken over by St. Thomas Aquinas. Considered from a different angle, under their political aspect, as a limitation of the powers of the state and recognized by the state, Human Rights are the result of the spiritual and political struggle for freedom against absolutism, conducted since the fourteenth century (Marsilius of Padua) and especially since the seventeenth century (opponents of the monarchy, Althusius). The effect they have had on world history comes primarily, since John Locke, from their essentially religious foundation. Since Rousseau, they have been based on the concept of the original and immutable nature of man.

3. This concept, born from an ancient tradition of freedom, has been used

---

[*] Alfred Weber was a German economist, sociologist, and politician, and the younger brother of Max Weber. Alfred Weber was 79 years old at the time of the UNESCO human rights survey, having just resumed lecturing at the University of Heidelberg (he had resigned from his professorship in 1933 in protest against the Nazi takeover of power). After the war, Weber was active in local politics in Heidelberg for the new Social Democratic party. He died in 1958 at age 90. His most important works include *Theory of the Location of Industries* (1909), *Germany and the European Cultural Crisis* (1924), *Cultural History as the Sociology of Culture* (1935), and *Farewell to European History: Or, the Conquest of Nihilism* (1946). This piece was translated from the French by Romana Iorga.

in the West to arrive for the most part at the definition of "the rights of the free man." This thus led to incorporating the notion of property, regarded not as the product of capitalism but as the fruit of labor and as the material condition of equal opportunities in the pursuit of freedom.

4. While in the West, in America as in Europe, we have conceived and continue to conceive of equality as guaranteeing freedom, that is to say, the enjoyment of equal rights and equal opportunities, the adoption of the principle of equality has, in the region that is now Soviet territory, led to a social notion of equality regarded as the abolition of exploitation of man by man. Human Rights have been and still are viewed in this region as a collective deliverance to which are sacrificed the individual aspirations to freedom.

5. A reconciliation between these two views, the Western and the Eastern, and a fusion of them into a single formula, is impossible unless we give up the hefty definition that has been given to the "Rights of the free Man" in the West. This reconciliation is impossible because the desire for freedom takes on fundamentally different forms in the two cases, and because by "equality" we understand absolutely different things in the two cases. So it seems fair that each of these two regions should separately develop its own "Human Rights," especially as the Soviet region has, because of its simplified design, a particular need to adapt expressive formulas.

6. The ideas that were strengthened in the Asian East, such as those of Mahatma Gandhi, are in turn founded on principles that are very different from those of the West or of Russia. For Gandhi, they are based on a conception of humanity that already existed in Buddhism. These ideas must adapt to the conditions of the historical evolution of these regions. So you have to let the Asians determine to what extent they intend to bring home the Russian or Western conceptions of Human Rights and the specific character they intend to give to these conceptions.

7. As a result, we cannot reasonably do anything other than examine, concerning the expression that Human Rights have received *so far in the West*, to what extent their historical evolution and, particularly, their social and political evolution require a redesign of the different principles of these Rights as they were first formulated about a hundred and fifty years ago.

8. In this regard it should be noted that:

—A new expression of Human Rights must consider, firstly, the fact that since the late eighteenth century, capitalism has modified the previous structure of ownership and has given rise to new possible forms of human slavery. It is in opposition to this fact that we must define Human Rights.

—Secondly, this new expression must take into account the fact that since that time, the West has gone through a period of national collectivism and national imperialism, along with the excesses that that entails. In view of these new facts, the question arises regarding the extent to which we can claim to guarantee Human Rights. . . .

MATERIAL SECURITY AND SPIRITUAL LIBERTY
Don Salvador de Madariaga[*]

I.

No discussion of "the Rights of Man" can yield fruitful results when the subject is so limited both to the rights and to the individual; and the very form of words is to be avoided. It dates from the era of the French Revolution, which bred a combative, biased and therefore limited outlook. Historically this attitude was only too natural and even justified. A similar attitude has been fostered by the cruel oppression millions of men and women have suffered in the last two decades. But true constructive work in the field of *Social nature* can be achieved only if and when the matter be approached objectively and not aggressively. The first result of this change of outlook is that the word and concept of *Rights* is found to be too narrow, for it only represents one aspect of the relations between the individual and the society in which he lives.

It is a commonplace—but an often forgotten one—that there is no such thing as an absolute individual, i.e. that no human being exists who does not contain a social element as well. Man is a synthesis which might be described as *individual-in-society*; and an individual without a society is no more thinkable than a society without individuals. It seems, therefore, that the right approach" to

---

[*] Don Salvador de Madariaga was a Spanish diplomat, academic, writer, and liberal internationalist. He was trained as an engineer in Paris, but moved to London before the First World War to write for *The Times*. After the war, he moved to Geneva to take up a position in the League of Nations, where he directed the disarmament section from 1922 to 1927. In 1928, he was appointed the first King Alfonso XIII Professor of Spanish Studies at Oxford, but he resigned that position three years later to begin a series of ambassadorial postings for the Spanish government, including postings to the United States and to France. A longtime opponent of General Franco, Madariaga was in de facto exile from Spain from 1936 until 1976. He was the author of many works, including *Englishmen, Frenchmen, Spaniards: An Essay in Comparative Psychology* (1929), *Anarchy or Hierarchy* (1937), *The Heart of Jade* (a novel, 1942), and *Latin America, Between the Eagle and the Bear* (1962).

the problem usually defined as that of "the Rights of man" should be that of the right political relations between the individual and the society to which he belongs.

In our day, the political society in which we are set has become one. For a number of well known reasons, nations, the separate societies of the past, have become merged into a world-society; and the chaos in which we all live is due to the fact that this world society being still without its State, or governmental institutions, the several nations seek to meet the trouble by the disastrous expedient of strengthening their respective authorities. The recrudescence of governmental regulations and the raising of frontier barriers of all kinds are direct, though paradoxical results of the growth of world solidarity.

This paradox can be solved easily once the distinction has been made between objective and subjective solidarity. The owners of—or passengers in—all the cars in a traffic jam are in as "thick" solidarity as the drops of water in a pipe: but their subjective solidarity is probably nihil, and each and every one of them is perhaps wishing the others were dead and in hell. The present chaos is due to the fact that while the objective solidarity of nations has rushed ahead with the increase in the speed of physical and mental communications, their subjective solidarity has lagged behind.

Of the three stages of social nature, man, nation, mankind, it is therefore the middle stage which most requires control and restraint. For it is the nation which, both towards the individual and towards the world society, turns an absolutist face. Towards the individual, the nation, once absolutist on the strength of the divine right of Kings, remains absolutist on the strength of "the will of the people." Towards the world society, the nation remains absolutist entrenched as it is in the doctrine—and practice—of national sovereignty.

The problem first understood as that of "the Rights of Man" thus reveals itself as one of the proper relations between man, nation and world community.

II.

This conclusion raises a fresh problem: what is meant by "proper relations"? In other words, what are the standards which are to guide us in our enquiry. The complete answer must ultimately depend on the faith, the philosophy or the *Weltanschauung* of the enquirer. The atheist-materialist-Marxist, the agnostic-liberal, the undogmatic Christian, the dogmatic Catholic will each provide a different answer. This fact might of itself render illusory any hope of agreement on so capital a subject were we to insist on a thorough-going definition of our criteria and a rigid formulation of their consequences. Yet, the door remains open for some kind of compromise or common ground of all doctrines; and it is as a contribution to this compromise that the following observations are put forward.

The atheist-materialist-Marxist asserts that there is no life after death; the believer puts this life after death at the forefront of his philosophy. We need not decide the point. If we base our conclusions on the assumption that we do not know and do not prejudice the eschatological issue, we need conflict with neither of the two extremes and dogmatic schools. All we need is the agreement of both on the principle that every individual human being is a singular and precious unit of life with a fate of his own, and with rights and duties towards himself. True, when we come to define what this unit-of-life's chief aim is, differences appear: "the pursuit of happiness" proclaim the fathers of the American revolution; "the salvation of the soul" preach the fathers of the Church. Could we again bring them together on a non-committal ground? Let us define man's chief right-duty in life as that of seeking, and if possible, finding himself in experience, i.e. of understanding as much as he can of the world, of himself and of the true relation between the two.

This conclusion leads to the first political right of man: that of freedom to live and learn in his own way. It is a primary right, inseparable from that of merely living. For in fact when we lay down the right to live as the first and fundamental right of man, we assume that what is to live *is* a man; and therefore the right to learn by experience is no attribute super-added to, but part and parcel of the right to live which no society can deny its members.

It will be seen therefore that liberty of personal experience—with all the consequential rights that flow from it—is at the very basis of all rights of man, and that it need never be justified, but follows automatically from the very fact that man lives.

All limitations to this fundamental right must be justified before they can be accepted. They fall under three heads:

limitations of individual liberty for the sake of the individual liberty of others
limitations of individual liberty for the sake of the nation
limitations of individual liberty for the sake of the world community

III.

If we come now to consider the first of these limitations, we might be tempted at first to dismiss all discussion of the subject on the ground that a balance could and would automatically be struck between all those equivalent rights. The matter is, however, more subtle than that. For the rights of the individual are of different qualities and values, and it is important that a scale should be set up and agreed upon so that no limitation of the higher or of the essential rights is permitted in favor of lower or less important ones.

It is clear from all that precedes, that the first right of man is to live; and that this right includes: that of living as a body, i.e. of ensuring his subsistence, and that of living as a mind and soul, i.e. of ensuring the freedom of his experience. In the exercise of their remaining rights, other individuals must not overstep the boundaries of these two primary rights, and should they attempt to do so, we know in advance that their claims cannot be legitimate.

It should be noticed that the two primary claims might, and, in fact, do enter into conflict, and not merely as between man and man, but even when one only individual is considered. For the body can be, and often is, the enemy of the mind and soul; and, particularly in our day, the trend of things favors the right to live as a body against the right to live as a spirit, or, in other words, the claims of security against those of liberty. This trend is unfortunate and decadent: a minimum guarantee against starvation is to be proclaimed as the *first* right of man; but the *foremost* right of man is a guarantee that he will be free to live his life in his own way.

IV.

No other limitations of individual liberty can be admitted from the point of view of the nation than those required by the very existence and healthy life of the nation itself. Chief among them are internal order and external peace, both indispensable also for the exercise of individual liberty. But in this respect two important considerations arise: one, mostly connected with order, touches on the administration of justice and the police; the other one refers to the army and to military service.

Order cannot be of the healthy kind which allows the free use of individual liberty if it does not rest on a wide basis of national assent. It follows that the rights of man must include: *government by the spontaneous, free and well-informed consent of the majority of the citizens, and with adequate guarantees for the freedom and opinions of the minorities. This implies objective justice and a non-political police*. The point need hardly be elaborated that, in their turn, these conditions require a *free press*. Without a free press no rights are worth the paper on which they are written.

The second point refers to the rights and duties of man with regard to international peace. When we admit the right of the nation to limit individual liberty for the sake of national defense, we have to bear in mind that nations have a way of covering under those words any designs, however aggressive, they may harbor. The problem thus created in the individual conscience was first discussed in the 16th century by Francisco de Vitoria in his *De Indis*. It is possible to adapt his conclusions to a modern setting. The citizen has the right, indeed the duty, to refuse military service if and when he is satisfied that the issue is against his conscience; but the decision is so grave that the citizen must not take it without listening first to the advice of the wise men. That is Vitoria's doctrine. In his day, when an orthodoxy was recognized by the overwhelming majority of Europeans, the "wise men" were eminent churchmen. In our day, we must endeavor to find some objective standard. The solution might be to lay down the right of all citizens to refuse military service in any war in which his country's side would have been declared in the wrong by a majority vote of the Security Council of U.N.

It is clear that a country ready to go to war in defiance of the international authority can hardly be expected to respect the right of its citizens to refuse service for such a war. Nevertheless the right must be stated, for it may act as a deterrent, particularly if, the war over, the statesmen responsible for its violation are made to pay for their guilt. Furthermore, persons having authentically expressed their unwillingness to serve would, if falling in the hands of the other side, be treated as friendly aliens, and not as prisoners of war.

V.

The discussion of the relations between the citizen and the nation does not exhaust the problem set by the existence of these two forms of human life: nation and man. What, for instance, of the right of immigration and emigration? This question is only too often discussed with a background and an understructure of feelings which deprive it of clarity. The point of view of the nation should be borne in mind, both on grounds of theoretical justice and of practical politics. *A nation has a right to exist.* And this might well be the best moment for establishing it on objective grounds. We start from the individual as the only tangible and concrete thing there is; and we re-assert that his chief purpose in life is to find himself in experience, i.e. to acquire a *culture*. Instruction, information, craft, are all excellent for earning a living and as elements of culture. But culture—a merely relative concept—is the degree of realization, of awareness of adequate relationship between himself and the world a man has reached.

Now, the nation is the best setting for most human beings to rise up the slope of culture. It is the depository of tradition, the "cup" in which the subconscious life of a community is held and accumulated; the setting of individual experiences. This function it is which gives the nation its *raison d'être*.

It follows that the nation has the right to persevere in its being, as Spinoza would have said. And therefore it is plain that the right of moving about and settling anywhere of any one man must be balanced against the right of any nation to remain what it is or to become what it wants to become.

VI.

There remain the limitations to individual liberty to be accepted in the name and for the sake of the world community. They include barriers against acts injurious to the healthy life and peace of the world community as a whole; and checks on individual acts against nations. In both cases, it is extremely unlikely that individuals, without the backing of a powerful nation, may threaten the peace or interests of the world or of another nation; so that this section practically merges with the next.

VII.

A section on the rights and duties of nations towards each other and towards the World Commonwealth should be considered as an integral part of the projected Charter. This field has been already covered twice; by the Covenant of the League of Nations and by the Charter of U.N. Neither recognized the existence of the World Commonwealth, the logical outcome of the World Community. The problem turns on the issue of national sovereignty.

This issue is too often simplified into what is known as "surrender" of national sovereignty to a higher authority. Such a thing can never happen except under duress as the outcome of a defeat. National sovereignty can be enlarged so as to include wider territories and populations, but only when the awareness of a common solidarity and destiny is so enlarged first. Sure this is a process which *must happen in life*; no "Charter" can bring it about. The projected charter should therefore be limited to a modest outline of the rights and duties between nations and the co-operative of sovereignties the UNO may be said to represent.

THE RIGHTS OF MAN
Frank R. Scott[*]

I should like first to comment upon the approach to the problem contained in the *aide-mémoire* which was attached to the material sent to me by Professor Huxley. In this *aide-mémoire* it seems to be suggested that two main conceptions of human rights are contending for acceptance, namely the one started from the premise of individual rights, and the other which was based upon Marxist principles. It is even suggested that one of the tasks immediately ahead for UNESCO is "to effect a reconciliation of the two opposites in a higher synthesis." May I suggest that this is a great over-simplification of the real problem. There are several currents of thought and belief in the western world which are neither Marxist nor individualist, and which are equally asserting a faith in human liberties. There is, for example, the democratic socialist philosophy from which contemporary Marxism is an historical derivation. Catholic philosophy would be another. The task ahead of us is rather to seek out the common elements in respect of human freedom which underlie all the main philosophic and political systems that hold an important place in the modern world (excluding of course Fascism and Nazism). It would be unfortunate if any documentation from UNESCO were to appear to accept a division of the world into two intellectual camps when in fact the situation is more complex.

I am not sure how far it is helpful to attempt to answer the very difficult questions which are posed in the *aide-mémoire* regarding the philosophic and social basis of human rights. On such questions there would inevitably be wide differences of view. It seems to me more practical and useful to concentrate upon the foundations of the particular freedoms and rights and to find the phraseology which will find the widest acceptance without sacrifice of principle. It would be proper, I think, for UNESCO to urge that the United Nations consider such a formulation as a minimum standard of national conduct and not as a fixed

---

[*] Frank R. Scott was a Canadian legal scholar and academic, public intellectual, political leader, and poet who played an important role in establishing both literary modernism and socialism in Canada. During the Great Depression, Scott was one of the founders of the League of Social Reconstruction, an organization modeled after the British Fabian Society. In 1947, at the time of the UNESCO human rights survey, Scott had just been elected to the Royal Society of Canada. Scott joined the law faculty of McGill University in 1928 and remained at McGill until his retirement in 1964, by which time he was serving as dean. Scott was a friend and colleague of John P. Humphrey, who was also on the law faculty at McGill. When Scott submitted his response to UNESCO in the late spring of 1947, Humphrey had already written the first, and most important, draft of the Universal Declaration of Human Rights.

maximum which is static and rigid in its application. What we want to create is the notion that human rights should be always expanding as man's control over his own behavior and the forces of nature make possible an enlargement of opportunities for human development.

One last thought occurs to me. It is not difficult to formulate the rights; the problem is to secure their enforcement. For some time this must remain primarily the responsibility of each Member state. Nevertheless, a study of techniques and procedures which have been found effective in various countries and the protection of these freedoms would be most valuable. I suggest that an organized plan of research be undertaken in this branch of comparative constitutional law. For example, England's development of the Writ of Habeas Corpus has had a world-wide influence. France developed a system of administrative law which affords a fine example of the manner in which administrative action may be controlled when it injures the individual citizen. Russia's policy toward her various nationalities is a remarkable example of cultural freedom to minority groups. One could find other examples in other countries, but my point is that an interchange of ideas and experience in these fields would help all nations to improve the procedures by which they may implement the Declaration of Rights when it is finally adopted. *Ubi remedium, ibi jus.* [Where there is a right, there is a remedy. Ed.]

JUST TO WRITE SOME PIOUS SENTIMENTS WILL SERVE LITTLE PURPOSE
*Jawaharlal Nehru**

External Affairs Department,   Air Mail
INDIA D. O. No. F.387-P.S./E.6
New Delhi
14th May 1947

Dear Dr. Huxley,

I must apologize to you for the delay in answering your letter of the 26th March. I am attracted by your project and I would gladly associate myself with it. But when you ask me to write something on the subject of human rights, I feel a bit diffident. There is no point in my writing unless I can say something

---

* Jawaharlal Nehru was the first prime minister of India. The architect of independent India, he was reelected three times, serving until his death in 1964.

worth while which has not been said by others. Just to write some pious sentiments will serve little purpose.

Apart from this, we have to face at present very difficult and intricate problems in India and I have the misfortune to be tied up with these problems. I cannot find the time for any quiet consideration or writing. You will therefore forgive me I hope if I do not send you a contribution.

I might inform you that our Constituent Assembly has recently been considering the question of fundamental rights to be incorporated in our constitution.

You mention in your letter that you were enclosing a letter to Mahatma Gandhi. No such letter reached me. Mr. Gandhi is not easy to reach always as he has been working in rather distant parts of India and, as always, he is frightfully busy. He is going to come here in about ten days time and I shall then mention this matter to him. Certainly I shall urge him to write something, for his approach to these problems is always novel and interesting. Whether he finds time to do so or not, I cannot say.

I am glad to learn from your letter of the 3rd April that you were trying to get the U.S.S.R. to join the UNESCO. I hope you will succeed. I am quite sure that it is desirable for the U.S.S.R. to be associated with the UNESCO.

With all good wishes,
Yours sincerely,
(Sd.) Jawaharlal Nehru

Specific Freedoms

HUMAN RIGHTS AND THE PRISONER
Margery Fry [*]

In considering the rights of the individual in relation to the State in which he lives, the limiting case is, in peace time, that of the person accused or convicted of breaking the law of that State. From very early times, long before the formation of organized Governments, the community has assumed the right to protect itself, by corporate action, against these enemies within its borders, by law, as it does in war against exterior foes. And, though in very primitive times, it is largely ritual offences, transgressions of taboos and customs of the tribe which are thus punished, still the private injuries, which at first were the subject of individual revenge, very early came to be considered as equally the concern of the whole community.

It has often been pointed out that the individual in a primitive society has an extremely small range of free action, and perhaps the growth of early law should be regarded rather as a definition and consequently a limitation of the power of the community over the individual than a limitation of the freedom of the individual in the interests of the community.

The history of this definition and limitation is the history of criminal law. The formulation of that law, the definition of the actions which justify the State in interference with the citizen has, in all civilized epochs, engaged some of the best minds; very much less attention has been paid to the question of what limits should be set to the forfeiture of his rights by the lawbreaker. Far too often this forfeiture has been regarded as complete, involving life itself. Where life is spared, to what length is the State entitled to go in stripping an offender, permanently or temporarily, of his other freedoms? Has a human being some rights which the community has no moral sanction in mulcting him of?

---

[*] Margery Fry was an English Quaker prison reformer and anti-death penalty activist. Although requests were sent to several other women, Fry was the only woman to submit a response to the UNESCO human rights survey. She studied mathematics at Oxford, later becoming the librarian of her college, Somerville. In 1921, she was appointed one of the first female magistrates in Britain. She returned to Somerville College in 1926 as principal. Fry also served as a governor of the British Broadcasting Corporation. At the time of the UNESCO human rights survey, Fry was 73 years old. She died in 1958 at age 84.

Such questions have been fully recognized only during the last 200 years, and to Beccaria belongs the credit of being the first writer to bring them prominently before the notice of the civilized world. Himself stimulated by the French philosophers of the 18th Century, he, in turn, greatly influenced them.

. . . Beccaria had proclaimed the measure of crime to be the injury done to society. Offences against God which do not endanger public security should be left to divine justice, and the object of punishment should not be the infliction of pain, but simply to deter the offender and others from future crimes. Thus he disclaimed—as did his followers—a semi-theocratic duty laid upon the State to punish moral depravity as such. The doctrines of these penologists of the period at the end of the eighteenth and beginning of the nineteenth centuries have never been either refuted or put into practice in their entirety. It is impossible to consider without horror the immensity of the needless human suffering which could have been saved if their views had really prevailed. "Wherever the laws suffer a man, in certain cases, to cease to be a *person* and to become a *thing*, there is no liberty," wrote Beccaria. The history of the last twenty years in Europe has illustrated this only too vividly. They have, moreover, shown that where no limit is set to the power of the State over those who break its laws, where no rights at all are acknowledged to be universal, a definite international tension is likely to be set up. The minority of one country is often attached by racial or political links with the majority of another, and inhumanity in the treatment of such a minority convicted of breaking laws intended for the benefit of the majority has aroused, again and again, extremely bitter international hatreds.

It was perhaps partly this aspect of the case, though it was not oblivious of its humanitarian side also, which determined the League of Nations to place the question of Penal Administration upon its agenda in 1929, and to request the co-operation of the International Penal and Penitentiary Commission in framing a set of Minimum Rules for the Treatment of Prisoners. These, after circulation to States (members and non-members of the League) were finally approved by the League as constituting a minimum below which no State's penitentiary system should fall (1934). The International Penal and Penitentiary Commission thus called into consultation by the League of Nations is itself an expression of the common interest of States in the proper administration of penal sanctions, i.e. of the ultimate relation of the State to the individual law-breaker. It had been in existence since 1872 as a standing body of penal experts appointed by various Governments, and had organized ten International Conferences on penal questions. The minimum rules which the Commission proposed for the treatment of convicted prisoners were thus the result of long and wide study of legal punishment over the greater part of the civilized world.

Though not framed in the form of a statement of "rights," these rules would, if carried out in their entirety, ensure that the man in prison should not "become a thing" but should retain at least some of the conditions without which life becomes intolerable, even though the exercise of most of his cherished liberties were denied him. In fact, taking the list in UNESCO's Memorandum on Human Rights, even if the Rules were scrupulously observed, the only freedoms reserved to the prisoner (during his incarceration) are numbers 1 and 14—unless it be urged that "the good life" can be pursued "even in a gaol" as well as "even in a palace."

It is to be observed that the right to decent treatment as a prisoner is not identical with (18) the right to justice, since the offender who has been justly condemned should not thereby forfeit all claims to a tolerable existence.

Actually, so far from these rules being completely observed, with all their recommendations, it is doubtful whether any country has even attained these so-called "minimum" standards. The degree of attainment varies immensely from country to country, and in all countries which have directly suffered from the effects of the war conditions have, in general, gravely deteriorated in spite of a few notable exceptions. Some of these exceptional modern experiments tend to show that the limitation of normal freedoms, the suffering (though not as a rule physical suffering) deliberately inflicted by States for the prevention of crime is usually in excess of what, upon a utilitarian calculation, is justifiable, since other methods can be found as efficacious for maintaining observance of the law.

The "Minimum Rules" dealt mainly with the treatment of convicted persons, but abundant evidence was forthcoming that the treatment of untried or unconvicted people in custody was, in many countries, at least as gravely in contradiction with elementary human rights. The League of Nations was engaged in collecting, from the technical organizations with which it was in communication, proposals for regulations "to protect witnesses and persons awaiting trial against the use of violence, and any other forms of physical or mental constraint." These proposed rules were actually discussed at a meeting of the same organizations in June 1939. This piece of work remained unfinished (but more than ever necessary) at the outbreak of war.

Both the practical extent and the guarantees of the minimum rights of the prisoner vary very greatly from country to country. In many the existence of capital punishment is an assertion that in the last resort the individual may forfeit every right.

The question of guarantees is peculiarly difficult in the case of prisoners. Their voice, as against that of those in authority over them, cannot make itself heard through the prison walls; their statements are often suspect. Safeguards through the admission of qualified persons to the prisons are most important.

The surest guarantee against abuses lies in an alert and well-informed public opinion. Such an opinion the United Nations is eminently qualified to guide. The acceptance by the United Nations of definite standards for the treatment of those who are deprived of their liberty was a step in the right direction. Unfortunately the absence of any system of international inspection and reporting allowed this acceptance to be, in too many cases, a purely verbal one. But it will be an irreparable loss to the world if the foundations already laid are allowed to disintegrate before a new and lasting structure for the defence of the rights of a peculiarly defenceless part of the human race is erected upon them.

London, April 1947

EDUCATION AND HUMAN RIGHTS
Isaac Leon Kandel[*]

A study of recent statements on Human Rights reveals the curious paradox that the one condition which is essential to their realization and proper use is hardly ever mentioned. Perhaps the omission of any reference to education can be explained on the assumption that it is taken for granted as a human right and as the essential foundation for the enjoyment of human rights. The history of education, however, provides ample evidence that education has not been regarded as a human right nor has it been used as an instrument for developing an appreciation of the importance of human rights for the fullest development of each individual as a human being. Historically two motives have dominated the provision of education. The first and the earliest motive was directed to indoctrinating the younger generation in the religious beliefs of their particular denominations. The second motive, which came with the use of the national state, was to develop a sense of loyalty to the political group or nation. In both cases the ends that were sought emphasized acquiescent discipline rather than education for freedom as a human being.

---

[*] Isaac Leon Kandel was one of the founders of the field of comparative educational studies. Although Kandel was English, he was born in the Romanian city of Botoşani, birthplace of Nicolae Iorga, the most influential Romanian historian, and Mihai Eminescu, Romania's national poet. Kandel received his PhD in 1910 from Teachers College, Columbia University, and in 1913 joined the faculty, where he remained until 1947. At the time of the UNESCO human rights survey, Kandel was a professor at Teachers College and one of the leading educational theorists and historians in the world. His many books include *History of Secondary Education* (1930), *Comparative Education* (1933), *The Cult of Uncertainty* (1943), and *The New Era in Education* (1955).

. . . Because education has not yet been recognized universally as a human right, it is essential that it be included in any declaration of human rights that may be drawn up. The right to education needs greater emphasis than it is given in the [Memorandum on the] Rights of Man, prepared by UNESCO. One of the tragic results of the traditional organization of education into two systems—one for the masses and the other for a select group—is that, even when equality of educational opportunity is provided, certain social and economic classes feel that the opportunities are not intended for them. The provision of equality of educational opportunity demands in some countries measures to change the psychological attitudes produced by the traditional organization. Thus M. Henri Laugier in discussing plans for the reconstruction of education in France, wrote:

> So many generations in France have lived in an atmosphere of theoretical equal-
> ity and actual inequality that the situation has in practice met with fairly gen-
> eral acceptance, induced by the normally pleasant conditions of French life. Of
> course, the immediate victims of the inequality are barely conscious of it or do
> not suffer from it in any way. It does not occur to the son of a worker or an
> agricultural labourer that he might become the governor of a colony, director
> in a ministry, an ambassador, an admiral, or an inspector of finance. He may
> know that such positions exist, but for him they exist in a higher world which
> is not open to him. Most frequently this situation neither inspires nor embitters
> him, nor does it arouse in him a desire to claim a right or to demand a definite
> change![1]

. . . The recognition of education as a human right is, however, only one aspect of the problem as it concerns the Rights of Man. Free access to education at
all levels may be provided without affecting either the content or the methods of
instruction. Traditionally, the quality of elementary education differed from the
quality of secondary education; the former was directed to imparting a certain
quantum of knowledge, most generally to be acquired by rote and resulting in
what the French call *l'esprit primaire*; the latter was intended to impart a liberal
or general cultural education. In neither case was there, except by indirection,
any deep-rooted training for the use and enjoyment of those freedoms which
are included in the list of Human Rights. The emphasis, particularly, since most
types of education were dominated by exigencies of examinations, was rather
on the acceptance of the authority either of the printed word or of the teacher.

---

1. In *Educational Yearbook, 1944*, of the International Institute, Teachers College, Columbia
University, p. 136 f, edited by I.L. Kandel. New York, 1944.

When the pendulum began to shift from an emphasis on discipline, indoctrination, and authoritarianism to an emphasis on freedom, it was too often forgotten that freedom is a conquest and that education for freedom of any kind demands a type of discipline in learning to appreciate the moral consequences of one's actions. Education for freedom does not mean, as it has frequently been thought to mean, a *laisser faire* program of content or of methods of instruction, but the intelligent recognition of responsibility and duty. If this principle is sound, it also means a change in the status of the teacher and of teaching. If the teacher is to be more than a purveyor of knowledge to be tested by examinations, then the traditional limitations placed upon him by courses of study prescribed in detail, by prescribed methods of instruction, and by control through inspection and examinations must be replaced by a different concept of the preparation that is desirable for the teacher. That preparation must be raised to the same level as preparation for any other liberal profession. If the efforts of the teacher are to be directed to the development of free personalities and to education for freedom of speech, expression, communication, information and inquiry, the teacher through his preparation should become professionally free and recognize that freedom without a sense of responsibility easily degenerates into license.

Before the Rights of Man can be incorporated into programs of education, another change is essential. In the past, education has been used as an instrument of nationalistic policy, which too frequently meant indoctrination in either national or racial separatism and superiority. And even where the humanities formed the core of the curriculum, so much attention was devoted to the scaffolding that the essential meaning of humanism was lost. The common goals inherent in the ideal of the Rights of Man can only be attained as programs of education and instruction are based on the realization that there is no national culture which does not owe far more than is usually admitted to the influence of the cultural heritage of man of all races and of all ages. It is upon this foundation that the freedoms included in the Rights of Man can be laid; it is only in this way that the true concept of humanism as an end in education can be developed. Their attainment, finally, depends upon training in the methods of free inquiry. Education for the various freedoms demands discipline. To paraphrase Rousseau, man must be disciplined to enjoy the freedoms which are his rights.

June 1947

THE RIGHT TO INFORMATION AND
THE RIGHT TO THE EXPRESSION OF OPINION
René Maheu[*]

It is an error to continue to regard freedom of information as an extension of freedom of expression, the latter itself proceeding from freedom of thought. The individualist concept implicit in this classical sequence, contemporaneous with a largely hack press, not merely lags behind the concepts of modern political sociology; the economic and technical realities of today clearly involve the adoption of an entirely different viewpoint.

Whether it be the press, news agencies, the cinema or broadcasting, information today is only to a limited degree an expression of opinion. Essentially it is the pre-conditioning (or the satisfying) of opinion. It either precedes or follows opinion. Moreover that opinion is the opinion of the public and not of news operators, whose task it is in most cases to suppress their personal views. It is a question of mass opinion, and mass behaviour; the techniques of modern news belong to the field of mass psycho-sociology, and not of individual psychology.

The conditioning or exploitation of mass opinion and mass behaviour is today a major industry, whose operation is only to a minor degree affected by the individual views and reactions of its producers and even consumers: that is the social fact which we must take as our starting point.

* * *

Neither ethics nor politics can disregard this formidable mechanism. The task is to humanize it. I believe that is one of the major problems of this age.

If we are to prevent what too often occurs, the large-scale alienation of the masses, the same revolution must be achieved as regards information in this century as took place in education in the last century. Information must be a right (hence, too, a duty) and that right must belong to those whose thought is at stake.

---

[*] René Maheu was a French philosopher who had a long and distinguished career at UNESCO. At the time of the UNESCO human rights survey, Maheu was serving as director of the Division of Free Flow of Information. He was asked to contribute to the survey almost as soon as the Phil/1/1947 documents were drafted, since he worked in the same office. Maheu had been a close friend of Jean-Paul Sartre and Simone de Beauvoir when they were all students in Paris in the 1920s. Maheu helped de Beauvoir prepare for the all-important *agrégation*, the rigorous exam for France's public education system, for which she gave him the nickname "my Lama." Maheu later became the first director-general of UNESCO to serve for two consecutive terms (1962–1974). He died in 1975.

The inclusion of the right to information among the Rights of Man means more than seeking a mere increase or improvement in the knowledge available to the public. It involves radical reconsideration of the function of information. It means that the products, the methods and even the organization of the news industry must be reassessed from the point of view not of the interests or prejudices of those who control its production, but of the human dignity of those who henceforth are justified in expecting of it the means of free thought.

From the moment that information comes to be regarded as one of the rights of man, the structures and practices which make of it an instrument for the exploitation, by alienation, of the minds of the masses, for money or for power, can no longer be tolerated; information becomes, for those who impart it, a social function in the service of intellectual emancipation.

The right to information is a natural extension of the right to education, and that very fact makes it possible to define its concrete content.

That content is sometimes defined as "facts" or raw news, i.e., news not interpreted. There should be no illusion about the practical value of the traditional distinction between fact and opinion. What is a fact? A piece of evidence. And the selection of a fact is an implicit expression of opinion. There is nothing more misleading than the chimera of mechanical objectivity. Nor can human liberty look for salvation to the impersonal.

A better definition of information would probably be a detached presentation of materials capable of use by anybody in the formation of an opinion. Whereas an expression of opinion—whether persuasive or challenging—is always militant, the characteristic of information, unlike propaganda or publicity, which proceeds by observation, is availability.

This being so, it will be asked whether a corollary of the recognition of man's right to information is not admission of the right of all to access to all sources of knowledge in all circumstances. Leaving out of account questions of physical impossibility, this straightway suggests to the mind the many restrictions imposed for the protection of the most legitimate political, economic or personal interests: secrets of State, manufacturing secrets, domestic privacy.

But the proclamation of the right to education does not *ipso facto* mean that the child has a right to learn anything, at any age, and anyhow. It only means that it is the duty of adults to give the child the knowledge necessary for his development in the light of his needs (and capabilities) at his age. A right is no more than an instrument—an instrument for building up Man in man's mind. And an instrument is only an instrument if it is related to needs.

The same is true of the right to information as of all other rights: its legitimate content must be defined in terms of real needs. Conditionally, of course,

on the word "needs" being understood to mean the needs of human development, and not of self-interest or passion.

Of their very nature those needs involve a large measure of recourse to human
fraternity and to exchanges between men, an appeal that will always extend far
beyond mere egotism. It is true, however, that, as there are great variations in
living conditions and modes of development, the needs of human groups are not
identical at all points in time and space. These groups do not all need the same
information.

There must be no fear of introducing into a consideration of the rights of
man this element of historical and sociological relativity. So far from putting in
peril the effective achievement of those rights, only a realistic appreciation in the
light of that relativity can give them concrete meaning for the men who must
fight to make them triumph.

* * *

The right to the expression of opinion is much more closely geared to historic
relativity. While the right to information must be numbered among the conditions of democracy and thus has the force of a principle, the right to the
expression of opinion is part of the exercise of democracy and, as such, shares
the relativity of all political realities or practice. A regime blessed with stable
institutions and with a body of citizens apathetic or tolerant or whose critical
faculties are highly trained, can give the freest rein to the expression of individual
views. Indeed it must do so, in the sense that, more than any other, it needs that
indispensable stimulus to maintain progress.

Against this a democratic order in peril in a State torn by passion or possessed of the devils of credulity or, again, a democracy fully committed to a
revolutionary or systematic process of reconstruction, is justified in imposing
considerable limitation on the freedom of individual expression, the exercise of
which is necessarily hostile to complete unity.

Recognition that the right to the expression of opinion must be conditioned
by the historical perspective of a particular democracy, is not sacrificing a human
right to reason of State. On the contrary, that right is thus given its full meaning
by refusal to sacrifice to an abstract concept the merits and chances of success of
a concrete undertaking.

Nor is it a question of limitation from outside, as when human liberty is
assailed by Fascism or any other tyranny, whether forcibly or by fraud. What
is meant is the self-imposed restraint inherent in liberty, which is known as the
sense of responsibility.

Just as it is derived from liberty through a twofold internal relationship, so that responsibility is itself twofold.

Firstly, all liberty exists in relation to a certain situation and consequently assumes that situation wherefrom it emerges, at the very moment when by its operating it affirms its power to repudiate it. Thus any expression of free opinion, to be valid, to be its true self, must have regard to the historical and sociological background against which it stands.

Secondly, any expression of free opinion is an attempt to affect the liberty of others. That expression is in essence far more an appeal directed to other free men than the mere exteriorization of an inner conviction. If I express my thought, I do so partly, no doubt, to clarify or demonstrate my own views, but mainly to convince others. But I cannot, without danger of self-contradiction, use my liberty to appeal to the liberty of others without treating their liberty as liberty, i.e. without respecting it.

Thus recognition of the perspective of the historical moment of society and respect for the liberty of others impose on every citizen in the expression of his views a twofold set of imperatives, whereby he must judge the possibilities; these are summed up in the single word responsibility. Responsibility decides the extent to which the right to the expression of opinion is valid. And hence that extent is relative like responsibility itself.

In strict ethics only the subject can and may assess his responsibility, and consequently a term to the exercise of his liberty in the act of expression of opinion.

But politics replace the disintegrated particles of absolute individual subjects by an ideal collective subject modeled on the framework of the State. Democracy is the reign of the "general will" of the individual citizens. Whether that "general will" is a real force in a living being or a regulating fiction, is a matter of philosophic theory. In practice it is enough that in normal conditions that "general will" be identified by hypothesis, with the majority vote, though capable—in extraordinary periods, e.g. during a revolution—of being embodied in a minority. Thus in a democracy there is a recognized judge of the individual's responsibility in the expression of his views. To be a democrat is to acknowledge that judge.

Admittedly, as no one can be fully a democrat save in a democracy already achieved, and as there are only imperfect potential democracies, it is at all times the citizen's right—and even his duty—to judge his judge. It is the fear of that ultimate appeal which holds back the steps of majorities along the path of tyranny. And similarly it is always ultimately the citizen who decides freely in his own mind whether this is the time for law or for revolution.

That is where politics finally yield to ethics and are absorbed in them. Doubtless in such an appeal ad infinitum, where rules and safeguards successively pass away, there are growing risks of errors. But is there any liberty without risk? Risk abides in the heart of man, for man exists only by inventing himself.

Paris, July 1947
(Translated from the French)

FREEDOM OF THOUGHT FOR CHILDREN
Albert Szent-Györgyi[*]

It is, in my opinion, a sign of respect for an absolutely essential freedom not to create in children, at an age when they are defenseless, any conditioned reflex (psychological or otherwise) that they would subsequently be incapable of making disappear.

Respect for this freedom has as a corollary the prohibition against anyone teaching the child anything as an absolute and unquestionable truth that is not recognized as such by the majority of educated adults. This applies to religion as well as history. For example, if most educated adults do not admit that the world was created in seven days, that is an idea that should be erased from the textbooks intended for children and presented only as the opinion of a small group or a folkloric tradition. It is the same for all religious matters (existence and number of gods, etc.).

In the field of history, if at any time a national group devastated another country and if the largest number of educated adults worldwide does not agree that humanity has gained by that particular invasion, then we should not teach children to consider it as an ideal or a claim to fame. That would instill in them imperialism, hatred, and national prejudices.

June 4, 1947

_____

[*] Albert Szent-Györgyi was a Hungarian medical scientist and biochemist. Although he began his research career somewhat inauspiciously, publishing his first article on the humble epithelium of the anus in 1913, he later went on to become one of the most important medical scientists of the twentieth century, winning the Nobel Prize in Medicine in 1937 for discovering Vitamin C. Szent-Györgyi's education was interrupted by the First World War, during which he used his detailed knowledge of human anatomy to shoot himself in his own arm with relative safety, in order to be released from active duty. In 1939, when the Soviet Union invaded Finland, he donated his Nobel medal (206 grams of 23-carat gold) to support Hungarian volunteers fighting in the short lived Winter War. After serving in the Hungarian anti-Nazi underground during the Second World War, Szent-Györgyi later emigrated to the United States, where he was director of the Institute for Muscle Research at the Marine Biological Laboratory in Woods Hole, Massachusetts and founder of the National Foundation for Cancer Research. He died in 1986 at the age of 93.

From Repudiation to the Play of Fancy

WE ARE FINISHED WITH THE ERA OF PASSING GENERAL
RESOLUTIONS IN REGARD TO LIBERTY AND FREEDOM
*Morris L. Ernst**

April 29, 1947

Mr. Richard P. McKeon
The University of Chicago
Chicago 37, Illinois

My dear Mr. McKeon:

I have just come out of the hospital and am still under doctors orders. I am
not in a position to answer your questionnaire in detail. On the abstract level, I
think you can get an idea of my approach in a book I recently did entitled THE
FIRST FREEDOM, published by Macmillan Company. In the early section
you will see that I have traced for popular consumption the transition from
natural rights through the Darwinian era into the Holmes-Brandeis pragmatic
market-place theory.

My main concern is one which obviously does not interest Huxley, with
whom I have discussed the matter. It seems to me that we are finished with the
era of passing general resolutions in regard to liberty and freedom. I am not
opposed to the creation of new, neatly worded symbols for man to use as goals.
But the continued yapping of Kent Cooper [General Manager of The Associated

---

* Morris L. Ernst was an American civil liberties lawyer and political activist. Ernst was one
of the founders of the American Civil Liberties Union (ACLU) and was involved, over a long
career, in some of the most celebrated and consequential American legal cases of the twentieth
century. Among the most significant cases was his defense of James Joyce's *Ulysses* in 1933 against
charges that it was obscene and his intervention during the mid-1950s in the Trujillo Affair, in
which his report controversially cleared the Dominican dictator Rafael Trujillo of complicity in
the kidnapping and murder of the Basque nationalist intellectual Jesús Galíndez in New York City.
He was also the author of many books, including *To the Pure: A Study of Obscenity and the Censor*
(1929), *Hold Your Tongue! Adventures in Libel and Slander* (1932), *The Censor Marches On: Recent
Milestones in the Administration of the Obscenity Laws in the United States* (1940), and *Privacy: The
Right to Be Let Alone* (1962).

Press], Eric Johnston [President of the Motion Picture Association of America], etc., for the free flow of thought seems to me at this time to be doing little more than creating cynicism.

Unless the mind of man can be reached there can be no peace in the world. There are two barriers to the mind of man: one, political or governmental; and the other, economic. On this level I have written a piece for the Survey Magazine, a copy of which I am enclosing, outlining in some detail a proposed treaty. In that instance I have used Czechoslovakia as an example. I tried to get some thinking started in those hundreds of apparently insignificant items which originally excited practically no one around UNESCO, but which in my opinion are worthy of genuine consideration. I refer to little items such as tariffs on news reels and books, postage rates on newspapers, currency restrictions on magazines, etc. From conversations I have had with heads of governments abroad during the Spring of 1946, I am thoroughly convinced that bilateral agreements can be reached between various nations which believe in the free market place of thought. The difficulty in the situation is that the main craftsmen who know the field are the heads of the big enterprises which, a la Sarnoff [President of the Radio Corporation of America], Cooper and Johnston, really want to divide up the world rather than overcome *all* barriers. For example, within this country we have no quota law on movies, but see what happens among the five big companies which own the dominant theaters when you try to get distribution of a foreign picture, or, for that matter, of a picture produced by an independent United States producer.

I am sorry to have to be brief. I know this letter is not a real answer to your questions, but it gets off my chest an approach which I think has been lacking. I have gone over it with Benton's boys and with Huxley's staff in England. The men below in these great organizations seem to me to be in agreement with my emphasis. Huxley, wonderful dream boy that he is, is obviously not excited about small concepts like postage barriers or customs rates. And Benton [Assistant United States Secretary of State for Public Affairs], I have concluded, has a background which makes him timid in dealing with the giants which dominate the American market place of thought in radio, movie and the press. And when I say "dominate," it is not too harsh. I can refer you to Federal Court decisions calling the leaders of these industries enemies of free enterprise.

If you are in New York and care to see me, I may have enough energy to discuss this with you further.

Sincerely yours,
Morris L. Ernst

THE RIGHTS OF MAN
Arnold Schoenberg[*]

I

It is sad to admit that most men consider it their right to challenge the rights of others and even fight them. What is even sadder is that the present configuration of the world does not offer any hope for improvement in the near future.

This should not however stifle our aspiration to a world in which the sanctity of the Rights of Man would be intangibly self-evident to everyone. Humanity has never been able to access this kind of happiness except when a growing number of individuals fervently pursued a long-conceived ideal to its achievement. All of the progress in social thought or social sentiment that has allowed for an orderly communal life has only been possible through the strength of such aspirations.

We must not give that up.

The heathens will always be able to deny the immortality of the soul, and yet the believers will nonetheless not stop holding it to be certain. Even if the heathens were right today, the power of the believers' faith means that one day the soul will be immortal.

It will be the same with the Rights of Man if we do not cease to believe in their existence, even though they may remain unrecognized and ill-defined for a long time.

II

If there is a difference between common law, civil law, and the rights of man, it should be limited to this:

a) The rights of man seek to balance powers and resistance even in areas where common law has not yet found solutions.

b) We must find a minimum of rights that are valid for all peoples and all races.

---

[*] Arnold Schoenberg, who grew up in Vienna but later moved to Berlin to continue his musical training and career, was an Austrian-American composer and one of the most influential musical innovators of the twentieth century. As the Nazi party gained power in Germany, Schoenberg, who was Jewish, emigrated to the United States. Schoenberg invented the twelve-tone method in music, in which all twelve notes of the chromatic scale are given equal prominence in a composition. He taught music at the University of Southern California and the University of California, Los Angeles and was a prolific painter. He suffered for many years from triskaidekaphobia, the fear of the number 13, and was the author of many works of musical theory, including *Theory of Harmony* (1922). This piece was translated from the French by Romana Iorga.

The task of formulating a declaration of the Rights of Man is clearly incumbent on an organization that purports to be at the "vanguard" of the progress of the common law.

III

It is only to a very small degree that the law proposes to establish a balance. In reality it is almost always the expression of power. It is true that the rights of the weak have to some extent been able to find a foothold in the world, but this was done in the manner of power. When, overcome by pity, we allow unintended consequences, an opposition arises: we have sparked a Reaction.

IV

The difficulty of defining rights lies in the opposition between the interests to be protected. Galileo, who questioned Genesis, and the Church, which does not admit any attack on God's word, are both equally in need of protection and have an equal right to it.

In our vaunted civilization, people are no longer burned at the stake. Everyone can say what they want, to a certain degree (but let us not forget the restriction, "to a certain degree"). Pasteur and Zola did not have to suffer in their body, but they did in their spirit, and the doctor who discovered a new theory of diabetes a decade too soon has lost nothing except a few customers.

War, the mother of all things, has forced the world to adopt new methods. Annoying or excessively uninhibited opinions are wiped out, along with their proponents. The former are diminished and the latter are hanged, stark naked. The generals along with the rest. All shame is ignored, because "the Law is what benefits Germany." Everything else is "the rights of man."

V

There is no certainty, in a battle, that 51% will prevail over 49% of the combatants, but in an election, those 51% take power over the minority and subjugate and enslave them.

We recognize the rights of the minority when the balance of power is 98% against 2%. But a minority of 49% no longer has any rights. Often, it does not even retain civil rights.

Yet we never forget these tiny minorities that are reduced to a single representative, of which there are examples even in the countries that share our civilization, five or ten per century at the most.

VI

A civilization and a culture based exclusively on scientific knowledge should, when their progress is complete, have arrived at a balance among competing interests. This will not happen until after long centuries, no doubt, because powerful forces oppose it; moreover, not all of the interests involved are known or recognized in time. But the study of rights has increasingly refined instruments at its disposal and an increasing number of requirements it must satisfy.

This leads us to the protection of honor.

The archbishop could afford to slap Mozart in the face without wondering whether he would thereby enter into the history of music.

Who could guess then that the sense of honor associated with the artist would assume such proportions in the future? Who could have predicted that this or that artist would become disgusted with life after having surprised himself with unworthy thoughts?

But, on the other hand, who could have envisioned that the insults heaped on Wagner, Ibsen, Strindberg, Mahler, and others by the critics would ultimately be considered a mark of honor? Without such enemies, one cannot be truly great.

When, then, will the rights of man—without of course being able to prevent the fact that people are forced to participate in injustice—cause others to understand the shame that is involved in inflicting such suffering?

VII

Every scientist, engineer, inventor, poet, painter, musician, etc. . . . who benefits from the efforts of a predecessor (whether he himself has invented something or whether he is content to imitate or use what has been done before) contributes to the progress of his specialty. We must not underestimate sincere disciples nor overestimate creators. No one can flatter himself that he owes everything to himself.

Should we, however, tolerate that the users always receive a higher reward than the inventor, from whom they took a loan they will never repay? This is basically a problem of secondary importance.

However, it often happens that the true inventor is scammed by the imitator, when the latter was able to create skillful propaganda for himself. In this case we have a falsification of spiritual history—but who, besides the victims, takes any interest in that?

VIII

A gold mine, an oil well, a store, a bank, a factory, or even a picture cannot be taken away from the most distant descendants of its original owner. But for

works of the mind and for art, property rights are exercised only for a specified period, during which the act of stealing the work from the producer or
the creator is considered a misdemeanor; not, truth be told, because theft is
immoral and dishonorable in itself, but because it undermines powerful and
fearsome interests. But after that specified period, competition forces the publisher to sell the work more cheaply, which will however not prevent him from
making an honest profit, since he no longer has to pay royalties. Indeed, after
that period, the work supposedly belongs to the community, but in reality it
belongs to exploiters. Therefore, you will no longer incur punishment when
appropriating what is not yours—but that does not mean it is any less a theft.
And the only ownership title that the community possesses in this case is that
conferred on it by its strength. It is absurd to allow these works to fall into
the public domain, not only from a moral but also from an economic point
of view, because society's interest in them is too limited to justify the fact that
we thus expose the descendants of a man of genius to the same misery which
he himself had to suffer.

IX
It is tragic that the Rights of Man are, like democracy, unable to defend themselves against attacks and destruction. All that could be undertaken on behalf of
these rights would indeed undermine the rights of the aggressor. Just as everything that tends to consolidate democracy is undemocratic.

There is therefore nothing left to do but to resort to persuasion.

X
It seems that the Rights of Man should be limited to a smaller number of claims
than this ambitious notion would lead us to believe.

XI
Most forms of belief are exclusive and antagonistic, sometimes even combative,
provocative, aggressive. It would be suicide to them to be tolerant. Let us think,
for example, of the Communist or Fascist States, where belief is a governing
instrument.

XII
Does man have the duty to believe what is true? Does the right to believe a false-
hood deserve to be protected?

XIII

The Ten Commandments are undoubtedly one of the first declarations of the Rights of Man that were ever formulated. They guarantee the right to life and the right to property; they protect marriage, oath taking, and labor; but, as there is only one God, they deny any freedom of belief.

XIV

"How can I truly love good without hating evil?" Strindberg asked himself. This is the source of the desire and even the obligation to fight evil.

This is why some believe that they must fight against "bourgeois" art and others that they must combat the Palestinian style, which is foreign to our race and began with the great Adolf Loos.

The warrior has the desire and the duty to vanquish, the desire and the duty to oppress the vanquished.

But what is then to become of the human rights of those who believe in the art forms or the ideas that have been vanquished?

XV

It appears as though what music expresses, in its language, is only musical information or, as most Aesthetes think, information that has to do with the senses or the imagination. Let us set aside Richard Strauss's joke, namely "Move a pencil from one place to another and I will express it in music," that is not the language of a musician who engages unconsciously, formulating thoughts that he would shudder to hear—if he did not know that no one would be able to discover the hidden meaning of his words.

But one day the great-grandchildren of our psychologists and our psychoanalysts will have managed to decipher the language of music. Woe, then, to the improvident, who had thought they could so carefully hide their most intimate and most secret thoughts and who will now have to open to the profane the most secret recesses of their consciousness.

Woe to you then, Beethoven, Brahms, and Schumann, and to all of you, the so far "unknown,"[1] who will fall into such hands; you who have only used the human right to express oneself freely in order to silence your thoughts all the more.

Does the right to silence one's thoughts not deserve to be protected?

---

1. Under the title "Unknown XXX," an author has tried to tarnish the image we have of composers.

XVI

We must also recognize the rights of the cannibal. They are based on the instinctive feeling that blood provides blood and flesh provides flesh. In consideration of the rudimentary instruments that have been used to establish this scientific truth, we must reserve a place of choice for this instinct, which is more reliable than some "tests" that allow suffering humanity to be overwhelmed with remedies whose harmfulness is often already obvious within a year.

XVII

Is the right to be born one of the rights of man? Or is the right to control births one of them? And does one have the right to allow those who are born, if there are too many of them, to die of hunger?

What do religions say about this?

XVIII

Let us also consider the Indians. They starve by the millions, but they would not even think of slaughtering a cow, a sacred cow. How, without blushing, can we explain the "rights of man" to people and populations who possess such faith and how can we expect that they will believe in them, these people who die calmly rather than infringe upon their sacred beliefs.

Perhaps we could offer them as an example that old lady, who, intending to have one of her chickens for her evening meal, began by caressing and kissing it tenderly, then, handing it into the good care of the cook, whispered, "Poor chicken! But you will be so good with gravy."

XIX

These are serious problems that could turn us into pessimists.

Nevertheless, we must not give up our desire to bestow a sacred and universal character on the rights of man.

We have in our hearts the strength of desire combined with a creative intensity.

Los Angeles, July 21, 1947

REFLECTIONS ON FREEDOM AND ART [2]
W. H. Auden [*]

Freedom means freedom of choice. A man exercises his freedom when, confronted by two or more possible alternatives, he realizes one and excludes the rest. Free choices are definite choices. Liberal theologians were foolish to get excited over Heisenberg's Principle. Vagueness of behavior may be good enough for electrons, it is not good enough for free men.

Choices are of three kinds:

1) choices of action. A thirsty man in a desert is unfree, not because he cannot satisfy his craving for water, but because he cannot choose between drinking and not drinking.

2) choices of value judgment; good or evil, true or false, beautiful or ugly, absolute or relative, required or forbidden.

A man who has seen only one picture is unfree to decide whether it is beautiful or ugly. A man in a passion of anger or fear is unfree because he is no longer conscious of any alternative state and so cannot judge his anger or his fear.

3) choices of authority: this God or man or organization is to be believed or obeyed, that is not. Here again, if there is no consciousness of possible alternatives, there is no freedom.

The cravings of man's spirit are totally unlike the appetites of his nature, such as hunger and sex. There are two of them; to be free from conditions and to be important. These can and often do conflict, for the former senses anything that is "given" whether by his own nature of by the world about him as a limitation on his freedom and longs to act gratuitously, yet it is precisely and only from the

---

2. Although Auden's name first appears in a letter of April 1947 from Stephen Spender to Julian Huxley, in which Spender says that "W. H. Auden should certainly be asked" (that is, to contribute to the human rights survey), in the end it was Richard McKeon who contacted Auden, mostly likely because Auden was living in the United States at this time (McKeon wrote to Auden at his summer house on Fire Island, New York) [ed.].

[*] W. H. Auden was an English poet, essayist, and playwright and one of the most influential literary figures of the twentieth century. After Auden emigrated to the United States in 1939, his reputation continued to grow; his poetry, in particular, played a significant role in shaping the development of modernism. Auden won the Pulitzer Prize for Poetry in 1948 for *The Age of Anxiety* and was a finalist for the Nobel Prize in Literature in 1963, 1964, and 1965. Some of his better-known poems include "Funeral Blues," "Musée des Beaux Arts," and "September 1, 1939." Auden died in Vienna in 1973 and a memorial stone was placed for him in Poets' Corner at Westminster Abbey a year later.

"given" that he can derive a sense of importance. Absolute arbitrariness would at the same time be absolute triviality.

One of man's attempts to satisfy both is the criminal *acte gratuit*, the breaking of a given law for the sake of breaking it, where the law supplies the importance, and the act of breaking it asserts the freedom. Another is play where the laws governing the game are kept by the player because they are chosen by him. At bottom, all art, all pure science, all creativity is play in this sense. The question What is Art? and the question Why does the artist create? are different questions.

It seems to me that the basic impulse behind creativity of any kind is the desire to do something that is quite necessary: the desire that the result should turn out to be important comes second.

The rules of a game give it importance to the player by making it difficult to play, a test and proof of an inborn gift or an acquired skill. Given that a game is morally permissible, then whether or not one should play it depends simply on whether or not it gives one pleasure, i.e., whether or not one is good at playing it. If one asks a great surgeon why he operates, if he is honest, he will not answer "Because it is my duty to save lives" but "Because I love operating." He may perfectly well hate his neighbour and nevertheless save his life because of the pleasure it gives him to exercise his skill.

One must say therefore that, in the profoundest sense, art and science are frivolous activities for they depend on the chance possession of special talents. The only serious matter is concerned with what every human being has alike, a will, namely that one shall love one's neighbor as oneself. Here one cannot speak of a talent for love nor in terms of pleasure and pain. If one asks the good Samaritan why he rescues the man fallen among thieves, he cannot answer, except as an ironical joke, "Because I like doing good" since pleasure or pain are irrelevant and the point is obeying the command: "Thou shalt love."

There are three kinds of human groups.

1) *Crowds*, i.e., two or more individuals whose sole common characteristic is togetherness, e.g., four strangers in a railway carriage.

2) *Societies*, i.e., two or more individuals united for the purpose of carrying out an action which requires them all, e.g., a string quartet.

3) *Communities*, i.e., two or more individuals united by a common love for something other than themselves, e.g., a room full of music-lovers.

Societies have a definite size and a definite structure and the character of the whole is different from the simple sum of the characters of the parts. Consequently the will of the individual member is subordinate to the general will of the society however that is established. Someone in the string quartet must have the authority to decide whether it is to play Mozart or Beethoven and the rest must obey whether they agree with the choice or not. A society may at the same time be a community but not necessarily. It is quite possible that the cellist of our quartet hates music and only plays to earn his living. A society is a free society as long as the member who exercises authority does so with the free consent of the other members. Societies function best when they are free, but in certain cases coercion can and indeed must be applied to compel a recalcitrant member to contribute his partial function, the moral justification depending on two factors:

1) the importance of the function the society discharges

2) the degree to which the recalcitrant member can or cannot be replaced by another more willing individual.

Communities, like crowds, have no definite size. It is impossible therefore to speak of the "general will" of a community since the individuals who belong to it cannot disagree; they are a community precisely because as individuals they all love the same thing (unlike members of crowds who have no love in common). In Time Magazine for June 23rd [1947, Ed.], Mr. Vladimir Kosetsky was reported as having said at the U.N. Conference on Human Rights: "Man should have no rights that place him in opposition to the community. Man opposed to the community is nothing." If the translation is correct, Mr. Kosetsky was talking nonsense.

An individual can be in opposition to a society, e.g., if the cellist plays out of tune, but if the rest of the quartet love the music of Mozart and he detests it, this simply means that there are two communities, a community of Mozart lovers and a potential community of Mozart haters for a community can begin with a single individual while a society cannot exist until all its members are present and correctly related.

There are two kinds of communities: closed or unfree, and open or free. The members of a closed community have a common love but they have not chosen it for they are unaware of any other love which they could prefer to or reject for the love they have. The members of an open community have consciously chosen their love out of two or more possible loves.

If I understand either the myth of Orpheus or Aristotle's doctrine of catharsis correctly, the Greeks held what is, to me, a false theory of art which has plagued the world ever since, namely, that art is a magic device for arousing desirable emotions and expelling undesirable emotions, and so leading to right action. If this were so, then I think Plato's censures of art in *The Republic* and Tolstoy's in *What is Art?* are unanswerable. For me the correct definition is Shakespeare's holding the mirror up to nature, i.e., art does not change my feelings but makes me conscious of what I have in fact felt or what I might feel, and of actual or possible relations between my feelings. The world of art is a looking-glass world, i.e., a possible image of the actual world where emotions are observed, divorced from their origin in immediate passion[3]. It is the business of the artist to make a mirror which distorts the world as little as possible and reflects as much of the world as possible. Bad art distorts; minor art reflects only a small or trivial corner of the world.

Art has two values: firstly it gives pleasure, the pleasure of idle curiosity; secondly, it enlarges the field of freedom. If man had no imagination, he could not make a choice between two possible courses of action without taking both, or make a value judgment about a feeling of his until he had felt the opposite.

Art does not and cannot influence the choice or judgment he actually makes, it only makes it more of a conscious choice.

Reading *Macbeth*, for instance, cannot prevent a man from becoming a murderer, but the man who has read *Macbeth* knows more about what becoming a murderer would be like than the man who hasn't, so that, if he chooses to become one, he is more responsible.

Art, in other words, is never a means for converting a bad community into a good one, it is one of the great means by which closed communities are turned into open communities.

Art can do harm in two ways. Firstly by failing to be good art and giving the wrong kind of pleasure thereby. If the reflection of the world which it offers is distorted, if it flatters the spectator by omitting the possibilities of evil or draws him to despair by denying the possibilities of good, (which, surprisingly enough, can also give pleasure) then it injures him.

Secondly and more seriously because the better the art the greater the danger, it may ensnare the spectator in the luxurious paralysis of self-contemplation so that, like Hamlet, he fails to choose at all. The danger of great art is Narcissism. Narcissus does not fall in love with his reflection because it was beautiful but because it is his own in all his endless possibilities.

One can tell the myth in another way: Narcissus was a hydrocephalous idiot; catching sight of himself in the pool, he cried: "On me it looks good." Or again: Narcissus was neither beautiful nor ugly but as commonplace as a Thurber husband; catching sight of himself in the pool, he said: "Excuse me, but haven't we met before some place?"

---

3. For this reason art cannot deal with experiences which are destroyed by reflection, e.g., the sexual act or the Mystical Union.

Art can encourage the formation of two kinds of bad communities, the community of those with false pictures of themselves, and the parody of a free community in which the knowledge of good and evil is turned against the will till it becomes too weak to choose either.

Every work of art is the focus of the potential community of those individuals who love it or could love it. Such a community is free if the artist could have created something else but chose to create this work, and vice versa, the spectators or readers could have chosen to look at or read another work but chose to look at or read this. If the artist creates a work which no one but he appreciates or a spectator cannot find any work which he likes, there is no lack of freedom, but simply no community. Freedom can be curtailed in two ways; the artist may be forced to alter his work so that the character of the community is other than it would have been if he were left alone; or people may be prevented from becoming acquainted with his work so that the community is smaller than it might have been.

Censorship can be of two kinds, an unplanned economic censorship where the artist cannot afford to create as he wishes or the public cannot afford to become acquainted with his work, and the planned censorship of authority. Economically the freedom of art is best attained if there is as great a variety of publishers, booksellers, libraries, galleries, etc. as possible and if some, but not all, of these are large-scale organizations. If there are too few agencies, above all, if there is a state monopoly, the variety of works distributed invariably declines even if there is no deliberate censorship. If all are on a small scale, costs are too high for some of the potential public.

The obstacle on which liberalism has so often come to grief is the fact that we find it easier to respect the freedom of those to whom we are indifferent than the freedom of those we love. A parent or a government who believe something to be good or true know well enough that it is possible for their children or their people to choose what, to them, is evil or false, and that, if the wrong choice is made, those they love will suffer and they themselves will suffer with them; further, they and those they love will no longer belong to the same community. However, to love one's neighbor as oneself means precisely to be willing to let him make his own mistakes and suffer with him when he suffers for them, for no man can himself consciously wish not to be responsible for his thoughts and actions, at whatever cost. Every man knows for himself that right and duty are not identical, that he has a duty to choose the good, but a right to choose the evil, that, as Kafka says: "A man lies as little as he can when he lies as little as he can, not when he is given the smallest possible opportunity to lie."

Authorities who are more concerned that their charges should do the right thing than that they should choose it are always tempted to look for a short cut.

In the short run, a man in a passion acts quicker and more effectively than a man who has reached the reflective stage of desire. Usually therefore, authorities would like the artist to arouse in others a passion for the good instead of making them conscious of good and evil; they would turn him, if they could, into Plato's Noble Liar. Art has hardly ever been censored for aesthetic reasons because artists have rarely been in authority, which is perhaps just as well. In my own day-dream state, for example, people caught reading Shelley or listening to Brahms are sentenced to the salt-mines, and the possession of a juke-box is a capital offence.

The usual reasons for censorship are two: either that the work is immoral, i.e., will incite the public to act immorally or illegally so that society ceases to function properly; or that it is heretical, i.e., will induce the public to adopt other values than those held by the authorities, causing them to desert the latter's community for a new one. Censorship always implies two things: that there is a potential public for the work and that its members are incapable of making a responsible choice. It is therefore only permissible under two conditions: for minors who are legally presumed to be as yet incapable of responsible choice; and for adults who have chosen their censor and are free to disregard him if they cease to believe in his authority. The Roman Catholic Church, for example, does not violate the freedom of its members by putting books on the index, because no one is obliged to be a Roman Catholic and to choose to be one necessarily implies believing in the authority of the Church to decide what the faithful may read.

No State has such a right because one becomes a member of a political society by being born, an act of chance, not a choice.

Each major revolution in history is concerned with some particular aspect of human freedom, and has its representative human type. Each establishes its kind of freedom once and for all. The success of each is threatened by its own false claim to be *the* revolution, i.e., that the aspect of freedom with which it is concerned is the only freedom that matters.

Since the particular aspect with which any revolution is concerned is one conspicuously ignored by the revolution before it, it is apt in its just criticism of the latter's failing to be hostile to the freedom for which it fought. Nevertheless the fates of all revolutions are bound up with each other; they stand or fall together: if the preceding revolution had not won its battle, its successor could not be fighting its own. In any revolution, therefore, the gains of the revolutions before it have to be defended if the present revolution is to succeed.

The Papal revolution of the 11th and the 12th centuries established the freedom of an individual to choose between loyalties, his right to leave one community and join another, his right to belong to two communities at the same time. Its typical figures are the contemplative international priest and the activist local soldier.

The revolution of the Reformation in the 16th century established the freedom of the individual to choose his career, his right to leave the society to which his father belonged and join another. Its typical figure is the professional man.

The French and Industrial Revolutions of the 18th and 19th centuries established the freedom of the individual man of talent to develop himself freely and compete for public attention, the right of the individual mind to change the community or lead a society if he can. The typical figure is Figaro.

> L'esprit seul peut tout changer.
> De vingt rois que l'on encense
> Le trépas brise l'autel
> Et Voltaire est immortel.

> [Only the mind can change everything.
> For twenty kings who wear a crown
> Death breaks the altar,
> But Voltaire is immortal. - Ed.]

Our revolution of the 20th century is trying to establish the freedom of the individual body to determine its satisfactions, to grow and be healthy. Its typical figure is the anonymous naked man with a dog-tag number, not yet a member of any society or any community, but simply one of the world crowd.

Hence the preoccupation of our time with medicine and economics, its activism, its hostility to the achievement of the French Revolution, freedom of speech and thought which it sees as a threat to unanimous action. At the physical level all are really equal in their needs and individual differences of temperament or talent are irrelevant.

In our revolution, therefore, focused on winning freedom from physical want, all the freedoms gained by preceding revolutions are threatened as never before. The French Revolution is denied wherever there is a controlled press and a censorship of art and science; the Reformation is denied wherever a state dictates what career an individual citizen shall follow; the Papal Revolution is denied wherever a monolithic state claims unconditional authority.

The talented individual today is being punished for the airs he gave himself in the past two centuries. Poets are not the unacknowledged legislators of the world and never were and it is a good thing that they should be made to realize this. Those who preached a doctrine of Art for Art's sake or Art as a luxury were much nearer the truth, but they should not then have regarded the comparative frivolity of their vocation as a proof of their spiritual superiority to the useful untalented worker. In actual fact the modern censor and the romantic artist are alike in thinking art more important than it is.

> "Once he looked rosy, now he looks blue.
> Nurse is wondering What shall I do?"

sings the poet in the sick room. If patient or nurse were to say to him "For God's sake, stop humming and fetch some hot water and bandages" it would be one thing. But neither says this. The nurse says: "Tell the patient I am the only one who can cure him and I will give you a passport, extra ration cards, and free tickets to the opera. If you tell him anything else, I shall call the police." And the poor delirious patient cries: "Persuade me that I am looking and feeling fine and I will give you a duplex apartment and a beautiful mistress. If you can't do that, I shan't listen to you."

Perhaps the poet, if he really loved the patient and the nurse as himself, would be silent and fetch the hot water, but as long as he continues singing, there is one commandment which his song must obey, "Thou shalt not bear false witness against thy neighbor."

> W. H. Auden

STATEMENT ON HUMAN RIGHTS
Melville Herskovits[*]

The problem faced by the Commission on Human Rights of the United Nations in preparing its Declaration on the Rights of Man must be approached from two points of view. The first, in terms of which the Declaration is ordinarily conceived, concerns the respect for the personality of the individual as such,

---

[*] Melville Herskovits was an American anthropologist who was a professor of anthropology at Northwestern University at the time of the UNESCO human rights survey. He had founded the department in 1927. Herskovits was a student of Franz Boas at Columbia University and was throughout his career one of the most energetic proponents of Boasian anthropology, an approach that emphasized the importance of history, ethnographic fieldwork, and the principle of cultural relativism. Herskovits had been asked to contribute to the survey by Richard McKeon, further contributing to the heavy representation of respondents from the Chicago area. Herskovits's area of specialization was the culture and history of Africans and African-Americans, and he founded the first program of African studies in the United States at Northwestern in 1948. He was the author of many books, including *The American Negro* (1928), *The Myth of the Negro Past* (1941), and *The Human Factor in Changing Africa* (1962).

and his right to its fullest development as a member of his society. In a world order, however, respect for the cultures of differing human groups is equally important.

These are two facets of the same problem, since it is a truism that groups are composed of individuals, and human beings do not function outside the societies of which they form a part. The problem is thus to formulate a statement of human rights that will do more than just phrase respect for the individual as an individual. It must also take into full account the individual as a member of the social group of which he is a part, whose sanctioned modes of life shape his behavior, and with whose fate his own is thus inextricably bound.

Because of the great numbers of societies that are in intimate contact in the modern world, and because of the diversity of their ways of life, the primary task confronting those who would draw up a Declaration on the Rights of Man is thus, in essence, to resolve the following problem: How can the proposed Declaration be applicable to all human beings, and not be a statement of rights conceived only in terms of the values prevalent in the countries of Western Europe and America?

Before we can cope with this problem, it will be necessary for us to outline some of the findings of the sciences that deal with the study of human culture, that must be taken into account if the Declaration is to be in accord with the present state of knowledge about man and his modes of life.

If we begin, as we must, with the individual, we find that from the moment of his birth not only his behavior, but his very thought, his hopes, aspirations, the moral values which direct his action and justify and give meaning to his life in his own eyes and those of his fellows, are shaped by the body of custom of the group of which he becomes a member. The process by means of which this is accomplished is so subtle, and its effects are so far-reaching, that only after considerable training are we conscious of it. Yet if the essence of the Declaration is to be, as it must, a statement in which the right of the individual to develop his personality to the fullest is to be stressed, then this must be based on a recognition of the fact that the personality of the individual can develop only in terms of the culture of his society.

Over the past fifty years, the many ways in which man resolves the problems of subsistence, of social living, of political regulation of group life, of reaching accord with the Universe and satisfying his aesthetic drives has been widely documented by the researches of anthropologists among peoples living in all parts of the world. All peoples do achieve these ends. No two of them, however, do so in exactly the same way, and some of them employ means that differ, often strikingly, from one another.

Yet here a dilemma arises. Because of the social setting of the learning process, the individual cannot but be convinced that his own way of life is the most desirable one. Conversely, and despite changes originating from within and without his culture that he recognizes as worthy of adoption, it becomes equally patent to him that, in the main, other ways than his own, to the degree they differ from it, are less desirable than those to which he is accustomed. Hence valuations arise, that in themselves receive the sanction of accepted belief.

The degree to which such evaluations eventuate in action depends on the basic sanctions in the thought of a people. In the main, people are willing to live and let live, exhibiting a tolerance for behavior of another group different than their own, especially where there is no conflict in the subsistence field. In the history of Western Europe and America, however, economic expansion, control of armaments, and an evangelical religious tradition have translated the recognition of cultural differences into a summons to action. This has been emphasized by philosophical systems that have stressed absolutes in the realm of values and ends. Definitions of freedom, concepts of the nature of human rights, and the like, have thus been narrowly drawn. Alternatives have been decried, and suppressed where controls have been established over non-European peoples. The hard core of *similarities* between cultures has consistently been overlooked.

The consequences of this point of view have been disastrous for mankind. Doctrines of the "white man's burden" have been employed to implement economic exploitation and to deny the right to control their own affairs to millions of peoples over the world, where the expansion of Europe and America has not meant the literal extermination of whole populations. Rationalized in terms of ascribing cultural inferiority to these peoples, or in conceptions of their backwardness in development of their "primitive mentality," that justified their being held in the tutelage of their superiors, the history of the expansion of the western world has been marked by demoralization of human personality and the disintegration of human rights among the peoples over whom hegemony has been established.

The values of the ways of life of these peoples have been consistently misunderstood and decried. Religious beliefs that for untold ages have carried conviction, and permitted adjustment to the Universe have been attacked as superstitious, immoral, untrue. And, since power carries its own conviction, this has furthered the process of demoralization begun by economic exploitation and the loss of political autonomy. The white man's burden, the civilizing mission, have been heavy indeed. But their weight has not been borne by those who, frequently in all honesty, have journeyed to the far places of the world to uplift those regarded by them as inferior.

We thus come to the first proposition that the study of human psychology and culture dictates as essential in drawing up a Bill of Human Rights in terms of existing knowledge:

1. *The individual realizes his personality through his culture, hence respect for individual differences entails a respect for cultural differences.*

There can be no individual freedom, that is, when the group with which the individual identifies himself is not free. There can be no full development of the individual personality as long as the individual is told, by men who have the power to enforce their commands, that the way of life of his group is inferior to that of those who wield the power.

This is more than an academic question, as becomes evident if one looks about him at the world as it exists today. Peoples who on first contact with European and American might were awed and partially convinced of the superior ways of their rulers have, through two wars and a depression, come to reexamine the new and the old. Professions of love of democracy, of devotion to freedom have come with something less than conviction to those who are themselves denied the right to lead their lives as seems proper to them. The religious dogmas of those who profess equality and practice discrimination, who stress the virtue of humility and are themselves arrogant in insistence on their beliefs have little meaning for peoples whose devotion to other faiths makes these inconsistencies as clear as the desert landscape at high noon. Small wonder that these peoples, denied the right to live in terms of their own cultures, are discovering new values in old beliefs they had been led to question.

No consideration of human rights can be adequate without taking into account the related problem of human capacity. Man, biologically, is one. *Homo sapiens* is a single species, no matter how individuals may differ in their aptitudes, their abilities, their interests. It is established that any normal individual can learn any part of any culture other than his own, provided only he is afforded the opportunity to do so. That cultures differ in degree of complexity, of richness of content, is due to historic forces, not biological ones. All existing ways of life meet the test of survival. Of those cultures that have disappeared, it must be remembered that their number includes some that were great, powerful, and complex as well as others that were modest, content with the *status quo*, and simple. Thus we reach a second principle:

2. *Respect for differences between cultures is validated by the scientific fact that no technique of qualitatively evaluating cultures has been discovered.*

This principle leads us to a further one, namely that the aims that guide the life of every people are self-evident in their significance to that people. It is the principle that emphasizes the universals in human conduct rather than the absolutes that the culture of Western Europe and America stresses. It recognizes that the eternal verities only seem so because we have been taught to regard them as such; that every people, whether it expresses them or not, lives in devotion to verities whose eternal nature is as real to them as are those of Euroamerican culture to Euroamericans. Briefly stated, this third principle that must be introduced into our consideration is the following:

3. Standards and values are relative to the culture from which they derive so that any attempt to formulate postulates that grow out of the beliefs or moral codes of one culture must to that extent detract from the applicability of any Declaration of Human Rights to mankind as a whole.

Ideas of right and wrong, good and evil, are found in all societies, though they differ in their expression among different peoples. What is held to be a human right in one society may be regarded as anti-social by another people, or by the same people in a different period of their history. The saint of one epoch would at a later time be confined as a man not fitted to cope with reality. Even the nature of the physical world, the colors we see, the sounds we hear, are conditioned by the language we speak, which is part of the culture into which we are born.

The problem of drawing up a Declaration of Human Rights was relatively simple in the Eighteenth Century, because it was not a matter of *human* rights, but of the rights of men within the framework of the sanctions laid by a single society. Even then, so noble a document as the American Declaration of Independence, or the American Bill of Rights, could be written by men who themselves were slave-owners, in a country where chattel slavery was a part of the recognized social order. The revolutionary character of the slogan "Liberty, Equality, Fraternity" was never more apparent than in the struggles to implement it by extending it to the French slave-owning colonies.

Today the problem is complicated by the fact that the Declaration must be of world-wide applicability. It must embrace and recognize the validity of many different ways of life. It will not be convincing to the Indonesian, the African, the Indian, the Chinese, if it lies on the same plane as like documents of an earlier period. The rights of Man in the Twentieth Century cannot be circumscribed by the standards of any single culture, or be dictated by the aspirations of any single people. Such a document will lead to frustration, not realization of the personalities of vast numbers of human beings.

Such persons, living in terms of values not envisaged by a limited Declaration, will thus be excluded from the freedom of full participation in the only right and proper way of life that can be known to them, the institutions, sanctions and goals that make up the culture of their particular society.

Even where political systems exist that deny citizens the right of participation in their government, or seek to conquer weaker peoples, underlying cultural values may be called on to bring the peoples of such states to a realization of the consequences of the acts of their governments, and thus enforce a brake upon discrimination and conquest. For the political system of a people is only a small part of their total culture.

World-wide standards of freedom and justice, based on the principle that man is free only when he lives as his society defines freedom, that his rights are those he recognizes as a member of his society, must be basic. Conversely, an effective world-order cannot be devised except insofar as it permits the free play of personality of the members of its constituent social units, and draws strength from the enrichment to be derived from the interplay of varying personalities.

The world-wide acclaim accorded the Atlantic Charter, before its restricted applicability was announced, is evidence of the fact that freedom is understood and sought after by peoples having the most diverse cultures. Only when a statement of the right of men to live in terms of their own traditions is incorporated into the proposed Declaration, then, can the next step of defining the rights and duties of human groups as regards each other be set upon the firm foundation of the present-day scientific knowledge of Man.

UNTITLED
Theodore Johannes Haarhoff[*]

GENERAL

There is one great overriding consideration in all human relationships and that is the question of values. If the various groups retain their present selfish and nationalistic outlook (or, rather, if the leaders of the groups do this) no amount

---

[*] At the time of the UNESCO human rights survey, Theodore Johannes Haarhoff held the Chair of Classics at the University of the Witswatersrand. Haarhoff was a leading international expert on the Roman poet Virgil and Haarhoff himself published several volumes of poetry in his native Afrikaans. Outside of his academic work, Haarhoff was involved in debates in South Africa over race relations. He took a cultural and historical approach to race and used his knowledge of the classical period to examine the development of racial identity throughout history, a perspective he explored in his 1938 book *The Stranger at the Gate: Aspects of Exclusiveness and Co-operation in Ancient Greece and Rome, with Some Reference to Modern Times.*

of organisation or of intellectual analysis will be any good. The first task of education in the world must be moral education, in the widest sense. People must *want* to build a unified world even if it means loss in material values or in prestige. Only on that basis will the important work of spreading knowledge bear fruits and the schemes for organisation be successful.

Moral values must be recognized as *real* and not relegated to the realm of religious talky-talk.

In the formulation of human rights there can ultimately be only one standard, that of the New Testament, which implies the ultimate unity of mankind and respect for all human personality. But different grades must be recognised. People who are backward must grow and not be shot into political and social positions for which they are not ripe. Here economic, social and cultural levels must be considered.

Personal and group relations (e.g. in South Africa) have been altered for the worse by the advent of modern nationalism and theories of racial superiority. The theory of British racial superiority in the days of Old Imperialism (which still persists) provoked the Afrikaner Nationalist Movement, which in turn has developed this superior air towards the English and towards the non-European races. The inferiority complex has turned into a superiority complex. On both sides there is still a failure to share and understand fear, lack of imagination and laziness being the main causes.

In the economic field the "Labour" Party upholds the Colour Bar. Here again the whole situation could be altered if the element of selfishness was eliminated and moral values changed. As long as the fight proceeds on a purely material basis, there is no solution. If the selfish people were capable of taking a long view, they would see that the moral principle will pay them materially in the long run and benefit the whole community by raising the purchasing power of the nations.

Unesco might explain and demonstrate the relation between moral principle and economic gain for the community. The whole question of rights and duties revolves round moral principle. Labour will not claim a "right" to an excessive share and Capital would not exploit the working man, if both saw their duty in terms of service. A real conception of service to mankind would counteract the fanatical loyalty to an ideology instead of to human values, that we frequently see to day.

The only sort of freedom that we should suppress is the freedom that actively undermines or destroys the right to be free. The negative and poisonous freedom that causes confusion by spreading prejudice, wrong views we can only oppose by counter-action; and we can try to convert its authors. Yet in granting political and social freedom account must be taken of stages or development, both in the case of the privileged class and in the case of the unprivileged.

Freedom of movement has been found to be most important in South Africa. Long distances often keep people isolated and isolation means ignorance and fear leading to suspicion and strife. Where contact has been established and people have worked together in the right atmosphere, difficulties (imagined or real) have been cleared away and co-operation became possible. Certain political powers rely on isolationism to strengthen their policy; others refuse to get out of their one track rut through sheer laziness and lack of imagination. The school is the place where these tendencies should be broken down. Here one of the barriers is language, and some of us have been working to establish the bilingual school but will enable English and Afrikaans children to be educated in the same institution.

Here again, recognition of the moral principle would overcome most of the difficulties that have been raised. It would also ensure the right of justice for all and protection for the weak. Once the moral values have been established by systematic education, it is honestly recognised that it is wrong for nations and groups to be selfish, intelligence and hard work should enable Unesco to build a new world.

ON HUMAN RIGHTS
Ernest Henry Burgmann[*]

Any "declaration on the Rights of Man for the entire world" immediately meets the obvious difficulty of being intelligible to peoples of vastly different traditions and cultures, at different stages of growth and development. The sophisticated European is busied with many thoughts that an African villager would find incomprehensible, and an intense communist has little in common with an easy going liberal. A form of words that might excite the passions of one people might well leave another completely cold.

---

[*] Ernest Henry Burgmann was an Australian Anglican bishop, social activist, and essayist who took a particular interest in Freudian psychology. During the 1920s, Burgmann was active in socialist and workers' movements and taught regularly through the Workers Education Association. During the Depression, he wrote newspaper columns and gave public speeches in support of miners and steel workers. In 1934, he became Bishop of Goulburn. Burgmann was known in the Australian media as the "Red Bishop." He retired in 1960 and died in 1967. Burgmann published many books, including *Religion in the Life of the Nation* (1930), *Justice for All* (1933), *The Faith of an Anglican* (1943), and *The Christian Revolution* (1959).

If we are to speak to the whole world we must find a common ground of appeal. It may be sought in our common humanity or in a pictured goal to which all would subscribe. It is not likely that in our common humanity we can find anything sufficiently tangible and stable to be made the basis for a universal appeal. Whatever we may have in common is so related to our particular circumstances and traditional outlook at any moment that the expression in verbal form would seldom, if ever, appeal to all. Well fed Americans and Australians may be very ready to sing the joys of freedom and proclaim the sanctity of equality and fraternity (with no particular thought of taking them too seriously), while hungry Europeans would feel that they would barter large quantities of liberty, equality, and fraternity, if they had them, for a sure supply of daily bread. The 18th century declaration of the Rights of Man came at a moment in human history when the emerging individual felt that for him the day of opportunity had dawned. With great energy, but with little concern for any rights but his own, the capitalist took the stage and played his part. Those who were not capitalists in fact strongly desired to be so. It was the effective myth of the age, and the common desire protected the successful minority. Successful capitalists fascinated even those whom they exploited, and in that fascination lay their security. It has ever been so. Kings lasted as long as their sanctity held the imagination of their peoples. The reign of the "Bill of Rights" was not in the fact that people understood it, and consented to it, and served it. The fact was that it gave verbal clothing to the dominant mythology of the day, and on the tide of emotion released by the whole complex historical situation the most enterprising spirits of the times rode to power. That tide has spent itself. It shows reluctance at ebbing. It may well leave behind large pools of water, even lakes, that will remain for a time to become stagnant and pollute the stream of history.

It would seem to be clear, therefore, that the search for natural rights of sufficient definiteness to be useful in giving verbal expression to the universal Rights of Man is not a very hopeful quest. There is too much relevancy to particular situations to make this line of search profitable. But if we cannot find a basis for human rights in what men are by nature, we might be more successful if we consider what they hope to become. There might be some possible agreement on the point at which they hope to arrive.

The vision of an ideal future has a powerful fascination for those who are possessed by it. Thousands of years ago Jewish leaders created the myth of the holy land, a land promised to their fathers, where every man may sit under his own vine or fig tree or orange grove. That vision still possesses the minds and hearts of many Jewish people with tragic intensity. The Russian Communist is busy creating a similar mythology. Moscow, the Third Rome, is becoming a New

Jerusalem with a worldwide appeal. A powerful vision, unconsciously held and therefore immune from rational criticism, is the strongest thing that can possess a man. If we had a satisfactory one, that had universal appeal, we would be able to make a "Declaration of Human Rights" with confidence. The difficulty arises from the fact that large sections of the human race hold competing and mutually exclusive visions. These visions are clothed in myths and rationalized into ideologies. They are then served with idolatrous passion. They are, in fact, the idols of the modern world, and the faith that is usually associated with religion is in them all. Rational criticism can make little impression upon them. They hold millions, not by reason but by faith. Any effective declaration of human rights must find a similar form. It must speak to the heart of man, and at the same time satisfy the rational judgment of the thinking minority. The result will be a work of art rather than a product of scientific thought. All possible help must be given by scientific thought, but we need an effective myth not a formula, and by "myth" we mean a theme that stirs the heart of man and pulsates with the life of a vital community.

But is there any theme that has such universal appeal that the whole world will respond when it is clothed with verbal imagery and translated into the languages of the race? Is the world of men hungry for any one thing? Different peoples are hungry for different things, and the hungers of vast multitudes count for little because they lack the institutions sufficiently strong to influence governments effectively. Spanish republicans might hunger for a change of government in Spain. That hunger might be sustained by a vision of peace beyond civil strife, but in the meantime freedom, brotherhood, and all the rest are laid aside as not immediately relevant. And so it is across the world. Different peoples are at different stages of need. It reminds us of St. Augustine's prayer, "Lord, give me chastity, but not yet." The different peoples of the world pray, "Give peace, but not till we have power." Every universal vision comes up against and is spoilt by the power problem. No one feels secure unless he can call on adequate power to protect him. He wants the power to be reliable beyond question, and as things are, have been, and are likely to remain for a long time, security for one people means insecurity for another. Russia and America are our tragic illustrations today. Both peoples want peace, but they also expect their governments to secure peace by power. The peoples trust in the power of their respective states for peace, not in each other's good will. They would, no doubt, be happy to trust in each other's good will if they only dared to take the chance, but neither side has the courage to do it. Here we touch on the dilemma of the modern world. If Russia decided to trust America, would she be able to count on receiving a fair share of Persian oil and open highways to the oceans of the world? And if

America decided to trust Russia, would America be sure of free access to the Middle East for trade in oil and other commodities? In the present condition of international morality, America would expect Russia to make herself militarily secure in the Middle East, and because of this state of mind America is prepared to use her present advantages of power to get in first. Thus we are bedeviled.

It is in and to such a world that we must speak if we speak at all about Human Rights. The natural rights of man as man are not universally acknowledged, neither is there any vision of the future that is universally acceptable. No statement can be made that will not appear partisan to large sections of the human race. There is no foreseeable future where conditions can be expected to be otherwise. It may well be that the Human race will always be in a condition of unrest because man's personal aspirations and ambitions have reached a point where they cannot find satisfaction in the physical environment in which they are committed to live. Man has outgrown his physical clothing and is bound to remain uncomfortable. Our job is to tackle the next problem at hand. There is no finality in things human. If we can set our faces in the right direction, we shall have achieved much.

If there is anything in this line of thought, might it not be the way of wisdom to accept it as a fact that man is destined to love and grow, that growth will ever be painful and dangerous, that there can be no end to the process while the earth bears life, and that the highest possible form of excellence must be sought and as widely distributed as possible, and the development of the race be steered, as far as may be, away from what has been found to be merely destructive and erroneous into sources that contain premise of further development or are at least worthy of experimental tests?

The catch in this line of thought is in the fact that we cannot get the steerman to agree on the course for the future. American Capitalists will not give up the wheel to Russian Communists, and British pilots believe that if either of these get all their own way, they will surely drive the ship of humanity onto the rocks. What is needed is a convincing philosophy of history, but rising peoples, who are youthful because they are growing, will never listen to a philosophy of history, or any other philosophy. They want mythologies, and by a mythology they will live, grow, and possibly make shipwreck. The myth of Britannia incarnated a mighty theme that has no doubt had its most recent great individual representative in Winston Churchill. But Churchill today is like the dove from Noah's Ark. He can find no place for his spiritual feet. His attempt to arrest history at the point where his soul could find peace shows the futility of clinging to any myth beyond its day. The communist myth of a classless utopia is doomed to the same disappointment, and the American form of the Capitalist mythology is already threatened with the storm clouds of internal unrest that will surely violently disturb its Indian Summer.

The pace of modern history has been vastly accelerated by modern industry. There seems to be no possible escape from a turbulent period of human activities. The road will be rough and dangerous over which the car of man's destiny must be driven. If we cannot have a philosophy of history, which we most sorely need, can we give the driver a myth, a great living theme, an inspiration, a faith, a hope, a song in his heart that will contain as much truth as human wisdom in its most inspired moments can provide? Can we sing of one world and of the brotherhood of all men with conviction, hoping that the theme will grow in man's imaginations to the point where an appeal for action will be accepted as a natural thing? Any declaration of Human Rights must take hold of something already present in human hearts, some latent desire, something we may feel is too good to be true, but if it were possible of achievement it would be seen to be obviously both true and good. We must take hold of an aspiration which will also be a challenge. Many who first sang the song of freedom ended in gaol, and it has always remained a dangerous song to sing universally. Any modern declaration of human rights that is vital and relevant will tell of things that will make the largest vested interests of the moment uncomfortable and almost certainly dangerous. There is no need to declare anything that is not being resisted. Liberty, equality, and all the rest were violently resisted in the years of their birth and growth even if the currents of history were running in their favour. As the "Bill of Rights" served its day, so a new declaration must serve a new day. But it must meet a new day and be a new declaration. Old men brought up in Western liberalism and feeling all its genuine virtue in their bones will need to be reborn before they can speak to the present occasion. We must never forget that the West in the last forty years has been powerless to avert two world wars, countless revolutions, and a worldwide depression of enormous magnitude. If this indictment is not enough to discredit a civilization and its leaders it is difficult to see how any regime can be held to be discredited. The themes on which the Western World rose to world power were not good enough as a basis on which to organize the world's life. Western man could sing of freedom while ruthlessly exploiting the rest of the world. That does not make freedom a bad thing but it means that no rational state or class group is at all likely to give freedom to any subject group until it is compelled in its own interests to do so. The West has believed in war and still sees no way out. War is the crucial question now. Whatever road we take in considering human problems we always come back to the problem of power to wage war. The influence of this power on the human soul invariably coarsens and corrupts. The men who handle power institutions soon learn to think impersonally. Men and women become items and things not persons. Controllers of power machines feel that the power institution must be made stronger and stronger. While more than one power group is playing the game none can feel safe. There is no end to this process except the trial of strength which eventually takes place. This has been the story of the Western World and now its evil heritage has passed over to the whole world. The West has destroyed itself, and if its example in this respect is followed it will lead to the destruction of the whole human race.

The difficulty is to see an alternative to the Western way of life which always has war in the background. The American version is unconvincing. There is so much subordination of the spirit of man to the technical processes of industrial production that a general cultural impoverishment would seem to be inevitable. This could easily mean as inordinate trust in industrial power and an exaggerated emphasis on standardization which would fatally inhibit creative cultural processes. Technological development can easily mean cultural impoverishment. America with superior technical efficiency and inferior political wisdom would be the world's greatest menace.

Soviet Russia would seem to be playing the Western power game with oriental astuteness. Russia is difficult to assess. She is where East and West enter into most intimate union. At the same time she is Russia, which is neither East nor West but whose historical background was fashioned by the Russian version of Eastern Orthodoxy. Russia for her present purposes has laid hold of Western and especially American ideas of technical production and is driving them with revolutionary fury. Just how long the Russian people will endure this pressure of what is really an alien influence remains to be seen. She is finding new interest in her own national history and in her great 19th century literature. If the authentic Russian spirit asserts itself and keeps the materialistic technology of the West in balance, the cultural achievements might be very great indeed, but her evident determination to make a vigorous response to the challenge of the West, and especially of America, on traditional Western war lines, might well result in a destructive and inhuman over-emphasis on the importance of the power machines.

Unless the competition in power between America and Russia can be resolved there is no escape from a head-on collision with disastrous results to the whole world. Each would seek a knock-out blow which would give the victor a temporary world supremacy. This is one way by which the one world could be achieved, but it would be a vast delusion and the beginning of untold woes. The victor would be driven by fear to trust more and more in repression. Secret police would make life intolerable and rebellion would be inevitable. War would be more deeply rooted in the soul of man.

Is there an alternative to this? Can the soul of Europe experience a resurrection or a rebirth? We do not want merely to resuscitate the old body of Europe. That would simply mean more war. We need a Europe risen to a new mission and reborn for a new purpose. She has had her fill of war. Surely she realizes now that war is not the way to life for man. Has she the spiritual resources to lead the world into the ways of peace? She has not the material power to resist or measure up to Russia or America, but among her cultural treasures are some of the finest things the race has known. She has known the love of truth, she has felt the urge to righteousness, she has experienced the satisfaction of neighbourly cooperation in all forms of cultural achievement. In music, architecture, literature, sport, and religion, Europe knows what unity means. Can these forces of the spirit of man be reborn for united action in a great work? Is the death of the old war-fevered Europe sufficiently convincing to make spiritual resurrection real?

Along this line is a ray of hope, possibly the best hope in the world today. But it must be realized that it will be difficult and costly beyond words. It is going to be hard to convince Europe that she must definitely accept the death of those things she has loved inordinately. The million marching men and panoply of war of Germany, the glory of France, the complacent superiority of Britain, all these things die hard. But die they must, if Europe is to be of any further use in human history.

Can we then from the spiritual resources of Europe find material for a declaration of the Rights of Man which will appeal not to Europe only but to the large sections in America and Russia and eventually to the whole world? It must be a song of hope. The spirit in man has ever responded to hard blows and the best things have resulted from patient endurance. It will ever be so. The spirit that moves in history gives us no ground for believing that it or He is too much concerned about our comfort or our material prosperity. We explore life better under strain. Our education is the more effective when it is spiritually costly. Aeschylus of old observed that we learned by suffering. Europe can rise again, the important thing is the quality of the resurrection life she will bring as her contribution to the new world. She can gain a spiritual ascendancy over both Russia and America, and she may even prevail upon them to exercise power with moral restraint and for moral purposes. This would seem to be her historical vocation. She has had to die to qualify for it, but she may do for the new world a better job than Hellas did for the old. Europe in her agony, and because of her agony, is the only substantial hope in the world today.

What song then should Europe teach the youth of the world to sing? It must be a song that looks war in the face and yet continues to sing of better things. The heart must be strong enough to conquer hate, and the mind clear enough to see the Question from the point of view of the whole world. It will be the hardest song to learn that the race has ever been called upon to sing. . . .

CULTURAL CHANGES CAN NEVER BE BROUGHT ABOUT BY ANY PROCESS OF INTELLECTUALIST ASSENT
Herbert Read[*]

Julian S. Huxley, Esq.   19th April 1947
Unesco-House
Avenue Kléber
Paris 16e

My dear Huxley,

Many thanks for your letter of March 27th forwarding for my comment the proposed Memorandum on Human Rights. . . .

My main complaint is that the policy of Unesco has been conceived on a plane which is far too intellectualist or academic. This characteristic is well illustrated by the document which you now send to me. It must, of course, be viewed in relation to the rest of Unesco's activities, but I cannot conceive what practical purpose is served by the preparation of such abstract definitions. Even if the Commission on Human Rights can agree on all the philosophical implications underlying such a document and can express them in clear and unequivocal language, I do not see that the future of Western Civilization

---

[*] Herbert Read was an English poet, art critic, and anarchist who in 1947, at the time of the UNESCO human rights survey, had recently co-founded the avant-garde Institute of Contemporary Arts in London. Read served for three years in the British Army during the First World War and was decorated for valor in combat. Although he was considered to be in the front ranks of English modernist poets by the 1930s, his greater influence came through art criticism. Read's *The True Voice of Feeling: Studies in English Romantic Poetry* (1953) was credited with reviving interest in the Romantic poets. He utilized the theories of Carl Jung in his writings and rejected the Marxist approach to art, which saw it as simply another product of bourgeois society. In part because of his hostility to Marxist theories, Read's writings had become neglected by the time of his death in 1968, although his stature was eventually reaffirmed in later decades.

is made one degree securer. My own conviction is that cultural changes can never be brought about by any process of intellectual assent. Real change is always essentially molecular and effected on the physical and emotional level of society . . . .

AT PRESENT WE ARE, IN A COLLECTIVE SENSE, SAVAGES, AND NOT ENTITLED TO ANY HUMAN RIGHTS
Herbert Read

9 ; vii ; 47

My dear Huxley,

. . . I wanted to explain my failure to produce anything for the Human Rights enquiry. It has not been for any lack of goodwill—I have started at least half-a-dozen times to write something, but always failed to come to any realistic terms with the question. It seems too remote from any immediate realities. Rights and freedoms don't seem to me to exist on the universal scale which the document (Memorandum on Human Rights) envisages. The very words cannot be interchanged internationally without ambiguity and misunderstanding. These problems only become real for the person within the intimacy of his social group—his family, workshop, or locality. It might, of course, be interesting to say just that, but even such a limited definition of human rights has not much significance in view of the psychological inhibitions and frustrations which everywhere enslave mankind. I am inclined to think that there is only one problem which is fundamental—the cause and cure of sadism and aggressiveness—and that until we have done something about this problem, it is merely futile to discuss Human Rights. At present we are, in a collective sense, savages, and not entitled to any human rights. . . .

Yours very sincerely,

Herbert Read

A STATEMENT OF THE RIGHTS OF MAN,
UNLESS IT WAS A TISSUE OF AMBIGUITIES, COULD NEVER,
I THINK, BE FRAMED IN SUCH A WAY AS TO COMMAND
THE ASSENT OF ALL INTELLIGENT MEN
*T. S. Eliot**

April 18th, 1947
The Director-General
U.N.E.S.C.O.
Unesco-House,
19 Avenue Kléber
Paris, 16e

My dear Julian,

I have just received your letter of 27th March together with the draft memo-randum on human rights. It arrives at an unfortunately moment. I am leaving for New York in three days and I simply haven't time before my departure to give the document the attention which might lead to criticism of any value to you. I shall certainly return to it when I am back in London in June, but I imagine that any criticism would then be too late.

I will confess, frankly, however, that my first sentiment is one of astonish-ment that Unesco should be occupied with such a formulation. A statement of the rights of man, unless it was a tissue of ambiguities, could never, I think, be framed in such a way as to command the assent of all intelligent men. It seems, therefore, a more appropriate activity for philosophers as private individuals than for an official body of the universal scope of Unesco. I should have thought that Unesco would be better occupied in the more particular activities of be-neficence in helping injured countries to reorganize the higher part of their life.

As for the document itself, while I think that it could be improved by being rewritten in better English, the principal question is that of the assumptions on which it is based. But an attempt to probe into these would take considerable time and close study. But while I shall be interested in such an exploration I

---

* T. S. Eliot, born in the Midwestern United States, was an essayist, publisher, and among the most important poets of the twentieth century. In 1948, a year after sending his letters to Huxley and Havet regarding human rights, Eliot won the Nobel Prize in Literature. Among his best-known poems are "The Love Song of J. Alfred Prufrock" (1915), "The Waste Land" (1922), and "Ash Wednesday" (1930). Eliot died in 1965; a stone was placed for him in Poets' Corner in Westminster Abbey.

confess that the design seems to me to be futile, in so far as the consequences do not turn out to be positively mischievous.

Yours ever,
T. S. Eliot

I FEEL THAT IT IS VERY LATE IN THE DAY TO MAKE A DECLARATION ON THE ASSUMPTIONS OF THE LATER PART OF THE EIGHTEENTH CENTURY
T. S. Eliot

FABER & FABER LTD. Publishers
24, Russell Square, LONDON, W. C. I.
15th July 1947
Monsieur J. Havet
Philosophy & Humanistic Studies Section
UNESCO, Paris

Dear Monsieur Havet,[4]
I have to thank you for your kind letter of July 4th. Since my return from the United States I have reread twice the Memorandum on Human Rights.

I feel at a loss what to say about this document. In the first place the whole conception seems to me somewhat antiquated. I am sceptical first of the foundation and assumptions underlying this enterprise and second of its usefulness if carried through. I feel that it is very late in the day to make a declaration on the assumptions of the later part of the eighteenth century, and I do not myself believe that Human Rights can be considered apart from the general question of the nature of man and his place in the universe. It seems to me that such a document fails in both of two ways. First, by so limiting the question that a really profound philosophic examination is impossible, and second by formulating the questions so abstractly that they have little relation to realities. I do not think that we are likely to get anywhere by asking the twenty-five questions at the end of the Memorandum. The specific freedoms are, I think, identified first when we recognize violations of them. In other words it is from the specific violations of freedom that we should proceed to the abstract and not the other way about.

----

4. At the top right of this typed letter, Julian Huxley writes in pen "I think Havet has it in mind to break a lance with T. Eliot" [ed.].

If the various freedoms are put positively in this way, not one of them can be of any use in practice without a great deal of qualification.

For another thing I think it is important if you are going to pursue this enquiry at all that the right sort of qualified minds should be assembled. I do not think that economists, politicists, men of letters, are qualified to discuss such deep matters. I think that on the one hand you need the very best European theologians, and on the other hand the most intelligent and highly qualified semanticists. The latter are essential for discussing what words and sentences have meaning and what have not. In the Memorandum before me there is a good deal which an expert in language, for instance Professor I. A. Richards of Harvard,[5] would immediately demolish. The Memorandum, I am sorry to find, gives me the impression of seeming extremely conventional and jejune.

I think that the second paragraph for instance should be submitted to some such authority as Professor Barth.[6] I do not think that all orthodox Protestants would accept this account of the Reformation.[7]

In the third paragraph it would be necessary to ask why it is that the principle of religious freedom has been scarcely questioned in the Western democracies. It may be due to quite transient causes.

In the fourth paragraph I think that the term "freedom of the press" needs to be more fully defined. What human individuals are exactly meant here by the "press"?

I regret that I cannot be of more assistance, but, so far as I can see, this enterprise is not one which should be encouraged.

Yours very sincerely,
T. S. ELIOT

---

5. Professor of English at Harvard University and one of the founders of modern literary theory, who introduced linguistics, semantics, and problems of meaning into twentieth-century literary criticism [ed.].

6. Karl Barth, Swiss Reformed theologian whose theory of "dialectical theology" influenced many important religious thinkers and writers [ed.].

7. "Two historical events had been mainly responsible for preparing the way for th[e] formulation of human rights—first, the Reformation with its appeal to the absolute authority of the individual conscience, and secondly the rise of early capitalism with its emphasis on freedom of individual enterprise from the shackles of Church or State authority" ["Memorandum and Questionnaire Circulated by UNESCO on the Theoretical Bases of the Rights of Man": see Part II: Key Documents (ed.)].

Appendix
Notes on Sources and Guide for Further Research

At the time that the 1947–48 UNESCO human rights survey was rediscovered by human rights historians in the 1990s, most of the documents were confined to hardcopy archives. Despite the fact that various parts of this archival record are now available through UNESCO's electronic search function (UNESDOC), it is still necessary to consult the original archives at UNESCO House in Paris to gain a full picture of events surrounding UNESCO's involvement with human rights during these early years. The relevant archival reference is the following: UNESCO Archives, AG 8 Secretariat Records, Central Registry Collection, file Human Rights—Enquiry, Public Opinion 342.7 (100): 301.153 A 151.

These archives contain many interoffice memoranda, letters, lists of potential contributors, and other documents that constitute the archival record of the UNESCO human rights survey. However, there is one major omission: the actual responses to the survey. Although the archives are filled with letters of acknowledgment to the various respondents, the survey responses themselves were not found in the file.

Upon consultation with UNESCO archivists, several explanations for the missing responses were suggested, all linked to the key participants in the process: Julian Huxley, Jacques Havet, Jacques Maritain, and Richard McKeon. Research in the Huxley papers at Rice University in Houston, Texas revealed additional correspondence related to this short period in Huxley's international career, but no copies of the responses to the survey. Havet retired from UNESCO in 1980 and did not, it appears, make his professional papers available to the public. Given the fact that Maritain's introduction to *Human Rights, Comments and Interpretations* (UNESCO 1949) was an adapted version of his 1947 Mexico City speech, and did not discuss the individual contributions, we assumed that research in his papers (which are housed at the Jacques Maritain Center at the University of Notre Dame) would likewise not yield the missing documents. That left Richard McKeon, rapporteur of the Committee of Experts, author of "The Grounds of an International Declaration of Human Rights," and a figure who exercised considerable intellectual, institutional, and political influence over the process from the beginning.

Indeed, it turned out to be McKeon who had kept the original responses to the UNESCO human rights survey, documents that can be found in the McKeon papers in the special collections of the University of Chicago Library (along with other interesting materials, including the syllabus from the home study course he created based on the survey—see the chapter entitled "UNESCO in the Paradigmatic Transition" in Part I). The original responses are found in Boxes 183 and 184. Included in these archives is a transcribed copy of the letter Mahatma Gandhi sent to Julian Huxley and an extract from Herbert Read's substantive refusal to contribute (the full text of which is reproduced in "From Repudiation to the Play of Fancy," in Part III). In total, there are fifty-two responses in the McKeon papers. Gandhi's original letter to Huxley—written from a moving train en route from the Bhangi Colony—has never been found.

Acknowledgments

The publication of this volume would not have been possible without the fortuitous convergence of three developments. First, in the early months of my tenure at the University of Lausanne, I received generous funding and administrative support for a project that admittedly fell somewhat outside the main lines of research in anthropology that I was then pursuing. The second was the discovery of the missing UNESCO documents in the Special Collections of the University of Chicago Library, which enlarged the archival record and substantially revised the history of the UNESCO human rights survey. And finally, this curated history would never have seen the light of day without the early and enthusiastic support of Stanford University Press, which agreed with the proposition that a relatively obscure episode in the wider history of human rights was actually a story of surprising contemporary relevance.

The list of specific acknowledgments is unsurprisingly a long one, given that this project could not have coalesced without the collaboration of many specialists over the years.

The following scholars provided key information on Jacques Maritain, which clarified some early confusions and kept me from following the conventional wisdom in overstating his role in the UNESCO human rights survey: Professor John Trapani, President of the American Jacques Maritain Association; Dr. Walter Schultz, President of the Canadian Jacques Maritain Association; Anthony Simon, Director of the Yves R. Simon Institute; and Professor William Sweet, President of both the *Istituto Internazionale Jacques Maritain* and the *Union mondiale des sociétés catholiques de philosophie*.

Ian Clark, formerly the E. H. Carr Professor in International Politics at Aberystwyth University, led me to important background information on E. H. Carr during the time in which Carr was the chair of the UNESCO human rights experts committee.

I want to offer a special word of sincere gratitude to Mary Ann Glendon. It was in a spirit of incomparable intellectual and ethical generosity that she encouraged me to "figure out what really happened in that committee." I can only hope that what emerged from that inquiry will be seen to complement the landmark body of scholarship on human rights that she has produced over the decades.

I was fortunate to be able to discuss different aspects of the project during presentations to a number of institutions over the years, including the following: the Netherlands Institute of Human Rights and the Montaigne Centre for Judicial Administration and Conflict Resolution, Utrecht University (April 2017); the Minerva Center for Human Rights, Faculty of Law, The Hebrew University of Jerusalem (January 2017); the University of Michigan Law School (October 2016); the Venice Academy of Human Rights, European Inter-University Centre for Human Rights and Democratization (July 2016); the Graduate Institute of International and Development Studies, Geneva (March 2016); the Danish Institute for Human Rights, Copenhagen (May 2015); the Flemish Interuniversity Research Network on Law and Development, University of Ghent (July 2014), the Freeman Spogli Institute for International Studies, Stanford University (April 2014); and the Department of International Studies, School of Global and International Studies, Indiana University (December 2013).

On a more lasting basis, my participation as a member of the Leverhulme Trust International Network "Rights, Duties and the Politics of Obligation: Socioeconomic Rights in History" (2015–2018) has given me the opportunity to learn from leading human rights historians in the course of presentations on the UNESCO survey at the University of Warwick (May 2015), the Paris Institute of Advanced Studies (November 2015), Sciences Po, Paris (May 2016), and Harvard Law School (March 2017). I would like to thank a number of colleagues in this innovative initiative for their patience and intellectual guidance, including Christian O. Christiansen, Steven Jensen, Philip Kaisary, Samuel Moyn, Mark Philp, Sridhar Venkatapuram, and Charles Walton.

My debt of gratitude to UNESCO is obviously wide-ranging. UNESCO prides itself on making its extensive archives and research facilities readily available to researchers, a level of access and cooperation that has proven invaluable in the study of international institutions. Although many staff members lent their expertise and rendered assistance over the years, I must acknowledge several in particular: Petra van den Born, UNESCO librarian; Nooshin Dadmehr, UNESCO librarian; Adriano Gonçalves, UNESCO librarian; Adele Torrance, UNESCO reference archivist; Jens Boel, UNESCO Chief Archivist; and Ian Denison, Chief of UNESCO Publishing and Branding.

My research in the University of Chicago Library would not have been possible without the assistance of Barbara Gilbert from the Special Collections Research Center and the advice and counsel of Daniel Meyer, Director of Special Collections and University Archivist at the University of Chicago. The timely intervention of Amanda Focke from the Woodson Research Center at Rice University's Fondren Library allowed me to rule out the Julian Huxley papers as the location for the missing UNESCO documents.

The editorial and production team at Stanford University Press was unfailingly superb, including Anne Fuzellier, Stephanie Adams, Nora Spiegel, and especially Michelle Lipinski, without whose commitment and passion for scholarship this project would never have moved forward. A special word of thanks to the volume's intrepid copy editor, Marie Deer, who brought an experienced and insightful touch to a difficult manuscript.

It is a pleasure to acknowledge the participation of my wife Romana Iorga on the project. I am grateful that she agreed to translate the original French documents into English.

Although the formal permissions are listed below, I want to make special mention of the generous and revelatory support of Edward Mendelson, literary executor of the Estate of W. H. Auden and Lionel Trilling Professor in the Humanities at Columbia University. Professor Mendelson, the world's leading authority on Auden, shared a number of important details on the life and work of Auden during the time when Auden wrote his essay on human rights for UNESCO. In addition, Professor Mendelson confirmed that Auden's essay, which was found among the missing UNESCO documents in the Special Collections of the University of Chicago Library, had never been seen by Auden specialists, although its existence had been rumored.

I am honored that Samuel Moyn agreed to write the Foreword to the volume. His own scholarship in the history of human rights has played an incomparable role in rewriting that history. Although the broader implications of the UNESCO human rights survey are likewise open to a range of interpretations, some of which will likely be competing, my hope is that these various readings look as much to the present and future as they do to the past. If it is true that we are living in the end times of human rights, perhaps we might find some solace in the fact that it is only a *particular* understanding of human rights that is ebbing. Other understandings, other ways of imagining the potential of human rights in a world of diversity, violence, and inequality, are there to be found in alternative histories if we are only willing to look for them.

Finally, as always, I must acknowledge the enduring support and inspiration I receive from my ever-present muses—Isaiah, Dara, and Romana. *Vă iubesc din toată inima mea.*

* * *

The editor and publisher gratefully acknowledge the permission granted to reproduce the following copyright material in this book:

All content originally published as *Human Rights: Comments and Interpretations (A Symposium Edited by Unesco)*, UNESCO/PHS/3 (rev.), Paris, 25 July 1948. Copyright © 1948 by United Nations Educational, Scientific and Cultural Organization. Reprinted by permission of the United Nations Educational, Scientific and Cultural Organization.

The following unpublished responses to the UNESCO human rights survey:

"Comments on the Basic Human Rights" (Arthur H. Compton)
"Memorandum on the Rights of Man for the Commission on Human Rights of the United Nations" (Lewis Mumford)
Untitled (Ture Nerman)
"Contribution to Discussion on Declaration of Human Rights" (R. Palme Dutt)
"Economic and Social Rights of Man" (Maurice Dobb)
"Grammatical Analysis of the Rights of Man" (Marcel de Corte)
"Some Fundamental Ideas for the Declaration of the Rights of Man of the United Nations" (Pedro Troncoso Sánchez)
"Reply to the Questionnaire on the Rights of Man" (Inocenc Arnošt Bláha)
"Memorandum on the Rights of Man" (Hubert Frère)
Untitled (M. Nicolay)
"The Rights of Man" (Peter Skov)
"Corrected Project for a Declaration of the Rights of Peoples and Collectivities" (Emmanuel Mounier)
"Note Regarding the Proposed 'Declaration of the Rights of Man'" (Maurice Webb)
"The Rights of Man" (John Macmurray)
Untitled (Julius Moór)
Untitled (L. Horváth)
"Response to the Questionnaire and Memorandum about the Rights of Man" (Alfred Weber)
"The Rights of Man" (Frank R. Scott)
"Just to write some pious sentiments will serve little purpose," letter from Jawarharlal Nehru to Julian Huxley, May 14, 1947.
"Freedom of Thought for Children" (Albert Szent-Györgyi)

"We are finished with the era of passing general resolutions in regard to liberty and freedom," extract of letter from Morris L. Ernst to Richard McKeon to Jacques Havet, April 29, 1947.

"The Rights of Man" (Arnold Schoenberg)

"Statement on Human Rights" (Melville Herskovits)

Untitled (Theodore Johannes Haarhoff)

On Human Rights (Ernest Henry Burgmann)

Copyright © 1947, 1948 by United Nations Educational, Scientific and Cultural Organization. Reprinted by permission of the United Nations Educational, Scientific and Cultural Organization.

"Reflections on Freedom and Art" by W. H. Auden. Reprinted by permission of the Estate of W. H. Auden.

"Cultural changes can never be brought about by any process of intellectualist assent" and "At present we are, in a collective sense, savages, and not entitled to any human rights," extracts of letters from Herbert Read to Julian Huxley, April 19, 1947 and September 7, 1947. Reprinted by permission of the Trustees of the Herbert Read Estate.

"A statement of the rights of man, unless it was a tissue of ambiguities, could never, I think, be framed in such a way as to command the assent of all intelligent men" and "I feel that it is very late in the day to make a declaration on the assumptions of the later part of the eighteenth century," extracts of letters from T. S. Eliot to Julian Huxley, April 18, 1947 and July 15, 1947. Reprinted by permission of the Estate of T. S. Eliot.

Every effort has been made to trace copyright holders and to obtain their permission for the use of copyright material. The publisher and editor would be grateful if notified of any corrections that should be incorporated in future reprints or editions of this book.

Index

The authorized representative in the EU for product safety and compliance is:
Mare Nostrum Group
B.V Doelen 72
4831 GR Breda
The Netherlands

www.ingramcontent.com/pod-product-compliance
Lightning Source LLC
Chambersburg PA
CBHW081227020726
47503CB00011B/2930